Contemporary Studies in Scripture

An exciting new series from Greg Kofford Books featuring authors whose works engage in rigorous textual analyses of the Bible and other LDS scripture. Written by Latter-day Saints for a Latter-day Saint audience, these books utilize the tools of historical criticism, literature, philosophy, and the sciences to celebrate the richness and complexity found in the standard works. This series will provide readers with new and fascinating ways to read, study, and re-read these sacred texts.

The Vision of All

The Vision of All

Twenty-five Lectures on Isaiah in Nephi's Record

Joseph M. Spencer

GREG KOFFORD BOOKS
SALT LAKE CITY, 2016

Greg Kofford Books
P.O. Box 1362
Draper, UT 84020
www.gregkofford.com
facebook.com/gkbooks

Also available in ebook.

2020   19   18   17   16   5   4   3   2   1

———————————————————————————

Library of Congress Control Number: 2016952722

Contents

Preface

We Latter-day Saints are all trying to make sense of Isaiah. We naturally feel the weight of those moments in the Book of Mormon where we're told to take this prophet seriously, but we also naturally feel the enormity of the task of understanding the prophet's message. Perhaps we put off getting serious about Isaiah for a number of years, or we put it off for the first handful of times we work our way through the Book of Mormon. But at some point we start to feel a little guilty, and we start making commitments: "You know what? I'm going to see if I can't begin to make some sense of Isaiah this year!" Resolutions made, we turn to the Book of Isaiah in the Bible, or perhaps to the Isaiah chapters in the Book of Mormon, and we start reading. We begin by reading slowly, paying careful attention to chapter headings and cross-references in the footnotes. But it doesn't take long before we're convinced that our work isn't getting us very far. The chapter headings are too short, the cross-references often confusing, and we're still entirely unsure of what at least half of the verses we're reading could possibly mean.

And so we turn to books—some more and some less scholarly in nature—in the hope that we can get a little help. We're looking for someone to get us started, as well as to give us some pointers during the more confusing moments in Isaiah's writings. Of course, most of us have few grand ambitions. We're not looking to become Isaiah scholars. We just want to have a decent sense for what's going on. And we're hoping that people who write books know enough about the subject to get us oriented. We're happy to let them feast on the sumptuous banquet of Isaiah's prophecies while we just gather some of the delicious crumbs that fall from the table. Perhaps, if that helps us to see what all the fuss is about, we'll look for a place at the table or ask ourselves over for dinner. But first we're really just interested in getting a taste—enough of a taste to feel like we know what we've been missing.

Are we really missing anything? Is the spread so remarkable at the Isaianic table? I think so. I don't know that I'm too frequent a guest at that table. I certainly don't have a reserved seat, and I doubt the waiters know me by name. But I attend the feast as often as I can get away with it, and

I'm startled by the richness of the experience every time. Perhaps what startles me the most is that the experience is richer every time I return. The food only gets better. Or perhaps my palate just gets more refined, making it so that I can appreciate the food better each time I return. Either way, I'm not only *happy* each time I attend the feast, I'm *happier* than I was the last time. That doesn't make me intellectually or spiritually superior, of course. I've just come to love Isaiah. I find his writings endlessly fascinating, and I can't stop reading about him. And the more I read Isaiah's own words, and the more I read in the massive library of things written about Isaiah's words, the more I love this difficult prophet. He's no longer inaccessible to me, and I think I get why Nephi was so taken by his prophecies. In fact, as I've worked on the Book of Mormon's use of Isaiah, I've come to see that this one Hebrew prophet's writings are far more central to the Restoration than we generally recognize. And I inevitably find myself wanting to share with others what I've learned.

So I've written a book, and you've decided to open it and start reading. What can you expect in the following pages? Well, let's be clear from the very beginning that I won't try to simplify Isaiah here. It seems to me a bit deceptive to try to give people a taste of Isaiah's delicious prophecies by stripping away the fat or by replacing the honey with high fructose corn syrup. I don't want highly processed and preservative-laden foods to be substitutes for the real thing. I want my readers to get a real taste of Isaiah, even if their palates aren't yet accustomed to what they experience.

How to accomplish this? Rather than attempt a line-by-line commentary (which gets dull fast and alienates most readers) or an overview and introduction (which remains too abstract to be of much use), I've written a series of twenty-five lectures, each of which could be delivered in forty-five minutes. This format has forced me to keep my writing informal or even chatty, as well as relatively clear, even though I'm dealing with topics of great depth and complexity. It's also forced me to leave off using footnotes and other distracting scholarly tools. (I *do* mention occasional books and articles of interest in the course of discussion, and full bibliographical information for all of these can be found at the end of the book. But that's the only piece of scholarly apparatus in the whole volume.) Finally, this format has forced me to keep focused, to get to the point quickly, and to leave out overly technical points of discussion. As for what this format means for you, I hope it invites you to be an active participant with me, rather than just a passive reader. That is, I hope we explore these texts *together*. So whenever it's possible, it would be beneficial for you to have your scriptures out and ready, just as you would in a class setting. (And don't worry, while I occasionally suggest some resources and outside readings, I don't assign you any homework.)

In addition to using the format of a lecture series, I've limited the scope of what's to be covered in this book. Rather than attempting to review the biblical Book of Isaiah (sixty-six chapters long!), I've kept my focus just on Isaiah as he appears in Nephi's writings (that is, in First and Second Nephi, the first two books of the Book of Mormon). This focus allows me to give my attention to a good deal less of Isaiah's writings, but it simultaneously requires me to say a lot about Nephi and his approach to Isaiah. In the end, however, I think this is useful for most Latter-day Saints. We're more interested in Isaiah in the Book of Mormon than we're interested in Isaiah in general, and we're often genuinely perplexed by Nephi's deep interest in this prophet. More importantly, perhaps, by giving my attention primarily to Nephi and his approach to Isaiah, I'm free to ignore many other approaches to Isaiah that are unquestionably important but of much less interest to many Latter-day Saint readers. I'm relatively sure that most of us wish above all to learn just how to read Isaiah like Nephi.

To read Isaiah like Nephi! It's a worthy goal. I can only hope I'll help to make such a thing possible for some few readers through this project.

This book, like every book, owes much to many. I'd like, though, just to mention four sources of assistance and inspiration in particular.

First, I'd like to thank Karen, my wife, who's done a great deal to encourage this project. Every time I've said aloud that I'm planning to do some work on "my Isaiah lectures," she's responded not only supportively, but with visible excitement. Her confidence that this book could do some good has meant much to me, and it's kept me working on it consistently.

Second, I'd like to thank Sharon Harris and Jenny Webb, both of whom took the time to read through the manuscript to provide feedback and encouragement. They're among my best friends, and their investment in what I'm doing means a great deal to me. I'd also like to thank Loyd Ericson at Greg Kofford Books for his interest in the project. His consistent support for my work has been sustaining.

Third, I'd like to thank the Neal A. Maxwell Institute for Religious Scholarship. The idea for this book took shape while I was a Hugh W. Nibley Dissertation Fellow, during the academic year of 2014–2015. The financial resources made available to me by the Maxwell Institute that year allowed me to acquire numerous sources on Isaiah I'd not had access to before that point. This book (and all of my work on Isaiah) is richer for their support.

Finally, I'd like to thank students and audiences in dozens of different classrooms and lecture venues where I've worked through my ideas about Isaiah out loud. This book likely owes more to them, nameless here, than it does to anyone else. In early-morning seminary classes, in Sunday School lessons, in Book of Mormon courses at Brigham Young University, in bookstore-sponsored lectures, in academic conference venues—all over the place I've found a host of willing and interested Latter-day Saints eager to make sense of Isaiah. Their questions and their reflections, all in response to what I've tried to piece together of Isaiah, have helped me to give shape to my thoughts. If I've said anything valuable here, it's largely due to such interactions.

For that reason above all, I dedicate this book to my students.

Lecture I

Nephi's Vision

Two Reactions to Isaiah

Admit it. The very mention of Isaiah's name is enough to put you in a mood. I don't know which mood, since that depends very much on who you happen to be. But *some* kind of a mood. Perhaps a certain bemusement settles over you. Or maybe a state of anxiety overtakes you. Likely you prepare yourself for exasperation. Or, let's be frank, some degree of (justified) annoyance at—perhaps suspicion of—those strange souls who get excited about Isaiah. Or maybe you happen to be one of those strange souls, one of the few who like it when someone brings Isaiah up. Then it might be a bit of pride you begin to feel at the mention of Isaiah's name— a sense of accomplishment or even spiritual superiority.

Why all these moods? Why can't we simply be indifferent to Isaiah? Well, that's easy to answer. *Because the Book of Mormon won't let us be indifferent to Isaiah.* It's not just that certain Nephite prophets quote Isaiah. It's that they say things like this from Nephi: Isaiah's writings "shall be of great worth unto them in the last days, for in that day shall they understand them" (2 Ne. 25:8). Or this from Moroni: "Search the prophecies of Isaiah" (Morm. 8:23). Perhaps we *could* ignore these kinds of things, but we *can't* ignore the fact that *Jesus himself* has something to say about Isaiah when he comes to visit Lehi's children: "Ye had ought to search these things," he says right after quoting from Isaiah. "Yea, a commandment I give unto you that ye search these things diligently—for great are the words of Isaiah" (3 Ne. 23:1). How could we get around that?

Well, we can't. Instead, we tend to develop one of two problematic relationships to Isaiah. Either we feel a kind of guilt about the fact that we don't give much attention to Isaiah's writings, or we feel a kind of pride about how hard we work at understanding Isaiah. Nephi says that "the words of Isaiah . . . are plain unto all they that are filled with the spirit of prophecy" (2 Ne. 25:4), so we either fret and worry that we're not spiritual enough to have that gift, or we pat ourselves on the back since the work we've put into understanding Isaiah seems to mean that we're worthy of that gift. Let's call this the Isaiah complex, an illness peculiar to those who cherish the Book of Mormon. My aim, over the twenty-five lectures you've volunteered to sit through, is to start the process of healing that illness. You can find a lot of material on Isaiah out there written and published by Latter-day Saints, but it's chiefly aimed at producing just an intellectual understanding of Isaiah's writings. I suspect the authors hope that developing some understanding will *eventually* lead to healing. But maybe we could reverse things here. I probably won't succeed, but I aim first to set right our collective relationship to Isaiah—that is, to get us started on healing—and *then* to see if understanding doesn't follow quite naturally.

How's that for a cute beginning to the lecture series? It's probably too cute. So let's get down to business. The question I'll be asking and doing my best to answer in our meetings is this: *What's Isaiah doing in the writings of Nephi?* Notice a couple of things about this question. First, it deliberately limits how much we'll try to tackle together. Isaiah shows up in crucial places in the Book of Mormon outside of Nephi's writings, but I think it's clear we can't actually get any work done on those other places until we've made some basic sense of what's going on with Nephi. It's Nephi who's first interested in Isaiah in the Book of Mormon. And his project is so intricate and so robust that we barely have time to cover even the basics of what he's up to. A second thing to notice is that my basic question assumes that Isaiah's *doing something* in the Book of Mormon. We're wrong to assume, as we often do, that Nephi just quotes chapters from Isaiah that he happens to find interesting. And we're especially wrong to assume, as we often do, that something changes when we come to the Isaiah material in Nephi's record—as if we could divide Nephi's investment in Isaiah from his desire to tell his own life's story or from his emphasis on the dreams and visions he and his father had. I'll see if I can't convince you that Nephi's whole project is a package deal, and that Isaiah's there in the text for discernible reasons.

So you see where we're going. Now let's start going there. I want to make sure we have enough time in this first lecture to set up the stakes of the project.

Nephi Sees a Book

Let's start gently, by setting Isaiah himself aside for a few minutes to look at something more familiar. Do you remember Nephi's apocalyptic vision in 1 Nephi 11–14? You'll certainly remember Lehi's dream of the tree of life, recorded in 1 Nephi 8. Nephi tells us that, after he heard about the dream, he had a deep desire to "see and hear and know" what his father had seen (1 Ne. 10:17). And you'll remember that he was rewarded with a visionary experience of his own, but one that was quite a bit more expansive than Lehi's (at least as Nephi tells the story).

The focus of Nephi's expanded vision is the situation of Christianity at the height of what historians call the Enlightenment, but for our purposes, we might say the situation of Christianity shortly after the American Revolution. Now, what Nephi tells us is that Christianity at that time and in that place was founded on "a book." Here are Nephi's words: "And it came to pass that I, Nephi, beheld that they"—that is, "the Gentiles which had gone out of captivity" and "were delivered by the power of God out of the hands of all other nations"—"that they did prosper in the land. And I beheld a book, and it was carried forth among them" (1 Ne. 13:19–20). Once Nephi sees this, his angelic guide focuses him on the book and provides him with a complex explanation of it:

> Knowest thou the meaning of the book? . . . Behold, it proceedeth out of the mouth of a Jew. . . . [It] is a record of the Jews, which contain the covenants of the Lord which he hath made unto the house of Israel. And it also containeth many of the prophecies of the holy prophets. And it is a record like unto the engravings which are upon the plates of brass—save there are not so many. Nevertheless, they contain the covenants of the Lord which he hath made unto the house of Israel; wherefore, they are of great worth unto the Gentiles. (1 Ne. 13:21, 23)

There's the first bit of the angel's explanation of the book. Let's say a few things about just this much of the text before turning to what else the angel has to say.

I don't know about you, but I'm struck first by the angel's question at the outset of this explanation: "Knowest thou the meaning of the book?" The angel's explanation, it seems to me, is supposed to answer this question, so we ought to make sure we understand it. The book Nephi sees, the angel suggests, has a *meaning*—but perhaps not a meaning in the way we'd assume. Today, the most common meaning of the word "meaning" is "sense" (to ask what something means is to ask what its sense is), but at the time Joseph Smith was working on the translation of the Book of Mormon, this wasn't its most common signification. Let's quote the handy 1828 edition of Webster's Dictionary, shall we? "Meaning": "that which exists in the mind, view or contemplation as a settled aim or purpose, though not directly expressed"; or again: "intention; purpose; aim; with reference to a future act." When Nephi's angel asks Nephi about the "meaning" of the book—and then goes on to answer his own question, he's asking primarily about the book's *purpose,* its implicit aim.

And what can we say of its purpose, if we read the angel's words closely? Well, one major feature of the book gets mentioned twice, both at the beginning and at the end of what the angel says in answering his own question. It "contain[s] the covenants of the Lord which he hath made unto the house of Israel." So it seems that what the book means to accomplish, what it's meant to do, is first and foremost to make known or at least to clarify what we usually call the Abrahamic covenant, the covenant made with Israel. Perhaps this helps to explain why, in the angel's words, the book "proceedeth out of the mouth of a Jew." What Nephi sees in vision is a Jewish book intended from the start to say something about the covenant given to Israel thousands of years ago. The book is a container of sorts (that's how the angel puts it, right?), and what it contains is a basic exposition of the Abrahamic covenant.

The angel also says that the book contains "many of the prophecies of the holy prophets." No surprise there. The chief purpose of the prophetic writings in the Hebrew Bible—that is, in the Old Testament—is *also* to clarify the status of the Abrahamic covenant. And can you guess which prophet this is truest about? Yes, a certain Isaiah of Jerusalem. Isaiah's book is unquestionably the most sustained and the profoundest engagement with the idea of the Abrahamic covenant that you can find in scripture. So when the angel mentions the Jewish prophets, he makes perfectly clear that the chief aim of the book from Nephi's vision is to alert the world to the stakes and status of Israel's covenant.

The Gentiles and the Book

So far, so good? Now here's the weird part. All this talk of the covenantal nature of the book, emphasized by the identification of its author ("a Jew") and some of its contributors ("the holy prophets"), culminates in the following—the very last words of the angel in the bit of the text we've already quoted: "wherefore, [the book is] of great worth unto the Gentiles." A quintessentially Jewish book, filled with quintessentially Jewish writings, focused on a quintessentially Jewish question—and it's *therefore* particularly useful for *non*-Jews? What's the angel getting at? We'll have to make this clearer as we go along, but this much should be apparent already: that the book Nephi sees in his vision is a Jewish book aimed at clarifying for non-Jews the heart of Judaism's historical encounter with God. This is what makes for the "great worth" of the book, or at least its "great worth" specifically for non-Jews—and it's they who actually *have* the book, who carry it around with them, in Nephi's vision.

Alright, so what *is* this book? Simply put, it's the Christian Bible. If you read further along in 1 Nephi 13, that's entirely clear. Remember the context. Nephi's seeing in vision "the Gentiles which . . . were delivered by the power of God out of the hands of all other nations." We'd simply call these people the inhabitants of the Colonies and then of the United States, from the seventeenth century up until about the Civil War. And they've got a cherished book they carry around with them. What could it be but the Bible? So the point of the angel's words is to help us understand the *real*—but generally overlooked—purpose of the Bible. The book these Americans cherish is actually a Jewish book about Israel's covenant, and it's what the book says about the covenant that makes it particularly precious for non-Jewish peoples. But, oddly, this isn't why the *Americans* Nephi sees cherish it. They've got their own reasons, and they seem to be oblivious to the real reasons it's of so much worth to them.

So why do they misunderstand the nature of the book? Well, this is what the angel explains next, in a rather complex passage. Let's see if we can't make it easier by taking it in bits and pieces.

First, the angel recapitulates what he's already said to Nephi about the Bible, but adding a few details:

> Thou hast beheld that the book proceeded forth from the mouth of a Jew. And when it proceeded forth from the mouth of a Jew, it contained the fullness of the gospel of the Lamb—of whom the twelve apostles bare record. And they bare record according to the truth which is in the Lamb of God. Wherefore, these things go forth from the Jews in purity unto the Gentiles, according to the truth which is in God. (1 Ne. 13:24–25)

Here again there's talk of the Bible's proceeding "from the mouth of a Jew." And here again it's clear that the book eventually finds its way into the hands of "the Gentiles." But the angel adds a few other details that make clear that this so-very-Jewish book we've been discussing is *also* a Christian book. It proceeds "from the mouth of Jew" even as it contains "the fullness of the gospel of the Lamb," and the Lamb is the one "of whom the twelve apostles bare record." Here, then, the angel makes clear that the Jewish book is a Christian book as well.

Actually, let's nuance this point a bit. It's not so much that the Bible is both Jewish *and* Christian. Rather, the angel makes clear that the line we usually draw between Judaism and Christianity is fuzzier than we think. Remember that Jesus, all his earliest disciples, and most or all of the earliest believers in Christ were Jews. Christianity began as a Jewish movement, a sect within Judaism. It was only a century and a half into Christianity's history that there began to be attempts—both by non-Christian Jews and by non-Jewish Christians—to distinguish Christianity from Judaism in a definitive way. There's so much we could say about this, but we'll have to see if there's time to go into the details later. For the moment, let's just make sure this much is clear: the Jewish book Nephi sees in vision concludes in some way with the testimony of the (Jewish) apostles, at which point the thing is taken to non-Jews, "the Gentiles."

One final detail from this first part of the angel's further explanation. The Bible goes "from the Jews in purity unto the Gentiles, according to the truth which is in God." When the book initially goes from the Jews to the Gentiles, it does so "in purity," in fact "according to the truth which is in God." You can already sense what's coming, can't you? The Bible won't remain in this state of "purity" and "truth." But the angel wants to make perfectly clear in advance that any impurity or falsehood to be found now in the Bible gets introduced into it only after it goes to the Gentiles. The prophets and the apostles whose writings are found in the Bible executed their offices righteously. If things go wrong at some point, it's only after the prophets and the apostles have done their work.

Okay, now let's look at a little more of the text. Here the angel lays out the unfortunate fate of the Bible once it's fully under Gentile control:

> And after that they go forth by the hand of the twelve apostles of the Lamb— from the Jews unto the Gentiles—behold, after this thou seest the formation of that great and abominable church, which is the most abominable of all other churches. For behold, they have taken away from the gospel of the Lamb many parts which are plain and most precious—and also many covenants of the Lord have they taken away. And all this have they done that they might pervert the right ways of the Lord, that they might blind the eyes and harden the hearts of the children of men. Wherefore, thou seest that after the book hath gone forth through the hands of the great and abominable church, that there are many plain and most precious things taken away from the book, which is the book of the Lamb of God. And after that these plain and precious things were taken away, it goeth forth unto all the nations of the Gentiles. (1 Ne. 13:26–29)

Here we have the story of how the original "purity" of the Bible ends up compromised. And this we have to read most carefully.

Great and Abominable

Notice, at the beginning of this sequence, that the angel refers Nephi back to something he's already seen earlier in his vision, namely "the formation of that great and abominable church." You'll remember that from your own readings of First Nephi, I assume. But don't be too quick to assume anything about the identity of this church. Years ago now, Stephen Robinson—of *Believing Christ* fame—wrote a nice study of 1 Nephi 13– 14 that rightly warned against equating this church with any particular organization, and especially with the Catholic Church. The best biography of David O. McKay—written by Greg Prince and Robert Wright a decade ago—also recounts how the popular (and sometimes semi-official) equation of the great and abominable with Catholicism deeply troubled President McKay and how he tried to work against it. You can go review those discussions as you'd like; we just need to be clear here that we're not going to jump to any quick conclusions about the historical referent of "the great and abominable church" discussed in Nephi's vision.

We can, however, say a few things about this church. Nephi witnesses its formation "among the nations of the Gentiles" (1 Ne. 13:4), and he sees "the devil, that he was the founder of it" (1 Ne. 13:6). What we're dealing with, clearly, is a Gentile phenomenon—or really, a specifically European phenomenon—and we're to understand that it's the devil's work. That's what Nephi already knew from an earlier part of the vision. Here what he learns in addition is that this church has something to do with the Bible's perversion. What makes this church "the most abominable of all other churches," according to the angel, is that "they have taken away from the gospel of the Lamb many parts which are plain and most precious." These are taken from the gospel, and more particularly from the Bible. The angel explains that "there are many plain and most precious things taken away from the book, which is the book of the Lamb of God." The abominable church manipulates the biblical text.

So, now we have the basic outline of this part of the angel's words. Once the Jewish book that's meant to bring Israel's covenants to the attention of the Gentiles actually comes into Gentile possession, there's something like a systematic attempt to transform it—or at least to control the way it's read. But here's the key question we need to ask: What exactly gets "taken away" from the biblical text in Nephi's vision? Well, given all we've said about the nature of the Bible as the angel describes it, it'd seem that the worst thing that could be done to it would be to strip it of its covenantal bearings, no? What makes the book so valuable for the Gentiles is what it has to say about the covenant made to Abraham, the profoundly Jewish message of this book aimed at bringing salvation to the Gentiles. Now note this. The only thing the angel says by way of specifying or clarifying the nature of the "plain" and "precious" things taken away from the book concerns the "covenants of the Lord." Here's the text again, drawn from the part of the angel's words we're still in the middle of interpreting: "they have taken away from the gospel of the Lamb many parts which are plain and most precious—and also many covenants of the Lord have they taken away." Did you catch that? The abomination of the great and abominable church would seem to be *this*, above all: that they reframed the Bible so that its message concerning the Abrahamic covenant effectively disappeared.

This, I think, is the story the angel wants to tell. The biblical text originally has a kind of purity about it, but it then gets manipulated by early Gentile Christianity. And the ways in which it's manipulated specifically concern what the book has to say about the covenantal status of Israel.

Now, I'm not a trained historian, and I'm certainly not an expert on early Christian history. But the reading I've done on the subject convinces me that we can tell a historically responsible story about when and how what the angel describes here actually happened. Over the course of the second century A.D., there was a complex and almost systematic effort by Gentile Christians (who were by that point the majority) to downplay the covenantal status of the Jews. A troubling interpretation of the covenant came to dominate Christian self-understanding, namely—that the *earlier* covenant people (the Jews, or Israel more generally) had *lost* their status as a covenant people, and so they'd been *replaced* in full by a *later* covenant people (the Gentiles, or at least those among the Gentiles who embraced Christianity). The anti-Semitic rhetoric of those who developed this notion in their writings is terrifying. I don't want to name names, but I suppose I'd better. I'll cite for the moment only Justin Martyr (see his *Dialogue with Trypho*) and Tertullian (see his *Against the Jews*), and I'll note that a close eye has to be kept on a complicated guy by the name of Marcion. But let's not go into those details today. Suffice it to say that it was arguably this development, the series of events through which Christianity came to define itself both *against* and *in the place of* Judaism, that Nephi sees in vision and that his angelic guide calls "the formation of that great and abominable church." (And don't ignore the fact that these events take place about a century and half before it's even possible to speak of the Catholic Church. We're dealing with something further back in history than the scapegoat of certain traditional apostasy narratives.)

Quickly, before summing up and turning to the third and final sequence of the angel's elaboration of the fate of the Christian Bible, I want to make one other note about this story of corruption. It's often assumed that the process of removing the plain and the precious from the biblical text was one of direct tampering with texts, or perhaps of ensuring that certain writings didn't make it into the canon. That's entirely possible, and I've become more convinced myself in recent years that there's a responsible way to tell the story of corruption along those lines. But let's be clear that it isn't at all necessary to tell the story that way. It would be enough, I think, to tell a story about how the transformation of early Christianity's general understanding of the Abrahamic covenant made it largely impossible for believers to make any real sense of the biblical record, even if the text hadn't really been tampered with. You're all postmodern enough to believe that your biases determine in part what you get out of a text, right? Perhaps things were "taken away" primarily because a new, noncovenantal bias was put in place, which made it difficult to understanding the Bible's real purposes. That'd be sufficient for the angel's words to be verified, I think. Of course, it might be that there *was* actual manipulation of texts. I don't want to deny that at all, just to keep our options open.

Okay, let's gather up the details and then read a bit more from the text. So far, we've got a quintessentially Jewish book, focused chiefly on the Abrahamic covenant and aimed at bringing the light of that covenant to the Gentiles. But then we've got a situation in which the Gentiles who become the caretakers of that book systematically distort its meaning, reassigning sole covenantal status to themselves. And then we've got this final bit from the angel's words we've looked at so far: "And after that these plain and precious things were taken away, [the book] goeth forth unto all the nations of the Gentiles." The general circulation of the Bible happens only once it becomes impossible for Gentile Christianity—its principal audience by that point—to understand its real importance and purpose.

Then comes this last part of the angel's discussion of the book's fate:

> And after it goeth forth unto all the nations of the Gentiles—yea, even across the many waters (which thou hast seen) with the Gentiles which have gone forth out of captivity—and thou seest because of the many plain and precious things which have been taken out of the book, which were plain unto

the understanding of the children of men, according to the plainness which is in the Lamb of God—and because of the things which are taken away out of the gospel of the Lamb, an exceeding great many do stumble—yea, insomuch that Satan hath great power over them. (1 Ne. 13:29)

The Book in the New World

This brings us back at last to where we began with Nephi's vision. Remember that the angel first begins talking about the Bible because Nephi sees it among the Gentiles in the New World—that is, among Protestants of European descent who came to establish a nation in the New World in the age of the Enlightenment. Here we come back to that moment and see what all this talk of the corruption of the Bible is really about. The Bible on which American Christianity is founded is apparently essential for those who love it and live by it, but not for the reasons they think it is. Remember that the angel tells Nephi that the book's covenantal contents are what make it "of great worth" to the Gentiles in the New World. But then the story the angel goes on to tell makes clear that the Gentiles necessarily fail—entirely fail!—to see the worth of the record they cherish. In effect, they cherish the Bible for all the wrong reasons. Not for *bad* reasons, of course, since they find in the biblical text a lot about Jesus Christ. But nonetheless for the *wrong* reasons, since it's the message of the covenant that they're especially supposed to be attuned to, or that they're supposed to embrace alongside the Christian gospel. (It's this *larger* picture that the angel seems to have in mind when he speaks of "the fullness of the gospel.")

So this, according to the angel, is what Christianity would come to by about the time of Joseph Smith. But, also according to the angel, God wouldn't let this situation continue forever. The Gentiles must be alerted to the true meaning of the Bible, and all of Israel—the Jews, but also the unknown remnants of Israel, like those among the native peoples of the New World—must also be brought to a real understanding of both the covenant and its entanglement with Jesus Christ. And what tools could be used for all this repair work? The angel relays a message from the Lamb of God addressed to Nephi: "I will manifest myself unto thy seed, that they shall write many things which I shall minister unto them, which shall be plain and precious. And after that thy seed shall be destroyed and dwindle in unbelief, and also the seed of thy brethren, behold, these things shall be hid up to come forth unto the Gentiles by the gift and power of the Lamb" (1 Ne. 13:35–36). There you have it, as straightforwardly as possible: the solution to the problem posed by the Bible's problematic history of reception is nothing other than the appearance, in nineteenth-century America, of the Book of Mormon.

You get what that means, I hope. The purpose of the Book of Mormon, according to Nephi's vision, is to refocus Christianity on its Abrahamic foundations, to restore to Christianity the idea that the Gentiles aren't a kind of replacement Israel, but that they're to be grafted into the everlasting covenant that's still vouchsafed to Jacob's children. This shouldn't be a surprise to us, though it usually is. Take a look at what the very title page of the Book of Mormon has to say about its primary purpose. It's "to show unto the remnant of the house of Israel how great things the Lord hath done for their fathers, and that they may know the covenants of the Lord, that they are not cast off forever." As we often note, it's certainly "also" meant to convince "the Jew and Gentile that Jesus is the Christ, the Eternal God," but it's first focused on the covenant. And Nephi's vision makes this perfectly clear. Long before the Book of Mormon would take shape, its first prophet saw in vision what the record's ultimate purpose would be. And its purpose is to launch anew the covenantal project that began with Abraham's call thousands of years ago.

Now, you've probably long since begun to wonder what all this has to do with Isaiah. Well, here's the short version. It's this vision of the Book of Mormon's purpose (to save Christianity from itself!) that drew Nephi's attention to Isaiah. In Isaiah's writings, Nephi found—as anyone who reads Isaiah carefully can find—the most brilliant available biblical explanation of the complex relationship between covenantal Israel and non-covenantal Gentiles. The book that bears Isaiah's name is nothing if it isn't a kind of systematic attempt to make sense of Abraham's covenant in the richest way possible. The only potential rival to Isaiah's attempts to think through the covenant would be Paul's letters in the New Testament, but we'd have to launch a second lecture series even to begin to talk about Paul. Maybe we'll have to do that at some point. (Or maybe you could read my book *For Zion* . . . .) For now, it's enough to take a stab at Isaiah, and especially at Nephi's interest in Isaiah.

And we've got a decent starting place. For the moment, you're probably just taking my word that Isaiah has something to do with the angel in Nephi's vision. But we'll soon enough be making as clear as we can how this all works. Let's hope I've given you enough for now to get you to come back for my next lecture!

Lecture II

The Book of Isaiah

Nephi's Motivations

We spent the bulk of our last lecture looking at just a few verses from 1 Nephi 13. The point of that exercise was double, really. We had just enough time as we wrapped up to state the first point (albeit without any real justification), which was basically that Nephi found in Isaiah a clear prophetic outline of exactly the things he saw in vision. If you're intimately acquainted with Isaiah's writings, you'll naturally see why Nephi would've become obsessed with him. But you probably aren't intimately acquainted with Isaiah's writings, so let me say something about them. Isaiah's book—especially the parts that find their way into Nephite scripture—is all about the production of a record, that is, of a series of prophecies uttered in one era but then written down and sealed up for later, more receptive readers. And the focus of Isaiah's written-and-then-sealed prophecies is principally, if not exclusively, on the complex relationship between the people of the covenant (Israel, Abraham's heirs) and the all the other peoples of the world, those without immediate access to the covenant (the Gentile nations). This is what Nephi found in Isaiah, and he seems to have seen it as a kind of interpretive key for making sense of what he'd seen in his own visions.

So there's the first point of beginning last time with 1 Nephi 13. The second point we didn't actually get to mention last time, but it's simple enough. We saw that Nephi learned from his vision about the crucial role that would eventually be played by what we call the Book of Mormon. His distant descendants would live to witness a visit from the resurrected Christ who would reveal plain and precious things to them. Then they'd write those things up in a sealed record that would be preserved until the opportune moment—apparently between the American Revolution and the Civil War—when the book's coming forth would begin the process of turning Gentile Christianity as a whole back to its Jewish roots, back to the Abrahamic covenant. There's the purpose of the Book of Mormon as laid out in Nephi's vision. Now here's the twist we didn't mention last time: Nephi saw all this concerning the fate of the Book of Mormon, but he seems to have been entirely unaware for a long time that his own writings would end up being included in that book. He knew that his descendants at the time of Christ's resurrection would have the task of producing a crucial record, but he seems not to have known at first that his own small plates would be a part of that record.

Now, why is this second point important? Well, it helps us begin to nail down Nephi's purposes in writing his record. And if we can get clear about what Nephi was trying to do when he wrote, we can begin to get clear about why he inserts long stretches of Isaiah in his writings. Basically, Nephi's aim was to do anything possible to ensure that his descendants would survive long enough to be present when Christ would make his visit—and to ensure that they wouldn't for any reason refuse Christ's teachings. If anything prevented Nephi's descendants from meeting and believing Christ, the promised Book of Mormon wouldn't be written. And that would be disastrous! Now, Nephi seems to have been divinely assured that his children would survive until the time of Christ. In the same vision we talked about last time, he saw his descendants receiving Christ at the time of his resurrection (1 Ne. 12:5–12), and later in his record he tells us that he received a divine promise that his children would be around to see the visiting Christ (2 Ne. 25:21). But apparently Nephi still worried that his children, even after surviving to see Christ come to visit them, might reject the Lord and his message. This is clearest in 2 Nephi 25:23–30, where Nephi pleads with his children to understand the deadness of the Law of Moses. Perhaps we'll have time to come back to this point in a later lecture.

Okay, so here's what we've got in hand after our last lecture's preliminaries. First, we've begun to recognize that what Nephi saw in the part of his vision we've given attention to bears a close relationship with certain crucial parts of Isaiah's writings. That is, we have reason to believe that it's possible to map what Nephi saw in vision to the writings of Isaiah. Let's summarize this first point this way: *Nephi had prophetic motivations for his deep interest in Isaiah.* And second, we've begun to see that specific purposes underlie Nephi's writing of his own record, purposes that should help us to get clear about why Nephi would include such long stretches of Isaianic material in his writings. That is, we have reason to believe that discernible intentions guide the organization of the material that makes up Nephi's record, and this should bear on our understanding of what

Isaiah's doing there. Let's summarize this second point this way: *Nephi used Isaiah in his writings for very particular reasons.*

With these two points, we have something like the alpha and the omega of Isaiah's place in Nephi's record. We see—or at least we see the possibility of seeing—why Nephi became interested in Isaiah in the first place. And we see—or we see the possibility of seeing—the ends that guided Nephi's inclusion of Isaiah in his writings. So we're *not* setting out on a fool's errand here. We've got from the outset a kind of double promise that we'll get somewhere, if we're careful enough. There are good reasons to think we can figure out what Nephi's doing with Isaiah.

But how to get started? I think the best place to begin is with questions of structure, that is, questions of how Nephi organizes the material making up his record. If we can convincingly identify the basic outline of Nephi's writings, I think we'll be well on our way toward understanding what he's doing with Isaiah.

But I'm actually going to put off questions of structure for next time. Let's take the remainder of our time together today to back up from Nephi's record a bit and say something about resources and strategies for reading Isaiah—for reading Isaiah on his own, so to speak. Although Nephi's intentions with Isaiah will help us immensely, we won't really get very far with them if we don't have a few tricks of our own up our sleeves. How would we recognize the correlation of sorts between what Nephi sees in vision and the basic shape of the Book of Isaiah if we don't have at least some familiarity with Isaiah's writings in the first place? And how would we be moved by Nephi's brilliant uses of Isaiah for his own ends if we don't have a sense for what Isaiah seems to be talking about all on his own? So let's begin with a few words about Isaiah himself, leaving the structure of Nephi's record for next time.

The Book of Isaiah

Of course, it's easy to begin with a few biographical details—that Isaiah of Jerusalem lived in the eighth century before Christ (that is, a hundred and fifty years before Nephi), that he prophesied during a time of major political turmoil, that he seems to have been trained in the literary arts and was an exceptional poet, and that he clearly occupied an elite social position in the kingdom of Judah. All this is true, but unfortunately, it hardly gets us anywhere near the Book of Isaiah. Instead, we've got to begin with a handful of rather more complicated considerations.

Let's begin instead, therefore, with a few words about the Book of Isaiah *as a book*. Do we know anything about how this book came into existence, apart from the rather obvious fact that it had its beginnings with a prophet from eighth-century Judah? It turns out that this is a question to which a great many scholars—more or less none of them Latter-day Saints—have been dedicating focused effort for a very long time. It used to be that the chief focus of scholarship on Isaiah was historical. That is, scholars tried to establish the original historical setting for each oracle or saying or narrative in Isaiah, and they tried to fix as exactly as possible the identity of the guy who created the oracle or saying or narrative in the first place. In short, the point was to get back *behind* the Book of Isaiah *to Isaiah himself* (or to whomever else might have usurped the name of Isaiah, so to speak, somewhat deceptively landing their teachings in the book that bears Isaiah's name). This used to be the focus of scholarship. But things began to change some decades ago—really, half a century ago now!—and scholars working on Isaiah these days pay attention less to historical questions than to more strictly literary questions. They—I'll give you some bibliographical information later—want to know about the basic shape of the book and about the way that shape determines the meaning of the prophet's words. Of course, the historical work of two centuries hasn't been forgotten or disparaged in the meanwhile. Rather, what historians reconstructed has been used extensively by those who work on literary questions, since all that proves useful for reconstructing the processes by which the literary forms of the Book of Isaiah originally took shape.

Now, what's been the result of all this literary work? You might well guess that it's difficult to summarize. And of course, this more recent sort of scholarship is still relatively young, with the result that there isn't as much consensus in the field as we'd probably like there to be. Maybe that's a virtue, in a way. Anyway, it lets us as readers of Isaiah in the Book of Mormon look at a host of incompatible proposals regarding the structures and literary intentions of the Book of Isaiah and then evaluate them in part based on their usefulness for making sense of, say, Nephi's use of Isaiah. That's really kind of nice. It is nice, but don't let me give the wrong impression there. I don't mean to say—in fact, it'd be absolutely incorrect to say—that the shift toward a literary approach in the study of Isaiah means that we've now got a mass of highly subjective proposals regarding the correct interpretation of Isaiah, and that this lets us bring our own merely subjective interests to the study of Isaiah. What I mean is rather that literary study of Isaiah is still taking definitive shape. Specific proposals haven't yielded any consensus yet, methodologies are still hotly debated, and no one agrees about exactly how to understand the relationship between the historical and the literary. But the discussion is nonetheless maturing. And while it's doing so, those interested in the Book of Mormon find themselves confronted with a wide variety of proposals that might prove useful for making sense of how Isaiah works in Nephite scripture.

So let me outline a couple of really interesting proposals to be drawn from work on the literary structure of the Book of Isaiah.

Two Halves of Isaiah

The simplest or most obvious literary feature of the Book of Isaiah is the fact that it comes in two halves. It's still a point of discussion as to exactly *where* the first half of Isaiah gives way to the second half. It's clear at least that chapters 1–33 are in the first half and that chapters 40–66 are in the second half. What's still under discussion is whether chapters 34–39 belong to the first half (that's the older idea, almost universally accepted for a long time), or whether they belong to the second half (that's the newer idea, gaining a good deal of attention lately). But whether we divide the book between chapters 33 and 34 or between chapters 39 and 40, what's important for our purposes is the fact that the two halves are literarily and theologically different. The first half of the book is taken up primarily with the theme of judgment (both of covenant peoples and of Gentile nations), while the second half of the book is taken up primarily with the theme of restoration (of the covenant people thanks in part to the assistance of the Gentile nations). Other major prophetic books are similarly organized, with prophecies of peace and restoration coming after prophecies of destruction and judgment. And it's recently been noted by Edgar Conrad that the whole collection of the minor prophetic books—Micah and Jonah and Malachi and the like—are collectively organized the same way.

So the pattern of judgment-and-then-restoration appears often in the Old Testament, but there seems to be something special about the internal coherence of the Book of Isaiah in this regard. In Isaiah, it's not just that judgment gives way to restoration. The prophecies of judgment in Isaiah have deliberately been shaped to anticipate the prophecies of restoration in a remarkable way, and the prophecies of restoration hark back to the prophecies of judgment in a similarly remarkable way. So there's a tightness about the Book of Isaiah that wasn't achieved by the compilers or editors of other prophetic collections. And there's something particularly relevant to the Book of Mormon about the way this tightness is achieved in Isaiah. Or really, there's something particularly relevant about it to Nephi's record.

In the first half of the Book of Isaiah, primarily focused on judgment, there's a strong emphasis on *writing*, on the actual work of writing prophecies down. It's an essential theme, since Isaiah was among the earliest of the Hebrew prophets whose oracles were put into writing. Before his era—that is, before Amos (his near-contemporary and the earliest of the so-called "writing prophets")—prophecy seems to have been considered a kind of in-the-moment affair, an oral business that was supposed to accomplish something important but basically temporary. So what we get with the prophets before Isaiah's day are really just stories. We have *stories* about Elijah, but no *book* of Elijah. But something about Hebrew prophecy changed at the time of Isaiah. Early in the twentieth century, Gerhard von Rad closely analyzed the passages in Isaiah that focus on writing and provided a brilliant explanation of this shift from oral to written prophecy. In a nutshell, he says this: Isaiah's task as prophet was (as Isaiah 6 makes clear) to address himself to a people hardened in advance against his message, with the result (as Isaiah 8 makes clear) that he found it necessary to write and then to seal up his prophecies for a later generation that would be prepared to receive them. Because he was called to prophesy, but to a people who couldn't receive his word, he helped to launch an era during which prophecy was understood to be directed to a later age rather than to the prophet's own people. And that's why it was to be written down. This is a theme all through the first half of Isaiah.

Then here's the fascinating thing. Early in the second half of Isaiah, there's a *new* prophetic call, a kind of repetition of the prophetic call from the first half, found in Isaiah 6. That is, Isaiah 40 repeats Isaiah 6, with the prophet being commissioned all over again. But where the commission in the first half of Isaiah forces the prophet to turn to the future by committing his prophecies to writing, the commission in the second half of Isaiah forces the prophet to turn to the past, opening the sealed prophecies of the earlier era to read them among a people finally prepared to receive them. Thus the second prophetic commission, found in Isaiah 40, finds the divine voice calling on the prophet to "Read!" Unfortunately, the Hebrew word that could and, I think, should be translated "Read!" has been translated as "Cry!" in most renderings, but the Hebrew word is actually ambiguous. (If you want the full argument for this reading, take a look at Edgar Conrad's book *Reading Isaiah* or Hugh Williamson's book *The Book Called Isaiah*.) On one literary reading, at any rate, the second half of the Book of Isaiah finds the prophet opening the sealed book of the first half and speaking peace to a people that's so far only heard prophecies of destruction and judgment.

So, the first half of Isaiah gives us this: "Write the vision and seal it up!" And then the second half gives us this: "Open what's been sealed and start reading!" It's beautiful that as we move from the first half to the second, we leave off divine wrath and devastating judgment for divine comfort and restorative deliverance.

Now, a second major feature of the Book of Isaiah supplements this first one. *Generally* speaking, the first half of the book focuses on the history of the eighth century B.C., while the second half of the book focuses on the history of the sixth century B.C. In case you're unfamiliar with ancient Israelite history, let me say a bit about what that means. The first half of the Book of Isaiah for the most part addresses problems that arose in connection with the rise of the Assyrian empire. The eighth century before Christ witnessed the advance of the then-apparently-invincible Assyrians into the region where Israel was settled. Assyria's center was located to the east of Palestine, but the road that led through Palestine to Egypt followed an arc that forced the Assyrians north first, so that their conquest of the lands surrounding Israel began at the north end of Palestine and then progressed southward toward Egypt. While Isaiah was an active prophet in Jerusalem, Assyria obliterated the northern kingdom of Israel, made up of ten of the twelve Israelite tribes—which resulted in their being, as we often say, lost. And then, while Isaiah was *still* active, Assyria pushed its campaign further to the south, causing all kinds of trouble for the southern kingdom of Israel, known simply as Judah ("the Jews"). All this is reflected in the first half of the Book of Isaiah, where the prophet gives intense attention to Judah's fate during the Assyrian campaign.

But then things change pretty drastically in the second half of the book. All too suddenly, it seems as if the Assyrian threat has disappeared, and the prophet turns his attention to Babylon. But this marks a turn from one era to another. Babylon didn't take its rise into imperial domination until well into the seventh century, some time after Isaiah had already died. And Babylon didn't become a serious threat for Judah—which just barely survived the Assyrian onslaught—until late in the seventh century, about the time Nephi and his brothers would have been born. But what interests the prophet in the second half of the Book of Isaiah isn't the Babylonian *threat*; it's rather the possibility of redemption or restoration *after* Babylon has already wreaked all kinds of havoc for Judah. The focus in the second half of the book, in other words, is on Judah's predicted return from Babylon—its *return from exile*. This didn't happen until the sixth century, and only once the Persians and the Medes overthrew the Babylonian empire. Lehi's family was fully settled in the New World by the time these events took place. So as we move from the first half to the second half of the Book of Isaiah, we move from the Assyrian threat of the eighth century to the return from Babylonian exile in the sixth century.

In a certain way, this second feature shouldn't surprise us too much. We've already seen that the whole of the Book of Isaiah is organized around a certain transformation of the idea of prophecy, with the result that prophecies uttered in one era are written and sealed up to be read in another era—an era in which God's people are prepared to understand their importance. Since such prophecies are written and sealed up in the first half of the Book of Isaiah and then opened and read carefully in the second half, there's nothing too shocking about the fact that the focus shifts from one era to another.

Here's the problem, though. This drastic shift in the second half of the Book of Isaiah has led the vast majority of Isaiah scholars—and for a long time—to conclude that the two halves of Isaiah were produced by at least two distinct prophets working in fundamentally different historical and geographical settings. Isaiah was the originator of the most historically trustworthy materials found in the first half of the book, certainly. But scholars have consistently argued that a so-called *second* Isaiah was active as a prophet in Babylon during the Exile, and that he was the chief author of the materials making up the second half of the book. Actually, that was the proposal some two hundred years ago. In the wake of Bernhard Duhm's work in the late nineteenth century, it's come now to be generally thought—though this remains a point of historical debate—that the second half of the Book of Isaiah should be further divided, with Isaiah 40–55 as the work of the second Isaiah and Isaiah 56–66 as the work of a *third* Isaiah, a prophet working in Judah only after the return from Babylonian exile. Among historians working on Isaiah, the most common opinion has come to be that the Book of Isaiah is the product of what's called the "Isaianic School," a series of prophets joined by a tradition that had its origins in the eighth century with Isaiah, but that generated new prophetic activity periodically as Judah's circumstances changed. The writings of the whole Isaianic School were worked by theologically motivated disciples and whole communities of interpretation into a single collection now presented in the Bible under Isaiah's name. In its most mature form (as in the work of Joseph Blenkinsopp, for instance; take a look at his three-volume commentary on Isaiah published as part of the *Anchor Bible Commentary*)—this approach believes the Book of Isaiah to have taken shape over the course of at least six or seven centuries, achieving final form only in third century or so before Christ.

Now, it's long been recognized that if the conclusions of the best scholars working on Isaiah are right, it spells serious trouble for the Book of Mormon. If the prevailing theory is right, major parts of the Book of Isaiah that appear in the Book of Mormon shouldn't have been produced until well after Lehi took his family away from Jerusalem. It'd therefore be impossible for those parts of Isaiah to be on the brass plates where Nephi says he found them. Isaiah chapters 2–4, 13–14, and 48–55 (Isaiah texts that all appear in the Book of Mormon) wouldn't seem to have been composed before at least a couple of decades after Lehi's family left Jerusalem—some of them still later. And even those Isaiah texts in the Book of Mormon that *would* seem to have originated before Lehi's time (such as chapters 5–12 and chapter 29) aren't regarded as having achieved their *final* form—the form in which they appear in the Book of Mormon—until well after the Lehites took their leave from the Old World. Simply put, modern Isaiah scholarship seems rather straightforwardly to work against the Book of Mormon's historical claims.

Skepticism about Scholarship

This has understandably led to a good deal of skepticism among Mormons toward Isaiah scholarship quite generally. I wonder, though, if we haven't been too hasty in certain ways here. I'm as committed to Book of Mormon historicity as anyone, and yet I think there's much to learn from solid non-Mormon scholarship on Isaiah. And I want to suggest, in fact, that the Book of Mormon itself gives us reasons to take at least *some* of the scholars' conclusions quite seriously. Somehow, it seems to me, we as Mormons have to find a complicated balance between the consensus among Isaiah scholars and the conclusions we're bound to because of our belief in the Book of Mormon's truth.

Here's a deeply suggestive detail. The Book of Mormon quotes extensively from the writings scholars today trace back to Isaiah of Jerusalem.

And it quotes extensively from the writings scholars today trace back to the so-called second Isaiah, active in Babylon during the Exile. But note this: *The Book of Mormon never quotes, not even once, from the writings scholars today trace back to the so-called third Isaiah.* Two things make this especially striking, I think. First, scholars working on Isaiah have noted a lot of literary connections between Isaiah 1 and Isaiah 65–66—that is, between the opening and closing bits of the Book of Isaiah. This may suggest that Isaiah 1 is actually the work of the third Isaiah. Now notice this. The Book of Mormon not only omits all of Third Isaiah, all of Isaiah 56–66; it also—and somewhat surprisingly—omits Isaiah 1. You might remember that when Nephi quotes thirteen chapters straight of Isaiah in Second Nephi, he begins with Isaiah 2, as if Isaiah 1 didn't exist at all. That's quite interesting, I think.

And now here's a second thing I find striking. There are two passages from Second Isaiah that receive particular attention in the Book of Mormon: Isaiah 49:22–23 and Isaiah 52:7–10. The first of these you'll likely remember: Gentile kings as nursing fathers and Gentile queens as nursing mothers, carrying redeemed Israel on their shoulders as they restore them to their promised lands. Well, here's the interesting thing. The most remarkable commentary on that passage that's available in the biblical text is to be found in Third Isaiah, in Isaiah 60. When Book of Mormon authors—both Nephi and Jacob at different times—comment on Isaiah 49:22–23, drawing on a host of other biblical and Isaianic texts to clarify its meaning, they never once draw on the most obvious source for developing it at length. They never quote from Isaiah 60. It's as if they're in fact entirely unaware of Isaiah 60, completely oblivious to the best possible source for making their pet passage fully clear to their audience. It seems to me downright odd that the Book of Mormon doesn't draw on Isaiah 60, especially when early revelations to Joseph Smith made clear allusions to it (as in, for instance, D&C 42:30–39).

Now, why are these two points striking? They suggest to me that the Book of Mormon could well be read as confirming the scholarly conclusion that Third Isaiah indeed had its origins only after the departure of Lehi's family from Jerusalem. There's reason to think that the Book of Mormon wants us to believe that Isaiah 56–66 was in fact missing from the brass plates that Lehi's family carried with them into the wilderness. This partial corroboration of what Isaiah scholars generally believe is suggestive, to say the least. Of course, the Book of Mormon certainly *doesn't* corroborate other conclusions drawn by most Isaiah scholars—for instance, that anything included in the Book of Isaiah with a focus on the Babylonian exile had its origins too late for the Lehites to have been aware of them. But the fact that it corroborates *some* conclusions in surprising ways, even as it fails to corroborate *others*, should draw our attention.

So I think we have reason to believe that the scholars are actually pretty good readers of Isaiah. They seem to have come to some conclusions using just the resources of textual and historical criticism that we might come to using primarily the commitments of our faith. And so, while someone committed to the Book of Mormon's historical claims can't uncritically accept every conclusion drawn in the best scholarship on Isaiah, we *can* certainly engage critically with the literature—and, I think, learn a great deal along the way.

Yikes! We've gone down a rather long tangent here, haven't we? But here's where it's led us. Let's recognize with the best of Isaiah scholarship that there's a strong shift from prophecies focused on the eighth century to prophecies focused on the sixth century as we move from the first to the second half of the Book of Isaiah. There's no need for such recognition to commit us to certain historical reconstructions of how the Book of Isaiah came into final form. We're free to suspend judgment on that point. But it seems we'd do best to see that there really is a turn from the Assyrian era to the post-Babylonian era as we work through the Book of Isaiah.

And in fact, it's rather obviously *because* of this shift that Isaiah's writings interested Nephi. Remember that Nephi opens his record by talking about how his father prophetically announced the exile to Babylon, as well as the subsequent return. If there was a second Isaiah, perhaps he prophesied in Jerusalem during Lehi's time, and his writings were included in the Book of Isaiah because of the way he tried to connect his prophecies to those of Isaiah. I don't know. I'm not a historian, but I suspect a solid historian could begin to construct a responsible account along these lines. Or, of course, it might simply be that at least major parts of the Book of Isaiah *were* in fact original to Isaiah himself and were written in the eighth century. There are respected Isaiah scholars today who argue for such a position—John Oswalt and Alec Motyer, for instance. They aren't part of the consensus, but their conclusions are recognized as important contenders.

Alright, we've nailed down two major features of the Book of Isaiah as a text, both focused on the fact that the book seems to divide pretty evenly into two halves. The Book of Mormon is selectively interested in material from both halves. A number of its contributors exhibit interest in writings from the second half of Isaiah, but only those usually attributed to the work of the second Isaiah. And Nephi exhibits peculiar additional interest in writings from the first half of Isaiah. We'll be looking in later lectures at some of the details here, asking questions about exactly which passages are taken up by whom and why.

For the moment, perhaps we've begun to get a sense for the Book of Isaiah. Perhaps. There's much more to say. I said before that I'd leave the structure of Nephi's record for next time, but I think it'd be best if we dedicate another session to making some preliminary points about Isaiah's writings. I'd like to be able to say a few things about how to go about reading Isaiah carefully, and we've been too bogged down in complex questions of structure and history to leave any time for that today. And I'd also like to say a bit more about the theological themes of each of the two halves of the Book of Isaiah we've isolated today. So let's turn our attention to these matters next time.

Lecture III

Themes and Strategies

Well, we're learning pretty quickly how much—or really, how little—ground we can cover each lecture. I'd hoped to say twice as much as I ended up saying last time. Let's see if we can remedy that today. And then we'll have to start moving more quickly, I suppose.

The Theology of Isaiah 1–39

I promised last time to say something this time about theological themes in Isaiah. Along with that, I'd like to say just a few things in a kind of practical vein about how to read Isaiah. First, though, theology. We've already become clear, I think, about the fact that the Book of Isaiah divides pretty evenly into two halves, each with a rather different set of emphases and intentions. Another marker of the division between the two halves is the fact that they exhibit rather different theological interests and investments. There are some excellent studies out there of these theological interests. Let me recommend, as a good starting place, John Goldingay's *The Theology of the Book of Isaiah*. Here, of course, we just want to highlight a couple of basic points. Let's say a bit about the first half of Isaiah first.

Two themes are often said to frame the theology of the first half of the Book of Isaiah: the inviolability of Jerusalem and the centrality of the Davidic dynasty. As for the former, it's essential that Isaiah's prophecies of judgment against Judah never predict the fall of the place where the Lord's temple stood. Assyria lays Judah waste, but Jerusalem—what Isaiah often calls simply Zion—remains. As for the second theme, that of the Davidic dynasty, note that Isaiah mingles often in the record with Judah's kings, and that his prophecies focus on the promised power of those kings as David's descendants. Now, these two themes intertwine in Isaiah's prophecies and stories regarding Hezekiah, the righteous Davidic king, who saw

Jerusalem through its most perilous encounter with the Assyrian empire, in the last years of the eighth century.

So there's the double focus of the first half of Isaiah. But let's be clear that this double focus on Jerusalem and the Judean monarchy really only helps to set up a still more central theological concern in the first half of Isaiah. Behind the prophet's confidence in Judah's exceptional status lies a larger investment in a certain conception of history. Key words in Isaiah's prophecies are "counsel" and "work." Well, those are the words as the King James Version renders them. The former, *'etsa* in Hebrew, would perhaps be better rendered as something like "plan" or "intention." "Work," however, is a good translation of the Hebrew terms *'abodah* and *ma'aseh*, which appear often. Now, what do these words express at the theological level? At least this: Isaiah has real confidence in the Lord's sovereignty over history, and he fully believes that all historical and political events bear witness to that sovereignty. As history unfolds, the divine plan makes itself known. God, it turns out, is up to something with all this messy history.

Think, for instance, of an Isaiah text I hope is relatively familiar. Assyria, Isaiah says, is "the rod of [God's] anger," and God intends to "send him against a hypocritical nation" (Isa. 10:5–6). The result will be the performance of God's "whole work upon mount Zion and on Jerusalem," but thereafter God will need to "punish the fruit of the stout heart of the king of Assyria, and the glory of his high looks" (v. 12). Why? Because Assyria's king thinks that it's his *own* strength that's behind his success, "for he saith, 'By the strength of my hand I have done it, and by my wisdom'" (v. 13). The Lord's response through Isaiah to this bit of nonsense is classic: "Shall the axe boast itself against him that heweth therewith? Or shall the saw magnify itself against him that shaketh it?" (v. 15). It turns out that all the pomp and glory of Assyria, the most impressive empire the world had known at the time of Isaiah, were just the byproduct of the Lord's historical intentions. And the Lord's intentions weren't focused on imperial power. Rather, they were focused on accomplishing something with and through the covenant people of Israel and Judah. Assyria, like every nation, was nothing more than a tool in God's hands.

For the Isaiah of the first half of the book, then, God has a *work* to accomplish, something he aims to get done by manipulating history. Apparently Isaiah spoke of this "work" often enough to be ridiculed for it. In one passage you might be familiar with, Isaiah concedes that God's work is a "strange work," his act a "strange act" (Isa. 28:21). In another, perhaps also familiar, Isaiah finds it necessary to respond directly to his critics, and he does so by pronouncing a woe on them for their mockery of his exposition of God's "work": "Woe unto them . . . that say, 'Let [God] make speed, and hasten his work, that we may see it: and let the counsel of the Holy One of Israel draw nigh and come, that we may know it!'" (Isa. 5:18–19). Isaiah's criticizing his critics here. They couldn't believe that God was actually pulling the strings of history, but Isaiah upbraids them for their lack of faith. Well, lack of faith and then some. In a neighboring passage, Isaiah describes these same critics as those who "follow strong drink" and enjoy music "in their feasts," even as "they regard not the work of the Lord, neither consider the operation of his hands" (Isa. 5:11–12). It would seem they thought they had better things to do, more important matters to attend to: *pleasure*.

The Remnant

So what *is* God's work, according to the first half of the Book of Isaiah? It's rather unpleasant perhaps. God's use of foreign powers against the covenant people is aimed at producing what Isaiah, drawing on a larger Israelite (and even more generally ancient Near Eastern) theme, calls "a remnant." (There's an excellent study available of how this theme developed before it funneled into its most remarkable manifestation in Isaiah's writings. Go take a look at Gerhard Hasel's book, *The Remnant*.) Here's a text from Isaiah that provides a basic exposition, found in the context of Isaiah's prophecy of what Assyria would do to Judah:

> And it shall come to pass in that day, that the remnant of Israel, and such as are escaped of the house of Jacob, shall no more again stay upon him that smote them [that is, upon Assyria]; but shall stay upon the Lord, the Holy One of Israel, in truth. The remnant shall return, even the remnant of Jacob, unto the mighty God. For though thy people Israel be as the sand of the sea, yet [only] a remnant of them shall return: the consumption decreed shall overflow with righteousness. (Isa. 10:20–22)

Hopefully that's clear enough in the King James rendering (and we'll say more about translations in a minute!). The point of God's working through Assyria is to prune the house of Jacob back so that it's made up just of those who will "return . . . unto the mighty God." (The word "return" here has, in Hebrew, a strong sense of repentance or conversion.) There's thus a "consumption"—a destruction—that's planned, but one that will nonetheless "overflow with righteousness."

God's work, then, is to reduce Israel to a righteous remnant. In light of all we said last time about the basic division between the two halves of the Book of Isaiah, we can already begin to guess at *why* God aims to produce a righteous remnant. These survivors of Israel's devastating history are those who will be prepared—at last!—to read the sealed book. In Isaiah 29, a chapter that's definitely familiar, Isaiah immediately follows his discussion of the sealed book with his announcement that the Lord "will proceed to do a marvellous work" (Isa. 29:14). So here we can see, it seems, that God's work, according to Isaiah, is double. He aims to produce *both* an Israelite remnant *and* a book they're prepared to read. *That's* the Lord's "whole work" on Zion.

The Theology of Isaiah 40–55

Can we let that suffice, for now, for theological themes in the first half of the Book of Isaiah? What, then, of the second half? In many ways, the theological themes of the second half of Isaiah are much clearer, or at least more readily discernible. They're nicely captured in isolated passages that don't require a lot of work to unpack. A good example is Isaiah 52:7–10, a passage the Book of Mormon deals with in several different places and at some length. Perhaps it's best if we just begin with an examination of that passage and then see whether there's much more that needs to be said about the themes of so-called Second Isaiah.

Here's the text:

> How beautiful upon the mountains are the feet of him that bringeth good tidings, that publisheth peace; that bringeth good tidings of good, that publisheth salvation; that saith unto Zion, "Thy God reigneth!" Thy watchmen shall lift up the voice; with the voice together shall they sing: for they shall see eye to eye, when the Lord shall bring again Zion. Break forth into joy, sing together, ye waste places of Jerusalem: for the Lord hath comforted his people, he hath redeemed Jerusalem. The Lord hath made bare his holy arm in the eyes of all the nations; and all the ends of the earth shall see the salvation of our God.

What's going on here? We open with an exclamation regarding beauty, and what overwhelms the speaker is the beauty of someone's *feet*. That might seem strange, but the point is actually pretty simple. What's celebrated here is the *coming* or the *arrival* of a messenger of peace (hence the praise for his feet, for what's brought him here). He's bounding across the mountains, almost dancing for joy as he approaches a besieged city. What does he bring?

"Good tidings." The Hebrew word, like its Greek rendering in the New Testament—which we in turn usually translate as "gospel"—has reference to the announcement of victory. The text thus presents words of praise and glory shouted when the besieged city realizes that an approaching figure bears victorious news. The war's over, and we've won! All the messenger can get out of his mouth before he's carried off to some kind of feast is this: "Thy God reigneth!" Deliverance for the city marks the benevolence of God, of the God the people of city have been praying to.

But then we note this crucial detail. The city receiving the messenger is Zion, Jerusalem. It's the covenant people who've been delivered. It's their God who's been proven faithful. And the surrounding chapters (and other details in this verse we'll come to in a moment) make perfectly clear exactly *what* deliverance is meant. It's deliverance from captivity or exile in Babylon. The announcement is brought from Babylon to Jerusalem: "Good news! The Lord has toppled the Babylonian power! Your people will return!" The city besieged, left desolate for far too long, now knows that it'll soon be inhabited again. So there's no surprise at the response inside the city, among what few inhabitants it has left. Its "watchmen . . . lift up the voice" and "sing." They sing redeeming love. And the prophet begins to call on all of Jerusalem—its ruins even, its "waste places"!—to join in the chorus. "Break forth into joy, sing together!" And why? Because "the Lord hath comforted his people, he hath redeemed Jerusalem."

All this is glorious enough, but there's one further detail in this passage that's essential to understanding the spirit of Second Isaiah. The passage ends with these words: "The Lord hath made bare his holy arm in the eyes of all the nations; and all the ends of the earth shall see the salvation of our God." The point here is, I think, relatively clear. The deliverance that's been accomplished has taken place in the midst of the Gentile nations, far away from Israel's promised lands. The result? The Gentile nations have witnessed the whole affair. All the ends of the earth have seen with their own eyes that Israel's God is *actually* God. The Lord's "holy arm"—a classic Hebrew image for God's might—has been bared before the entire world. As the Persians prepare to send the Jews back to home from exile, the first seeds of Gentile conversion have been planted. Non-covenantal peoples have begun to recognize that there's a God in heaven who makes and keeps covenant, and that he summons all people to worship together before him, leaving off their petty nationalisms to join Israel and be numbered among the covenant people.

That, in a nutshell, is the theological theme of Isaiah 40–55. There's more to say, of course, concerning how Isaiah presents the theme, and concerning the felt need to reprimand the covenant people for their faithlessness—and concerning the role of the Gentile nations in assisting Israel's actual redemption. But none of these further points of clarification make any sense if one doesn't already have the basic picture clear. The second half of the Book of Isaiah, especially in the earlier parts, focuses on the return from exile, announcing good news to Jerusalem and broadcasting the fact that non-Israelite peoples have begun to see the real nature of the covenant God.

That much is clear, then, but let's nonetheless say a couple of things about the details just mentioned. How does the text present the central theological theme of Isaiah 40–55? Through a reinvigoration of the exodus tradition. You're all quite familiar with the exodus from Egypt, through the Red Sea and the Sinai wilderness, which lands Israel—eventually—in their Promised Land. The second half of Isaiah is obsessed with that story, using its imagery again and again to tell its own story, making of the escape from exile a new exodus, and of the resettlement in Palestine a new conquest. In many ways, this makes reading Second Isaiah a rather simple affair. Familiar imagery keeps the story moving. This also makes clear why the prophets might think that Israel *again* needs reprimanding. Just as Israel wandering in the Sinai wilderness needed constant berating to keep them focused on the God who'd delivered them, so Israel leaving Babylon to return to Judah requires chastening. Perhaps I can leave that point just at that.

But at least a few words need to be added about the role the Gentiles play in the restoration of Israel. It's of course God who does the actual work of delivering the Jews from exile. But because that deliverance is worked out through the rise of a Gentile nation that's willing to assist Israel's return, the Gentiles end up playing a central role in the story. To make the point clear, we might just quote one further passage from these chapters of Isaiah, another one that's familiar—and to which we already made reference last time:

> Thus saith the Lord God, "Behold, I will lift up mine hand to the Gentiles, and set up my standard to the people; and they shall bring thy sons in their arms, and thy daughters shall be carried upon their shoulders. And kings shall be thy nursing fathers, and their queens thy nursing mothers: they shall bow down to thee with their face toward the earth, and lick up the dust of thy feet; and thou shalt know that I am the Lord: for they shall not be ashamed that wait for me." (Isa. 49:22–23)

That passage seems to be Nephi's favorite. And in many ways it's self-explanatory—but not in all ways, since we have a tendency to flatten its meaning as Latter-day Saints, applying it *just* to missionary work. But notice the point of the text. The Lord summons the *Gentiles*—Persians and others—to redeem *Israel*. Gentile monarchs, in fact, carry the covenant people home to their own lands on their shoulders. It's a beautiful image, and it marks the peculiar role played by the Gentiles in this story. It's not just that Israel gets home. The Gentiles play a role in their redemption, and it's *that* that plants the seed of Gentile conversion.

Strategies for Reading

Okay, let's say that's enough to cover the ground of basic theological themes in the two halves of the Book of Isaiah. With what time we have left today, let's turn our attention to a more general question. How does one go about *actually reading* Isaiah? Some of the historical, literary, and theological points we've made should help, of course, but there are deeply practical questions that need answering, too. How does one go about making sense of particular texts in the concrete work of reading?

A first point might—but also might not—go without saying: *Use alternative translations.* If you can read Hebrew or have the time to learn, that's great. But chances are, you don't, and you won't be learning too much Hebrew any time soon. So it's best to become familiar with a few of the better translations of the Bible so that you can look at Isaiah in a couple of different renderings. Here are my recommendations, for what they're worth. I particularly like the New Revised Standard Version, or the NRSV. It's both ecumenical (it wasn't produced from any particular Christian denomination's perspective) and scholarly (informed by variants in the manuscripts and deeply aware of the best scholarship on the relevant ancient languages). And of course it's very easy to read, relatively speaking, because it's in modern English. It's not nearly so necessary to keep an English dictionary nearby as when you read something like the King James Version. Similar in many ways is the English Standard Version, the ESV, and I think it's to be recommended as well. A third you might keep in mind is the Jewish Publication Society's rendering, or the JSP. As the name suggests, this is a specifically Jewish rendering. It's far less literal than many other translations, but it's built on centuries, even millennia, of Jewish reflection. It's one worth keeping an eye on when you're reading something like Isaiah. So these are some translations you might consult. And they're all available online for free in one place or another.

Now, why bother with alternative translations? Well, *you've* read Isaiah in the King James Version, and you've likely thrown up your hands in frustration at the complexity of the language! A large part of that is due simply to age. The King James Version is four centuries old already, and it often uses older constructions or terminology that's long since out of date. Further, the translators were excellent writers who recognized the beauty of the underlying Hebrew or Greek of the richest biblical texts, and so they often produced beautifully poetic renderings that trip up modern readers. So you could use a little help. And that, by the way, is how to use other translations. Don't take them as the direct and unfiltered word of God, as if they weren't also translations. But I recommend reading them *alongside* the King James Version, seeing how they help you to make sense of the sometimes-awkward renderings in the translation you're used to. If you find that the translations are deeply different in places, then you'll realize that there are difficulties in the Hebrew text, difficulties that make the translators scratch their heads. Also, don't assume that translators all have suspicious agendas—whether religious or political. Just recognize that biblical Hebrew is a difficult and long-since-dead language. Even the best scholars struggle with how to make sense of Isaiah in many places.

So take a look at some other translations, and see if you can't make more sense of Isaiah than you usually do. But that's only a start. You'll find that reading Isaiah is still easier if you become acquainted with a bit of an- cient history. I realize that this is where a lot of eyes start rolling, since no one has time to study big scholarly books on complicated ancient history. But it's nothing like so difficult as you might think it is. Let me recom- mend three quick sources that can get you acquainted in a basic way with the context for Isaiah. First, take a look at an excellent Latter-day Saint publication. A few years ago, Richard Holzapfel, Dana Pike, and David Seely published a solid but gentle introduction to Israelite history with Deseret Book, titled *Jehovah and the World of the Old Testament*. About two hundred and fifty pages into the book, you'll find chapters on the his- tory leading up to Isaiah's time, beginning from just after Solomon's reign. The book is richly illustrated with interspersed sections on specific histori- cal events or important historical figures. You'll learn a lot in just a couple hours of reading, and you'll have the broad setting of Isaiah quite clear. A second option, somewhat more scholarly in presentation and not written by Latter-day Saints, is the *Oxford History of the Biblical World*, edited by

Michael Coogan. Chapters 6 and 7 cover all the history you'd need to know. Finally, a *really* great option is simply to get your hands on a solid commentary on Isaiah, and I'd recommend a relatively conservative one. Commentaries work passage by passage, and so a good commentary will back up from the text to provide historical context whenever things get confusing. I recommend conservative commentaries when you're looking at history because more liberal commentaries tend to get downright obsessed about history in a way that proves unhelpful for many readers, and because they're much more likely to draw conclusions at odds with what the Book of Mormon suggests about ancient history. Let me recommend, then, either John Oswalt's two-volume commentary, titled *The Book of Isaiah*, or Gary Smith's also-two-volume commentary, just called *Isaiah*.

Okay. Alternative translations and some historical familiarity. These are good first resources. I've just recommended a couple of commentaries for purposes of sorting out the history, but let me say just a bit more about commentaries in a general vein. It's a *great* idea to use commentaries. Obviously, you aren't looking to build a library, so let me just recommend two commentaries that might help you the most. If you're struggling to make sense of some particular passage, look up what's said about it in *both* of the following two commentaries: Oswalt's *The Book of Isaiah*, which I just mentioned, and Blenkinsopp's three-volume *Isaiah*. Oswalt is a very conservative commentator, while Blenkinsopp is among the most liberal. Taking a look at the two extremes isn't a bad idea. It'll give you a sense for the range of interpretations, and you might begin to find your way toward a solid middle-of-the-road position. Plus, these two commentaries are both substantive, and each provides its *own* translation of the text, with notes on the Hebrew. There's a lot to work with if you have these in hand.

What else needs to be said? Shall we tackle the most difficult bit of advice? Let's do. Here it is, put far too strongly at first: *Stop looking for Jesus in Isaiah.* We've been trained by a long Christian tradition to think that the prophets of the Hebrew Bible frequently spoke in anticipation of Christ. And the result has been a Christological approach to understanding Isaiah. All too often, we read Isaiah, talking to ourselves in something like this way: "This doesn't make sense. Nor does this. Oh, that sounds like Jesus! Okay, this doesn't make sense again. Nor that. Oh, Jesus again! Now this doesn't make sense. . . ." You see, the passages from Isaiah we're most comfortable with are the ones we associate directly with Christ: "a virgin shall conceive," "unto us a child is born," "the Lord hath laid on him the iniquities of us all," and so on. The rest of Isaiah we find too obscure to make much sense of. I think that's in part because we're wondering what the rest has to say about Christ. We read about the virgin conceiving, and we feel like we're on solid ground. But the passage then goes on to talk about eating butter and honey, about foreign kings, about flies and bees, about hired razors, and so on, and we feel like everything stopped making sense. That whole text actually becomes relatively simple if you wait a bit before trying to find Christ in it, figuring out what Isaiah himself is saying first. You see, there's a difficult political situation in Isaiah's day, and Judah's king is acting out of fear as it unfolds; Isaiah tells him not to fear because a soon-to-be-born baby won't know how to speak before the enemy has been deposed; but then the real tough times will come beyond that, and largely because the king has acted faithlessly—and so on. This is a relatively clear story (we'll be telling it in detail in a later lecture), but it's clear only if we don't try too quickly to force it to tell us something about Christ. It'll do that in good time.

Now, let me be perfectly clear on something: Christ *is* there in Isaiah, I think. There are very good Isaiah scholars who find messianic anticipation in Isaiah's prophecies, even if there are others who don't. (I actually find *the latter's* arguments a bit obtuse.) And we'll see later that *Nephi* insists that certain Isaiah passages have something to say about Christ. Abinadi's even stronger on that point. But here's the trick, I think. It's essential *first* to get clear about what Isaiah says without trying to import into it anything you know about Christ from the New Testament. Try to figure out what he's saying on his own terms. And *then*, if what he's saying strongly anticipates a redeemer to come, a kind of royal or priestly figure, you're probably right to read it as an anticipation of Christ in some way or another. But don't start from the New Testament. My experience is that it'll only confuse you. And there's a reason for all this. Isaiah's chief purpose wasn't to predict the Messiah. His chief purpose—we'll be making this clearer and clearer—was to outline the stakes and status of the Abrahamic covenant in history. Obviously, the Messiah plays an important role in that, and Isaiah knew that. But the Messiah is only *part* of the story for Isaiah, and we'll miss Isaiah's point if we make the Messiah *the whole* or even *the most important part* of the story. We've got to focus on what Isaiah was focusing on, if we want to get what he's trying to tell us.

Is that clear enough? You can guess why I'm a bit nervous about it. It's not terribly common to hear someone tell you to *stop* looking for Jesus in the scriptures. But I think that's a necessary thing to do in this case.

Alright. What else needs saying? We're rapidly running out of time, so let me give just one more bit of advice for the moment. We'll have to make other points about reading Isaiah as we're going along in our work in later lectures. But this one's probably worth getting on the table from the outset: *Don't get lost in the details.* One of the difficulties people experience in reading Isaiah is that he uses *a lot* of imagery. And that imagery comes from his culture, which is of course profoundly foreign to us. So when you come to an image that doesn't make sense to you, don't worry about it. See instead if you can make sense of the larger passage. And if you can make decent sense of a whole chapter, with a few image-heavy verses sticking out like uninterpreted sore thumbs, that's fine. For example, let's say you begin to make sense of Isaiah 7 in general, which we were just talking about above. There's a serious threat of war, and Isaiah tells the king not to fear. His enemies will be conquered. But then Assyria will come through Judah and cause a great deal of trouble. Okay, that's clear enough. Now don't get too wound up about the passages that seem really odd: "butter and honey shall he eat" or "the hair of the feet" or "a man shall nourish a young cow and two sheep" or "all hills that shall be digged with the mattock." Let these go while you're getting clear about the general sense of the oracle. And then let alternative translations and commentaries help you make some sense of these more puzzling passages. It turns out that "butter and honey" is a sign of depopulation, with the survivors eating like kings. And "the hair of the feet" is a euphemism for pubic hair, which conquerors shaved off of the conquered in an act of humiliation. The cow-and-sheep thing is a subject of unsettled debate that's worth reviewing. And the hills digged with the mattock are cultivable hills, which will be overgrown with weeds. Commentaries can clear all this up pretty quickly once you've got a good sense for what's going on in general.

Especially beware of reading strange mystical insights into obscure imagery. Don't start asking weird questions about butter and honey, wondering whether there's some kind of deep mystery contained in the image. And don't assume that the "young cow" refers to some future prophet, while the "two sheep" are his counselors, or some such nonsense. Isaiah doesn't speak in mystical allegories, as is sometimes assumed. Keep it simple. I think you'll find, as you read other translations, that Isaiah's far simpler than you've imagined. Seriously.

We'll try, though, to make things more complex next time.

Lecture IV

The More Sacred Part

Matters of Structure

Well, I've been promising to get to questions of structure for a while now, so we should get right to it. With the last two lectures, we've hopefully got some kind of basic sense for what to expect from Isaiah. But what's to be expected from Nephi himself? What is he up to in his record? Well, we already saw in our first lecture that he's got some discernible purposes—even if we tend to read Nephi as if he were somewhat haphazardly sticking things together without any unifying vision. To the contrary, he does have a unifying vision, and we've got to begin to uncover it. And the key, I think, is structure.

Why structure? It's actually not terribly difficult, I think, to see why structure is important. If you set about some task, and you have the freedom to design its execution from scratch, most of your work is structural in nature. Let's say you're organizing an all-Saturday event for your community about the increasing difficulties associated with an extended drought. Once you've decided on some basic parameters (an all-day event, aimed at the general public), you set about organizing structure. What should the major components of the event be? How do you divide up the day? You want people to see that there are things they should start doing right now to help, so how do you make sure those get communicated? Do you have a public talk with an expert people would trust? If so, where should it be in the schedule so that it gets the best possible attendance? What other activities should be involved? Would it be better to have a kind of carnival with educational games to make sure families attend? Or would it be better to make it a more serious occasion, more like a science fair, so that it's mostly adults who come? And once these questions can be answered, it's necessary to decide when each part of the event should happen so that everything is as effective as possible.

No surprises here. This is everyday stuff. But now assume that *Nephi's* doing something like this. He's got an overarching purpose, and he's organizing his materials in order to accomplish it as effectively as possible. We learn from 2 Nephi 5:28–34 that he had *at least* thirty to forty years to reflect on things before he actually produced the record we have from him. This isn't something he dashed off in a couple of days, and it's certainly not something he wrote in bits and pieces as he went along, without any particular aim. Rather, after having kept a kind of aimless chronicle of events in his "large plates," he gathered his thoughts and created his "small plates," a deliberate record with specific points of focus. And so it's best if we recognize from the outset that he took up the task of writing with an eye to organizing his materials. I see him sketching out a variety of different possible approaches to his task, only eventually settling on the one we've got in the text. And he's careful to let us know exactly what he's up to.

Is that making sense? Nephi's got a purpose, and so he's got a structure. If we want to sort out his purpose, and especially if we want to see that purpose fulfilled as we read, we've got to keep a close eye on how he organizes his material. The structure of Nephi's record is absolutely key to everything he's doing.

So, what is the structure of Nephi's record?

Dividing Nephi's Record

Well, the most obvious and certainly the first thing we've got to say is simply that *Nephi divides his record into two major parts*, what we call "First Nephi" and what we call "Second Nephi." Have you ever asked yourself why? He doesn't seem to be trying to imitate the division of Samuel or Kings or Chronicles into two books in the Bible. (For one, it's not at all clear whether he knew *our* books of Samuel or Kings or Chronicles. His brass plates, he tells us, had a history of the Jews in it, but the historical books of our Old Testament seem to have been written—or at least finished and fully edited—only well after Nephi and his family left Jerusalem. That's not controversial at all and should be obvious when closely reading Samuel, Kings, or Chronicles.) Further, we should note that most of the Book of Mormon *isn't* divided into "First So-and-So" and "Second So-and-So." We don't have "First Alma" and "Second Alma," though it would have maybe made more structural sense to do it that way (the Book of Alma actually divides into two parallel halves quite evenly). We *do* have "Third Nephi" and "Fourth Nephi," but those were written by *different* men named Nephi, and these titles were given to them only by Orson Pratt anyway.

So there's something actually *surprising* about the fact that Nephi divides his record into two separable books. So we've got to wrestle with this first point. Why *First* Nephi and *Second* Nephi?

And we've got to wrestle with this first point right alongside a second point. Because it turns out that Nephi doesn't just divide his record into two *books*, right there between 1 Nephi 22 and 2 Nephi 1. He also divides his record into two *parts*, let's call them: a part he calls "the more sacred things" and that's located in 2 Nephi 6–30, and a part that should be called, he seems to imply, "the less sacred things," made up by everything else in his record: all of First Nephi, and then chapters 1–5 and 31–33 of Second Nephi. I'll be justifying this claim in a moment here, but let's make this point clearly first: Nephi divides his record in two *twice*, and *in a different place in each instance*. That's weird. There's the division of Nephi's record into two books—First Nephi, Second Nephi—and then there's the division of Nephi's record into two parts—more sacred (2 Ne. 6–30) and less sacred (the rest of the record). So we've got to wrestle with this second point right alongside the first. Why *more* and *less* sacred parts of the record, clearly delineated?

And between these first two points is a third one, making us ask a third and especially difficult question: *Why don't the two ways of dividing the record map onto one another?* If there's a "more sacred" part of the record, why not just make it into one of the two books? And if there's a "less sacred" part, why not just make it into the other book? Why this mismatch between the two ways of dividing up the record? I've been wrestling with this question myself for a long time, and I think I've finally begun to come up with some answers. I gave some preliminary answers, largely useless, in my first book, *An Other Testament*. We'll see if we can't go well beyond them today.

More and Less Sacred Parts

But let's get back to the second way Nephi divides up his record. You can all see that the record's divided into two books, First and Second Nephi. But I doubt you all see that it's also divided into "more sacred" and "less sacred" parts. To see this, we've got to look in great detail at a couple of passages, on which I've done some work that's available in print. (You can check out *An Other Testament* if you're interested.) So let's turn to 1 Nephi 19, where we'll look at the first handful of verses.

Here's the context: Nephi and his family have just arrived in the New World after a complicated journey. 1 Nephi 18 closes with their arrival, and with their discovery of all kinds of resources there—fertile land and useful animals and, especially relevant to our interests, "all manner of ore, both of gold and of silver and of copper" (1 Ne. 18:25). Nephi puts all this ore to good use, as he explains in the first verse of 1 Nephi 19: "And it came to pass that the Lord commanded me, wherefore I did make plates of ore that I might engraven upon them the record of my people." More or less upon arrival in the New World, Nephi produced a record, including in it his father's record, as well as some account of the journey. And he included both his father's and his own prophecies, as he goes on to tell us in that same verse.

What record is Nephi describing here? Well, this is what we usually call Nephi's "large plates," but what he himself usually calls his "other plates." Let's refresh our memory here, since Nephi goes on to give a kind of general description of these large plates in verses 2 and 4:

> The record of my father, and the genealogy of his forefathers, and the more part of all our proceedings in the wilderness are engraven upon those first plates. . . . [These things] are of a truth more particularly made mention upon the first plates. . . . I, Nephi, did make a record upon the other plates, which gives an account—or which gives a greater account—of the wars and contentions and destructions of my people.

It's perhaps that last detail that's most familiar: Nephi's large plates gave much more space than his small plates did to what we might call the secular—to historical matters, to wars and the like, and to his father's experiences. It clearly included religious material as well (like Lehi's prophecies), but the large plates were apparently a good deal more inclusive than the small plates. And of course, *we're* familiar only with the small plates. (You'll remember that Mormon made an abridgment from Nephi's large plates, apparently calling it the Book of Lehi. But that was part of what was lost when Martin Harris let the first manuscript get out of his hands.)

Okay, so we've got the first record Nephi produced, the so-called large plates. And we're clear that he made that record quite soon after he and his family got to the New World. Now, what of his other record, the small plates, the thing we're reading? He tells us about it also in this passage. It comes up first in verses 2–3, where Nephi says this:

I knew not at that time which I made [the other plates] that I should be commanded of the Lord to make these plates. . . . And after that I made these plates by way of commandment, I, Nephi, received a commandment that the ministry and the prophecies, the more plain and precious parts of them, should be written upon these plates—and that the things which were written should be kept for the instruction of my people which should possess the land, and also for other wise purposes (which purposes are known unto the Lord).

Here's our introduction to the small plates. Note that they were made quite a bit later. Here Nephi doesn't yet tell us *when* they were produced, but just that he had no idea at the time he made the *large* plates that he'd later be commanded to produce the *small* plates. Nonetheless, he gives us a bit of information about the content of the small plates. When he was later commanded to produce them, the commandment was accompanied by some instruction about their content: "the ministry and the prophecies, the more plain and precious parts of them."

All this, I assume, is relatively old news. But the crucial point is still coming. Turning now to verse 5, we read this: "An account of my making these plates shall be given hereafter." Which plates? The small plates. Nephi's been consistent here, calling the large plates his "other plates" and the small plates "these plates." So here he tells us that he'll give us *only later* in his record an account of the actual production—the actual physical production and subsequent inscription—of the small plates. It might seem peculiar that he bothers to tell us this, but we'll see how important it is in a moment. So, where does he later tell us about making the small plates? It's not hard to find. Take a look at the last verses of 2 Nephi 5:

And I, Nephi, had kept the records upon my plates which I had made of my people thus far. And it came to pass that the Lord God said unto me, "Make other plates, and thou shalt engraven many things upon them which are good in my sight for the profit of thy people." Wherefore, I, Nephi, to be obedient to the commandments of the Lord, went and made these plates, upon which I have engraven these things. And I engravened that which is pleasing unto God. And if my people be pleased with the things of God, they be pleased with mine engravings which are upon these plates. And if my people desire to know the more particular part of the history of my people, they must search mine other plates. And it sufficeth me to say that forty years had passed away, and we had already had wars and contentions with our brethren. (2 Ne. 5:29–34)

That's a long passage, I realize, but you'll see why it's important in a moment. For now, let's just make this much clear. In 1 Nephi 19:5, Nephi notes that he'll later give an account of the actual physical production of the small plates, and then in the very last verses of 2 Nephi 5, he provides that promised account.

That's clear, then? And now you're asking why all this matters. The answer is back in 1 Nephi 19:5: "An account of my making these plates shall be given hereafter"—at, as we've seen, the end of 2 Nephi 5—"and *then*, behold, I proceed according to *that which I have spoken*." I've tried to emphasize two parts of that last bit. First, the word "then." "And then," Nephi says. Meaning what? I think it's clear. "Later on, at the end of 2 Nephi 5, I'll tell you about when I actually made the small plates," he says, "and *then*, beginning right after I've told you about that—hence, starting with 2 Nephi 6—I'm going to do something very specific." Good? That seems to be the force of Nephi's "then": "An account of my making these plates shall be given hereafter, and *then*, behold, I proceed according to that which I have spoken." There's a kind of break in Nephi's record at the border between 2 Nephi 5 and 2 Nephi 6. Something *new* is to be found beginning in 2 Nephi 6.

The second thing I've tried to emphasize in what I just quoted is "that which I have spoken." Whatever that phrase refers to is what Nephi promises he'll start doing when 2 Nephi 6 begins. And what's that? Well, as he puts it, it's the thing he's already "spoken" about with respect to the small plates. That makes it easy to identify: "the ministry and the prophecies, the more plain and precious parts of them" are supposed to be "written upon these plates." Nephi's telling us, pretty unmistakably, that 2 Nephi 6 marks the beginning of what he was divinely commanded to write on the small plates—the plain and precious parts of the ministry and the prophecies.

Interestingly, Nephi gives us a name for the material that begins only in 2 Nephi 6. He goes on in verse 5 to tell us this: "This I do"—he relegates the plain and the precious to a later, specified place in his record—"this I do that the more sacred things may be kept for the knowledge of my people." There's a whole lot we could do in thinking about what Nephi's saying with these words, but let's note just one point for our purposes. Nephi here calls the stuff to be found only beginning with 2 Nephi 6 "the more sacred things." However his organization of the record is supposed to ensure that these things are "kept for the knowledge of [his] people," we can see that he regards that plain and precious stuff to be found only later in the record as "more sacred" in some way than everything else that appears in his writings.

So, what have we got so far? In the opening verses of 1 Nephi 19, Nephi makes clear that there's a special part of his record, one that's more sacred than the rest—in fact, one that he produced by way of direct commandment from God—and this is to be found beginning only with 2 Nephi 6. But now we ought to ask a further question. Where does that "more sacred" part of the record end? Does it stretch all the way through the end of Nephi's record, right to 2 Nephi 33? I think we can find a clear answer to this, actually. Take a look at the last verse of 2 Nephi 30. Right as Nephi wraps up an extended prophecy, he says this: "And now, my beloved brethren, I must make an end of my sayings." And then the next chapter opens like this: "And now, I, Nephi, make an end of my prophesying unto you, my beloved brethren. . . . The things which I have written sufficeth me" (2 Ne. 31:1–2). Nephi here marks another seam in the text, making pretty clear, I think, that 2 Nephi 31–33, those final three chapters of the record, come only *after* the "more sacred things," as a kind of conclusion to the whole record. As we'll see in a moment, this makes really good sense of things.

All these details add up to the following, it seems to me. Nephi divides his record into a "more sacred" and particularly privileged part, which stretches from 2 Nephi 6 to 2 Nephi 30, and what we'd probably have to call a "less sacred" or at least less privileged part, made up of the whole of First Nephi, along with the first five and the last three chapters of Second Nephi. And now we find we have yet another question. What's to be said about the apparently less sacred material that makes up so much of Nephi's record? Why is it there at all? Does Nephi explain his inclusion of all this other stuff? Actually, I think he does. Let's go back to 1 Nephi 19 for one more minute. After all he says in verse 5 there about the "more sacred things," he begins to apologize, so to speak, in verse 6: "Nevertheless, I do not write anything upon plates, save it be that I think it be sacred." This comes across as an apology of sorts, doesn't it? He's just told us that 2 Nephi 6–30 makes up "the more sacred things," such that we'll only find what God specifically commanded him to write in that rather limited part of the record. But then he's sure to tell us that *everything* he writes is sacred, even if some of it technically qualifies as *less* sacred by comparison to the *more* sacred.

He goes still further in his apology, too. Still in the same verse: "And now if I do err, even did they err of old—not that I would excuse myself because of other men, but because of the weakness which is in me according to the flesh, I would excuse myself." Here Nephi recognizes pretty openly that he *might* be making a mistake in adding things to what God commanded him to inscribe. He's consciously taking a risk, consciously packing what God told him to write into a larger framework he's built up on his own. And he recognizes that he might be erring in doing so. But note this also: Nephi sees what he's doing as following a pattern that others before him have followed, "they . . . of old." Apparently, as he reads scripture, he finds other authors and editors doing much the same thing, carefully arranging the strictly prophetic into larger structural frameworks so that their readers won't miss what's most essential. This is perhaps a weakness that all producers of scripture share. Nephi worries right along with others, as he explains in the next verse, that "the things which some men esteem to be of great worth . . . others set at naught and trample under their feet" (1 Ne. 19:7). That's reason enough to couch the directly-commanded word of God in a not-directly-commanded package!

Okay, so now we know what to say about the "less sacred" material in Nephi's record as well. It seems it's included in order to make our reception of the "more sacred" a bit smoother. If we're careful readers of First Nephi, as well as of the opening and closing chapters of Second Nephi, we'll be all the better readers of 2 Nephi 6–30, the privileged core of Nephi's record. If we were just to begin with 2 Nephi 6–30, we'd likely miss the point of the whole project.

So the question we've got to ask now is simply this: What's to be found in 2 Nephi 6–30, and why is it so important to Nephi—or really, to God, to whom Nephi attributes the commandment he received to write those chapters?

The More Sacred Part

Have you ever noticed how we read Nephi? The parts we really don't like seem to be the parts Nephi wants to privilege, at least in light of what we've seen today. You know what I mean. We enjoy Nephi's writings immensely until we get to somewhere around 2 Nephi 6, and then we find ourselves bored or deeply confused until 2 Nephi 31 or so. There are parts of 2 Nephi 6–30 we don't mind. There are lots of fans of 2 Nephi 9, Jacob's major sermon on the atonement. And it isn't too hard to find people who really enjoy 2 Nephi 29, where Nephi rails against those who reject the Book of Mormon because they already have a Bible. But only two chapters out of twenty-five! We're not doing so hot. What is it about 2 Nephi 6–30 that turns us all off? That's easy enough to answer, and in just one word—or rather one name: *Isaiah*.

If we're right that Nephi sets apart 2 Nephi 6–30 as the "more sacred" and only divinely ordered part of his record, then we've got to grapple with this fact. *The core of Nephi's record is the part where he focuses extensively on Isaiah.* There's no way around this, I think. What Nephi most wanted us to have in our possession—actually, scratch that. What *God* most wanted us to have in our possession, thanks to Nephi's efforts at writing, is Isaiah. What we get in 2 Nephi 6–30, in those privileged twenty-five chapters, is Isaiah—Isaiah, Isaiah, Isaiah. And note that there's something essential about saying it three times—Isaiah, Isaiah, Isaiah—because we get Isaiah three times over. Here's a passage from Nephi's "more sacred things" that emphasizes this point:

> And now I, Nephi, write more of the words of Isaiah, for my soul delighteth in his words. For I will liken his words unto my people, and I will send them forth unto all my children. For he verily saw my Redeemer even as I have seen him, and my brother Jacob also hath seen him as I have seen him. Wherefore, I will send their words forth unto my children to prove unto them that my words are true. Wherefore, by the words of three, God hath said, I will establish my word. (2 Ne. 11:2–3)

The law of witnesses, right? Nephi emphasizes that he's giving us three witnesses concerning the Redeemer, that is, concerning the redemption of Israel: Jacob and Isaiah in addition to himself. In his beautiful book *Christ and the New Covenant*, Elder Holland says that in 2 Nephi 6–30 Nephi presents us with three angelic messengers who stand as sentinels at the gate of the Book of Mormon, prepared to admit us into the scriptural presence of the Lord.

But it's precisely this part of the Book of Mormon, this passage through the veil, as it were, that we want to avoid most. Why? Because it's *saturated* with Isaiah. It's not just that we get thirteen chapters drawn straight from Isaiah—that chunk of text we usually just call "the Isaiah chapters" (2 Nephi 12–24, drawn from Isaiah 2–14). It's that Jacob and Nephi *also* give us, in their respective contributions to this "more sacred" portion of the record, *more* Isaiah. Jacob comes first, and he's giving us a sermon that stretches over two days. His assigned topic, given him by Nephi, is a passage of scripture from—you guessed it!—Isaiah. Nephi has him speak about Isaiah 49:22–23. And in order to develop the meaning of the passage, Jacob not only provides some explanations in his own words, but he also quotes the rest of Isaiah 49, and then all of Isaiah 50–51, and *then* the first couple of verses of Isaiah 52! Perhaps we find some comfort in the fact that Jacob gives us a break from Isaiah in 2 Nephi 9, that sermon on the atonement, but he returns to things Isaianic in 2 Nephi 10, and we're forced to realize that the whole point of his sermon is to get us to understand certain among Isaiah's prophecies.

You're all too aware that Jacob's sermon on Isaiah is followed almost immediately by the longest single quotation of Isaiah in the Book of Mormon, that thirteen-chapter stretch we talked about a moment ago. Once that ends, Nephi takes over to provide us with his own contribution to this "more sacred" part of his record. And what does he do? He quotes and reworks more or less all of Isaiah 29 (he skips over just the first two verses)! And he concludes his contribution with a lengthy quotation of the heart of Isaiah 11! And, if you read carefully, you'll see that everything else in his contribution is built on a complicated web of further quotations of and allusions to Isaiah! (If you want to see these clearly, get your hands on Grant Hardy's *Reader's Edition* of the Book of Mormon. He italicizes and footnotes all the borrowings from Isaiah running through Nephi's prophecy. It'll startle you to see how much of Isaiah appears there in Nephi.)

So we don't get a break from Isaiah at all. Jacob gives us Isaiah. Isaiah *is* Isaiah. And then Nephi gives us more Isaiah. Isaiah, Isaiah, Isaiah.

If we believe Nephi, it's *this* part of his record that we're supposed to pay the most attention to. And what we're getting there is nothing but Isaiah. And if we start paying close attention to what's going on there, we start to realize that it doesn't just throw us in the deep end—except maybe in that thirteen-chapter stretch taken more or less straight from Isaiah. Instead, Nephi takes care to use his brother's and his own words to clarify and comment on Isaiah. We're not only being confronted with Isaiah, we're getting a bit of training in how to read Isaiah—at least in the way that Nephi wants us to read Isaiah. 2 Nephi 6–10 and 2 Nephi 25–30 make up two "manuals" of sorts, aimed at getting us to see what it means to read Isaiah's writings correctly. Nephi's helping us out all along the way.

But this much we shouldn't miss—can't miss, I hope. The point of Nephi's record is to bring us face to face with Isaiah, to get us to read Isaiah carefully. Will we do so?

Well, it turns out that Nephi's giving us a lot more help than already appears. We've already seen that everything in Nephi's record that *isn't* the "more sacred" part is there, it seems, to help us get ready for what *is* the "more sacred" part. So we ought quite naturally to ask what help, say, First Nephi might give us in making sense of Isaiah in Nephi's writings. The answer, it turns out, is that there's a lot there to help us, but we'll have to do more careful reading. We'll turn to this in our next lecture.

Lecture V

The Nature of First Nephi

Why First Nephi?

We covered *a lot* of ground last time. We've made this much clear, at least in a preliminary way: that the whole point of Nephi's record is to get us to read Isaiah carefully. Nephi explicitly distinguishes between two major parts of his record—a "more sacred" and a "less sacred" part—and the "more sacred" part is taken up entirely with presenting and interpreting Isaiah. Further, the "more sacred" part of the record is something God directly commissioned Nephi to write, but Nephi felt he could serve the Lord's purposes best by couching that divinely commissioned text within a larger setting—that is, by contextualizing it with some "less sacred" (but *still* sacred) textual material. The "more sacred" part, we've made clear, is to be found in the twenty-five chapters stretching from 2 Nephi 6 to 2 Nephi 30. The "less sacred" part is found chiefly in First Nephi, but also in the first and last few chapters of Second Nephi.

So we're left with a picture something like this. Second Nephi is the *real* core of Nephi's larger record. It opens with an introduction of sorts (2 Ne. 1–5) and it closes with a conclusion of sorts (2 Ne. 31–33), but all the rest of it makes up that hardest and most divine core of the record. The question that remains, then, is this: *Why First Nephi? Why does Nephi bother to give us this other book at all? How is this "less sacred" book supposed to help us?*

Let's make note of some obvious answers. The most obvious of all would be that Nephi *has* to tell us his story, doesn't he? If he were to jump right into his Isaiah project, we'd be beyond lost, wouldn't we? And since Martin Harris went and lost the Book of Lehi for us, it's *especially* necessary that we be provided with some explanation of how the Nephites got to the New World! Isn't First Nephi at the very least just a kind of contextualizing narrative, a story that explains who's writing this record, where he came from, and how he came to be a prophet? Isn't that reason enough for Nephi to have written his first book? Well, actually, no, it isn't. It's clear already that Nephi was willing to insert an introduction into Second Nephi. Why couldn't he just make the opening chapters of Second Nephi a kind of abbreviated record of how he and his family came to the New World? We could have had a cleaner abridgment than we've got, couldn't we? You can see the wisdom in that kind of approach, can't you? Imagine Nephi producing 2 Nephi 6–30 and then wondering how to introduce it to his readers. Rather than deciding to write all of First Nephi and then add the first chapters of Second Nephi, he writes just a couple of chapters of introduction to "the more sacred things." Here's who I am, who my parents are, where we came from; here's a brief account of how much trouble we had as a family, which led to a long-term schism; here's a quick story about how we got to the New World and settled in; and here's a word or two about what you're about to read. Why didn't Nephi do something like that?

So it turns out that we can't explain the existence of First Nephi just by saying that we need some background. But maybe another obvious explanation is better. It's obvious that the stories in First Nephi are there to show us a good example of obedience and faith, right? "Nephi was courageous," "I will go and do," and all that. Isn't the point of First Nephi to add a slightly less sacred narrative to the slightly more sacred sermons of Second Nephi, so that we have, in addition to prophecies about heady, abstract stuff, some concrete, readily applicable stories? It's Nephi himself, after all, who tells us we're to liken the scriptures to ourselves, and so he's given us a set of stories that so easily apply to everyday life that we can be better people by reading his record. Well, actually, this doesn't work either. Sure, there are some stories about obedience in First Nephi, and we certainly can learn important lessons from them, but that's hardly all that's there. In fact, it's not even *half* of what's there. There's Lehi's dream (ch. 8) and his later sermon on Christian history (ch. 10); there's Nephi's own apocalyptic vision (chs. 11–14) and his subsequent attempt to explain it to his brothers (ch. 15); there's the long sermon on Israelite history (ch. 17); and there's the first substantial quotation of Isaiah (chs. 20–21) and Nephi's attempt to explain that to his brothers (ch. 22). Really, there are just a few stories in First Nephi, and they're constantly interrupted by prophetic material that anticipates the focus of Second Nephi. Add to all this the fact that the stories in First Nephi are actually far more complex than we often make them, something we won't have time even to touch on in our lectures (though I'll note that I've given a sample of this in an essay of mine on René Girard).

So we can't say that First Nephi just provides necessary historical and biographical context for Second Nephi, and we can't say that it exists just to provide us with a set of spiritually-inflected stories. So what's it doing there? It seems we're going to have to be a good deal more careful if we want to answer this question!

Two Halves of First Nephi

We can start to get somewhere, I think, if we turn our attention to another moment in the text where Nephi talks about what he's doing structurally. A first such moment happens in 1 Nephi 1:16–17. Perhaps you won't remember this passage, so let me quote it in full. Nephi's here in the middle of his opening narrative, the story of Lehi's first visionary experiences—the ones that lead to his becoming a prophet and facing serious opposition in Jerusalem. Here's what Nephi says when he interrupts this story for a moment:

> And now I, Nephi, do not make a full account of the things which my father hath written. For he hath written many things which he saw in visions and in dreams, and he also hath written many things which he prophesied and spake unto his children—of which I shall not make a full account. But I shall make an account of my proceedings in my days. Behold, I make an abridgment of the record of my father upon plates which I have made with mine own hands. Wherefore, after that I have abridged the record of my father, then will I make an account of mine own life.

Alright, here we're seeing a move not unlike the one we looked at last time. Nephi's here telling us in simple prose about certain divisions in the structure of his text. Here he tells us about the basic structure just of First Nephi. It comes, it seems, in two parts. First we get "an abridgment" of Lehi's record. And "then," "after that," we get "an account" of Nephi's own life. So it seems that First Nephi comes in two halves.

That's simple enough, but where are the two halves? Where's the dividing line? That's actually *perfectly* clear. Take a look at 1 Nephi 10:1: "And now I, Nephi, proceed to give an account upon these plates of my proceedings and my reign and ministry." That's nothing if not a clear marker of the moment Nephi switches from the first half—the abridgment of his father's record—to the second half—the record of his own proceedings. This is confirmed by another detail, actually. Did you notice how he worded things there in 1 Nephi 10:1? He speaks, as in 1 Nephi 1:17, of his "proceedings," but he adds to it a reference to his "reign and ministry." Where's that coming from? Well, have you ever noticed that First Nephi has a subtitle? Look at the first page of the book. We're reading "The Book of Nephi, His Reign and Ministry." So here in 1 Nephi 10:1 we have an echo of the subtitle of First Nephi. We're clearly moving into the second half of the record, the part where we'll get Nephi's account of his own life—and of his reign and ministry.

Original Chapter Breaks

So this much we can say without any doubt. First Nephi divides into two clear halves: an abridgment of Lehi's record, found in 1 Nephi 1–9, and a record of Nephi's own proceedings and reign and ministry, found in 1 Nephi 10–22. But this only gets us started. What else can we find here? The key to getting any further with this might be surprising—at least, it surprised me when I first stumbled on it. To get further, we have to look at chapter breaks. I don't mean the chapter breaks we're all familiar with from current or even recent editions of the Book of Mormon, but chapter breaks that go much further back in the history of the printing of the Book of Mormon. Did you know that Joseph Smith dictated chapter breaks along with the text of the Book of Mormon—*and* that they're different from the ones you know so well? This is something Royal Skousen has made clear in his scholarship.

Are you familiar with Royal Skousen's work on the Book of Mormon? Skousen is a linguistics professor at Brigham Young University, and he's dedicated almost thirty years now to establishing a critical text of the Book of Mormon. He's done intensely close work on the original manuscript of the Book of Mormon—well, of what's left of it (it suffered a great deal of damage at one point). And he's done equally intensely close work on the printer's manuscript of the Book of Mormon, the copy of the text made for the use of the printer (and on which revisions were made for later editions). On top of that, he's looked carefully at every single printed edition of the Book of Mormon published by either of the two major branches of Mormonism—The Church of Jesus Christ of Latter-day Saints and Community of Christ (what used to be called the Reorganized Church of Jesus Christ of Latter Day Saints). In all this work, Skousen has tracked every variant in the texts and undertaken detailed analysis of what they might mean. And he has made guesses in other cases about where there might be variants without there being clear evidence of it. All this work has been published in a six-volume series, *Analysis of Textual Variants of the Book of Mormon*. Each entry in the *Analysis* concludes with a specific recommendation for how the text should read in a critical edition of the Book of Mormon. His aim has been to get as close as possible to what Joseph Smith originally dictated to Oliver Cowdery (and others).

A few years ago, Skousen finally put all of his findings together in an edition of the Book of Mormon, *The Earliest Text*, published by Yale University Press. It's a crucial resource. I've actually been using it whenever I've quoted the text of the Book of Mormon in our discussions here (though I've used my own punctuation, since that's a matter of interpretation, and I often differ from Skousen on how I'd point the text). If we're serious about looking at the Book of Mormon with a critical eye, we've got to use Skousen.

Now, why bring all this up? As I mentioned a minute ago, in his work on the critical text, Skousen has established firmly that Joseph Smith dictated chapter breaks along with the text of the Book of Mormon. Apparently, the chapters weren't numbered in the dictation. When Joseph would come to a break in the text, Oliver would write "Chapter," but without a number. When they were finished, they went back through the manuscript and inserted numbers for each chapter in order. But it's clear that Joseph told Oliver in the course of dictation when there were breaks in the text. Those chapter breaks were part of the original text of the Book of Mormon. They go back to Nephi, to Mormon, to Moroni. And we'll see that they're extremely helpful for making better sense of the text.

There's a problem for us, though. The original chapters of the dictated Book of Mormon were often rather long. That was maybe fine for the first fifty years or so of the book's publication, since it was published in a format that was something like a novel—in prose paragraphs, without verse numbers and the like. If what you're reading is presented like a novel, you're not terribly bothered if chapters stretch on for ten or twenty pages. But in the 1870s, it was decided to reformat the text of the Book of Mormon to make it look more like biblical scripture. Orson Pratt was given the responsibility to divide the text up into more Bible-like chapter lengths, as well as to add verse numbers and so on. The result was that the original chapter breaks were obscured. What we read now doesn't alert us to the chapter breaks of the original. Of course, you can find the original chapter breaks pretty easily. They're marked in Skousen's *Earliest Text*, just as they are in Grant Hardy's *Reader's Edition* of the Book of Mormon. Any Community of Christ edition has the original chapter breaks as well, since that tradition never reworked the chapter breaks. You can find them also in republications of pre-1870s editions. You've probably seen those 1830 edition reprints. And there's a Penguin Books edition of the Book of Mormon that reproduces the 1840 edition. And of course, you can look at images of early editions online in a variety of places, including the Joseph Smith Papers website. Any of these resources will give you the original chapter breaks.

What we'll see as we go along today is that the original chapter breaks in First Nephi are essential to understanding its purpose. In our current edition we have twenty-two chapters, but as Joseph originally dictated the book it had only seven. Here's how they map onto our current chapter-and-verse divisions: the original Chapter I is today's chapters 1–5; the original Chapter II is today's chapters 6–9; the original Chapter III is to-day's chapters 10–14; the original Chapter IV is today's chapter 15 (here's one Orson didn't change); the original Chapter V is complicated, consisting of today's chapters 16–18 and the first twenty-one verses of chapter 19; the original Chapter VI is also complicated, consisting of the last three verses of today's chapter 19, as well as all of today's chapters 20–21; and the original Chapter VII is today's chapter 22 (another one Orson didn't change). Here's all that again:

Chapter I	1 Nephi 1–5
Chapter II	1 Nephi 6–9
Chapter III	1 Nephi 10–14
Chapter IV	1 Nephi 15
Chapter V	1 Nephi 16:1–19:21
Chapter VI	1 Nephi 19:22–21:26
Chapter VII	1 Nephi 22

There we are. Seven chapters in the original. Now, why is all this supposedly helpful?

Well, let's first note that we can draw a line here between the two halves of First Nephi, which we've already discerned. 1 Nephi 1–9 makes up the first half of the book, while 1 Nephi 10–22 makes up the second half. That means that the first half of First Nephi originally consisted of just two chapters, the original Chapters I and II, while the second half of First Nephi originally consisted of five chapters, the original Chapters III through VII. How about another chart or table of sorts?

This is starting to look like a table of contents, no? And we'll see that it's actually quite helpful to look at it this way.

Two Stories in 1 Nephi 1–9

Now, to go further with all this, let's look for a moment just at the original Chapters I and II. There's a host of details here I'd absolutely love to spend some time on, but we just can't cover everything. So let's deal just with what's essential. The details concern the fact that Nephi himself marks the boundaries of each of the first two original chapters, making clear that he wanted them to be read as structural wholes, as separable units. What happens if we read them that way? We're used to reading 1 Nephi 1 as the story of Lehi's first vision, 1 Nephi 2 as the story of the journey into the wilderness, 1 Nephi 3 as the trek up to retrieve the brass plates, 1 Nephi 4 as the actual retrieval of the plates, and 1 Nephi 5 as the aftermath of that dangerous situation. But what if we read 1 Nephi 1–5 as *one* story, rather than as *five* stories? Well, then I think we find that it's just the one story of how the brass plates came into the Lehites' possession. 1 Nephi 1 and much of 1 Nephi 2 then become just the context or background for that story; the remainder of 1 Nephi 2 provides the Lord's word that focuses Nephi on the necessity of keeping commandments; 1 Nephi 3 tells the first part of the story of getting the plates, during which Nephi demonstrates his slightly problematic zeal without knowledge; 1 Nephi 4 tells us of how Nephi finally got things right concerning his relationship to the Lord and to his brothers; and 1 Nephi 5 provides us with a further reconciliation in the family, as well as with some explanation of the actual contents of the plates recovered from Jerusalem. But all this is just one story—complex and multi-layered, but a single story nonetheless.

Are we getting somewhere? It seems we're to read 1 Nephi 1–5, the original Chapter I, as a single story, and that story is focused just on how the Lehites came to possess the brass plates. What of the original Chapter II, now 1 Nephi 6–9? What if we read *that* as a unit, as just one story? We usually read 1 Nephi 6 as an aside about record-keeping, 1 Nephi 7 as the retrieval of Ishmael's family, 1 Nephi 8 as the dream of the tree of life, and 1 Nephi 9 as another aside about record-keeping. But what if we take it as one story? I think it's clear its chief focus is then on the dream of the tree of life, with the asides in 1 Nephi 6 and 9 just setting up the boundaries of the story and the narrative in 1 Nephi 7 just setting up the basic conflict between Nephi and his brothers that's then expressed in crucial ways in Lehi's dream. Forced to simplify a bit, we see that all of 1 Nephi 6–9 amounts to just one story: that of how the Lehites were first confronted with an image-laden dream that provided an outline of their own future history.

Let's put all this together. The first half of First Nephi, treated as two and only two stories told in two and only two original chapters, is aimed at distilling from Lehi's record just two points. In abridging his father's writings, Nephi wants us to know (1) how he and his family came to have a collection of Old-World prophetic writings and (2) how he and his family came to launch their own New-World prophetic tradition. From Lehi's experiences and writings, we're just to glean this: Nephi had in his possession the written prophecies of those they were leaving behind, and he had in his possession the oral prophecies of the leader of the colony they were themselves going to found. Two stories, nice and simple, which allow us to flesh out our little table of contents a bit more:

The Abridgment of Lehi's Record

Chapter I	How We Received the
(1 Nephi 1–5)	Biblical Prophetic Tradition
Chapter II	How We Started Our
(1 Nephi 6–9)	Own Prophetic Tradition

Parallels in 1 Nephi 10–22

Now, lest you think I'm just making stuff up as I go along, let's take a look at what we can say about the second half of First Nephi. Here, as we've already made clear, we have five original chapters to deal with. And it doesn't take much work to begin to see how they're organized. There's at least one clear bit of patterning here. Notice that in the original Chapter III (today's 1 Nephi 10–14) we have Nephi simply recounting some prophetic stuff, but then in the original Chapter IV (today's 1 Nephi 15) we have him attempting to explain that prophetic stuff to his brothers. And then notice that we have the same thing all over again later. In the original Chapter VI (today's 1 Nephi 19:22–21:26) we have Nephi recounting some more prophetic stuff, but then in the original Chapter VII (today's 1 Nephi 22) we have him attempting to explain that prophetic stuff to his brothers. So there's at least this much that needs to be said here: Nephi organizes his material in the second half of First Nephi in terms of a repeating pattern of just quoting prophetic stuff and then explaining that stuff to his brothers. The original Chapters III and IV and then the original Chapters VI and VII make this perfectly clear. And sandwiched between these two pairings of the prophetic and the explanatory is, quite simply, just the story of how the family finally traveled from the Old to the New World—the original Chapter V (today's 1 Nephi 16:1–19:21).

But we can get a good deal more specific about things here. Notice *what* the prophetic stuff is in the original Chapters III and VI. In Chapter III (today's 1 Nephi 10–14), we have Nephi outlining his own visionary experience of what his father saw in the tree-of-life dream. And in Chapter VI (today's 1 Nephi 19:22–21:26), we have Nephi quoting at length for the first time from the writings of Isaiah (specifically, from Isaiah 48–49). I assume you're already beginning to see what's going on here. Here we have Nephi drawing from the two sources whose provenance he recounted in the two stories making up the *first* half of First Nephi, the stories of the original Chapters I and II. In Chapter I Nephi told us how his family came to possess the brass plates, and in Chapter VI he begins quoting at length from that prophetic source. And then in Chapter II Nephi told us how his family sat around and listened to Lehi recount his dream of the tree of life, and in Chapter III he outlines his own prophetic experience of the same vision. And then in each case, he finds that he has to explain these things to his brothers—his own Lehi-like vision in Chapter IV and Isaiah's writings from the brass plates in Chapter VII. Do you see how close a relationship there is, suddenly, between the two halves of First Nephi?

So we can flesh out our table of contents even more, now. Here it is, with overly colloquial chapter titles:

The Abridgment of Lehi's Record

Chapter I   How We Received the
(1 Nephi 1–5)   Biblical Prophetic Tradition

Chapter II   How We Started Our
(1 Nephi 6–9)   Own Prophetic Tradition

The Record of Nephi's Own Proceeding

Chapter III   My Experience of Our
(1 Nephi 10–14)   Prophetic Tradition

Chapter IV   I Try to Explain It to
(1 Nephi 15)   My Brothers

Chapter V   Our Journey to the
(1 Nephi 16:1–19:21)   New World

Chapter VI   My Experience of the
(1 Nephi 19:22–21:26)   Biblical Prophets

Chapter VII   I Try to Explain It to
(1 Nephi 22)   My Brothers

Now, I think, we're really getting somewhere.

Anticipating Second Nephi

Lots of structure here, and all of it unquestionably right there, quite intentionally, in First Nephi. But now the essential question: *Why does any of this matter to us?* That's the key question. And here's a first answer. Remember the "more sacred" part of Nephi's record, positioned at the heart of Second Nephi. What's to be found there? In 2 Nephi 6–30, we get not only Isaiah's writings but a bunch of commentary on Isaiah's writings. And where does the inspiration for all that commentary come from? Quite simply, it comes from the visionary tradition that begins with Lehi's dream, that comes to a first culmination with Nephi's expansion of that dream in vision, and that continues with Jacob's much later experience of the same visions. What we get in Nephi's "more sacred things" is, precisely, a weave of two prophetic sources, one hailing from the Old World, and another hailing from the New World. The visions of Lehi and Nephi and Jacob serve as interpretive keys to reading Isaiah. And, in turn, Isaiah's writings serve as interpretive keys to understanding the stakes of the visions of Lehi and his sons. (Nephi lays out this close relationship in the clearest of terms in 2 Nephi 25, in a text we'll be looking at much more closely in a later lecture.)

Now, I hope you're beginning to see how all this works. There are two major purposes of First Nephi, each of them accomplished in one or the other of its two halves. The first half of First Nephi—the abridgment of Lehi—provides us with a basic understanding of *how the Lehites came to possess* the two prophetic resources that in Second Nephi work to interpret each other. And the second half of First Nephi—Nephi's own reign and ministry—provides us with *a first investigation into the contents and significance* of those two prophetic resources that form the crux of Second Nephi. If Nephi were to talk us through it, he might say something like: "Here's how we became aware of the written prophetic tradition of our forebears. And here's how God granted us our own prophetic tradition to supplement that. And now here's how our own prophetic tradition was expanded, and how I went about explaining its significance to my boneheaded brothers. And here's the sort of thing I found when I studied the written prophetic tradition that preceded us, and how I went about explaining its significance also to those same boneheaded brothers of mine. Now, if you see all this, you're quite ready to begin reading a little book God's commanded me to write, which weaves our own prophetic insights into the written prophecies we inherited. Are you ready?"

Now, there's one other major way First Nephi anticipates Second Nephi that we haven't yet mentioned, but it's essential. In the second half of First Nephi, Nephi gives a whole chapter in each case to describing how he explained his two prophetic resources to his brothers. Here's the key thing: *In each case, he explains the one prophetic resource by drawing on the other.* Let me make this perfectly clear. In the original Chapter III (today's 1 Nephi 10–14), Nephi provides us with his own visionary expansion of Lehi's dream. And then in the original Chapter IV (today's 1 Nephi 15), he explains Lehi's dream to his brothers. But look at this. When he really wants them to understand things, he tells us, he turned to the writings of Isaiah. Here's what he says in 1 Nephi 15:19–20: "And it came to pass that I, Nephi, spake much unto them concerning these things—yea, I spake unto them concerning the restoration of the Jews in the latter days. And I did rehearse unto them the words of Isaiah, which spake concerning the restoration of the Jews (or of the house of Israel)." I don't know if the vision wasn't clear enough already in Nephi's own words, but at any rate, Nephi tells us that he only really got his explanation of the vision off the ground when he wove Isaiah into it.

And then we find the same thing later. In the original Chapter VI (today's 1 Nephi 19:22–21:26), Nephi provides us with a first chunk of Isaiah's prophecy, quoted in full. And then in the original Chapter VII (today's 1 Nephi 22), he explains those Isaianic writings to his brothers. And how does he explain those writings? He doesn't give us a one-liner that refers to his vision—nothing like his one-liner about using Isaiah to explain the vision in 1 Nephi 15. But even a cursory reading of 1 Nephi 22 makes perfectly clear how it is that Nephi feels he can explain Isaiah. He's just using what he learned in his vision in 1 Nephi 11–14. The whole of his explanation of Isaiah to his brothers follows exactly the outline of his own prophetic experience. (And, actually, the first couple of verses of 1 Nephi 22 have him suggesting that he'd seen something on his own.)

So now we can add to what we've already said about how First Nephi prepares for Second Nephi. First Nephi not only gives us the provenance of the two prophetic resources that get woven together in Second Nephi. And it not only gives us preliminary expansions and quotations of those resources, along with relevant explanations of their significance. It *also* builds into all of this an intertwining of the two resources, making clear that each helps to interpret the other. By the end of First Nephi, if we're reading carefully, we see that Isaiah can't be interpreted without the Nephite visionary tradition, just as the Nephite visionary tradition can't be interpreted without Isaiah. And so you can see quite clearly that Nephi had a kind of program with his first book. It wasn't something God commanded him to write (like Second Nephi). Rather, he rightly saw a good deal of wisdom in putting it together and attaching it to Second Nephi, even if he hadn't been commanded to do so. And if we read First Nephi carefully, we're fully prepared to read Second Nephi, the plain and the precious.

Ack. We're well beyond out of time for today's discussion. We'll draw up a summary and see what's next when we meet next time.

Lehi as a Reader of Isaiah

We covered a lot of ground again last time, so we need to see if we can't draw up a map now. What did we learn in our discussion of First Nephi?

A Primer on Reading Isaiah

The question that set us in motion last time is one that at first seems to have little to do with Isaiah. Once we see—thanks to 1 Nephi 19:1–6—that Second Nephi contains the real core of Nephi's record (and apparently the only part of it Nephi was specifically commanded to write), it becomes pretty natural to want to know why Nephi bothered at all to produce his *other* book, First Nephi, and especially why he would think to place it *before* the "more sacred" part of his record. We might naturally guess that there's some essential difference between the basic content of First Nephi and that of Second Nephi. Since the latter is focused on Isaiah—long quotations of and commentaries on Isaiah—we might well assume that First Nephi is supposed to turn our attention to other, non-Isaianic concerns. Maybe Nephi wanted his readers to learn about *something* besides Isaiah? Perhaps he supplemented Second Nephi with First Nephi so as to supplement the Isaianic with the non-Isaianic?

So we might have guessed. But our investigations last time made perfectly clear that any such guess is wrong. Wrong, wrong, wrong. It turns out that, despite what surface reading and haphazard guessing might suggest, First Nephi is *also* all about Isaiah—though it's more subtle. It's clear now that Nephi produced his first book to prepare his readers to make full sense of Isaiah. You'll remember that Nephi says later that the key to Isaiah interpretation is "the spirit of prophecy" (2 Ne. 25:4). Well, he seems to have some *very* specific prophecies in mind when he says that: his own vision, his father's vision, and his brother Jacob's vision. The way Isaiah gets interpreted in Second Nephi constantly depends on those prophetic visions, as we'll see in great detail in later lectures. But in order to prepare us for that dependence long in advance, First Nephi is organized with an eye to interweaving these two prophetic resources: Isaiah's writings and Nephi's visions.

How does Nephi do it? He divides his first book into two halves. The first half he dedicates to two stories, focused respectively (1) on how he and his father came to inherit the written record of the Old-World prophets (Isaiah above all), and (2) on how his father inaugurated what would become a New-World tradition of oral prophecy. The second half of First Nephi then focuses on providing preliminary studies of each of these prophetic resources. Lehi's prophetic dream is expanded into a massive apocalyptic vision of the whole of the world's history, which Nephi then explains in a preliminary way to his brothers by quoting from the written prophecies of Isaiah. And, in turn, the writings of Isaiah are quoted selectively and suggestively before Nephi explains them, again preliminarily, to his brothers—in part by drawing on his own visionary experiences to help orient their meaning. And, of course, all this is grounded historically in the second half of First Nephi by organizing it around the account of the trek from the Old World to the New World, from the place where Isaiah's prophecies were first written to the place where Lehi's and Nephi's prophecies would come to fruition. As a kind of primer, a handbook on how to read Isaiah, First Nephi contains the prophetic visions of Lehi and Nephi you want on hand to make sense of Isaiah. Similarly, you've got to have Isaiah's writings also on hand if you want to make sense of those visions. Whether you're trying to explain prophetic history or whether you're trying to read Isaiah, you need the companion resource in order to get anywhere productive.

A few lectures back, we could already say that what Nephi is trying to do in his writings is to get us to see the way his own visionary experiences line up with Isaiah's writings. Now we can see, at least in a preliminary way, how that's so. Or at least we can see more or more clearly *that* that's so. Make no mistake: *We can't get serious about Nephi unless we get serious about Isaiah.*

Comparative Study

What's next, then? Here we're finally at the threshold, ready to enter into the actual work of reading Isaiah in Nephi's record. Nonetheless, let me ease your trepidation for one last lecture. Instead of coming directly at Nephi's (or, derivatively, at Jacob's) handling of Isaiah, whether in First or in Second Nephi, let's spend our time together looking at *another* reader of Isaiah. Here we want to begin to set up a kind of contrast with Nephi, one that's especially suggestive. Nephi and Jacob will launch their own interpretive tradition, we'll see. But in order to see that that tradition is definitively *theirs*, let's take a look today at how *their father* read Isaiah. In just a couple of places, a couple of fragments in Nephi's record, we see something of how Lehi approached the prophet. And I suspect we might see how unique Nephi's program is when we set it side by side with his father's far less systematic interpretive efforts.

Let's start with two general observations. First, it's got to be significant that Nephi never gives us so much as a possible allusion to Isaiah anywhere in 1 Nephi 1–9, that stretch of First Nephi that, he tells us, is an abridgment of Lehi's record. That's crucial. When we're getting something like a straightforward summary of Lehi's visions and teachings, there's not even a hint of Isaiah. (Well, maybe a *slight* hint in the broad parallels between 1 Nephi 1 and Isaiah 6. But that's complicated, and we'll deal with it in a later lecture anyway.) So let's take this as a first observation: Nephi seems to want us to see Lehi as largely uninterested in Isaiah. The second general observation we've got to make is this: in all the remainder of Nephi's record, we have only two places where Lehi *might* be borrowing from or alluding to Isaiah—and neither of them is terribly sure. After the abridgment of Lehi's record, we still get at least four and a half chapters of Lehi's teachings (1 Nephi 10, along with the first three and half chapters of Second Nephi). But in all that material, there are only two *possible* references to Isaiah. So not only does Nephi want us to think of Lehi as largely uninterested in Isaiah quite generally, he also demonstrates Lehi's lack of interest by quoting his teachings at length but without obvious ties to Isaiah's writings.

These two observations should already give us a general sense for the difference between Lehi and Nephi. It's only with Nephi that the Isaiah project gets off the ground. Lehi's doing other things with his prophetic gifts, or so Nephi wants us to believe. We can anticipate that wherever we *might* find Lehi touching on things Isaianic, they're going to be quite different from Nephi's treatment of the prophet.

Lehi Reads Isaiah 40:3

The first possible reference to Isaiah in what Nephi's left us of Lehi's teachings comes in 1 Nephi 10. It's perhaps significant that it comes there. Remember the structure of First Nephi. It divides into two halves, with 1 Nephi 10 marking the beginning of the second half,—where Nephi sets aside the task of abridging his father's record in order to get on with his own life and such. But then shouldn't it strike us as a bit odd that we get more of Lehi's teachings in 1 Nephi 10? Well, Nephi actually says something about that. So here's the first verse of 1 Nephi 10, which we quoted before because of the way it marks the transition from the first half to the second half of First Nephi: "And now I, Nephi, proceed to give an account upon these plates of my proceedings, and my reign and ministry." That's clearly transitional. But then he immediately goes on to say this as well: "Wherefore, to proceed with mine account, I must speak somewhat of the things of my father, and also of my brethren—for behold, it came to pass that after my father had made an end of speaking the words of his dream (and also of exhorting them to all diligence), he spake unto them concerning the Jews" (1 Ne. 10:1–2). Notice that Nephi *does* make the transition from the first half to the second half here, but he then lets his readers know that he has to open that second half with a little bit more concerning his father's preaching—and specifically preaching to his brothers. So it is that we get more of Lehi even as we leave the abridgment of Lehi's record behind.

It's actually quite clear why Lehi's further teaching has to appear there at the beginning of the second half of First Nephi. What Nephi records in 1 Nephi 10 is a kind of sermon on the then-future history of Israel. And that's the lens through which Nephi ends up looking when he has his own expansive version of the dream of the tree of life, which follows immediately on the report of Lehi's sermon of sorts. So Lehi's prophetic words in 1 Nephi 10 work as a kind of prophetic preface to Nephi's visionary experience. Here we get a first introduction to the themes that draw Nephi's most consistent attention. It's not something he simply stumbled on himself; rather, it's something he learned from his father.

Now, what we've said so far might well lead us to *expect* to find Isaiah referred to in 1 Nephi 10. We've already begun to see Nephi's program of using his vision in concert with Isaiah's writings to explain Israel's history. Here we have the first prophecy concerning Israel's history that appears in Nephi's record, so why shouldn't Isaiah show up there? But here's the weird thing. The possible reference to Isaiah (and remember that it's only *possible*) that appears in 1 Nephi 10 doesn't serve to clarify Israel's history in anything like the way Isaiah's writings do elsewhere in Nephi's record.

As Nephi summarizes things, Lehi opens his sermon in 1 Nephi 10 with a brief overview of the history of Israel from the time of the exile to the birth of Jesus Christ. He prophesies of the destruction of Jerusalem, captivity in Babylon, and return. And then he talks about the "prophet" to be raised up among the Jews: "even a messiah—or, in other words, a savior of the world" (1 Ne. 10:4). Interestingly, at first Lehi focuses less on messianic fulfillment as such than on the dawn of the messianic age. Here's the text: "And he spake also concerning a prophet which should come before the messiah to prepare the way of the Lord—yea, even he should go forth and cry in the wilderness: 'Prepare ye the way of the Lord! And make his paths straight! For there standeth one among you whom ye know not (and he is mightier than I!), whose shoe's latchet I am not worthy to unloose'" (vv. 7–8). Nephi then adds this editorial note by way of conclusion: "And much spake my father concerning this thing" (v. 8).

Nephi goes on to give us a bit more information about this prophet-before-the-prophet, this pre-messianic figure whose task is to prepare the way. But let's focus just on this first introduction to him—this summary statement that apparently leaves out a lot of detail. It's here, at any rate, that the first of Lehi's two possible references to Isaiah appears.

If there's an Isaiah text behind Lehi's prophetic description of the figure we easily recognize as John the Baptist, it's Isaiah 40:3, which reads as follows: "The voice of him that crieth in the wilderness, 'Prepare ye the way of the Lord, make straight in the desert a highway for our God.'" You can see some particularly close parallels if you read carefully. Isaiah speaks of the one who "crieth in the wilderness," and Lehi speaks of a figure who "should . . . cry in the wilderness." The only difference there is the mood and tense of the verb ("crieth," "should cry"). And then Isaiah says that the first words of this figure are "Prepare ye the way of the Lord," directly echoed in Lehi's prophecy: "Prepare ye the way of the Lord!" We get a slight change, however, when we look at the next line. Isaiah has the figure then cry this: "Make straight in the desert a highway for our God." Lehi has the figure say something slightly different: "And make his paths straight!" Both prophets have the figure speak of making something straight—but Isaiah refers to "a highway" while Lehi refers to "paths"; and Isaiah describes the highway as "for our God," while Lehi just uses the possessive "his" to attribute the paths in question to "the Lord." Here the texts seem to diverge slightly.

So it's clear that Isaiah 40:3 is *somehow* behind 1 Nephi 10:8, but it would seem that a few relevant differences might make us wonder *exactly how* the two relate. Actually, it's not very difficult to figure out what's going on here. The way the Isaianic prophecy is worded in 1 Nephi 10 follows exactly the way the same prophecy is worded in several parallel New Testament passages. Matthew and Mark and Luke all introduce John the Baptist into their stories by quoting the Isaiah passage (Matthew and

Luke cite Isaiah by name—as "Esaias" in the King James Version—while Mark speaks just of "the prophets," quoting Malachi and Isaiah together in a kind of confused blend). Here's how the one crying in the wilderness speaks in all three of those gospels: "Prepare ye the way of the Lord, make his paths straight" (Matt. 3:3; Mark 1:3; Luke 3:4). There's our clearest source. If Lehi borrows the language of Isaiah, he does it *through* the intermediary renderings of the New Testament.

This, of course, makes it a little difficult to know if Lehi is supposed to be *knowingly* or *intentionally* borrowing from Isaiah. Are we supposed to believe that he's been reading the brass plates and that he's using their language as he presents his prophecy concerning the Baptist? Or are we supposed rather to believe that he's seen in one of his visions something more like what the gospel-writers describe? Is he playing with Isaiah's texts, or is he quoting things seen in vision that themselves—perhaps unbeknownst to Lehi—borrow from and play with Isaiah's texts? The fact of the matter is this: *We can't know for sure that this is an intentional borrowing from Isaiah on Lehi's part.* There's certainly something Isaianic about his prophecy of John the Baptist, but it's not clear whether Lehi's in some kind of *direct* relation to Isaiah's writings there or whether he's just *indirectly* borrowing from Isaiah, perhaps without being at all aware of the fact. (I explored some of these questions in *An Other Testament*, and I don't think I like any of the answers I gave to them back then. I claim the privilege to change my mind substantially as often as I like!)

So where does all this leave us? It seems we have to say something like the following. It's possible that Lehi meant to borrow from Isaiah 40 in presenting his prophecy of John the Baptist, but it's just as possible—and perhaps even more likely—that he didn't actually have anything like Isaiah 40 in mind. But bracketing the latter possibility, what would we need to say if in fact Lehi *did* mean to draw on Isaiah 40 in presenting his prophecy? If that turns out to have been the case, then we'd have to say that, in the first of his two possible borrowings, Lehi finds in Isaiah's writings prophecies focused first and foremost on the messianic age. In something like the fashion of the gospel writers (if not in fact basically borrowing from them), Lehi sees the events surrounding the Messiah's coming as what Isaiah especially concerned himself with. Isaiah saw the time and coming of Christ in vision. Isaiah's prophecies would be fulfilled first and foremost when the messianic age would dawn and the redemption of the world would begin in earnest. In all this, Lehi reads Isaiah in something like the way Abinadi would later read him.

Lehi as a messianic reader of Isaiah 40, then? Well, we're moving too quickly, actually. The gospel writers certainly talk in something like the way we were just saying Lehi talked, and Abinadi would arguably talk in something like that way as well. But Lehi isn't so clear as these guys. If Lehi really had Isaiah 40 in mind, it's actually possible just that he saw in Isaiah's words a handy parallel to what he'd seen in vision, not that he actually saw Isaiah as prophesying of the same thing. Nothing in 1 Nephi 10 tells us that the prophecy of Isaiah 40:3 was to be uniquely fulfilled, directly and unequivocally, in the appearance of John the Baptist. Rather, Lehi's prophecy just uses the language of Isaiah 40 (mediated by the New Testament) to talk about the coming of John, though it might be used to describe other events as well. Where the gospel writers explicitly name Isaiah, attribute the prophecy to him, and then speak of its fulfillment through a specified event, Lehi just uses Isaianic language nonchalantly, as if it were simply an appropriate resource for clothing an otherwise naked prophecy of the Baptist. One could easily come to the conclusion that Lehi's reading in Isaiah provided him with some helpful language, with a passage to which he might allude, as he made sense for himself of something he'd seen in vision. That 1 Nephi 10 borrows directly from the language of the gospels might then be regarded as an incidental feature of the nineteenth-century translation of the Book of Mormon.

Okay, we've outlined three possibilities, none of them particularly sure. First, it might be that Lehi never had Isaiah 40 in mind in 1 Nephi 10, something perhaps indicated by the fact that the language of Lehi's prophecy actually relates more closely to passages in the New Testament than to Isaiah's own words (in the King James Version). Second, it might be that Lehi did indeed have Isaiah 40 in mind (the New Testament language being just a feature of the translation), and that he saw the Baptist's appearance as its direct fulfillment—since, presumably, that's what Isaiah saw in vision long in advance. Third, it might be that Lehi had Isaiah 40 in mind, but that he simply used the passage to enrich his own prophecy, without any presuppositions about whether Isaiah had seen something like the Baptist in vision. Those are the three possibilities, and because they are all genuine possibilities, any of them could work. Which of them appeals to you will depend on how you go about answering a host of separate questions. So perhaps, in the end, the possible borrowing from Isaiah in 1 Nephi 10 doesn't really get us anywhere. We simply can't say much in any definite sense about what Lehi's prophecy of the Baptist tells us about his relationship to Isaiah's writings.

We need to turn to the other possible allusion, then, since it's a good deal surer, and it's ultimately a good deal more illustrative. But before we do that, we can already make this general point, I think: Lehi's already different from Nephi in that we're faced with this host of ambiguities in his first possible allusion to Isaiah. Nephi is clearer than clear about what he's doing with Isaiah. There's a passage or two where things get ambiguous, and we'll have to see if we can't find some time to talk about them in another lecture. But on the whole, Nephi doesn't make these kinds of loose and only possible allusions to Isaiah. He gives us Isaiah's writings, and he gives us clear interpretations of them. Lehi's quite different from Nephi already.

Lehi Reads Isaiah 14:12

The other possible borrowing by Lehi from Isaiah comes in 2 Nephi 2. I think I can assume a little more familiarity with this passage. This is Lehi's remarkable sermon on law—on the necessity of opposition at the core of the creation, on the way such opposition undergirds the fall, and on the means by which the difficulties associated with such opposition can be set right by the atonement. After Lehi builds up some of his basic principles, he recounts the creation and the fall himself. With the fundamental opposition between "the forbidden fruit" and "the tree of life" in place (2 Ne. 2:15), he tells us that "man could not act for himself save it should be that he was enticed by the one or the other" (v. 16). Lehi then says this:

> And I, Lehi, according to the things which I have read, must needs suppose that an angel of God—according to that which is written—had fallen from heaven. Wherefore, he became a devil, having sought that which was evil before God. And because that he had fallen from heaven, and had became miserable forever, he sought also the misery of all mankind. Wherefore, he saith unto Eve—yea, even that old serpent which is the devil, which is the father of all lies—wherefore, he saith: "Partake of the forbidden fruit, and ye shall not die, but ye shall be as God, knowing good and evil." (vv. 17–18)

There's the key passage. And in it one finds the other possible borrowing from Isaiah. We're looking here just at three simple words: "fallen from heaven." Those seem rather clearly to come from Isaiah 14:12, which famously opens as follows: "How art thou fallen from heaven, O Lucifer, son of the morning!" It seems Lehi has this text in mind.

Notice a major difference that sets this possible borrowing apart from the other one we were just considering. Lehi here speaks of both "the things which I have read" and "that which is written," making clear that he's got *some text* in mind. In 1 Nephi 10, we were left to wonder whether or not Lehi had an actual text in mind, or whether we weren't just dealing with a feature of the translation—which often borrows from New Testament language. But there's no question here in 2 Nephi 2. Lehi's thinking of some passage of scripture. Of course, he doesn't tell us *which* passage he's got in mind, and there's some chance it's not actually Isaiah. And the fact that he doesn't mention Isaiah by name reminds us of a fact we just mentioned: that Lehi is less forthcoming than Nephi about his (potential) uses of Isaiah. In this particular case, nonetheless, it seems pretty sure that we're dealing with Isaiah, since we get a three-word sequence, "fallen from heaven," that appears identically in Isaiah and here in Lehi's words. It seems that Lehi reads Isaiah 14 as telling us something about "an angel of God" that fell from heaven and "became a devil."

Now, likely many of you think Lehi's interpretation of Isaiah 14 is the natural or even simply the correct one. There's a *very* long tradition of interpreting Isaiah's words regarding "Lucifer" as a description of how Satan became Satan. In fact, that tradition was already in place as early as the dawn of Christianity, two thousand years ago (see Luke 10:18). But let's be clear that this isn't the only or even the most obvious interpretation of the text. And in certain ways, it's probably necessary to say that it isn't exactly a *correct* interpretation, as scholars have been pointing out for five centuries. In the setting of Isaiah 13–14, it's perfectly clear that Isaiah's talking about the ruler of ancient Babylon, whom he compares to Helel ben Shahar (the "Star of the Dawning Day," as Blenkinsopp renders it), who was apparently a minor deity in the mythology of Israel's neighbors (at Ugarit, at the very least). The best reconstruction suggests that there was a popular legend about a deity, associated with the morning star, who had attempted to take the throne of the god who ruled over the entire pantheon, El Elyon. But just as the morning star fades when the sun rises, the would-be usurper deity was thrust down by the Most High. Isaiah seems to have drawn on this myth in composing a critique of sorts of Babylon's arrogant ruler. Like Helel ben Shahar, Babylon believed it could undermine the sovereign decrees of the true or highest God. And like Helel ben Shahar, Babylon would be eradicated for its arrogance.

Actually, in light of specifically Mormon theology, it's probably too strong to say that it's simply *incorrect* to link Isaiah 14 with the story of Satan's fall. Latter-day Saints are committed to a picture similar in interesting ways to that contained in the Ugaritic myth: a council of gods, one of whom attempts to thwart the plans of the head of the council, only then to be cast down. The unorthodox quality of Mormon theology maybe makes the connection more viable than for other Christians and their strict commitment to uncompromising monotheism. At the same time, historians argue that Isaiah wouldn't have had anything like the figure of Satan in mind when he (or someone else in Isaiah's name) produced this text. I don't want to get bogged down in the details, but the idea is basically that it was through contact with foreign religious ideas during the Exile that the Jews first stumbled on the idea of Satan. So it seems that Isaiah's words regarding the Babylonian ruler could only have taken on a strictly satanic cast during or after the Exile.

But perhaps all these details can help us notice something else about Lehi's treatment of Isaiah in 2 Nephi 2. Notice that, unlike us, he doesn't refer to anything like a *traditional* interpretation. He seems to think he's going out on a rather shaky theological limb. He doesn't simply say that there's an Isaiah text that describes how Satan became Satan. He says that he "must needs suppose" that some "angel of God," nameless in the text, "had fallen from heaven"—and all this "according to that which is written." Lehi seems to see himself as experimenting with the Isaianic text. He's not telling us what it unquestionably means; rather, he's telling us what he *supposes* it might mean, and that only after a good deal of careful study. And he then tries to fit what he thinks the text might be saying with other texts that seem clearer to him—the story of "that old serpent" who beguiled Eve. Where the story of Genesis 2–3 makes relatively good or clear sense to Lehi, the prophetic words of Isaiah 14 are relatively obscure and require careful attention and deep thought before an interpretation might be ventured. Lehi's being really careful giving his provisional interpretation.

Now, I see two aspects of Lehi's interpretation of Isaiah that should probably be distinguished from each other. On the one hand, we should notice the hesitancy or the provisionality of Lehi's interpretation. He in no way suggests that every reader will immediately recognize the meaning of Isaiah's words. Rather, there's a kind of mystery that requires close and careful interpretation if someone wants to get clear about what Isaiah means. This is what we've just been saying. On the other hand, though, we should also notice that Lehi seems to think he's stumbled on what ultimately is the true—and perhaps the only true—interpretation of the passage. Once he's come to an answer, he doesn't suggest that it's just a private interpretation, something like what you're always hearing in Sunday School: "This passage means *to me* that . . . ." No, Lehi seems to think that he's sorted out the text's real meaning. So let's hold these two aspects of

Lehi's interpretive relationship to Isaiah in their appropriate tension. He comes at the text humbly, fully aware of his own interpretive fallibility. But he also seems to believe that there *is* indeed a true or correct interpretation, and he's relatively sure that he's begun to hit on that interpretation.

We're quickly running out of time today, so let's stop here and say a bit about how Lehi's handling of Isaiah 14 in 2 Nephi 2 distinguishes his interpretive style from that of Nephi. I see two particularly salient points. First and rather generally, let's note a contrast due to the fact that Nephi finds in Isaiah strong anticipations of the *future*, of a future focused indelibly on *the Abrahamic covenant.* In 2 Nephi 2, however, in what seems to be Lehi's only sure attempt at interpreting Isaiah in the text, we see Nephi's father finding in Isaiah an indication about the *past*, a past that helps to explain *the general human condition.* Where Nephi seems to see in Isaiah a rather specific theological program that organizes and orients the whole Book of Isaiah—or whatever of it was contained in the brass plates—Lehi seems to see in Isaiah a looser collection of prophetic materials that help to articulate a rather general picture of what we'd call the plan of salvation. Perhaps we could say that Lehi seems to read Isaiah in something like the way we tend to read scripture: as a collection of inspired statements that, read carefully and correctly, help us to see the basic outline of the plan of salvation and our place in it.

But let's couple this with a second point. Nephi, we'll see, explicitly recognizes that he has his own theological program that guides his interpretation of Isaiah. He'll speak of *likening* the text, and he'll tell us a fair bit about what it means to liken Isaianic prophecy. Nephi, that is, recognizes a kind of gap between what might be called *the* meaning of text and what we should probably call the *possible* and *always-proliferating* meanings of the text. Nephi sees that texts can be adopted and used for one's own purposes, so to speak. But let's note that Lehi seems to think otherwise. What we've seen, anyway, suggests that Lehi thinks the text has a relatively stable meaning, however difficult it might be to discover it. He doesn't himself seem terribly interested in a complicated program of likening. He just tries to figure out the true meaning of the text. This is a second crucial difference between Lehi and Nephi. But it's one that suggests that we're perhaps today more naturally like Nephi than like Lehi. Perhaps.

Well, we've gone over time again! We'll draw up a balance sheet of our discoveries at the outset next time and see where we're then headed next.

Lecture VII

Preliminaries to Isaiah 48–49

Summary and Synthesis

We're always running out of time at the end of our discussions, and so we're always beginning our next discussions with necessary attempts to draw up balance sheets. It's just as well. I suppose this at least forces you to think each time about what we've done in previous lectures. I'll just have to hope you don't resent it.

I'm especially hoping you don't resent it because I think I'd like to take a bit *more* time today to summarize *all* we've done so far. I said last time that we've now dealt with all the preliminaries necessary before getting to work on the actual writings of Isaiah as they appear in Nephi's text. So let's pause just a moment longer and make sure we're all quite aware of what we've accomplished so far. Can you remember back to the first lecture? And what do you remember of all we've done since then? Let's see if we can't put everything together in a single picture.

Over the course of our discussions, we've developed a clear—if nonetheless hastily sketched—picture of what Nephi's up to in general. If he's telling us the whole truth, it turns out that only the second of his two books contains material he was explicitly commanded by God to commit to writing. Decades after he arrived in the New World, the Lord told him to make a special record for the ministry and the prophecies, and he tells us that that's to be found in Second Nephi, and more specifically in 2 Nephi 6–30, the "more sacred things." If we review those chapters, moreover, we see that what God wanted Nephi to put in writing for his children was a set of Isaianic texts, coupled with a bit of commentary drawn from the Lehite prophetic tradition. Nephi, however, seems to have been rather nervous about whether his children would have any idea what was going on in this record, so he added a number of supplementary things to it. In addition to a kind of introduction (2 Ne. 1–5) and a kind of conclusion (2 Ne. 31–33), he tacked on a whole other book, what we know as his *first* book, First Nephi. We've looked in especially close detail at that first book, which bears within it an unmistakable structure that makes fully manifest Nephi's purpose in appending it to the recorded produced by way of direct commandment. First Nephi is an extended introduction to Second Nephi, and it does its work of introduction by getting us acquainted with the two prophetic sources he brings together in 2 Nephi 6–30: Isaiah's writings from the brass plates, and the prophetic tradition that began with his father. What's more, it shows its readers at least preliminarily how those two sources are interrelated or inter-interpretive.

There's what we've learned about the genesis and structure of Nephi's record. But we've learned a good deal more than that. We've looked also both at the prophetic tradition Nephi inherited from his father and at the Book of Isaiah. And from our far-to-brief investigations we've already begun to see, in rather general terms, why these might be brought into a revealing relationship. Nephi's vision, as we saw, was focused on the Abrahamic covenant, and especially on how the covenantal underpinnings of the Christian Bible came to be dropped from the scriptures as European Christianity developed. And don't forget what Nephi and other prophetic members of his family saw in vision. They saw that a book produced by their own descendants would contain within it the full covenantal vision that Christianity had lost. The book would contain the words of the resurrected Christ visiting the New World, and it would have to be buried for centuries before it could be recovered for its world-historical purposes. That book alone could solve the problem with the Bible. This is what Nephi saw quite early on. And he seems almost immediately to have seen how intertwined it all was with the writings of Isaiah. In Isaiah we have a record divided into two parts that are nonetheless deeply entangled with one another. You'll remember that what scholars call First Isaiah focuses on prophecies of destruction, and they present a prophet who's forced to write and then seal up his prophecies so they can be kept for a later generation. But then what scholars call Second Isaiah focuses on prophecies of restoration, of the fulfillment of the Abrahamic covenant at last—all a consequence of the sealed book being opened and read among the faithful. Nephi saw his own vision mirrored rather perfectly in the writings of Isaiah, or he saw Isaiah's writings mirrored rather perfectly in his own vision.

Alright, so we've got the genesis and structure of Nephi's record. And we've got a set of clear parallels between the two prophetic resources that Nephi's record aims to put in close relation to one another. Really, that summarizes everything we did up until our last discussion. Let's be sure to keep al of this fresh in our minds as we turn to what Nephi actually does with Isaiah. But before making the plunge at last, let's also draw up a balance sheet of our discussion last time. So that we might have something with which to compare Nephi's interpretive method, we looked at how Lehi uses Isaiah—on those terribly infrequent occasions where we might be led to think that he *does* use Isaiah. We don't have a lot of data, of course, but we saw that there are differences enough between Nephi and Lehi when it comes to interpreting Isaiah, and those differences are remarkably instructive. So let's at least summarize our findings from last time.

A first point would be this: Lehi doesn't seem intent on letting anyone know when he's drawing from Isaiah. He seems to borrow from the prophet in at least two places, but in neither does he mention Isaiah by name. In one case, it's possible that Isaiah isn't actually in Lehi's mind, and in the other, he refers only to the fact that he's got *some* scriptural text in mind. We're left to make the connection ourselves. This is already quite different from Nephi. We've seen how explicit Nephi is about his interest in Isaiah, and, with just a couple of exceptions, he's emphatic about when he's using Isaiah's words. This is important. The contrast with Lehi allows us to see how deliberate, how intentional, Nephi's program is. He's most certainly not inheriting a way of working on biblical texts; rather, he's doing something novel, and he wants us to understand exactly what he's up to. That's essential.

A second point might be added: Lehi seems to recognize that there's a good deal of interpretive difficulty in making sense of Isaiah's writings, but he's convinced that he's come, in the end, to understand the meaning of the Isaianic text. He seems to experiment with Isaiah's writings, but with the idea in mind that the experiment can produce genuine knowledge. Here again we sense a real contrast with Nephi. For Nephi, Isaiah's writings are to be likened in a way that's often and intentionally at odds with a simple historical interpretation of the Old-World prophet's words. Nephi seems entirely clear that he's not giving us a scientific or even terribly responsible interpretation of Isaiah. But he sees what he's doing as nonetheless the task of a certain prophetic appropriation of the prophet. Where Lehi tries to make sense of Isaiah himself and seems sure he can come to correct answers, Nephi doesn't much bother with what Isaiah means in his original context; instead, he's happy just to use broader patterns in Isaiah's prophecy to see how it might shed light on God's larger dealings with the covenant people. Seeing that Nephi's quite explicit about his complex relationship to Isaiah is important.

Finally, a third point: Lehi seems to see Isaiah's writings as helping to clarify something like the general "plan of salvation." He finds in Isaiah's writings a haphazard collection of information that might be drawn on to make sense of what it means to be human, and that because Isaiah has things to say about matters taken up elsewhere in biblical scripture. For Lehi, it seems that Isaiah works in something like the way Latter-day Saints tend to think all scripture works: as a set of isolated texts that can be studied for their doctrinal and practical value. Nephi works with Isaiah in a drastically distinct way. He seems to see the whole of the Book of Isaiah—or whatever of it he had in his possession—as a systematic exposition of a single theme: the Abrahamic covenant. For Nephi, the point of reading through Isaiah is to think through just a few central concepts, and to see what they really mean. And this can only be done if you're tuned to the larger structural complexity of the prophet's writings. Nephi reads Isaiah systematically, but he does so without an interest in things like doctrine or practice. He seems more interested in developing a kind of theology of history, or a historical theology—as we'll see. And that requires sustained reading with an eye to questions that aren't about our everyday concerns, about living the life of faith.

Okay, is that enough by way of summary? Are we all on the same page? Shall we turn our attention, at last, to what Nephi actually does with Isaiah at the level of the details?

Distinct Approaches to Isaiah 48–49

Let's start, if we can, with what in the original dictation were Chapters VI and VII of First Nephi. Here's where Nephi first quotes Isaiah at some length and then provides a bit of commentary. And I think we'll see that it'll introduce us to a number of things we'll want to keep an eye on.

1 Nephi 20–21 (originally making up the bulk of Chapter VI) reproduces Isaiah 48–49. Generally, interpreters of Isaiah would likely find it odd that Nephi puts these two chapters together in this way. Why? Because there is a pretty standard notion among interpreters of Isaiah that the sixteen-chapter sequence making up Isaiah 40–55 divides into two halves: Isaiah 40–48 and Isaiah 49–55. Isaiah 48 is a kind of conclusion to what the so-called Second Isaiah has to say about the rise of Cyrus of Persia and his deliverance of the Judahite exiles from their captivity. Isaiah 49, however, marks the beginning of an extended reflection on the process of Jerusalem's consequent redemption, organized by alternating sections

focused on Zion or the Lord's servant. (There's a nice discussion of that alternating pattern in Patricia Tull Willey's *Remember the Former Things*, if you're interested.) So, with Isaiah 48 working as a kind of conclusion to one sequence of the text of Isaiah and Isaiah 49 working as a kind of introduction to another sequence of the text, we might well be surprised to find Nephi excerpting them and sticking them together.

Actually, though, there may be some good sense to this. In a way, Isaiah 48 introduces us to all the themes of Isaiah 40–48 without getting us bogged down too much in the historical particulars. And then there's *this* interesting peculiarity: Nephi never again quotes from or alludes to Isaiah 48. We'll see that bits and pieces from Isaiah 49 appear often in Nephi's own prophetic writings, as well as in Jacob's. In fact, along with Isaiah 11 and Isaiah 29, Isaiah 49 is among the most-quoted chapters of Isaiah in the Book of Mormon. But Isaiah 48 just appears here in 1 Nephi 20, and that's it. So it seems Nephi isn't much concerned about Isaiah 40–48 in general, and the inclusion of Isaiah 48 is driven by the need to have a kind of summary of the themes of those chapters without getting too invested in everything else we can find there. It's just an introduction of sorts to Isaiah 49–55, an introduction we can read through relatively quickly and get on to what interests Nephi and his descendants more deeply and more consistently.

So, we get Isaiah 48–49 together in 1 Nephi 20–21. But let's note this also: that Nephi doesn't treat them as a single text. Although they're sandwiched together, and although they even form parts of just one chapter in the original dictation, Nephi takes care to distinguish them. As he makes his transition from Isaiah 48 to Isaiah 49, he inserts an interruptive "and again," a short little phrase that's often used in the Book of Mormon to mark transitions between sections or units of text. We'll see as we go along that he might actually have added a good deal more by way of transition. But let's not get ahead of ourselves. For the moment, just note the added "and again" and recognize that Nephi seems fully aware that Isaiah 48 and Isaiah 49 don't form a single unit. He wants us to read them as distinct texts that he's placing side by side.

He might even give us some indication of *how* he sees these two Isaianic texts as differing from each other. Despite some differences between the opening of Isaiah 48 in Nephi and in the biblical text, both versions identify the audience of Isaiah 48 as the "house of Jacob, which are called by the name of Israel and are come out of the waters of Judah" (1 Ne. 20:1). But the audience of Isaiah 49 is different. I've just mentioned that Nephi seems to add a whole lot of material to the beginning of Isaiah 49. Again, we'll get to the details there later, but note for the moment that the apparently added material identifies a rather different audience for Isaiah 49. *At first* it looks like the audience is the "house of Israel," not much different from what's found in Isaiah 48, but *then* the text narrows the scope: "all ye that are broken off and are driven out because of the wickedness of the pastors of my people." And it goes on: "Yea, all ye that are broken off, that are scattered abroad, which are of my people, O house of Israel" (1 Ne. 21:1). This suggests that, at least in the Book of Mormon, Isaiah 48 is addressed to Israel quite generally, but only in their close relationship to Judah, while Isaiah 49 is addressed quite differently to the scattered branches or remnants of Israel, those at some geographical distance from Judah and the Promised Land. There's even talk here of the "isles" (v. 1).

That there's a difference of scope actually becomes clearer if we look at the content of the two chapters. The exhortations in Isaiah 48 to "go . . . forth of Babylon" and to "flee . . . from the Chaldeans" (1 Ne. 20:20) make clear that that chapter's meant to speak to those specifically who were in Babylonian exile at the time of Nephi. But Isaiah 49 focuses on the "isles of the sea" (1 Ne. 21:8) on "the north" and "the west" (1 Ne. 21:12), and so on—a rather broader geographical focus, no? It seems Nephi wants his readers to hear these two chapters from the Book of Isaiah as differently oriented, one with a narrower focus on Israel in and around the Holy Land, and one with a broader focus on Israel scattered across the whole earth. Since Nephi sees his own people as "a branch which have been broken off" from those at Jerusalem (1 Ne. 19:24), it wouldn't be at all surprising if he meant to draw exactly this sort of distinction.

In fact, there's still *further* reason to think that we're on the right track. In the last verses before the quotation of Isaiah 48–49 in First Nephi, verses that are now the last verses of 1 Nephi 19 but that were actually the opening verses of Chapter VI in the original dictation (clearly intended, then, to be a kind of introduction to Isaiah 48–49)—in *those* verses, Nephi distinguishes between Isaiah-in-himself, so to speak, and Isaiah-as-Nephi-interprets-him. We've already mentioned this distinction earlier today, in drawing a contrast between Nephi's and Lehi's ways of reading Isaiah. Lehi seems focused on figuring out what Isaiah himself actually meant, while Nephi seems intent rather on using Isaiah for his own larger purposes. Nephi calls this "likening," and this is what he lays out in those verses immediately preceding the quotation of Isaiah 48–49. He tells us that he spent his time likening Isaiah's writings to his own people, "that it might be for [their] profit and learning" (1 Ne. 19:23), but he also says this, which we quote far less often: "Hear ye the words of the prophet, ye which are a remnant of the house of Israel, a branch which have been broken off. Hear ye the words of the prophet, which was written unto all the house of Israel, and liken it unto yourselves, that ye may have hope as well as your brethren from whom ye have been broken off" (1 Ne. 19:24).

Did you catch that? Nephi twice says, "Hear ye the words of the prophet." In connection with the first, he makes clear that he (Nephi himself) is addressing "a remnant," "a branch" of Israel. But in connection with the second instance of the formula, he makes clear that to read the prophet from the perspective of the remnant or the branch, it's necessary to *liken* the text. It was written unto *all* of Israel, but a bit of likening can narrow the scope of the prophet's words so that it speaks also to the New-World branch of Israel. Does Nephi immediately go on to enact the program of likening he's just laid out? He gives us Isaiah 48 but leaves its original audience and context intact. Isaiah had a word for the exiles in Babylon. But then he gives us Isaiah 49 just after that, and he begins himself to do some likening by reworking the text, or at least by inserting at its opening a few words that focus the text on the remnant or the branch of Israel specifically. There, words that were most likely, just like those in Isaiah 48, intended originally to speak to those in Babylonian exile have been reworked in a preliminary way, allowing them to be more readily likened to other sorts of Israelites in exile—scattered across the earth.

Did all that make sense? I'm suggesting the possibility that Nephi divides Isaiah 48–49 into two successive sequences in part to illustrate the actual process of likening, which he recommends to his readers. He quotes Isaiah 48, but leaves it unlikened, a prophecy trapped in its historical context because it speaks primarily and in rather particular terms to those stuck in Babylon. But then he quotes Isaiah 49, and he reshapes the text in important ways so that it's well on its way to being likened, a prophecy recontextualized and somewhat generalized so that it speaks to other Israelites kept at some distance from the land promised to their ancestors. It seems that Nephi takes the opportunity in these last chapters of First Nephi to begin to *model* the interpretive program he's got in mind. "You should liken Isaiah. And here's *exactly* what I mean when I talk about likening. Here's what an *un*likened text looks like, Isaiah 48 taken as a rigid historical document, trapped in the past. And then here's what a *likened* text looks like, Isaiah 49 re-envisioned so that it can speak to much larger historical concerns than just those you might usually associate with such a text."

Isaiah re-envisioned—that's the program Nephi's after, reproduced in a kind of slogan. Perhaps we could take a couple of minutes and clarify just what it means to talk that way. Isaiah 49 provides a *perfect* illustration, so let's use it as an example.

Isaiah 49 opens with a few words about Israel, presented as the Lord's servant. Israel isn't terribly pleased with its situation, wallowing in lowly exile. Israel complains: "I have labored in vain! I have spent my strength for naught, and in vain!" (1 Ne. 21:4). The Lord's response to these complaints? "It is a light thing that thou shouldst be my servant to raise up the tribes of Jacob, and to restore the preserved of Israel. I will also give thee for a light to the Gentiles, that thou mayest be my salvation unto the ends of the earth!" (v. 6). Do you see the basic picture here? Israel's off in exile in Babylon, and they're not happy about it. They complain to God about the situation, and his response is that he's got bigger plans than they realize. He isn't interested solely in raising up and restoring Israel; he's interested in redeeming the whole world—the Gentiles included! And so he's drawn them away from their lands, away from their precious lands of promise, to situate them among the nations, among Gentiles who're watching them closely. There he can do something much bigger than Israel has ever anticipated. He can redeem them while everyone's watching, and then the Gentiles might join in the worship of the Lord also. Isaiah 49 will go on to predict this event in what's pretty clearly one of Nephi's favorite Isaiah passages, where the Gentiles carry Israel home on their shoulders, bowing in the dust and offering to be their servants. When Israel is redeemed *from among* the Gentile nations, the possibility of the Gentile nations becoming a part of the covenant becomes real.

Now, in Isaiah 49 *originally*, it seems all this is supposed to be an explanation of why Israel has found itself in exile in Babylon. But Nephi likens the text. Sure, there was this rather local deliverance of the covenant people among the Persians and the Babylonians, and maybe all of a few thousand Gentiles were converted as a result. Isaiah foresaw that. But Nephi seems to think we find in the very same prophecy a more general pattern, a way that God scatters bits and pieces of Israel all over the world, so that the redemption of each and every branch of Israel will gather in more Gentiles. And it's to this larger vision of history that Nephi wants, then, to liken the text. Can we see in Isaiah 49 the outline of a larger pattern of God's covenantal work? Can we see there a kind of vision of what it means for God to use Israel for the redemption of the whole world? If so, we're getting somewhere with the work of likening the text.

That's what I've got in mind when I refer to Isaiah re-envisioned. Nephi's interested in what Isaiah has to say, but he's interested because he sees there a basic pattern for God's working with Israel and the Gentiles quite generally. And he wants to see if he can't align Isaiah's text with that much, much larger history—the history he saw in his own visionary experiences outside of Jerusalem.

The Abrahamic Covenant

Okay, that was a lot. We need to start actually working on the *text* of Isaiah 48–49, but we're getting near the end of our time today. I don't want to be caught in the middle of things and end up keeping you over time *again*, likely far longer than usual! What to do? Actually, I've got an idea. And I can only hope we can do it in the time we've got left.

I've been making reference from day one to the Abrahamic covenant, and we haven't yet taken the time to step back and ask exactly what's meant by it. And we'll see that it's probably impossible really to get at the meaning of Isaiah 49 without getting clear about some particulars here. Here's what I propose to do with the remainder of our time today, then: to look in rather broad terms at the meaning of the Abrahamic covenant. This should do us all good anyway, since we as Latter-day Saints seem more than a bit confused about this notion. We all seem to know it's central or important in some way, but we're never quite sure what it really is or *why* it's supposedly so important. Every four years we give forty-five minutes to it in Sunday School, but we do little more than write up a list of things we see promised to Abraham in Genesis 12 or Abraham 2, but then we look at the list and we don't know what to do with it. Is that your experience as much as it is mine? So let's see if we can't get preliminarily clear about the Abrahamic covenant.

To make full sense of this thing, I think we need to give the opening chapters of Genesis a good, fresh read, keeping Joseph Smith's systematic reworking of the text (part of which we have in the Book of Moses) ready to hand. Let's begin with the fall. Adam and Eve end up ejected from Eden, and what's the result, the immediate aftermath of the fall? Violence. Cain and Abel, specifically, to start with, but then things rapidly escalate. Cain starts a whole tradition of secret murder, violence wielded as a tool to procure wealth. And by the time of Noah—especially after Enoch and his people have disappeared—things have gotten completely out of control. Do you remember why the Lord floods the earth? Here's how it's put in Genesis, just as it in the Book of Moses: "The earth also was corrupt before God, and the earth was filled with violence" (Gen. 6:11; see Moses 8:28). It's this that's the *primary* motivation for the flood: "The end of all flesh is come before me," God says to Noah, "for the earth is filled with violence through them; and, behold, I will destroy them with the earth" (Gen. 6:11; see Moses 8:30). We seem to be facing a kind of Jaredite-like situation of self-eradication, so the Lord floods the earth to allow for the salvation of a small remnant: Noah and his family.

After the flood, we find God setting up some rules for Noah's progeny, with the hope that violence can be curbed. Take a look sometime at the so-called Noahide laws, found in Genesis 9, where the focus is on ensuring that the violence and bloodshed of the antediluvian, or pre-flood, era would disappear. And with those rules solidly in place, God then makes a promise to Noah that he won't again flood the earth, that he won't again solve the problem of violence by eradicating the human population to start afresh. But of course, as soon as Noah's children have children, we end up with violence all over again. It takes a new form, however, after the flood. We don't get a lot of talk of secret combinations and universal violence. Instead we enter the age of the empires, massive nations slaughtering one another and wielding power by commanding control over life and death. We get the violence of national wars instead of the violence of fraternal conflicts. Or we might say that we get fraternal conflict now worked out at a kind of global level, the clash of nations in horrific displays of bloody power. And now we might say that God finds himself in a kind of dilemma. The earth is filling up anew with violence, but he's made a promise not to flood the earth and start over. A new strategy is necessary.

And so God calls Abraham. He takes one man and through him launches a *new* nation—or really a *non*-nation, a nation that won't *work like* a nation. Remember how the story begins, with God telling Abraham, "Get thee out of thy country, and from thy kindred, and from thy father's house" (Gen. 12:1). He's to strip himself of nationality, and then he's to go wandering. Through him a new nation would come into existence, but from the outset it's to be a rather different sort of thing from the other nations. *They* mark borders and claim lands, but *his children* are to do everything possible to establish peace among the nations. And they're to do so by blessing "all families of the earth" (v. 3). They're to rework the very order of the world, replacing the national with the familial, war with peace. This is what the stories of Abraham in the Book of Genesis are all about, remember. Abraham is the figure of hospitality and peace. He's the guy who makes peace with Egypt, with Lot, with the king of Sodom, with Melchizedek, with Abimelech, with Ephron the Hittite. He's the guy who welcomes the strangers in and feeds them, the same strangers that nearby nations (Sodom, Gomorrah) treat with terrible violence (rape as a way of putting the newcomers into their place). Abraham is the figure of faith and obedience, but also of hospitality, of peacemaking.

His children inherit this task. Israel is born, a whole nation that's supposed to be ready to assume the Abrahamic project. But the rest of the Bible is the story of their failure to understand this. They want to be a nation *like other nations*. They want kings and legal structures that mirror the other nations. They want imperial power and they hope to extend their borders. They see their covenantal relationship with God to mean that they're different from other nations *only in that God backs them up*. And so they find themselves in constant trouble. And God sends them prophets to get them out of trouble, or at least to call them back to their responsibilities. There's an especially important prophet who comes along in the eighth century when the covenantal status of Israel is under the most serious threat it's experienced since Egypt. You can guess his name: Isaiah. He lays into Israel, trying to call them back to their covenantal task, to the work of redeeming all the Gentile nations by teaching them peace. At the outset of his remarkable book of prophecy, there's an especially Abrahamic promise of what's to come when Israel finally fulfills its task. The Gentile nations won't be learning war anymore, because they'll be beating their swords into plowshares and their spears into pruning hooks. Abandoning violence at last, they instead decide to join Israel in worshiping the Lord at his temple.

There's the fulfillment of the Abrahamic covenant. That's what everything in the Bible looks to, works toward. The whole of the New Testament is also obsessed with this, especially in the writings of Paul. Paul spends his time thinking about the status of the covenant people after the Messiah's advent, about what it means finally to see Israel and the Gentiles worshipfully working together to establish universal peace. And this is the burden of the gospels as well. We don't have time to go into it all.

In fact, we're basically out of time. I've given you just a sketch of the Abrahamic covenant, but hopefully it's enough to see what's going on. It'll prove really important for making sense of Isaiah 49. We'll look at that next time. At any rate, it's got to be perfectly clear that it's this covenantal theme that drives Nephi's interest in Isaiah. He'll certainly say as much in 1 Nephi 22, when he tries to explain Isaiah to his brothers. What Isaiah describes, he says there, is "the making known of the covenants of the Father of heaven unto Abraham" (1 Ne. 22:9). There's the focus of everything Nephi has to say about Isaiah.

This will become perfectly clear next time, I hope.

Isaiah 48–49 in Summary

"Hear ye the words of the prophet!" Nephi says. "Hear ye the words of the prophet!" (1 Ne. 19:24). I don't know about you, but I'm getting more than a bit eager to get on to following his advice. Let's take the plunge, shall we?

Isaiah 48 in Summary

Nephi gives us Isaiah 48 first. That's a bit of a surprise. I think I mentioned last time that Nephi never comes back to Isaiah 48. He quotes it in 1 Nephi 20. But then he never again, not even once, refers back to it. And recognize that that's quite unusual. Much of what Nephi quotes from Isaiah shows up all over his writings—a little allusion here, a brief quotation there, occasionally a longer selection. Isaiah 48, however, he gives us just in this *one* form, its full quotation in 1 Nephi 20. I suggested last time, moreover, that he quotes it here as an example of an unlikened Isaianic text. He seems to leave it trapped in its original historical context, refusing to begin the work of adapting and appropriating it for his own theological purposes. It's almost as if he wants us to encounter Isaiah 48 as a kind of museum piece, carefully preserved and certainly not to be touched.

So what does it say?

It's clear from the outset of Isaiah 48 that we're dealing with wayward Israel. It opens with a command to the "house of Jacob," those "called by the name of Israel," to "hearken and hear" (1 Ne. 20:1). And then we're given this description of the state of Israel's relationship to the God to whom they're bound in covenant. They "swear by the name of the Lord and make mention of the God of Israel, yet they swear not in truth nor in righteousness" (v. 1). Or again: "They *call* themselves of the holy city, but they do not stay themselves upon the God of Israel" (v. 2). Here we have a basic motivation for the prophet's intervention. Israel needs to hear a few words of rebuke. They aren't much exemplifying faith in or fidelity to the Lord, even as they outwardly identify as his followers, his covenant people. In what circumstances? Well, we'll come to that. For the moment, it's enough to recognize that such a word could have come to Israel at a great many points in their recorded history, just as it could come to us at a great many points in our recorded history.

Having indicted Israel in these general terms, the prophet next describes the lengths the Lord has to go to keep the covenant people from wandering too far astray. This comes in two sequences. The first focuses on "the former things" (1 Ne. 20:3), on things "declared" to Israel "from the beginning" (v. 5). The second then focuses on "new things" (v. 6), on things "created now and not from the beginning" (v. 7). The Lord, it seems, has found it necessary to employ a double strategy to keep Israel in check. First, knowing Israel to be "obstinate" (v. 4), he made a number of things known to them by the prophets long in advance. In the Lord's words, "before it came to pass, I showed them thee" (v. 5). And his reason for doing this he states clearly: "I showed them for fear lest thou shouldst say, 'Mine idol hath done them'" (v. 5). Some words attributed to the Lord, it seems, had to be in circulation from ancient times so that Israel couldn't claim that their fulfillment was a function of whatever new-fangled idolatrous cult they happened to have discovered quite recently. There's the first part of the strategy. But it's not enough, because Israel might well respond by saying that such ancient prophecies are just common knowledge. "Who cares about the old? Take a look at the new!" Hence the Lord's second strategy. Knowing Israel to be "a transgressor from the womb," prone to "deal very treacherously" (v. 8), the Lord *still* sends prophets, ones who now declare "new things from this time," things Israel could "not know" (v. 6). The Lord has his own new things, and so he can trump Israel's tendency to respond to the ancient with "Behold, I knew them" (v. 7). And so at least some prophetic words have to be as new as possible, supplementing more ancient prophecies, so that Israel can't squirm its way out of the situation. They're to deal with a God who calls himself, just a few verses later, both "the first" and "also the last" (v. 12).

It should be no surprise that all this necessary strategizing leaves the Lord less than impressed with the covenant people. In fact, Isaiah says clearly, it leaves him in a state of "anger" (1 Ne. 20:9). So why does the Lord put up with Israel at all? Isaiah gives the Lord's response: "Nevertheless for my name's sake will I defer mine anger, and for my praise will I refrain from thee, that I cut thee not off" (v. 9). The Lord sticks with Israel, but not because Israel deserves it. It's for God's own purposes, much broader and richer than anything Israel has in mind, that he keeps working with them. It seems he's got a plan. And drawing from our discussion at the end of our last lecture, we can already say something about what that larger, more expansive plan seems to be. It concerns the Abrahamic task to which Israel *should* be dedicated, but which it almost systematically ignores. The Lord will hold to Israel, wearing himself out in strategically thwarting Israel's waywardness, so that he can accomplish his larger purposes in the world. "For mine own sake—yea, for mine own sake—will I do this" (v. 11).

But I hope you're asking yourself, at this point, the following question: *What* will the Lord do? What *concrete* shape does his double strategy take? Can we actually say anything *specific* about "the former things," these ancient prophecies that predict rather specific events? Or can we actually say anything specific in turn about "the new things," these novel prophecies that apparently also predict rather specific events? I think we can. And in fact, we get our first hint at concrete content at the very moment that the Lord explains that he's got his own larger purposes. Isaiah quotes him thus: "For behold, I have refined thee. I have chosen thee in the furnace of affliction" (1 Ne. 20:10). This doesn't sound good. And in fact, we *might* at this point begin to feel compassion rather than disgust at Israel's wonted waywardness, condemned so forcefully at the outset of the chapter. They might be wayward, but the Lord himself seems to make clear here that they're in a difficult situation, passing through "the furnace of affliction." Suddenly, the story looks rather different. Before this point in Isaiah 48, we might feel like we're listening to the Lord chastising unrepentant Israel, fat and happy in their own land. Suddenly we realize that we're listening to the Lord chastising a people experiencing intense pressure.

It gets worse, though, because soon Isaiah identifies the exact situation Israel is in. The Israel Isaiah's talking to is the Israel that's wallowing in Babylonian exile. They've seen their monarchy fall, they've watched their temple's destruction, they've witnessed the slaughter of their people, and they've experienced the loss of their land as they've been resettled in foreign territory. And *there*, in that most difficult situation, Isaiah dares to quote words of chastisement from the Lord! But note that he always and inevitably couples such words of chastisement with words of comfort. At the very moment we begin to realize that Isaiah 48 is addressed to Israel in exile, we find the Lord making promises through Isaiah. They're in the furnace of affliction, yes, but there they've been chosen. The Lord is refining them. And Isaiah makes this crucial promise: "The Lord . . . will fulfill his word. . . . He will do his pleasure on Babylon, and his arm shall come upon the Chaldeans" (1 Ne. 20:14). *This*, it turns out, is the ancient word that's been in circulation for so long that Israel can barely remember when it was first spoken. Babylon will be overcome! It seems like we're supposed to be thinking here of Isaiah 13–14, Isaiah's oracle against Babylon to be found much earlier in the book, certainly one of "the former things." Or anyway, it seems quite likely that *Nephi* has Isaiah 13–14 in mind. Those two chapters make up the last bit of his lengthy quotation of Isaiah at the heart of Second Nephi.

So here we begin to get concrete. The ancient word is a promise that Babylon will fall. And what's the new thing that's happening now? That isn't made quite as clear in Isaiah 48 as it will be in Isaiah 49, but we can say something about it already. The new thing is that there's a secret purpose on the Lord's part for having Israel go into and then return from exile. It's not *just* a process of refinement that he's got in mind. And it's not just a kind of covenant faithfulness to a chosen people that he wants to maintain. The Lord's purpose is to put his faithfulness and his power on display before the nations. The whole world—according to what might well seem like a bit of hyperbole!—will witness Israel's redemption when Babylon falls, and the Gentile nations will get their first glimpse of what it might mean to turn from their idols to the true God. That, it seems, is the new thing, or at least the chiefest of the new things. But we'll say more about this theme in a bit, since, as I just said, it's a lot clearer in Isaiah 49.

Now we've got a concrete picture taking shape. Long before it could possibly seem relevant—indeed, long before Babylon was even a serious contender on the world political scene—the Lord gave his word that he'd redeem Israel by bringing Babylon to its knees. And this is supposed to keep Israel from being able to say that their deliverance is the fruit of their adhering to whatever recently adopted idolatrous cults have come into fashion among them. Because now it's all finally happening. The Lord's ancient word is coming true. But, lest Israel respond by saying that this is all then just a bit of old news, and that they've got little to learn from this situation, they're about to be confronted with some remarkable surprises, things the Lord has kept hidden so that they can't deny their dependence on him. And now it seems that we were wrong a moment ago to think of the opening part of Isaiah 48 as unfair or inopportune chastisement. What we're seeing here is the Lord's everlasting love and covenant fidelity being put fully on display. He's carefully thwarting their attempts to skirt their own covenantal obligations, preventing their tendency to swear by the Lord's name always and only in vain. He's about to do something of world-historical importance, and they're doing all they can to miss out on it. He won't let them. And that's a gesture of profoundest grace.

The rest of Isaiah 48 casts the resulting situation as a reboot of the story of the exodus from Egypt, but now, of course, it's an exodus from Babylon. First, just as in the ancient exodus, the Lord calls a servant to lead Israel from their bondage. It's no longer Moses, of course (in fact, we don't get any clear identification of the servant in Isaiah 48), but it's some leader nonetheless. Here are the Lord's words about the new servant as Isaiah quotes them: "I have called him to declare. I have brought him, and he shall make his way prosperous" (1 Ne. 20:15). This servant figure is, of course, also a prophet figure, just like Moses. This becomes apparent when Isaiah next quotes the servant himself: "Come ye near unto me. I have not spoken in secret from the beginning. From the time that it was declared have I spoken, and the Lord God and his spirit hath sent me" (v. 16). Lest Israel ignore this word, the Lord himself confirms it immediately: "I have sent him" (v. 17). So we've got a Moses-like figure set up to lead Israel out of exile. Next, as with the exodus, we're told that this situation should be understood within the larger frame of the Abrahamic history. Isaiah has the Lord cry out: "O! that thou hadst hearkened to my commandments! Then had thy peace been as a river, and thy righteousness as the waves of the sea! Thy seed also had been as the sand, the offspring of thy bowels like the gravel thereof!" (vv. 18–19). This is unmistakable Abrahamic language, language we're all quite familiar with. Of course, it's cast somewhat negatively here, since Israel *hasn't* kept the Lord's commandments to them, and so they *haven't* yet seen anything of the fulfillment of these promises. But Israel has another chance. Always another chance. They're given a new commandment: "Go ye forth of Babylon! Flee ye from the Chaldeans!" (v. 20). And with this commandment, the reboot of the exodus can begin in earnest. And so, third and finally, we get language that describes the new trek through the wilderness on the way to the Promised Land: "And they thirsted not. He led them through the deserts. He caused the waters to flow out of the rock for them. He clave the rock also, and the waters gushed out" (v. 21). You can't miss the allusions here. The exodus has begun anew.

There. That's Isaiah 48. And I think it's nothing like so obscure as we often take it to be. Let's review it briefly, shall we? It opens (verses 1–2) with the Lord making clear that Israel has been unfaithful, but this is immediately followed with an outline of the Lord's double strategy for keeping

Israel faithful: first by providing them with prophecies long in advance of fulfillment (verses 3–6a), and second by providing them with brand new prophetic things to think about (verses 6b–8). Isaiah follows this with an explanation of the Lord's patience, which is a product of his own larger purposes (verses 9–11) and a statement of the Lord's sovereignty (verses 12–13). And then we finally get the first clear indication of what all this is about, the Lord's ancient word that he'd bring Babylon's towering empire crashing to the ground (verse 14). From that point on, we watch the old exodus story play itself out in a new situation—in three sequences: a prophetic servant is raised up to lead Israel (verses 15–17), the Abrahamic context of the exodus is clarified (verses 18–19), and the actual trek through the wilderness is described (verses 20–21). We haven't mentioned the final verse in our discussion, but it's an ominous conclusion: "And notwithstanding he hath done all this—and greater also!—there is no peace, saith the Lord, unto the wicked" (1 Ne. 20:22). It's a fitting conclusion.

And with that, I think we can move on to Isaiah 49. We're making decent time today for once, so perhaps we'll get all the way through it too!

Isaiah 49 in Summary

Isaiah 49 opens with one of the four so-called "servant songs" that can be found in Isaiah 40–55. A whole lot has been written about the servant songs, from the time they were first isolated from their literary contexts by Berhard Duhm at the end of the nineteenth century to the time, quite recently, when they've been pretty definitively set back into their literary contexts by, among others, Trygvve Mettinger. Here's the short version. At different points in Isaiah 40–55, there's talk of a servant, and at a few places there appear extended poems focused on the servant. The first of the four that have been traditionally identified doesn't appear in the Book of Mormon, but the other three do—one of them here in Isaiah 49. (The others appear in Jacob's quotation of Isaiah 50 in 2 Nephi 7 and in Abinadi's quotation of Isaiah 53 in Mosiah 14—as well as in a few scattered quotations by Christ in Third Nephi.) Much of the scholarly work that's been done on the servant songs addresses the identity of the servant, a question that seems especially pressing in the fourth and final servant song. We can ignore more or less all of that debate for our purposes here, since Nephi never quotes from the fourth song. He seems satisfied with the straightforward identification of the servant in Isaiah 49. And so we'll start there, with the Lord addressing the servant as follows: "Thou art my servant, O Israel, in whom I will be glorified" (1 Ne. 21:3). Let's leave the whole question of the servant songs at that, for now, with the equation of Israel with the servant in Isaiah 49. That seems to be all that matters to Nephi.

In the opening verses of Isaiah 49, we're told that God's purposes with his servant Israel have been long in the making: "The Lord hath called me from the womb. From the bowels of my mother hath he made mention of my name" (1 Ne. 21:1). And for what purpose? Well, Isaiah attributes to Israel *one* understanding of the Lord's purposes. He has Israel say of the Lord that he "formed me from the womb that I should be his servant to bring Jacob again to him" (v. 5). On Israel's account, it seems, the Lord's intention is that they look out for themselves, that they fulfill their obligations to the Lord so that they can receive all the blessings promised to them. That would glorify the Lord, and it's in his servant Israel that the Lord "will be glorified" (v. 3). Nothing here seems *terribly* offensive yet, since we might hear in what Isaiah puts in Israel's mouth at this point little more than what we hear in an average sacrament meeting talk. God loves us, and he wishes us to be righteous so that we can receive the blessings promised to the obedient. But there's a kind of sinister note here, since Isaiah also has Israel saying that the Lord's made them "like a sharp sword," a dagger that's then hidden "in the shadow of [the Lord's] hand" (v. 2). Or again, Israel understands itself to be "a polished shaft," an arrow hidden in the Lord's "quiver" (v. 2). These are more violent images, and one can't help but wonder whether Isaiah means to suggest that Israel has understood its task to be one of military might. They're to look out for themselves, not only in obedience, but in rising to power and prominence in a world of war and violence.

If that's so, then we can understand Israel's eventual response: "I have labored in vain! I have spent my strength for naught and in vain!" (1 Ne. 21:4). All that their chosenness seems to have earned them by the time of Nephi is exile in foreign territory, their lands taken from them and their temple laid waste. Some dagger in the hand of the Lord! Does he not know how to strike an enemy down? So here we find ourselves back where we were in Isaiah 48, with Israel in exile wondering at the Lord's failure to redeem. And as before, naturally, we're going to get the promise that redemption is about to happen at last. But we're going to get something more this time as well. We're going to get a *larger* purpose for the exile. And we get this in a first form pretty early in Isaiah 49. In response to Israel's lament, Isaiah quotes the Lord as saying these remarkable words: "It is a light thing that thou shouldst be my servant to raise up the tribes of

Jacob, and to restore the preserved of Israel. I will *also* give thee for a light to the Gentiles, that thou mayest be my salvation unto the ends of the earth" (v. 6). With these words, Isaiah offers a crucial corrective to Israel's self-understanding. They seem to think that their whole work is to look out for their own redemption, to see that they do what's necessary to secure the Lord's blessing. But when they express their inevitable frustration at failing, the Lord responds by making clear that there's a bigger picture. It's too "light," too easy, just to redeem Israel. God's got his eyes on *the whole world.* You see, Israel isn't there with the task of redeeming itself, but of being "a light to the Gentiles," of being God's "salvation unto the ends of the earth." That's a much grander affair.

This becomes only clearer as the text of Isaiah 49 goes on. Isaiah quotes the Lord describing Israel as "him whom man despiseth" and "him whom the nation abhorreth," a mere "servant of rulers" (1 Ne. 21:7). But then he announces that "kings shall see and arise," that "princes also shall worship" (v. 7), and that Israel will be given "for a covenant of the people to establish the earth" (v. 8). Humiliated in foreign exile for a moment, Israel will be redeemed with a strong hand, and the whole world will witness the Lord's glory and power. And Israel will less *have* a covenant that puts them in relation to God than *be* a covenant that puts all human beings in relation to God. There's the bigger plan. And once it's laid out, Isaiah starts to give us material familiar from Isaiah 48: exodus talk that describes the return of Israel from exile. When Israel leaves Babylon, "they shall feed in the ways" (v. 9), and "they shall not hunger nor thirst" because the Lord will "guide them" to all "the springs of water" (v. 10). Israel will be gathering from every place of exile, "from the north and from the west," some even "from the land of Sinim," the far east (v. 12). And all this is reason, indeed, to rejoice: "Sing, O heavens," Isaiah exults, "and be joyful, O earth!" (v. 13). Even the mountains are to "break forth into singing," because "the Lord hath comforted his people and will have mercy upon his afflicted" (v. 13). This is an old story by this point, but now we've been introduced to the larger context in which it's supposed to function—a larger story about the possibility of drawing non-covenantal peoples into the covenant.

And then Isaiah tells us the same thing all over again, but, of course, in a different way, giving us the same story from a rather different perspective. It's a *really* different perspective. It's that of the *land.* The land of Zion speaks up: "The Lord hath forsaken me! And my lord hath forgotten me!" (1 Ne. 21:14). That's what Zion says, but neither Isaiah nor the Lord will have any of it. Isaiah retorts, "But he will show that he hath not!" (v. 14), and the Lord responds with a famous rhetorical question: "Can a woman forget her sucking child?" (v. 15). This is then followed up with a word of encouragement to the forsaken land to open her eyes, because there's a massive crowd already gathering for resettlement: "Lift up thine eyes round about, and behold all these gather themselves together!" (v. 18). The reunion is to be a kind of wedding feast, with the once-abandoned land clothing itself "as a bride" (v. 18). And the marriage is to be a fruitful one: "Thy waste and thy desolate places . . . shall even now be too narrow by reason of the inhabitants. . . . The children which thou shalt have after thou hast lost the other shall say again in thine ears, 'The place is too strait for me! Give place to me that I may dwell!'" vv. 19, 21). There won't even be room in Jerusalem for all the peoples that will occupy it after the redemption of Israel from exile!

And now we get to the crucial moment of this retelling from the perspective of the land. When the once-forsaken finally looks up to see the approaching multitudes, *she doesn't recognize their faces*. This, at least, the land says to herself within her heart. Isaiah explains: "Then shalt thou say in thine heart, 'Who hath begotten me these, seeing I have lost my children, and am desolate, a captive and removing to and fro? And who hath brought up these? Behold, I was left alone—these, where have they been?'" (1 Ne. 21:21). Here we have repeated the moment from the first part of Isaiah 49, where Israel, wallowing in exile, whines that all its work in seeking its own redemption has yielded nothing. And you remember the response from the Lord, right? That there's a much bigger picture Israel fails to see, a story that's as much about the non-covenantal Gentiles as about covenantal Israel. We get the same thing here. The forsaken land looks in the faces of the approaching people, gathered from all over, and she recognizes none of them. But then the Lord explains what's going on in what turns out to be among Nephi's favorite passages in Isaiah:

> Thus saith the Lord God: Behold, I will lift up mine hand to the Gentiles and set up my standard to the people, and they shall bring thy sons in their arms, and thy daughters shall be carried upon their shoulders. And kings shall be thy nursing fathers, and their queens thy nursing mothers. They shall bow down to thee with their face towards the earth and lick up the dust of thy feet. And thou shalt know that I am the Lord—for they shall not be ashamed that wait for me! (vv. 22–23)

There's a whole lot going on in this verse, so let's slow down and spell it out.

The forsaken land looks up and stares at the faces of those approaching for resettlement, but she recognizes none of them. Who are these people?

The Lord responds, essentially, by telling the land to look higher. "Don't you see? Of course you don't recognize the faces of the people walking toward you. *Your children are riding on their shoulders!* The people whose footsteps you're tracing are Gentiles, non-Israelites, but *they're carrying your children back to you!* Your children aren't coming home alone, but with hosts of others who seek redemption!" Here again, as earlier in the chapter, Isaiah clarifies the breadth and scope of the Abrahamic covenant. Here again, it's too light a thing for Israel to be redeemed alone; the point is to set up the covenant people as a standard, a banner that waves before all the non-covenant peoples to invite them to join in the worship of the true God. And it's worked. Israel comes home to its beloved land, carefully tended by the very kings and queens of the Gentile nations. Even Gentile royalty lies prostrate before Israel, licking up the dust of their feet with their tears and kisses. Waiting for the Lord's faithfulness has proven more than worth it.

Isaiah 49 ends with a few words of confirmation. The predicted redemption of Israel along with the Gentiles is miraculous indeed. It's like "prey be[ing] taken from the mighty" (1 Ne. 21:24). And it's God who's done it: "I will save thy children," he says (v. 25). And the chapter thus ends with these beautiful words that announce the theme that's at the heart of Isaiah 49: "All flesh shall know that I, the Lord, am thy savior and thy redeemer, the Mighty One of Jacob" (v. 26). Israel's redemption has set the Lord's goodness before the whole world. And there the prophecy ends.

Shall we summarize things again like we did with Isaiah 48? I think that's useful. And here it's perhaps even easier. In Isaiah 49, we get the same story twice over, the story of Israel's redemption from exile. And in each telling of the story, the point is to correct Israel's terribly narrow view of the covenant that binds them to the Lord. Their focus is consistently on just their own redemption, their own benefit. But each telling of the story finds Israel corrected by the Lord on this point. It turns out that their covenantal status is part of a larger project, one that's meant to make of their eventual redemption a kind of beacon to the whole world. *Here* the nations can find a God who keeps covenant and redeems people. *Here* the nations can find a God who seeks to establish real peace. *Here* the nations can find a God who would have all people reconciled in genuine worship. Israel's task is to let God redeem them in a way that puts God's grace on display before the whole world. And that's to happen, in each telling of the story, right in Israel's miraculous return from Babylon.

There's Isaiah 49 in a nutshell. Now before we wrap up—and we're already almost out of time—let's add just one further point. Remember from last time that Nephi treats Isaiah 49 somewhat differently than Isaiah 48. He leaves Isaiah 48 unlikened, a story solely about Israel's redemption from Babylonian exile. But he simply *can't* leave Isaiah 49 untouched. Throughout his quotation of this chapter, there are differences between what he says and what appears in the King James Version of Isaiah 49, and some of them at least seem to be Nephi's own alterations of the text—moments where he's changing the text in order to begin the work of likening it. And what he sees in Isaiah 49 is of major importance to him. He sees something much, much bigger than just the return to Palestine from Babylon, accomplished with some fanfare but in relative obscurity in the sixth century before Christ. He finds there at least the outline of a larger pattern, a pattern that just as well describes the events he's seen in vision: the eventual redemption of all the scattered branches of Israel from among the Gentile—that is European—nations. And that's where Nephi goes as soon as he gets a chance to explain the meaning of Isaiah 49 to his brothers in 1 Nephi 22. He wants to see in this remarkable chapter a series of allusions to events, of which escape from Babylon is only a foretaste. Something just like return from exile is coming, but it'll *actually* be before all the nations of the world, and it'll *actually* result in massive numbers of Gentiles joining with Israel to worship the Lord. And, I hope and pray every day, it'll also *actually* result in the cessation of war and violence, that source of almost all of human misery still today. Nephi sees in Isaiah 49 reason to look forward to genuine transformation of the whole world.

I think I see it there too.

Lecture IX

Variants in Isaiah 48–49

Variants in Book of Mormon Isaiah

Last time, we tried to get our first taste of Isaiah's actual writings. And maybe we've got something of a preliminary sense for them—*only* preliminary, of course, but real and worthwhile. But today I want to begin by noting that we actually *didn't* really read last time from the writings that appear in the Bible under the name of Isaiah. We read from the writings that appear in the Book of Mormon under the name of Isaiah. There are differences—a *lot* of them—between Isaiah in the Bible and Isaiah in the Book of Mormon, and we want to spend our time today taking a first look at those differences. We'll stick with Isaiah 48–49 for now, doing a bit of compare-and-contrast. How do these two chapters read in the Book of Mormon when set side by side with the same two chapters in the Bible? It turns out that there's much to learn here.

We've got a few preliminary points we'll have to make if we want to get much of anywhere with this, of course. First, let me just quickly note that there's not much out there by way of literature on this subject. John Tvedtnes published a preliminary study of the variants in the Book of Mormon's Isaiah texts way back in 1981, available for free on the Maxwell Institute website. But as Tvedtnes has more recently noted, it's now very much out of date, both because there's been a great deal more Isaiah scholarship in the years since and because Royal Skousen has since done his work on establishing a critical text of the Book of Mormon. More recently (but not since Skousen completed his work), David Wright wrote up a lengthy study of the Isaiah variants, but from a skeptical point of view, attempting to show that the variants in Book of Mormon Isaiah texts suggest that they were the product of Joseph Smith's mind. There are other scattered attempts at looking at textual variants in Book of Mormon Isaiah, but these are the two that reflect the most depth and are built on the best training. They're both out of date, and one of them begins with an antagonistic bias that often colors the interpretations it presents. So there's much to learn from these resources, but there's nothing definitive about them. And, as we'll see, they take up a different approach than we'll assume ourselves.

A second preliminary point, already implicit in what I've just said about the available literature, is that we won't get very far if we aren't paying very careful attention to at least Royal Skousen's efforts at establishing the critical text of the Book of Mormon. There are variants in Book of Mormon Isaiah texts that have been introduced accidentally or inadvertently over the years by fallible scribes and printers, and then some actual variants in Book of Mormon Isaiah texts have been occasionally replaced with the readings that appear in the King James Version of the Bible. If we're serious about looking at textual variants in Book of Mormon Isaiah, we have to do our best to be sure we've got all and only the actual variants dictated by Joseph Smith in 1829. For that, we *must* be dependent on textual critical work like Skousen's. In this connection, let's note that Joseph Smith did some editing of the Book of Mormon text for the 1837 and the 1840 editions. The vast majority of such work focused on fixing the grammatical problems of the original dictation, but a few more substantial changes to the text were made. Joseph made changes in a few instances to the Isaiah texts, and in one case the change made to the text was quite substantial. You'll likely remember it. Isaiah 48 opens in your current editions of the Book of Mormon by referring to Israel as a people "come forth out of the waters of Judah," which the text then clarifies with "or out of the waters of baptism" (1 Ne. 20:1). That clarification is something Joseph inserted only in later editions of the Book of Mormon; it wasn't part of the original dictation, and it doesn't appear in the 1830 first edition. It seems that at one point at least in his rereading of the manuscripts for the Book of Mormon, while preparing a new edition, Joseph thought he might add an interpretive gloss to the text. But that interpretive gloss is probably best understood as reflecting Joseph's interpretation. It seems unlikely that it was something Nephi would have himself added to the text, and there's little reason to think it was part of any pre-Nephi version of Isaiah. So here's a second preliminary point. Wherever we find Joseph Smith himself altering the texts of Isaiah in the Book of Mormon after the fact, it seems best to assume that we should keep our focus on the original dictation rather than on the subsequent alterations.

A third preliminary point is somewhat more difficult than the preceding two. We have to ask the question of whether we're to understand the variants in Book of Mormon Isaiah texts as faithfully reproducing what Nephi and other Book of Mormon authors found in the brass plates, or as reflecting what Nephi and other Book of Mormon authors sometimes erringly copied down from the brass plates, *or* as reflecting what Nephi and other Book of Mormon authors produced as they inventively reworked what was in the brass plates. The evidence, let's note, points in several different directions at once. Much of what Nephi gives us from Isaiah is littered with variants, sometimes more frequent, sometimes less. (We'll see, for instance, that Isaiah 48–49 is *filled* with variants.) But then when Abinadi quotes the whole of Isaiah 53, it's more or less without *any* (significant) variants. Does that suggest that the Nephites are supposed to have had an Isaiah text rather like what we have in our Bibles, but that Nephi was inventive in his rendition of the text while someone like Abinadi felt it inappropriate to alter the text? Something like a reworking of the text is suggested by the fact that Christ himself, in Third Nephi, quotes a passage from Isaiah 52 twice, first quite faithfully to what you find in the biblical version and then with some clearly deliberate alterations. And let's note also that Nephi manipulates Isaiah 29 extensively and unmistakably in 2 Nephi 26–27. At the same time, Nephi doesn't tell us when he's altering the text, so perhaps we're to understand some or even many of the variants reflected in his quotations of Isaiah as faithful reproductions of the original as contained in the brass plates. It's excessively difficult to know what we should decide about these matters, and perhaps it'll come down to particular cases. We'll see we have some reasons to think that some of the variants in Nephi's version of Isaiah 49 are his own alterations of the text. But we don't have any particular reasons to think that he's manipulating other parts of Isaiah when he quotes them. So we'll have to decide as we come to individual variants what exactly we have before us.

Okay, one last preliminary. (So many preliminaries!) How much attention should we be giving to the variants in ancient versions of Isaiah? We have a number of Hebrew manuscripts of Isaiah, and they don't all agree. And then there are all kinds of variants if we consider the great variety of translations of Isaiah into other ancient languages: Aramaic, Greek, Syriac, Latin, and so on. There's a whole academic discipline out there focused on looking at all these ancient versions of Isaiah in the hopes of reconstructing the original. Of course, we have no manuscripts of Isaiah in any language that go back before a century or two before Christ. At least five centuries passed between the death of Isaiah of Jerusalem and the production of the earliest copies we have of the text. Do the variants we have in the Book of Mormon map onto the variants that can be found in the ancient world? That, by the way, was Tvedtnes's question, and you can read his work to see a number of instances where he concludes that, yes, there are links between variants in the Book of Mormon Isaiah texts and variants in other ancient versions of Isaiah. Wright's essay was written in large part to contest a number of Tvedtnes's conclusions, so you can also look there to see another way of reading the evidence. What'll *we* do? Well, I'm not an expert in ancient texts and languages, so I won't pretend to improve on either Tvedtnes's or Wright's work. That's not my field. We'll leave to others to weigh in on how the variants we'll discuss here might or might not map onto ancient versions of Isaiah. We'll focus just on asking what these variants suggest about Isaiah as Nephi understood him. We're aiming solely at getting clear about what Nephi seems to have hoped to teach his readers through his use of Isaiah. The point in looking at the variants *as* variants is, for us, to see how the differences between Book of Mormon Isaiah texts and biblical Isaiah texts might be instructive. What do they suggest about Isaiah's meaning, as Nephi apparently conceived of it?

That's enough—more than enough!—by way of preliminaries. Let's get to work.

Variants in Isaiah 48

We'll start, of course, in Isaiah 48. In a lot of ways, that chapter's easier to deal with, anyway, since, as we've already noted, we've got reason to believe that some of the textual variants we can find in Isaiah 49 are Nephi's deliberate alterations to the text. We have some reason, on the other hand, to believe that Nephi meant to leave Isaiah 48 in more or less the state he found it, so we can probably assume that the variants we find there are *supposed* to be variants—that is, not things Nephi himself changed in the text of Isaiah. And what do we find?

Well, the first thing we might note is that there are *a lot* of variants in Isaiah 48. Of the twenty-two verses that make up the chapter, only two appear identically in the King James Version and the Book of Mormon—verses 18 and 19. All the rest present differences that call for our attention. That's a high frequency of textual variation, even if a good many of the variants are quite minor in nature. We'll see that there are chapters of Isaiah in the Book of Mormon with very few—and some even with no—variants, so the differences between Isaiah 48 in the Bible and Isaiah

48 in the Book of Mormon should strike us as quite suggestive. Let's take them a handful of verses at a time. To make this easiest on us, let's consider in order the several parts of Isaiah 48 as we identified them at the end of our review of the chapter last time: (1) the Lord accuses Israel (verses 1–2), before he outlines his double strategy of (2) providing Israel with prophecies long in advance (verses 3–6a) as well as (3) providing them with new prophecies just prior to acting (verses 6b–8); (4) Isaiah then gives us an explanation of the Lord's patience (verses 9–13) before (5) he tells us about the new leader that will take them from Babylon (verses 14–17) and (6) predicts the exodus-like trek back to the promised land (verses 18–21); finally, (7) the chapter concludes with a warning to the still-wicked (verse 22). Seven sequences we'll consider in order. And let me warn you: We're going to move fast!

In verses 1–2, we get the Lord's accusation against Israel. What sorts of differences do we find? Things start off simply, with the biblical text's "Hear ye this!" rendered as "Hearken and hear this!" A technically unnecessary pronoun disappears, and the verb "hear" is doubled with "hearken," perhaps suggesting a stronger emphasis. That's relatively minor. But then a series of other differences follow, all bent on making a good deal clearer the accusatory nature of the passage. This is especially evident in the differences between the two versions of verse 2. Verse 1 ends with a pretty clear accusation, but the biblical verse 2 then opens with "for" and goes on to say things that make Israel sound faithful: "they call themselves of the holy city, and stay themselves upon the God of Israel." In the Book of Mormon, the "for" becomes "nevertheless," disrupting the connection suggested in the biblical text. And then a clarifying clause that doesn't appear in the biblical text turns what would otherwise be a word of commendation into a word of condemnation. In the place of the Bible's "they call themselves of the holy city, and stay themselves upon the God of Israel," we find "they call themselves of the holy city, but they do not stay themselves upon the God of Israel." Suddenly, Israel's self-description as being "of the holy city" becomes hypocritical, and the accusatory nature of the opening verses becomes perfectly clear.

A rather different set of differences are to be found in verses 3–6a, where the Lord explains that he's given Israel prophecies of events long in advance. There are several minor differences here—an inserted "behold" in verse 3, for instance, or an extra "and" in verse 5. But then there are major differences also, more suggestive differences. Most of the differences between the two versions here seem to focus on exactly *when* the prophecies in question were to have been fulfilled. In the biblical version of verse 3, for instance, it reads as if the Lord in ancient times not only revealed but also "did" the things prophesied of; "and they came to pass," he says. In the Book of Mormon version, however, the clause "and they came to pass" entirely disappears, and the word "did" becomes "did shew," so that it's only said that the Lord *showed* things in vision anciently, not that they were also accomplished at that time. Fulfillment of these prophecies, it seems, was to wait for the time of Isaiah's audience. A difference in verse 5 follows this same pattern: "and I shewed them for fear" appears before "lest thou shouldest say, 'Mine idol hath done them.'" Here again emphasis is laid on showing rather than doing, so that what's said to have taken place anciently was just the giving—not the fulfillment—of prophecy. A slight difference in verse 6 seems significant here also. The word "it" becomes plural, "them," in the Book of Mormon text ("will ye not declare them?"), with the suggestion that Israel has been maliciously keeping the prophecies in question secret. All this is quite rich.

Relatively fewer differences show up in the next sequence of the text, verses 6b–8, where the other half of the Lord's strategy appears. The most important difference, by far, is the presence in the Book of Mormon rendering of a whole clause, "they were declared unto thee," explaining what took place "even before the day when thou heardest them not." The text in the Book of Mormon is rather difficult to interpret, but it's certainly of importance that these extra words provide the Book of Mormon Isaiah text with an additional instance of the verb "declare," a word central to verses 5 and 6, and a word about which we said something just a moment ago. There's a larger, richer story about declaration in the Book of Mormon text of Isaiah 48, a story about what the Lord declares to Israel when, and about whether and how Israel goes on to declare such things to others. It seems the Book of Mormon version of Isaiah is more closely attuned to this theme than the biblical version.

Hurrying on, let's take a brief look at verses 9–13, where Isaiah gives us an explanation of the Lord's patience with Israel, rooted in his own covenant obligation. Here most of the differences are pretty minor: a clarifying "nevertheless" at the outset of verse 9, a connective "for" opening verse 10, an instance of "yea" replacing "even" in verse 11, a couple of conjunctions in verse 12, a more natural word ordering in verse 13. Here, it seems, there are fewer substantial differences between the two versions of Isaiah. Let's nonetheless notice one striking difference. In verse 10, the Book of Mormon rendering drops a whole clause, "but not with silver" (which follows "I have refined thee" in the biblical version). There's some obscurity in the biblical text here. What does it mean to refine Israel *with* silver? Alongside or in the same crucible as silver? Certainly we're not to understand that silver is used in order to refine Israel, are we? Such difficulties disappear in the Book of Mormon text. We're straightforwardly told that the Lord has refined Israel, chosen them in the furnace of affliction—a simpler, more readily understandable text. Perhaps we're to understand that Nephi corrected or simplified what he recognized to be an impossible reading. Or perhaps we're supposed to have access here to a text that hadn't been rendered problematic by some well-meaning but errant scribe?

Then come verses 14–17, where Isaiah prophesies of a new leader for Israel, someone to lead them from exile. Here again we find relatively minor differences between the two versions of the text, just as here again we find some more substantial differences. Going straight to the latter, let's note that the most substantial differences here concern the verb "to declare," something we've already seen in earlier parts of the chapter. In verse 15 in the biblical text, the servant is simply "called," but in the Book of Mormon rendering he's "called . . . to declare." And then in verse 15, several differences result in another additional reference to declaring in the Book of Mormon Isaiah text. A command to "hear ye this" disappears from the text, allowing for a strong emphasis on declaration; and then "from the time that it was, there am I" becomes "from the time that it was declared have I spoken." In the Book of Mormon version uniquely, the servant's responsibility is principally to declare something, and that declaration marks the public nature of the Lord's interventions in Israel. There's almost something systematic about the differences between the two versions at this point.

The next stretch of text, verses 18–21, is almost entirely without variants. There are none in verse 18, and the variants in verses 19–21 are quite minor—none substantially changes the meaning of the text. This in itself is an interesting thing, since it seems that there needn't be differences at every turn in the two versions. Apparently, the theme of the exodus stands firm in the biblical text from Nephi's perspective. But then let's note that there's a pretty major difference between the two versions of Isaiah 48 when we come to the last verse, the warning that there's no peace for the wicked. The verse opens in the Book of Mormon with the following words, entirely absent from the biblical version: "and notwithstanding he hath done all this—and greater also!" Here we have a remarkably substantive difference, with the Book of Mormon version marking a much stronger transition between the preceding verses and this final warning. The additional words in the Book of Mormon Isaiah text make clear that the final warning doesn't simply come out of nowhere, which is more or less how the text feels in the biblical rendering.

Alright, this has been more than a bit hurried and harried. Of course, the point has been less to do an exhaustive investigation of variants in Isaiah 48—that would take a whole lecture series of its own!—than to provide a kind of surface-level survey of variants, outlining the basic sorts of differences we can find between the biblical and Book of Mormon Isaiah texts. And we've already become clear about a couple of things at least, I hope. There are a good many variants that are pretty minor in character—added conjunctions, supplementary transition words, synonymous substitutions, slight reorderings of words, and so on. But there are also variants that are far more substantial in nature, clarifying or delimiting or expanding the meaning of the text—often in a way that leads to a more systematic presentation of a consistent message. And among these latter sorts of variants, we've seen variants that seem collectively bent on bringing out of the Isaiah text certain themes—the theme of declaration in Isaiah 48, for instance—that can be developed in greater detail. We find similar patterns everywhere else we might go in Book of Mormon Isaiah. That's significant.

Of course, there's still a pretty major question of what to make of all this. Historical-critical interpreters trained in biblical studies would almost surely see the patterns we've already identified as indicating that the Book of Mormon aims to *clean up* the Isaiah text—that is, that it begins from the Isaiah text found in the Bible (and really, from the Isaiah text as found specifically in the King James Version of the Bible) and then tries to develop it into something clearer in presentation, more consistent in theme, and deeper in content. That's an issue we may want to take up in a few minutes. For the moment, we're just making a preliminary survey and seeing what we might say in rather general terms about the differences between the Isaiah text of the Bible and the Isaiah text of the Book of Mormon. And we've got our first data set in hand.

Variants in Isaiah 49

So, shall we move on to Isaiah 49? I can tell already that we'll run out of time before we get through if we try to do with Isaiah 49 what we've just done with Isaiah 48. So let's take a different tack. Rather than work through the text in order, let's step back from it and see what we can see when we look at the differences between the biblical and the Nephite presentations of Isaiah 49 on the whole. And it's actually pretty easy to decide where to start, since there's a *massive* difference between verse 1 in the two versions of Isaiah here. The Book of Mormon text opens with forty-eight words that don't appear in the biblical text at all. That's reason enough to start there, and it turns out that close study of this major difference will allow us to raise a few essential questions that might help to make sense of what we've already found with Isaiah 48.

We've talked a bit about Nephi's rendering of Isaiah 49:1 in a previous lecture, but that shouldn't stop us now. Here's how he starts: "And again . . . ." It seems pretty clear to me that that's just Nephi, not even pretending to be quoting from the actual text of Isaiah. I take it that his point with these two words is just meant to mark a transition from one quotation (that of Isaiah 48) to another (that of Isaiah 49); this is how "and again" is used generally in the Book of Mormon. But then Nephi goes on: "Hearken, O ye house of Israel, all ye that are broken off and are driven out because of the wickedness of the pastors of my people—yea, all ye that are broken off that are scattered abroad, which are of my people, O house of Israel . . . ." We're still not done quoting Nephi's rendering of Isaiah 49:1, but I want to stop here for a moment to note that everything I've just read appears only in the Book of Mormon version. This isn't there in the biblical text. And note that we can interpret this in at least three rather different ways. First, it *could* of course be that these words appear right on the brass plates, that these were at one point part of the writings attributed to Isaiah but were subsequently deleted or somehow lost. Second, though, and I think more likely, Nephi might have deliberately added these words to the text—along with other bits and pieces we'll consider in Isaiah 49—in an attempt to shape the text for his immediate audience, his rebellious brothers. Let me make that clearer. It might be that Nephi is deliberately altering Isaiah's words for his own purposes, as we'll see he might be doing further along in the text as well. And then a third possibility should be mentioned. It's possible also that these words are simply to be read as an introductory word, entirely Nephi's own, that precedes the quotation of Isaiah 49—something he meant to be understood as a separate, introductory word rather than an interpolation directly into the Isaianic text. (Note that we pretty clearly have something like that in 1 Nephi 19:24, introducing Isaiah 48.)

Three possibilities, then. They're all entirely possible, but I find myself pretty strongly inclined to the second option, that Nephi's here beginning to adapt Isaiah's text directly for his own purposes—his stated purpose of "likening" the text, for instance. We said a bit by way of justification for this interpretation in an earlier lecture, but let's note now that there's a kind of pattern of this sort of thing in Isaiah 49, one that suggests that we're likely on the right track here. Let me assemble a brief catalog of sorts. Verse 7: The Book of Mormon version of the text drops two whole clauses: "and the Holy One of Israel, and he shall choose thee." Why drop all these words? In context, it seems that they're meant to make Isaiah 49 speak directly and perhaps only to Israel exiled in Babylon. With its removal, the passage seems actually to speak to Israel in whatever condition or conditions it might be—including a widely scattered or dispersed condition. Verse 8: Immediately after the change just noted, the Book of Mormon version has a little insertion, "O isles of the sea." Right after removing a bit of text that seems to make the focus of the prophecy quite narrow and specific, the Book of Mormon version adds a bit of text that generalizes the prophecy's application to Israelites scattered on all the "isles of the sea." Verse 12: Here there's a prediction of Israel's return to the promised land, which in the original seems to be directly from Babylon to Palestine. But the Book of Mormon version opens with "And then, O house of Israel," which suggests that it's less to the empty *land* that Israel as a whole returns than to the non-scattered *house of Israel* that scattered Israel comes in an event of gathering. (This strongly highlights the already implicit sense of this verse, by the way, which seems to imply a scattered condition on Israel's part, despite the narrow focus of the prophecy in its biblical form.)

All these differences between the biblical and the Nephite versions of Isaiah 49 are suggestive of the same thing, namely that this New-World version anticipates less a *return* than a *gathering*, worrying less about *exile* than about *dispersion*. We've got, I think, two quite distinct versions of Isaiah 49, even if we ignore the two dozen or more minor variants in the Book of Mormon text. These more substantive differences between the two texts gives them widely differing scopes. The biblical prophecy seems focused only on the situation Israel faced in Babylonian exile. The Book of Mormon prophecy is clearly focused on something broader, a situation where bits and pieces of Israel have found themselves scattered across the whole earth, from which they must all be gathered back to their lands of promise. Babylonian exile might be included in that picture, but it would have to be interpreted as only one small part of it.

Now, we could, naturally, interpret all of this in two different ways. On the one hand, as I've already suggested, we can assume that Nephi has himself doctored the Isaianic text for his purposes—doing a bit of what he calls likening in the very moment he copies Isaiah into his record (or reads Isaiah aloud to his brothers), collapsing into one stage the two stages of likening (understanding the text, then adapting it). I've made clear that I'm inclined toward this interpretation. But note that we *could*, of course, interpret all this in an almost opposite fashion. Why not assume that Nephi's copying down the text of the brass plates more or less exactly as he found it, and that what we have in the biblical text is rather the doctored version—a manipulated version of Isaiah that was meant to obscure the broader focus of the prophet's words? Some have certainly made a case along these lines. I'm thinking of a book by Clay Gorton called *The Legacy of the Brass Plates of Laban*, which interprets most every difference between the biblical and the Nephite texts of Isaiah as evidence of corrupt and designing ancient Israelites. Perhaps somewhat less conspiratorially but no less forcefully, might we not rightly assume that ancient Judah would have done their own work of likening, and that the biblical version is a product of their own narrowing of the Isaianic prophecy to fit their unique circumstances? (One might even get excited about how such an interpretation might secure a pre-exilic date for this part of Second Isaiah.)

This second interpretation can't be ruled out, and there are ways I find it quite attractive. Indeed, I'd love to see someone work it out at length and make the best possible case for it so that I can see if it would convince me. In the meanwhile, I still find myself inclined toward the idea that Nephi is likening the text, changing it as he reads it aloud or as he copies it down, applying the text to what he's already seen in his own visionary experiences. At the very least, I'm inclined in this direction because of the fact that Isaiah 48, even as Nephi quotes it, seems focused specifically on Israel in Babylonian exile. There's something nicely symmetrical about Nephi quoting two prophecies that originally addressed just that situation—but then leaving one in an unlikened state while transforming the other into a fully likened text right before our eyes. That feels to me like something Nephi would do. But I don't know that that's anything like proof. Only further and closer work will get us closer to a final answer.

Well, we're out of time. No surprises, and we really only got started on a first, rather general point as regards Isaiah 49. We didn't get to say anything about verse 13, which is really quite exciting in its Book of Mormon version. And I'd hoped to say something about how all the manipulations we've tracked in Isaiah 49 appear only in the first half of the chapter—an interesting fact that's suggestive in all kinds of ways. And so on. Always we have to say far too little, far less than we'd like to. And we'll have to leave this question of variants behind us for now, because we want to look at questions of actual interpretation next time, turning our attention to 1 Nephi 22.

I'll hope, nonetheless and somewhat naively, that we've made a few salient points along the way today, and that you've all got something of a sense for what it might mean to look at textual variants in Book of Mormon Isaiah. This is a field that's white and quite ready to harvest. I'd love to see some folks start laying these things up in store!

Lecture X

Nephi's Explanation of Isaiah 49

Focus on Likening

Are you getting sick of Isaiah 48–49 yet? This is now the *fourth* lecture we'll have dedicated to looking at what Nephi's doing with just those chapters! But you'll get no apologies from me. *I* didn't sign you up for this! And anyway, you're still here. So we'll keep moving forward. But perhaps I should warn you that we won't finish with Isaiah 48–49 even today. We'll have to say at least a little more about Isaiah 49 in one further lecture, since it's a focus all over again in 2 Nephi 6 and 2 Nephi 10.

But what have we accomplished so far in our work on Isaiah 48–49? Three lectures back, we looked just at a few preliminary questions, chiefly at what Nephi seems to mean when he talks about likening as well as a few words about the Abrahamic covenant rather generally. In our last lecture, we put a *much* finer point on likening by looking at some of the variants in Nephi's quotation of Isaiah 48–49. That in turn built on what we did two lectures ago, where we took some time just to read through Isaiah 48–49 in broad terms, getting familiar with the themes and turns of phrase, and with what Isaiah has to say about the story of the Abrahamic covenant. Taken all together, then, our last three lectures have given us a sense for what Nephi's up to, I hope. We've begun to see that the writings that appear in the Bible under Isaiah's name are deeply focused on what we'd call the Abrahamic covenant. Apparently, the chapters we're considering now—like the rest of Isaiah 40–55—originally focused on a quite specific part of covenantal history, namely Judah's exile in Babylon during the sixth century, coupled with their glorious return as witnessed by impressed non-covenantal peoples. And *then* we've begun to see that Nephi sees this rather specific moment in the history of the Abrahamic covenant as a kind of figure for a much larger pattern, one that God uses with branches and remnants of Israel as much as with exiled Judah. And so he's begun, under inspiration, to tamper with Isaiah's writings, clearly in an attempt to get his readers to see what it would mean to read Isaiah as speaking to *all* of scattered Israel. How might they *also* be redeemed by and from among the Gentiles in a way that might bring salvation to the whole world?

That's what we've seen so far. But note that Nephi's only really just begun, since all he's done by way of likening to this point is to have altered Isaiah's own text so that it can be read as speaking to the remnants and branches of Israel scattered across the globe. But he hasn't yet begun *to explain* what that really looks like—in his own words, I mean. He's given us Isaiah's writings in a proto-likened form, but if he's really going to convince his readers that he's onto something here, he's going to have to take them by the hand and walk them through his reading of, say, Isaiah 49. "Alright, Nephi. We can see that Isaiah could be read as talking about the remnants of Israel. But what do you think we're supposed to expect to see happen to the remnants? The Gentiles will redeem them. Fine. *But when?* Can't you give us a little more information about this?" We're lucky Nephi's so obliging. He's apparently quite happy to walk his readers through this, quite patiently. And that's what he does in 1 Nephi 22. And he's got a resource he hasn't yet drawn on to explain what likened Isaiah means, though he's given us a good deal of information about that resource. It's his vision, that massive apocalyptic vision in 1 Nephi 11–14. That's what 1 Nephi 22 is all about. How does what Nephi's already learned from that vision help to clarify a bit of Isaiah's text, if we're likening it to a rather specific remnant or branch of Israel: the latter-day Lamanites?

There's where we're headed today.

Isaiah's Scope

Nephi's just finished quoting Isaiah 48–49 at length when his brothers—Laman and Lemuel? or Jacob and Joseph? or who?—come to him with a question: "What mean these things which ye have read? Behold, are they to be understood according to things which are spiritual, which shall come to pass according to the spirit and not the flesh?" (1 Ne. 22:1). Nephi's hardly shy about jumping in to explain, and he immediately clarifies that "all things" are "made known unto the prophets" by "the Spirit" (v. 2)—something he can say from his own experience. In fact, he seems to refer to his *own* prophetic experiences a moment later when he says this: "For it appears that the house of Israel, sooner or later, will be scattered upon all the face of the earth—and also among all nations" (v. 3). "It appears." Is that a rather humble way for Nephi to refer to his own visionary experiences? Or is he trying to avoid referring to his own visions, so that his brothers can learn just to read Isaiah? At any rate, his source for understanding Isaiah will become perfectly clear as he goes along.

Actually, Nephi comes to the things he saw in his own apocalyptic vision only after a few words that broaden the historical picture drastically. Let's give at least a couple of minutes to these verses. Here they are in full:

> And behold, there are many which are already lost from the knowledge of they which are at Jerusalem. Yea, the more part of all the tribes have been led away, and they are scattered to and fro upon the isles of the sea. And whither they are none of us knoweth, save that we know that they have been led away. And since that they have been led away, these things have been prophesied concerning them—and also concerning all they which shall hereafter be scattered and be confounded because of the Holy One of Israel. For against him will they harden their hearts; wherefore, they shall be scattered among all nations and shall be hated by all men. (1 Ne. 22:4–5)

What's going on here? A couple of things to note. First, Nephi opens this passage by referring to "many which are already lost from the knowledge of they which are at Jerusalem." Is he thinking of the Northern Kingdom, crushed by Assyria at the time of Isaiah himself, and then scattered about the sprawling Assyrian kingdom? Or is he perhaps thinking of little groups like his own family, colonists of a sort who've been drawn away from Palestine at various points in Israelite history, about whom we know nothing? Well, the next line suggests that he means the latter: "The more part of all the tribes have been led away, and they are scattered to and fro upon the isles of the sea." Wait! What? "The more part"? That's a big part. And these are people who, Nephi says, have "been led away," not who've been scattered by a foreign power. These people are, it seems, *everywhere*. And Nephi sees Isaiah's words, in their proto-likened form, as addressed to all these bits and pieces of Israel, relocated in little colonies all over the place thanks to the God's getting involved. And notice that Nephi also gives us a timeline. These little colonies left early, before Nephi's time, such that "these things have been prophesied concerning them" only "since that they have been led away."

All this leaves my head spinning. It seems Nephi wants us to understand that his little colony is one of *many*—tens? hundreds? thousands?—spread out all over the world, led away by the Lord from the covenant people and their promised land to remote places. Most of these, it seems, are supposed to have left Palestine even before Nephi's time, such that

Isaiah's prophecies—the key to understanding all those little colonies' futures—were only first uttered or written down after they'd already left to settle elsewhere. Even so, Isaiah's prophecies should be likened to every one of these little colonies, to all these little branches of Israel.

Isaiah 29 in 1 Nephi 22

But notice that as we come to the end of the passage I've just quoted, Nephi narrows in on the group that *wasn't* led away—those who would "hereafter be scattered and be confounded," by which he clearly means to refer to Judah, returned from exile and treated horrifically by the Gentiles around and especially after the time of Christ. "They shall be scattered among all nations, and shall be hated by all men." Nephi, however, dwells on Jewish history only for a moment (it's Nephi's brother Jacob that gets particularly excited about Jewish history, while Nephi keeps his eyes on a broader Israelite history, generally speaking). He begins to speak about the redemption of the Jews, but he quickly broadens it, and it's here that we start to hear echoes of Nephi's apocalyptic vision with real clarity. Moreover, it's here that we get our first *clear* references back to the Isaiah texts Nephi's just read to his brothers. He paraphrases Isaiah 49:22–23, referring to Israel's being "nursed by the Gentiles," of the Lord's setting the Gentiles "up for a standard," and so on. And then he says that "these things . . . are temporal, for thus is the covenants of the Lord with our fathers, and it meaneth us in the days to come—and also all our brethren which are of the house of Israel" (1 Ne. 22:6). There, at once, Nephi gives us both his vision regarding the future of his particular branch or remnant of Israel ("us in the days to come") and the writings of Isaiah (the "it" of "it meaneth"). To get at the meaning of Isaiah, we've got to draw on what Nephi's seen in vision.

Now, lest it prove difficult for us to reconstruct exactly what he's after in the passage just referred to, he gives us a full explanation next:

> And it meaneth that the time cometh that, after all the house of Israel have been scattered and confounded, that the Lord God will raise up a mighty nation among the Gentiles—yea, even upon the face of this land—and by them shall our seed be scattered. And after that our seed is scattered, the Lord God will proceed to do a marvelous work among the Gentiles which shall be of great worth unto our seed. Wherefore, it is likened unto the being nursed by the Gentiles and being carried in their arms and upon their shoulders. (1 Ne. 22:7–8)

Here, of course, we've got a clearer outline of Nephi's vision: the confounding of Israel consequent to the rise of a mighty Gentile nation in the Americas, and then a marvelous work that turns the Gentiles to the task of caring for the very Israelites they've trodden down in their zeal to inherit the New World for themselves. And Nephi's quite clear that all this is what's to be understood by Isaiah's talk of Israelites "being nursed by the Gentiles and being carried in their arms and upon their shoulders." Again, we've quite clearly got the content of Nephi's vision and the form of Isaiah's writings brought together here. That Nephi thinks his vision provides the substance of a solid likening of Isaiah's writings couldn't be much clearer.

But let's notice that Nephi does something *further* in the passage we've just quoted. He not only draws together the substance of 1 Nephi 13 and the form of Isaiah 49, he also inserts *other* Isaianic language. Did you catch it? "The Lord God will proceed to do a marvelous work among the Gentiles." That's Isaianic phrasing, but it's not from Isaiah 49. It's from Isaiah 29 (verse 14 specifically), a part of Isaiah's writings about which Nephi will have *a lot* to say later on, but from which he hasn't yet taken any of his Isaiah quotations. At this point, though, even when we're just beginning to work on the actual interpretation of Isaiah, Isaiah 29 is already to be regarded as a relevant text. Nephi gives us Isaiah 49 as a base text for this first endeavor in likening Isaiah to his people, but if he's going to explain it to us fully, apparently we've got to have Isaiah 29 in mind as well. And let's note that this is only the first of several allusions to Isaiah 29 that appear in 1 Nephi 22.

The next allusion to Isaiah 29 appears in verse 12 of 1 Nephi 22. Here Nephi is describing the redemption of Israel, and he tells us that they'll "be brought out of obscurity and out of darkness." This clearly borrows its language from Isaiah 29:18: "And in that day shall the deaf hear the words of the book, and the eyes of the blind shall see out of obscurity, and out of darkness." Here Nephi implicitly figures Israel as the deaf and the blind (in accordance, presumably, with Isaiah 6, another text we'll have much to say about in another lecture), but he specifically figures Israel as those among the deaf and the blind who "shall . . . hear" and "shall see." Of course, Nephi drops the direct references to deafness and blindness, and to hearing and seeing, but the allusion asks readers to keep the whole of the Isaiah text in mind. And then Nephi reconfigures the text in an interesting way. By claiming that Israel must "be brought out of obscurity and out of darkness," he seems to suggest that Israel's blindness and deafness is solely a result of their location. They're deaf and blind because their trapped in a place of obscurity and darkness. Their eyes have the capacity to perceive light, and their ears have the capacity to discern sound, but they're in a place without light and without sound. They have to "be brought" out of such a place so that their deafness and their blindness will cease. Notice the care with which Nephi handles the allusion to Isaiah 29. But notice above all that Isaiah 29 is there in Nephi's mind. The next allusion to Isaiah 29 comes just a couple verses later. In 1 Nephi 22:14, we find Nephi referring to Israel's enemies, "every nation . . . , all they which fight against Zion." This is the language of Isaiah 29:8, which refers to "all the nations . . . that fight against Zion." And Nephi predicts that such nations "shall be destroyed," just as Isaiah claims that these nations will pursue their murderous desires but find them unfulfillable. The same theme appears in 1 Nephi 22:19, which speaks again of "all they which fight against Zion," predicting that they'll all "be cut off." Here perhaps there's less to say about these allusions, apart from the fact that Nephi's again weaving his commentary on Isaiah 49 with his sustained interest in Isaiah 29. He doesn't seem to be showing quite as much as innovation at this point as he did in the last passage he alluded to. But the weaving together of Isaiah 29 and Isaiah 49 is striking.

And, of course, there's at least one more allusion to Isaiah 29 in 1 Nephi 22. It's a bit more complex. It comes in 1 Nephi 22:23, a passage Hugh Nibley used to cite often because Nephi there provides a list of the four worldly pursuits that ruin us, over and over and again and again. Nephi condemns churches that (1) "are built up to get gain," (2) "are built up to get power over the flesh," (3) "are built up to become popular in the eyes of the world," and (4) "seek the lusts of the flesh and the things of the world." What's to happen to such churches? According to Nephi, "the time speedily shall come" that they all "need fear and tremble and quake" because they "must be brought low in the dust" and "must be consumed as stubble." Where's the allusion to Isaiah 29? It's in the reference to these churches being "brought low in the dust." This echoes Isaiah 29:4: "And thou shalt be brought down, . . . and thy speech shall be low out of the dust." The link is even closer if we turn to 2 Nephi 26:15, where Nephi again uses the language of this passage from Isaiah 29. There he renders Isaiah's words as follows: "they shall have been brought down low in the dust." That's almost identical to what we have here in 1 Nephi 22: "they . . . must be brought low in the dust." Interestingly, where Isaiah's original oracle clearly refers to Jerusalem's destruction with these words, and where

Nephi's later quotation refers to the Nephites' destruction with these same words, here in 1 Nephi 22 he applies them to the corrupt churches, all those who "belong to the kingdom of the devil." And this, note, is more closely aligned with Nephi's apocalyptic vision from 1 Nephi 11–14. There he predicted the collapse of the great and abominable church, and here he describes that same event, but using the language of Isaiah 29. And, again, we shouldn't miss that he's woven these allusions to Isaiah 29 in with his discussion of Isaiah 49.

Is that enough to clinch the case that Isaiah 29 and 49 form the warp and the woof of the visionary tapestry Nephi's put on display before us? Some Isaiah texts interest Nephi more than others, or at least they appear in his writings more often than others, and usually woven together in the way we're seeing here. If he has a third preferred text, one that nonetheless doesn't make any particular appearance here in 1 Nephi 22, it's Isaiah 11. We'll come to that. For the moment, it's enough just to be clear that there are, as it were, Isaianic highlights for Nephi, bits of Isaianic prophecy he's especially keen on. And we should be clear that to understand how Nephi goes about likening Isaiah 49, we have to keep an eye on Isaiah 29 and perhaps even Isaiah 11 to make sure we've got the story. Really, we could just say that it's these three chapters that spell out the basics of Nephi's own vision, albeit in Isaianic language.

Isaiah and World History

But perhaps we're getting ahead of ourselves here. Let's get back to a sequential reading of 1 Nephi 22, shall we? We left off with 1 Nephi 22:7–8, where the first allusion to Isaiah 29 shows up. And there Nephi was doing something relatively simple still, namely setting side by side his own visionary knowledge (the future history of his own people, eventually redeemed by the New-World Gentiles) and the writings of Isaiah (concerning Gentile kings and queens caring for the covenant people). And now he adds this further point, one he might easily have drawn from either his vision or the writings of Isaiah: "And it shall also be of worth unto the Gentiles—and not only unto the Gentiles, but unto all the house of Israel—unto the making known of the covenants of the Father of heaven unto Abraham, saying, 'In thy seed shall all the kindreds of the earth be blessed'" (1 Ne. 22:9). Israel is to be redeemed by the Gentiles, and the Gentiles are to find a place in the covenant for their redemption of Israel. In short, universality is the theme here, with covenantal and non-covenantal peoples joined together. And that's the direct fulfillment of the Abrahamic covenant, which Nephi here quotes directly from Genesis 12.

But then we get a few further words of commentary from Nephi, and here we get Isaianic all over again. Here's what he says: "And I would, my brethren, that ye should know that all the kindreds of the earth cannot be blessed unless he shall make bare his arm in the eyes of the nations. Wherefore, the Lord God will proceed to make bare his arm in the eyes of all the nations in bringing about his covenants and his gospel unto they which are of the house of Israel" (1 Ne. 22:10–11). The point here is, I think, relatively simple. The kind of universal redemption Nephi has in mind—redemption for Israel, redemption for non-Israel—can only happen if the event prophesied of is of world-historical significance. It seems it can't be a minor, out-of-the-way affair. It's got to be something put on display "in the eyes of the nations" or "in the eyes of all the nations." It's this last thing that's particularly Isaianic. Nephi is using the language here of Isaiah 52—specifically of Isaiah 52:10. Interpreters of Isaiah more or less universally agree that Isaiah 52:7–10 forms the thematic climax of Second Isaiah, and it's a passage that pretty much obsesses the Book of Mormon. "How beautiful upon the mountains" and all that. It's the passage that ends with this: "The Lord hath made bare his holy arm in the eyes of the all the nations; and all the ends of the earth shall see the salvation of our God."

What's really interesting is that this passage shows up here in *Nephi's* writings. Different parts of Isaiah 52:7–10 show up throughout the Book of Mormon, but mostly outside of Nephi's record. The passage plays a major role in Abinadi's sermon (it's the passage the priests ask him to comment on), and it plays an equally major role in Christ's teachings during his visit to the New World (where discussion of it spreads out over several chapters). Parts of it make appearances in Mormon's commentary on Nephite preaching, and Alma uses the same parts to describe his own efforts at conversion. The language of Isaiah 52:10 shows up once in Enos too. But in addition to all this interest in the passage elsewhere in the Book of Mormon, it appears a few times in Nephi. A snippet of Isaiah 52:7 appears in 1 Nephi 13:37, where Nephi's quoting the angel quoting the Lamb. And then a little bit of Isaiah 52:10 appears in 1 Nephi 19:17, where Nephi attributes the words to "the prophet," an ambiguous reference that in context could mean either Isaiah or Zenos or even someone else. (Nephi attributes a good deal to "the prophet" in 1 Nephi 19, but only one such attribution—the one we're discussing—seems to come from any known text of Isaiah.) So this language isn't exactly foreign to Nephi's intentions more generally, though it's a text he seems to have paid less attention to, generally, than others in the Nephite tradition after him.

It's a nice passage nonetheless, at the very least because it suggests something of the enormity of the event Nephi has in mind. It's almost like he's here offering a defense of his likening, suggesting that it makes more sense of Isaiah than the original or the more strictly historical interpretation—the "unlikened" text. It seems to me there's an argument at work in Nephi's words, one we might reconstruct as follows:

(1) The promise from Genesis 12 associated with the Abrahamic covenant concerns all the kindreds of the earth, with the consequence that the Abrahamic covenant can't be fulfilled completely unless all nations come to see the strength and fidelity of the true God.

(2) What seems at first to be the immediate historical context for Isaiah 49 is, as with Isaiah 48, that of Judah's redemption from exile in Babylon during the sixth century before Christ. That redemption was indeed accomplished before certain Gentile nations, and in such a way that they joined with Israel to some (limited) extent in worshiping the true God as they assisted in returning the covenant people to their promised lands. Nonetheless, the experience of the redemption from Babylonian exile was necessarily limited in scope, such that it couldn't really be said to have accomplished the fulfillment of the promises made to Abraham.

(3) Consequently, it can't really be said that the meaning of Isaiah 49 was exhausted by the Old-World events of the sixth century. It has to be said, rather, that Isaiah—whatever he himself might have understood by his own words—anticipated events of a much wider scope. And those more obviously world-historical events are the ones Nephi witnessed in vision.

If this is really what Nephi has in mind in 1 Nephi 22:9–11—and I'm pretty convinced it *is*—it almost seems as if he's at this point suggesting that his likening is *more than* likening, that it's actually a *better* interpretation of the text than the apparently obvious but nonetheless historically limited interpretation. And it seems Nephi comes to this interpretation only because he sees the relevance of Isaiah 52:7–10 to the meaning of Isaiah 49.

We're starting to see something of a pattern, no? Nephi's only quoted two chapters of Isaiah for us so far—and he seems really to be interested only in *one* of the two he's quoted—but he brings to the task of interpreting what he's quoted a host of other resources. Lying behind every interpretive move he makes, of course, is his visionary experience recorded in 1 Nephi 11–14. It's there he first glimpsed the complicated future history of the covenant people through which he's making sense of Isaiah's writings. But he doesn't seem to be applying that vision directly to just the one chapter from Isaiah he's quoted in earnest. That is, it isn't *immediately* to Isaiah 49 that Nephi applies what he's learned in vision. Rather, it seems he's taken the vision as a lens through which to read the whole of Isaiah's writings, and he's found himself attracted to a couple of passages that suggest that—even if Isaiah didn't always see it himself—the Old-World prophet had in view events of major world-historical importance. And it's only once he's interpreted the whole of Isaiah (the whole of whatever he had of Isaiah, anyway) that he uses this more general Isaianic key to work out his narrower likening of specific Isaianic texts, like Isaiah 49, for instance.

We might generalize this even more, in fact. As Nephi goes on in 1 Nephi 22, we find him quoting Deuteronomy 18, and we find him using the language of Malachi 4 (curiously despite the fact that, on the Book of Mormon's own account, he shouldn't have had access to Malachi's writings at all). And there are other biblical allusions in 1 Nephi 22 as well. It seems, then, that the vision from 1 Nephi 11–14 has at this point become a lens through which to work up an interpretation of the Bible as a whole, an almost systematic way of making sense of biblical texts. And then this rather general lens is what Nephi uses to make particular sense of Isaiah's writings in an otherwise relatively narrowly focused text like Isaiah 49. Or, so it seems.

Isaiah 49 in 1 Nephi 22

Yikes, we're quickly running out of time. Only a few minutes left, and we've only gotten through 1 Nephi 22:11 so far! Even so, I'm pretty confident we've already got the general picture clear, yes? With our last couple of minutes today, let's do the following, then. Let's just note how much attention Nephi's giving to Isaiah 49 as he works his way through 1 Nephi 22. These are details one can easily miss, I think. We're not likely to miss the fact that Nephi paraphrases Isaiah 49:22–23 in the course of his discussion; we recognize talk of nursing fathers and nursing mothers, talk of a standard being set up for the Gentiles, talk of covenant children being carried on shoulders, and so on. It's the shorter, less obvious borrowings from, or references back to, Isaiah 49 that we're likely to miss. Let's just note them quickly—and let me note as we turn to this task that I'm not being inventive here, but more or less borrowing the insights of

Grant Hardy here, who's tracked all these borrowings and allusions and references in the footnotes of his *Reader's Edition* of the Book of Mormon.

Let's start with 1 Nephi 22:4, which we've already looked at earlier today. Here Nephi speaks of the groups led away from Jerusalem, but he says that they're "scattered to and fro upon the isles of the sea." That's the language of Isaiah 49, but we're likely to miss it. First, "to and fro"—that's the language of Isaiah 49:21, where Zion, failing to recognize the faces of the Gentiles carrying her children on their shoulders, describes herself as "desolate, a captive, and removing to and fro." That's a pretty subtle allusion, no? But it's the sort of thing we can find throughout 1 Nephi 22. There's another in the bit we just quoted. "Scattered to and fro upon the isles of the sea," Nephi says. Isaiah 49:1 refers to the "isles," and Nephi's likened rendering of Isaiah 49 makes verse 8 refer more fully to the "isles of the sea." Nephi's clearly referring back to the text, perhaps especially in its likened form. And these sorts of things show up again and again. 1 Nephi 22:7 draws on Isaiah 49:24–25. Nephi speaks of "a mighty nation" among the Gentiles, and Isaiah refers to "the mighty" whom even the Lord can control in order to accomplish his work of deliverance. And then 1 Nephi 22:12 draws on Isaiah 49:26. Nephi says that the house of Israel "shall know that the Lord is their savior and their redeemer, the Mighty One of Israel." Isaiah says that "all flesh shall know that I the Lord am thy Saviour and thy Redeemer, the mighty One of Jacob." The borrowing is clear.

And this pattern continues. 1 Nephi 22:13 draws also on Isaiah 49:26 with a reference to who are "drunken with their own blood." 1 Nephi 22:17 speaks of those who are "preserved," apparently referring to the promise of preservation spelled out in Isaiah 49:8. And so on. Nephi's quite consistent about this. He's quoted Isaiah 49 at length, adjusting it according to his program of likening so that his readers will feel the force of its relevance. But then he constantly refers back to the language of Isaiah 49 as he goes about explaining its basic import. He won't let us leave this text behind.

In fact, he *so* won't let us leave this text behind that he's going to make his brother Jacob give a sermon on it, to be recorded in 2 Nephi 6–10. We're just getting started.

Lecture XI

Approaching Jacob on Isaiah

Recapitulation

Alright, we've done *a lot* over our past few meetings. We've given our attention for maybe four lectures in a row to Nephi's introduction to, quotation of, slight tampering with, and almost systematic interpretation of Isaiah 48–49 in 1 Nephi 19–22. And don't forget what we did before all that. We saw, remember, that the whole of First Nephi is structured and organized in a way that's supposed to reveal that there's a larger purpose in 1 Nephi 19–22. Nephi's trying here to help us begin to make sense of Isaiah by seeing how his writings are interpretively linked to Nephi's own visions. But he's done all this in what's ultimately still just a preparatory fashion. The *real* treatment of Isaiah is still to come, since it's found in those "more sacred things" (2 Ne. 6–30) that First Nephi's just meant to get us ready for. We've really just started getting a first taste of what Nephi's up to, apparently so that we're basically prepared to read the stuff Nephi's *most* excited about.

Can we cull a few general points from these past few discussions? Or can we identify a couple of clear strategies we might find useful as we leave First Nephi behind to take a look at Nephi's more systematic presentation of Isaiah in 2 Nephi 6–30? I think we can, but we've got to remember that these'll only be provisional. We'll see Nephi change gears in important ways when we get to Second Nephi. Even so, we're certainly able to say a few things already about what to expect whenever Nephi deals with Isaiah.

First, we've been introduced to Nephi's program of likening. In rather general terms, the program is one of recognizing that Isaiah's prophecies were originally addressed to a historically determinate audience at a historically determinate time. Nephi doesn't seem to ignore that, despite the fact that we—apparently rather like his father, Lehi—often *do* ignore it. Nephi's what we might call a holistic reader. He's less interested in isolated or contextless passages of Isaiah than he is in larger swaths of the Isaianic text. He finds himself somewhat fixated by occasional passages, of course, but he's always careful to see these passages as particularly important moments integral with a larger context. And Nephi's attempts at likening always begin from those larger contexts. Only once he's really understood whatever he can reconstruct of the original meaning of the text, Nephi turns his attention to how Isaiah's words can be reapplied to other contexts—"likened." And Nephi's pretty consistent about what those other contexts are, the contexts to which Isaiah should be likened. He sees Isaiah as speaking originally to Israel as a whole, but because the scattered branches or remnants of Israel are thus included in Isaiah's scope, it's possible to apply Isaiah texts to those branches and remnants (such as the Lehite colony). Further, let's be clear that, even as Nephi turns from the original to the likened, he always keeps larger contexts in mind. He doesn't apply just this or that passage to his people, but the whole story laid out by larger excerpts of material from Isaiah. There are *lengthy stories* of God's dealings with the covenant people that Nephi feels are relevant to his own people.

So there's a first point: likening. A second point we might draw is that Nephi seems particularly interested—at this point at least—in Isaiah's prophecies regarding restoration and redemption. *So far*, Nephi is especially attuned to those later chapters in Isaiah's writings where Israel is being delivered from her enemies and restored to her promised lands. In the jargon of Isaiah scholarship, Nephi is especially interested in Second Isaiah. In a certain way, that's entirely unsurprising, because what Nephi has seen in his vision—the thing he wishes to place in some kind of intimate relationship with Isaiah's writings—is the future redemption of the Lehites and the other remnants of Israel that have been relocated all over the world. Because he's interested in their redemption, he's interested in Isaiah's prophecies of redemption. Further, let's remember that there's a relatively clear pattern in the stories such prophecies recount. Israel's languishing in exile, distant from her promised land. But it turns out that this is part of a strategy on the Lord's part, an attempt to force Israel to mingle with the Gentiles in such a way that redemption for Israel can lead to Gentile conversion. The Gentiles are to play a crucial role in Israel's redemption, and Israel is thus finally to fulfill its role in God's larger vision for the whole world's peace and salvation.

Let's call that point number two: a focus on redemption. Next, the third point: Nephi does his work of likening the text not only by way of *commentary on* but also by way of *interpolation in* Isaiah's writings. When Nephi copies down into his own writings lengthy stretches of Isaiah text, we readers who have a copy of the King James Version ready to hand can recognize without much difficulty that there are a good many differences between the two texts. Some of those differences we're of course meant to regard as actual textual variants, it seems. That is, some of the differences are things we're supposed to understand as going back to the brass plates themselves. Nephi and his family had access to a version of Isaiah that doesn't in every regard match up with our own Isaiah text. But then others of those differences it seems we're to understand as the product of Nephi's own inspired manipulation of the text. He's entirely prepared to do some of his work of likening Isaiah's words to branches and remnants of Israel by rewriting parts of Isaiah, or by inserting additions that refocus Isaiah. So we can't get terribly far into the Book of Mormon's Isaiah if we aren't raising questions about which differences between biblical Isaiah and Book of Mormon Isaiah we're to understand in which way.

There's point three, then: variants and interpolations. Now let's mark a fourth and final point before we decide where we're headed next. What's that? Nephi—like as we'll see with his brother—never quotes long stretches of Isaiah without at some point pausing to give us a bit of commentary. In addition to whatever interpolations he makes directly into the text of Isaiah, he also gives us a kind of running interpretation of the text. And there are several identifiable features of Nephi's interpretive style. For one, and perhaps most importantly, he's intensely focused on tying Isaiah's writings to his own prophetic visions. He finds in the latter a kind of hermeneutic key for the former. Further, we've seen that he undertakes his interpretations of Isaiah by keeping an eye on a host of Isaiah texts, and not just on those he's focused on at any particular moment. His favorites, we've seen, are apparently Isaiah 11, Isaiah 29, and Isaiah 49. But we'll see that he goes far beyond his favorites as well. *And* he brings in other biblical texts too, using Isaiah as a kind of lens through which to view the whole of the Hebrew Bible (and perhaps beyond!). Also, he uses all of these texts— yet again—in a holistic way, never by way of what we'd call prooftexting, but rather through careful attention to a much larger whole. Nephi would fit right in with today's "Unity of Isaiah" school of interpreters, I think.

Alright, there's a general picture so far. Where do we go next?

Motivations for Including Jacob

The most natural move for us to make next, it seems to me, is to turn our attention to Jacob's discussions of Isaiah 49 in 2 Nephi 6–10. This is natural for at least two reasons. First, the next chunk of Isaianic material in Nephi's record comes in Jacob's two-day sermon recorded in those chapters. If we're going to work sequentially through Nephi's treatment of Isaiah, it's Jacob's work on Isaiah 49 that comes next. Moreover, we should note that Jacob continues with a focus on the same chapter—Isaiah 49—to which Nephi gives his closest attention in 1 Nephi 19–22. Although Lehi's final sermons and a little bit of poetry and history intervene between 1 Nephi 22 and 2 Nephi 6, there's a pretty strong sense of continuity between Nephi's and Jacob's discussions of Isaiah 49.

But we need to do a bit by way of transition to make this leap, however much continuity there may be between where we're leaping from and where we're leaping to. For one, we're leaving First Nephi to turn our attention to Second Nephi. And then, of course, we're now to give some attention to what Nephi claims Jacob had to say about Isaiah, rather than directly with what Nephi himself has to say about Isaiah. So we're on new terrain with 2 Nephi 6–10, even if the particular text from Isaiah we'll be focusing on is the same we've already seen in the last part of First Nephi. Let's spend the rest of our time today approaching Jacob's treatment of Isaiah 49 in relatively broad terms, and then next time we can focus in a little more closely on some of the details.

We've already said quite a lot in previous lectures about how Nephi privileges 2 Nephi 6–30 among his writings, calling these "the more sacred things" in his record. What we've been considering in First Nephi just provides us with an outline of the project of bringing Isaiah's writings and Nephi's visions together into one coherent whole. The point in 1 Nephi 19–22 is really just to make clear to us what's at stake in undertaking this project. As we turn now to the first five chapters of these most sacred things, we shift from preparatory or introductory material to what we're supposed to be prepared for or introduced to. We're now coming to the real deal. With Jacob's treatment of Isaiah, we're getting our first real taste of what Nephi sees as the whole point of his record.

Here's a first question that might get us thinking: *Why does Nephi start with Jacob—rather than with, for instance, himself?* We might, of course, note that there's a pretty obvious basic structure to these "more sacred" materials in Nephi's writings. Their centerpiece is clearly the large stretch of Isaiah text drawn from Isaiah 2–14 (now to be found in 2 Nephi 12–24, with an introduction of sorts in 2 Nephi 11). It's flanked on either end by attempts to weave the Isaianic into Nephite prophecy, with Jacob's sermon coming before the block of Isaianic text (in, of course, 2 Nephi

6–10) and Nephi's own prophecies coming only after the block of Isaianic text (in 2 Nephi 25–30). We get something like this: Jacob on Isaiah, then Isaiah himself, and finally Nephi on Isaiah. Perhaps it makes sense that Nephi wants to have the last word, but why does he give the first word to Jacob? Maybe the explanation is as follows? Jacob's sermon focuses on a text from Isaiah that's already appeared in the last part of First Nephi, so we're given to feel a bit of continuity with what we've already read as we come to Jacob's sermon. That seems to work, except that Nephi's already suggested to us that he wrote the First Nephi material to get us ready for the Second Nephi material, and that seems to mean that he *first* planned to open his "more sacred things" with Jacob and only *then* wrote up First Nephi in such a way that it really gets readers ready for Jacob's opening treatment of Isaiah. So we're still left with this question.

And let's note this further point. Once Jacob's sermon is over and we turn to Isaiah himself, coupled with Nephi's subsequent commentary, our focus is exclusively on First Isaiah—that is, on texts from Isaiah 1–39—while Jacob's sermon focuses (as does First Nephi) only on Second Isaiah—that is, on texts from Isaiah 40–55. There's perhaps at least this reason for having Jacob's material appear first. Jacob's treatment of Isaiah, as prepared for by the treatment at the end of First Nephi, establishes the Nephite approach to the theme of restoration and redemption rather generally. Only *then* does Nephi give his attention to the less comforting prophecies to be found in First Isaiah. It's as if Nephi wants us to encounter the promise that lies *beyond* the consumption decreed for the whole earth, before we then have to deal with that decreed consumption. "Let's focus first on the fulfillment of the Abrahamic covenant, and *then* let's see how far Israel has to go to get to that point." Actually, as we'll see, it seems Nephi wants to read at least Isaiah 2–12 as a two-part story about precisely how that fulfillment takes place. So we start with the basic outline of fulfillment, and then we go back to see how it's accomplished through history. This seems to me a pretty sensible way of approaching Isaiah on Nephi's part. Perhaps we can assume that this is what's really going on.

Let's note that Jacob's focus on Isaiah 49 is a product of *Nephi's* genius. He opens 2 Nephi 6 by stating that he's setting aside his *usual* topic ("the words of my father," he says in verse 3) to address "words which my brother hath desired me that I should speak" (2 Ne. 6:4). And the words are, of course, "they which Isaiah spake concerning all the house of Israel" in Isaiah 49:22–23 (2 Ne. 6:5). So let's be quite clear as we turn to Jacob's treatment of Isaiah that his interest and investment in Isaiah derive from an assignment given him by Nephi. Even so, let's also be quite clear that Jacob doesn't *exactly* approach Isaiah in the same way Nephi does. We'll be tracing a few differences as we go along between their respect interpretive approaches. And we'll note also along the way that Nephi seems to have been influenced by Jacob's approach in certain ways. Themes central to Nephi's interpretation of Isaiah in 2 Nephi 25–30 don't at all appear in his interpretation of Isaiah in 1 Nephi 19–22, and those themes appear for the first time really in 2 Nephi 6–10, in Jacob's treatment of the Old-World prophet. It seems that Nephi includes Jacob's words on Isaiah not only because they're in part a response to his own request, but also apparently because he felt he learned something about the interpretation of Isaiah from them. We'll see this as we go along.

Now, as I just mentioned, Jacob's text in 2 Nephi 6–10 is Isaiah 49:22–23, those verses yet again in which Isaiah makes reference to the Gentile kings and queens nursing Israel as they carry them home to their lands of promise. But let's note this from the outset: Jacob's going to go far beyond just that two-verse quotation. He'll conclude 2 Nephi 6 by quoting a little more of Isaiah 49, as if to provide a larger context for the passage. And then he'll go on to quote the next two chapters (and a few extra verses as well) of Isaiah by way of further contextualization: Isaiah 50 (in 2 Nephi 7), Isaiah 51 (in 2 Nephi 8), and then the first two verses of Isaiah 52 (right at the end of 2 Nephi 8). It's interesting that Jacob never comes back to these *extra* chapters, however. In 2 Nephi 10, he says a fair bit by way of interpreting Isaiah 49, but he doesn't so much as allude back to Isaiah 50 or 51 or 52. Jacob seems entirely content just to let Isaiah 50:1–52:2 explain themselves, to let them stand on their own as if they needed no commentary. That's curious, to say the least! Of course, we might further note that Nephi follows his quotation of Jacob's two-day sermon by telling us that "Jacob spake many more things . . . at that time" (2 Ne. 11:1), so perhaps we should assume that Jacob went on to provide some kind of commentary on Isaiah 50 and 51. But even if he did, Nephi doesn't seem to think it's terribly important for his readers to have any of it.

So our focus here in Jacob's sermon *has* to be on Isaiah 49, and especially on verses 22 through 23. That's, at least, where Nephi's focus is as he edits and copies down Jacob's preaching. It's this kings-and-queens-of-the-Gentiles business all over again that we're to be learning from. And to find out what Jacob has to say by way of commentary on this passage Nephi loves so much, we have to focus more or less solely on 2 Nephi 6 and 2 Nephi 10—the first part of day one of Jacob's preaching, and the first part of day two of Jacob's preaching. We should, of course, ask some questions about how the uninterpreted texts from Isaiah 50, 51, and 52 are supposed to clarify Isaiah 49:22–23, but we have little guidance. But apparently there's almost nothing in 2 Nephi 9—that very-long aside about the resurrection and such—that'll be of use to us in seeing what Jacob's doing with Isaiah 49. We *might* have some minimal resources from other parts of Jacob's preaching, then, but we're largely left to struggle just with what little Jacob has to say in 2 Nephi 6 and 2 Nephi 10.

Next time, of course, we'll get into the details. Today we're just starting our approach, taking in the big picture. And perhaps we've been jumping around too much for that big picture to take shape clearly yet. Has it felt a bit scattered to you today so far? It has to me. So let's get a bit more systematic.

Jacob's Sermon in 2 Nephi 6–10

2 Nephi 6–10 gives us Nephi's highlights of a two-day sermon delivered at some unspecified time by Jacob to the Nephites. It's pretty easy to divide the sermon into two or three larger parts. At the broadest level, we can divide it into the parts Jacob delivered on day one and the parts Jacob delivered on day two. That gives us, on the one hand, 2 Nephi 6–9 and, on the other hand, 2 Nephi 10. Note that we get a good deal more of day one's preaching than we do of day two. Perhaps we actually get *all* of day one. 2 Nephi 6 certainly opens with the first things Jacob said that day, since it starts with a kind of introduction. And 2 Nephi 9 certainly closes with the last things Jacob said that day, since it closes with his announcement that he's quitting until then. So perhaps we've got more or less the whole of what Jacob had to say on day one. But we get only a truncated report of day two, as Nephi makes clear. We already quoted the passage, but here it is again (and more fully now): "And now, Jacob spake many more things to my people at that time—nevertheless, only these things have I caused to be written, for the things which I have written sufficeth me" (2 Ne. 11:1).

We can further divide Jacob's sermon, since Nephi himself divides the preaching from the first day into two parts. In the original chapter breaks—and we've seen already in earlier lectures how important these can be!—2 Nephi 6–8 make up one chapter, while 2 Nephi 9 makes up a separate chapter. And the break between 2 Nephi 6–8 and 2 Nephi 9 makes perfect sense. The former part focuses on Isaiah, while the latter part turns to the subject of the resurrection and related matters. Taken all together, what we've got from Jacob in 2 Nephi 6–10 looks like this (with original chapter numbers in parentheses):

Day One of Jacob's Preaching

About Isaiah 49	2 Nephi 6–8 (Chapter V)
About Christ and the Resurrection	2 Nephi 9 (Chapter VI)

Day Two of Jacob's Preaching

About Isaiah 49 (Again)	2 Nephi 10 (Chapter VII)

Despite the divisions in the text, there's a kind of flow from one portion to the next. At first it seems like 2 Nephi 9—the second part of the first day of Jacob's preaching—is a kind of odd tangent, a lengthy aside that leaves off Isaiah and the question of the covenant to focus on other things. But closer reading makes clear that there's a logic at work there. Let's say something about this.

First, note that 2 Nephi 9 opens with at least a few words about 2 Nephi 6–8. "I have read these things that ye might know concerning the covenants of the Lord," Jacob explains, because the Lord "hath spoken unto the Jews by the mouth of his holy prophets, even from the beginning" (2 Ne. 9:1–2). We'll have *much* to say next time about Jacob's focus on "the Jews" here and throughout 2 Nephi 6–10, but let's note for now just that this clearly sets up the context for what he talks about throughout 2 Nephi 9. He tells his hearers that he knows many of them have been searching "to know of things to come" (2 Ne. 9:4), and so he assumes they've come to "know that in the body [God] shall show himself unto they at Jerusalem," who will kill him: "For it behooveth the great Creator that he suffereth himself to become subject unto man in the flesh, and die for all men, that all men might become subject unto him" (v. 5). The transition from Isaiah (whose words Jacob interprets quite narrowly at first as applying specifically to the tribe of Judah—that is, to Jews)—to the story of the Messiah and his resurrection is pretty smooth.

Second, notice how smooth the transition from 2 Nephi 9 to 2 Nephi 10 is as well. 2 Nephi 9 ends with Jacob turning back from resurrection and associated matters to Isaiah kinds of themes. Right after announcing one last time the goodness of the God who redeems from death, he says this: "And behold how great the covenants of the Lord! And how great his condescension unto the children of men! And because of his greatness, and his grace and mercy, he hath promised unto us that our seed shall not utterly be destroyed according to the flesh—but that he would preserve them, and in future generations they shall become a righteous branch unto the house of Israel!" (2 Ne. 9:53). That's how 2 Nephi 9 ends. And look at how 2 Nephi 10 begins. Jacob starts off by stating that he's going to say something about "this righteous branch" mentioned at the end of the previous day's discussion (2 Ne. 10:1). And to get that off the ground, he goes on immediately to start talking again about the Messiah coming among the Jews, so he's right back where he was at the beginning of 2 Nephi 9. So, although there's *something* like a tangent in 2 Nephi 9, there's actually a good deal of continuity over the whole of Jacob's sermon as well. To get the entire story of Israel's redemption and their relationship to the Messiah, it's necessary to outline the consequences of the Messiah's intervention in matters of life and death.

So there's a flow in 2 Nephi 6–10, but at the same time, we can say that it's the first and last of the three parts of Jacob's preaching that focus particularly on Isaiah, or on things Isaianic. Like any good editor, Nephi makes sure to begin and to end his report of Jacob's sermon with the material he wants us to remember best, and that's the Isaiah material. And we've already seen that the chief focus in that Isaiah material falls on Isaiah 49:22–23, the passage already discussed in 1 Nephi 19–22, which Nephi further assigns to Jacob to address here in some detail. Jacob introduces that text early in 2 Nephi 6 (specifically in verses 6–7), and then he returns to it explicitly in 2 Nephi 10 (specifically in verses 7–9). It's thus pretty hard to lose sight of what Jacob's really after if we read carefully.

Another Approach to Likening

Okay, what else do we need to do by way of general approach? Let's say a bit, before we wrap up today, about what seems to be Jacob's relatively unique way of going about the task of *likening*. First, let's note the points of continuity with Nephi. Immediately before he quotes Isaiah 49:22–23, Jacob says the following, which should sound quite familiar to us at this point: "And now the words which I shall read are they which Isaiah spake concerning all the house of Israel—wherefore they may be likened unto you, for ye are of the house of Israel. And there are many things which have been spoken by Isaiah which may be likened unto you because that ye are of the house of Israel" (2 Ne. 6:5). Note how similar this is to what we've already seen from Nephi, back in the last verses of 1 Nephi 19. Jacob uses the same word we find in Nephi, "likening," and he seems to understand it to mean more or less the same thing. Isaiah's prophecies were originally directed to the whole house of Israel ("all the house of Israel," Jacob says), and for that reason precisely they can be applied to branches and remnants of Israel that happen to have been separated from the main body of Israel. Jacob's perhaps even more explicit about all this than Nephi, since he uses the word "because": "Many things which have been spoken by Isaiah . . . may be likened unto you because that ye are of the house of Israel."

So far, then, Jacob reproduces Nephi. Let's further note this other formula of sorts that can be found just one verse earlier in 2 Nephi 6. Jacob says, "I would speak unto you concerning things which are and which are to come, wherefore I will read you the words of Isaiah" (2 Ne. 6:4). I'm not sure quite how much we should read into that formula, but *I* find it striking. Jacob seems here to be saying relatively straightforwardly that Isaiah's words inherently have *two* meanings, one bound up with the original context of Isaiah's prophecy ("things which are") and one bound up with Nephi's likening of Isaiah's prophecies texts to the larger history of the covenant he's witnessed in vision ("things . . . which are to come"). Maybe that's reading too much into Jacob's words, but I like it, and I'm happy to use it as a helpful formula for making sense of the operation of likening.

Alright. So Nephi and Jacob seem largely to agree on the basic nature of likening. Where are we going to find a bit of innovation on Jacob's part? Well, at least in this: Jacob seems particularly interested in limiting the unlikened application of Isaiah's words to *Judah alone*, that is, to "the Jews." If you think back to what we've seen in Nephi's discussion of Isaiah 48–49, there's been more or less *no* discussion of "the Jews." The closest we got to that was a reference in 1 Nephi 22:5 to "all they which shall hereafter be scattered and be confounded because of the Holy One of Israel—for against them will they harden their hearts. Wherefore, they shall be scattered among all nations and shall be hated by all men." That's all Nephi says that seems to be focused specifically on "the Jews." And note that he gives those he speaks of no name. He doesn't there call them "the Jews" or "Judah" or "those at Jerusalem" or even "those from whence we came." He just makes a passing allusion to Judah before quickly moving on to his own interests. Jacob, however, focuses *intensely* on Jews in his sermon—intensely enough to say a few things that might well make us uncomfortable today. And this seems to underlie a somewhat unique conception of likening for him. He seems to think that much more needs to be said about the Jews before any program of likening like Nephi's can really get off the ground.

We saw that Nephi distinguishes the two stages of likening—or really, distinguishes between the unlikened text and the likened text—basically by giving us two chapters of Isaiah in succession, the boundary between them clearly marked, with one left in its original historical context and the other adapted in a variety of ways to the situation to which it's to be likened. And of course, Nephi then followed that up with a likening commentary. Let me be more specific and concrete. Nephi gave us Isaiah 48, but he left it in its original state, so to speak, trapped in the historical particularity of its original intentions. But then he gave us Isaiah 49, which he seems to have altered directly in a few ways, bending and shaping it so that even just the act of reading it begins to alert one to the possibilities of likening the text to a broader history. And then he added his own commentary in 1 Nephi 22, drawing on a variety of resources to accomplish a full likening of the text.

Jacob's approach is quite distinct. He gives us Isaiah 49:22–23 in two forms, unlikened and likened. But he gives us what might be called an *unlikened commentary* in 2 Nephi 6. He doesn't just let the unlikened text speak for itself. He tells us a whole lot about the original application or intention of the text, and it's this that focuses him so intensely on those he calls "the Jews." He provides what he takes to be a straightforward exegesis of the text. That's the point of 2 Nephi 6. But then, later, he undertakes the work of likening—in 2 Nephi 10. There he begins by coming back to the unlikened meaning of the text, reviewing it in some detail. But then, finally, he makes a clear transition and provides a likening that's more or less along the lines of what Nephi usually gives us. So Jacob's doing something slightly new. It seems he's much more interested than Nephi in the unlikened state of Isaiah's prophecy, much more concerned to make sure we understand Isaiah's original before we move to the adaptation of the text for specifically Nephite purposes.

That's perhaps peculiar. We'll have to say more about all this next time, obviously, when we turn to the details. For now, hopefully, we've done enough just to be ready for what we'll try to accomplish next time.

Lecture XII

Jacob's Isaiah

Well, as usual, we covered quite a bit of ground last time, so let's review a few things before we get moving today. Last time we *began* our approach to Jacob's treatment of Isaiah in 2 Nephi 6–10. You'll recall that the sermon was given over two days, and we've got in our possession what seems to be all of what Jacob said on the first day, but only the very first part of what he said on the second day. With his editorial work on Jacob's teachings, Nephi's made it so that what *we* have opens and closes with Jacob's treatment of Isaiah 49. And that's where our focus naturally needs to be, given our intentions in these lectures.

We saw that Jacob comes at Isaiah 49—a text assigned to him by Nephi—in a manner that's ultimately quite distinct from his brother. If I remember correctly, we marked two major ways we can say that his approach is different, despite a set of similarities we could enumerate as well. First, Jacob quotes a good deal of Isaiah text by way of contextualization, but he never says much of anything about that contextualizing text. He seems to think that its presentation without commentary is enough to help us understand the meaning of the text on which he does comment. Second, he spends a good deal more time on explaining the unlikened text of Isaiah in its original context or according to its original meaning before he moves on to likening. He seems to think that we ought to spend a good deal more time thinking about what Isaiah had to say directly to Judah before we go off exploring what Isaiah might be read as having to say to branches and remnants of Israel scattered all over the world.

These two differences between Nephi and Jacob are, I think, quite striking. Don't you think so? At any rate, I find myself struck by Nephi's willingness to put a variety of approaches to Isaiah on display before us, rather than simply to steamroll over us with his own unique approach, as if that were the only way one could possibly make sense of Isaiah. And don't forget that we've already seen before that Nephi gives us a couple of instances where Lehi seems to interpret Isaiah as well. Really, we're getting a handful of different approaches to Isaiah in Nephi—even if he gives by far the *most* attention to his own approach.

Okay, let's allow that quick summary to suffice for review. On to the details of Jacob's work on Isaiah!

An Emphasis on Jewish History

Let's start by highlighting Jacob's interesting postponement of the actual work of likening. Where Nephi gives us an unlikened text but then says nothing about it so he can move on quickly to the text he likens extensively—*and* also appears to manipulate the very words of the would-be likened text so that we never really get it in an unlikened state—Jacob makes us dwell for quite a while on the unlikened text. He seems to want us to wrestle with Isaiah's words in the original, and we're subjected to extensive commentary on its unlikened meaning. And for Jacob, the unlikened meaning of a text like Isaiah 49 has everything to do with what he calls "the Jews."

I want to make two quick caveats before we dive into this. First, let's be clear that Jacob *isn't* necessarily giving us insight into the *original* meaning of the Isaiah text he deals with, though we might find ourselves inclined to talk that way. (In fact, I've used that language myself along the way!) He's giving us insight into the *unlikened*, rather than the *original*, text of Isaiah 49. By looking at what Jacob has to say about Isaiah 49, we're not traveling with him back in time to find out what the actual prophet whose words appear in Isaiah 49 had in mind when he first uttered them—before they were subsequently gathered and shaped by their inclusion in a larger swath of text. We're not interested in *originals* here, but in what Jacob takes to be the rather obvious meaning of the text *in the final form*, but as yet *unlikened*. He wants to know, basically, how the text might be read in his day by non-remnant or non-branch Israelites—that is, by Jews still back in Jerusalem or perhaps by that point already in exile in Babylon. That's not necessarily an attempt to get back to anything original.

Second caveat: Jacob's discussion of "the Jews" in 2 Nephi 6 and especially 2 Nephi 10 might—and probably *should*—make you a bit uncomfortable. Some have pointed to some of the passages in Jacob's sermon as using language that smacks of anti-Semitism. And I don't think they're entirely wrong to do so. (If you want a decent summary treatment of these matters, you might look at Steve Epperson's *Mormons and Jews*.) Certainly, from a post-Holocaust perspective, it's natural to bristle at ways of talking about Jewish persons and practices that were at one point sadly regarded as socially acceptable. Now, perhaps there are also ways to defend the language used in the Book of Mormon to talk about Jews, but I'm not interested here in pursuing that. I'm fine with just feeling a bit uncomfortable with these matters—in something like the way we ought to be uncomfortable with the ways women are presented in ancient scripture—while nonetheless pressing forward with the task of interpreting texts we regard as containing probing revelations concerning God's purposes. So I'll take up Jacob's treatment of Isaiah and what he has to say about Judah without trying to sort out the ethical implications of such talk.

Okay, caveats out of the way. So what does Jacob see Isaiah 49 as actually being about? Let's notice this right off: Jacob spends 2 Nephi 6 outlining what he sees Isaiah 49 saying to and about Judah, and then he spends a bit of time in 2 Nephi 10 summarizing these same things all over again. Let's make this quite specific. Jacob provides his initial commentary on Isaiah 49:22–23 in 2 Nephi 6:8–15. (After that point, he begins his lengthy quotation of further parts of Isaiah 49, as well as all of Isaiah 50–51 and the first verses of Isaiah 52.) It's clear from the outset of 2 Nephi 10 that the purpose of the last chapter of Jacob's sermon is to shift attention to Lehi's seed, to "the promises which *we* have obtained," as Jacob puts it (2 Ne. 10:2). But he only actually gets to Lehi's seed in verse 10, a transition he marks clearly: "But behold, *this* land, saith God, shall be a land of *thine* inheritance" (2 Ne. 10:10). So we get in 2 Nephi 10:3–9 a summary review of 2 Nephi 6:8–15. Both of these passages— eight verses in 2 Nephi 6 and then seven verses in 2 Nephi 10—focus on the unlikened meaning of Isaiah 49, on what that passage is supposed to say to and about Judah regardless of any scattered remnants or branches of Israel. Jacob thus opens both Day One and Day Two of his sermonizing with commentary on the unlikened text, and we've already seen that he dedicates the bulk of Day One to continuing in the same vein. In the end, Jacob says a good deal more about Isaiah 49 and Judah than he does about Isaiah 49 and the Lehites.

So what does he have to say in these two stretches of commentary in 2 Nephi 6 and 2 Nephi 10? Maybe we could start with a quick skim of 2 Nephi 6:8–15. Jacob says the following (taking bits and pieces of his words, and slightly changing a verb here and there to smooth things out):

> They which were at Jerusalem . . . have been slain and carried away captive. Nevertheless . . . they shall return again, and . . . the Holy One of Israel shall

manifest himself unto them in the flesh. And . . . they shall scourge him and crucify him . . . . [And then] the judgments of the Holy One of Israel shall come upon them, and the day cometh that they shall be smitten and afflicted . . . ; they shall be scattered and smitten and hated. Nevertheless, the Lord will be merciful unto them, that, when they shall come to the knowledge of their Redeemer, they shall be gathered together again to the lands of their inheritance. And blessed are the Gentiles, . . . for behold, if it so be that they shall repent and fight not against Zion, . . . they shall be saved. . . . [But] they that fight against Zion and the covenant people of the Lord shall lick up the dust of their feet, and the people of the Lord shall not be ashamed. . . . [Finally] the Messiah will set himself again the second time to recover them—wherefore, he will manifest himself unto them in power and great glory, unto the destruction of their enemies . . . . And they shall know that the Lord is God, the Holy One of Israel.

Notice the clear story here, divisible into several parts: (1) exile and subsequent return of Judah; (2) appearance and crucifixion of the Holy One of Israel; (3) subsequent destruction and scattering of Judah; (4) recognition by Judah of the Redeemer and a resultant gathering; (5) Gentile responses of two sorts with appropriate consequences; and (6) final messianic recovery of Judah and globally visible manifestation of the Messiah. Throughout this story, the main character is what Jacob calls the people of the Lord, those who "still wait for the coming of the Messiah"—clearly, Jews (2 Ne. 6:13). But notice how much further Jacob sees this text going in its unlikened state than Nephi seems to have seen. So far as we could tell, Nephi saw the unlikened Isaianic word as telling the story just of the *first* of the six events Jacob recounts here: exile in, and then redemption from, Babylon. Jacob sees a longer story at work here, however—a longer story already there in the unlikened text. And he sees the moment in the story that's especially relevant to Isaiah 49:22–23 to come rather later in the story: at the moment where the Gentiles respond to Judah's *later* redemption (the latter-day redemption of Jews).

That Jacob sees Isaiah 49:22–23 to refer to these later moments in Judah's larger story is quite clear from the ways he uses the language of the Isaiah text as he tells his story. It's only late in the six-part story that he begins to use Isaianic terms. When he describes "the people of the Lord" as those who "still wait for the coming of the Messiah," he's clearly referring to the word Isaiah attributes to the Lord: "They shall not be ashamed that wait for me" (2 Ne. 6:7). Still more, it's only late in the story that Nephi brings in any talk of "the Gentiles," the chief focus of the passage from Isaiah (v. 6). Jacob, like Nephi, understands Isaiah to be talking about

Gentiles who assist in the redemption of Judah. But where Nephi seems to have understood the unlikened Isaiah text to refer pretty clearly to the redemption of Judah from Babylonian exile, Jacob sees it as referring to a much later, and much more globally significant redemption—one that ultimately results in all people "know[ing] that the Lord is God, the Holy One of Israel."

Jacob on the Gentiles

There's an interesting consequence of Jacob's different historical understanding of Isaiah 49:22–23. While Isaiah here seems quite straightforward in speaking only of repentant Gentiles, and while we've seen that Nephi seems straightforwardly to interpret him along those lines, Jacob takes the passage from Isaiah to refer to *two* distinct sorts of Gentiles: some repentant and some rebellious. Jacob refers to those who "repent and fight not against Zion," and he presumably has in mind those Gentiles who, Isaiah says, carry Israel's children on their shoulders (though it's interesting that he says nothing of this gracious act in 2 Nephi 6). But then Jacob goes on to speak of those Gentiles who in fact *do* "fight against Zion and the covenant people of the Lord," and he says that they "shall lick up the dust of [the Jews'] feet." Those last words are, of course, Isaiah's: "They shall bow down to thee with their faces towards the earth and lick up the dust of thy feet" (2 Ne. 6:7). As I said a moment ago, one gets the sense reading Isaiah himself that these words are supposed to describe the humble acts of repentant Gentiles. Jacob, however, apparently hears in these words a description of the humiliated acts of unrepentant Gentiles. And so he clearly understands Isaiah 49:22–23 as distinguishing between two sorts of Gentile responses.

So we've got two fascinating differences between Nephi and Jacob so far, when it comes to interpreting this passage from Isaiah. Both see it as applying originally to Judah, but Nephi apparently understands its scope as limited to redemption from Babylon, while Jacob clearly understands it as focused on the later, more global redemption of Judah from among all nations. Further, while Nephi seems to find in Isaiah's words only affirmative talk regarding the repentant Gentiles who get involved in Judah's redemption from exile, Jacob pretty clearly finds a distinction between Gentiles who humble themselves and assist in Judah's redemption and Gentiles who have to be humiliated and lick up the dust of Judah's feet. The Gentiles find themselves in a more obviously precarious situation in Jacob's commentary.

They're presented as naturally inclined to fight against the covenant people of the Lord, such that those who assist in Judah's redemption Jacob only negatively describes as those who "fight *not* against Zion" and "do *not* unite themselves to that great and abominable church." According to Jacob, it seems there are only a few Gentiles who refuse to vilify Jews and can thus "be saved" with them as part of the covenant.

So that's what we find in 2 Nephi 6. What of 2 Nephi 10, where Jacob tells this six-part story all over again? Interestingly, his story is somewhat shorter in review. He leaves off talk of the exile and the return, starting with Judah already re-established in the land. What Nephi takes to be the whole focus of Isaiah 49:22–23 Jacob entirely neglects to mention in his second bit of commentary on the passage! The focus is again on Jews and Gentiles, of course, but the tone, we'll see, has changed pretty dramatically. Where Jews are presented as those who faithfully wait for the Lord in 2 Nephi 6, while Gentiles are presented there as those who too-naturally fight against the covenant people of the Lord, here in 2 Nephi 10 it's almost the reverse. Notice that "the Jews" are now described as "they which are the more wicked part of the world," something Jacob says with this troubling explanation: "There is none other nation on earth that would crucify their God" (2 Ne. 10:3). And notice further that "the nations of the Gentiles" are now described as "great in the eyes of . . . God" (v. 8), and this Jacob explains by saying a peculiar thing: "The promises of the Lord is great unto the Gentiles, for he hath spoken it, and who can dispute?" (v. 9). *Clearly*, something's changed.

Presumably, what lies behind the change—from "the Jews are the faithful people of the Lord" to "the Jews are the most wicked of peoples," and from "the Gentiles do nothing but fight against the covenant" to "the Gentiles are great in God's eyes"—is the intervening account of Christ's death and resurrection. In 2 Nephi 9, between 2 Nephi 6 and 2 Nephi 10, Jacob reports on "the great Creator" who "suffereth himself to become subject unto man in the flesh and die for all men" (2 Ne. 9:5). For the most part, 2 Nephi 9 has Jacob saying beautiful and edifying things about that fact, but perhaps it's also left him with a sour attitude. Perhaps what he's seen there in vision, combined with an antipathy toward Jerusalem's people spurred by his family's being driven out before his birth, has led him to use language that's a bit disturbing to read. Again, I don't want to dwell on this point. Mostly, I want to highlight the change between approval of the Jews and disapproval of the Gentiles to approval of the Gentiles and disapproval of the Jews in order to note that this reversal seems to cause *another* reversal for Jacob. In 2 Nephi 6, the bit of Isaiah 49:22–23 that most draws his attention is the part that reports on rebellious or unrepentant Gentiles, those who will lick the dust from the feet of the Jews. But in 2 Nephi 10, the bit of the same Isaiah text that most draws Jacob's attention is the part that commends certain Gentiles for getting involved in the right way in the covenant.

Here's what Jacob says, then, in 2 Nephi 10:

> It shall come to pass that [the Jews] shall be gathered in from their long dispersion, from the isles of the sea, and from the four parts of the earth. And the nations of the Gentiles shall be great in the eyes of me, saith God, in carrying them forth to the lands of their inheritance. Yea, the kings of the Gentiles shall be nursing fathers unto them, and their queens shall become nursing mothers. Wherefore, the promises of the Lord is great unto the Gentiles—for he hath spoken it, and who can dispute? (vv. 8–9)

Before—quite against the grain of Nephi's commentary on Isaiah 49— Jacob failed to refer back to this nursing-fathers, nursing-mothers portion of the text. He had very little good to say about the Gentiles. Here in 2 Nephi 10, it's all he wants to talk about from Isaiah 49:22–23, with striking praise for the Gentiles rather generally. We've already seen that Jacob has a more complicated reading of the Isaiah passage. Now we see that that complicated reading distributes its two major elements across the gap between 2 Nephi 6 and 2 Nephi 10. This is peculiar, to say the least.

But let's not get bogged down here. We're going too slowly already today. So let's come back to the point that set us in motion here. Everything we've been talking about so far has, don't forget, been part of Jacob's *unlikened* interpretation of Isaiah 49:22–23. Even before he comes to the task of likening this text, he's got an interpretation that's a good deal more complex than Nephi's. He sees Isaiah's words as distinguishing between Gentiles who repent and Gentiles who rebel. And perhaps he sees the same words as distinguishing between Jews who prove faithful (and so have the very dust of their feet licked up by their enemies) and Jews who prove resistant (and so must be carried to the lands of their promise by humble Gentiles). Beyond these distinctions that are absent in Nephi, Jacob's approach to the text is also more complex because of the way he sees its unlikened application as focused on the eventual global redemption of Judah, rather than on the historically particular redemption of Judah from Babylonian exile.

Jacob's Likening of Isaiah 49

So Jacob finds he has a good deal more to say than Nephi regarding Isaiah 49 before it gets likened. What does he have to say about this text by way of actually likening it? Here he hasn't got a whole lot to say—or, at least, Nephi doesn't copy a whole lot of what Jacob has to say about it. We're short on time, so let's do another quick skim:

> But behold, this land . . . shall be a land of thine inheritance, and the Gentiles shall be blessed upon the land. . . . He that fighteth against Zion shall perish. . . . He that fighteth against Zion, both Jew and Gentile, both bond and free, both male and female, shall perish . . . , for I will fulfill my promises which I have made unto the children of men . . . . Wherefore, my beloved brethren, thus saith our God: I will afflict thy seed by the hand of the Gentiles—nevertheless, I will soften the hearts of the Gentiles that they shall be like a father to them. Wherefore, the Gentiles shall be blessed and numbered among the house of Israel. (2 Ne. 10:10–19)

That's a bit quicker a skim than I'd like to do (I've left out all the talk about kings here!), but hopefully it'll suffice. First note that Jacob makes clear that he's transitioning from all his commentary on the unlikened text to his likening commentary—marking the shift with a contrastive "but," an emphatic "this" (in "this land") and the possessive "thine" ("thine inheritance"). And then note that there's a kind of leveling, in this likening, of the covenantal/non-covenantal difference between Jews and Gentiles. They "both" might be among those who "fight against Zion" and so "shall perish." God's faithful fulfillment of his promises, focused here on the redemption of the *rest* of Israel, will proceed with or without Jews, despite all that's been said in previous passages. Finally, note that all this is followed by the likening itself, with the Gentiles being "like a father" to the New-World remnant of Israel, and with God making them a part of the covenant as a reward of sorts.

This story isn't exactly the one we've been getting from Nephi, is it? It's similar in obvious ways, but it's also got its own flavor. What's most remarkable, of course, is the way Jacob's *still* focused, even in his likening, on the complex relationship between Jews and Gentiles. There's a larger gap between unlikened and likened meanings for Nephi, we might say. He sees God doing more or less the same things with Judah and the rest of Israel—just at different times and through different groups of Gentiles, maybe. There's a pattern of God's involvement with Judah, and that pattern can be found operating also in the larger history of scattered Israel. Jacob seems to see the unlikened and likened versions of Isaiah as more closely entangled. Even in its unlikened form, Isaiah 49:22–23 exhibits for Jacob a kind of ambivalence about the respective statuses of Jews and Gentiles. Both deserve accolades, and yet both deserve condemnation—always in a kind of inverse relation the one to the other. And then he takes this ambivalence over into his likening of the text. Both Jews and Gentiles are without any real privilege, because Jacob sees something still *more* central to God's covenantal purposes than what's going to happen specifically with Judah. It's Jacob, after all, who places such a heavy emphasis on the Lehites finding "a better land" than the one they had "been driven out of" (2 Ne. 10:20). And it's Jacob who emphasizes how "great is the promises of the Lord unto they which are upon the isles of the sea" (v. 20). It seems clear that Jacob sees his own people as being in a kind of *superior* position to Judah.

This is a surprising turn. We've seen nothing of its sort in Nephi. But here's the really interesting thing: We *will* be seeing it in Nephi. In fact, we'll see that what Jacob has to say in 2 Nephi 6–10 seems rather generally to have had an impact on Nephi. In 2 Nephi 25–30, when Nephi will give us his concluding treatment of Isaiah, it'll look a good deal more like Jacob than like what we've seen so far from Nephi. That's really quite intriguing. And maybe *this* provides us with a better answer to a question we asked last time. Why does Nephi give the first word to Jacob here? It may be that he does so because he feels he's really learned a lot from Jacob. And it'd be best if we as readers get Jacob's peculiar focus on Judah before we come to Nephi's most mature treatment of Isaiah and the Abrahamic covenant. All we've gotten in First Nephi is a preliminary treatment, enough to whet our appetite and give us a basic sense for what it means to read Isaiah in a Nephi-like way. But then we've got to experience Isaiah through a Jacobite lens so that we're fully prepared to read him in the way Nephi wants us *ultimately* to read him.

Isaiah 50–51

Maybe all this is right. I think we're on to something here. We'll be revisiting these questions later, at any rate, once we get past the large chunk of Isaiah quotation in 2 Nephi 12–24 and get back to Nephi. So perhaps we can leave these matters relatively undeveloped for the moment. With our last few minutes today (time passes too quickly!), I want to say at least *something* about the quotation of Isaiah 49:24–52:2 in 2 Nephi 6–8. All we've said so far is that Jacob quotes them, apparently by way of providing Isaiah 49:22–23 with some context, but he does so without ever actually commenting on them. And we should note from the outset that Jacob himself never refers back to this rather lengthy quotation of Isaiah subsequently. Others in the Book of Mormon seem to do so—Nephi maybe once, Mormon a time or two, Christ himself at one point, and then Moroni for sure in his final farewell. Mostly, though, we're left just with Jacob's straightforward quotation without comment.

So what's to be said about Isaiah 49:24–52:2 in Jacob's sermon? Well, there's much that could be said about textual variants again. As Jacob quotes these chapters—or perhaps, like Nephi, copies them—they again differ materially from what's to be found in the King James Version. But in this case, *most* of the variants do little to change the meaning of the text. If there's a consistent pattern in Jacob's long quotation of Isaiah, it would simply be that he seems to drop whole lines with far greater frequency than can be found elsewhere in the Book of Mormon's quotations of Isaiah. Let me just provide a quick list to give you a feel. The last two clauses of Isaiah 50:10 disappear in Jacob's quotation, as does the third clause of Isaiah 51:1 and the final clause of Isaiah 51:2, and then whole prepositional phrases drop out of Isaiah 51:9 and Isaiah 51:15. Nothing like this frequency of simple disappearances of Isaiah text can be found anywhere else in the Book of Mormon. Is this supposed to be a feature of Jacob's preaching? Perhaps the circumstances of oral delivery lead him to drop lines here and there, whether intentionally or unintentionally? Some interpreters have played with this possibility. But maybe we're just to understand that these chapters of Isaiah received a number of minor expansions after the brass plates were produced? I don't know that we can really go into any of that sort of thing here. It's enough just to notice the pattern for now.

Let's give our remaining time just to a brief summary of these chapters, if for no other reason than that a bit of increased familiarity with them could do us all some good. We'll be leaving Jacob's treatment of Isaiah behind after this lecture, so we'll just conclude with a kind of running commentary of sorts—a rather brief one, unfortunately!

Jacob opens this quotation by starting with the verse immediately following Isaiah 49:22–23 (immediately following, that is, the passage given him by Nephi for comment). As a result, it opens with talk of the Lord contending with Israel's contenders, with a promise that he can recover "the captives of the mighty" (2 Ne. 6:17). This Jacob then ties to the questions that open Isaiah 50: "Have I put thee away, or have I cast thee off forever?" (2 Ne. 7:1). There we get a rhetorical reaffirmation of God's faithfulness to Israel, despite their waywardness. And immediately thereafter, we get a clear demonstration of that faithfulness: God's sent a prophet, one with "the tongue of the learned" who "should know how to speak a word in season" to Israel (v. 4). That prophet finds he doesn't have much of an audience, of course: "I gave my back to the smiters, and my cheeks to them that plucked off the hair" (v. 6). But the Lord comes to the rescue of his servant, which gives him some confidence. But then the discussion of the prophet-servant sent to Israel is brief, and the text soon turns again to speech directed to Israel in her waywardness. Rather nicely, that speech focuses on things Abrahamic in a forceful way: "Look unto Abraham, your father, and unto Sarah, she that bare you" (2 Ne. 8:2). Israel's task is to do the works of Abraham, of course, but they seldom do anything like that. So they're reminded of the Lord's perpetual faithfulness, his righteousness that "shall not be abolished" (v. 6) and his salvation that will be "from generation to generation" (v. 8).

Then the audacious response of Israel to all these prophetic commandments: "Awake! Awake!" they cry to God; "Put on strength, O arm of the Lord! Awake as in the ancient days!" (2 Ne. 8:9). Apparently disappointed in mediocre displays of divine power, they call on God to be like he was in the time of the Exodus. A few words of encouragement from the Lord follow, but then he returns the favor to his wayward hearers: "Awake! Awake!" he says right back to Jerusalem (v. 17). Then, weaving his way through a series of further promises, he comes once more to the same injunction: "Awake! Awake!" he says again (v. 24). Using their words against them, pointing out that *they're* the ones who're sleeping through everything, the Lord calls on Israel to get serious. And there the quotation ends, with the Lord calling Israel to put on "beautiful garments," to "sit down" on a throne, and to be free, finally, of its captive status (vv. 24–25).

Yikes. Somehow, we've got to let this terribly-too-brief review of a long quotation suffice. It's embarrassing. But we're out of time, and we've got to move on in our next lecture, since there's a lot more Isaiah material in the small plates we want to cover. Hopefully we've done something like justice to Jacob in these past two lectures. At any rate, we'll draw up a balance sheet of our work at the outset next time, as usual.

Lecture XIII

A Start on the Isaiah Chapters

Turning to the Isaiah Chapters

Alright, so we've spent our last two times together working on Jacob's sermon in 2 Nephi 6–10. And let's be clear that we've done it anything but justice. In fact, we've done it so little justice that I find myself wondering how to summarize our findings. Above all, I suppose I want to highlight something we haven't really yet discovered so much as anticipated. It seems that Jacob's words in 2 Nephi 6–10 had a pretty profound impact on Nephi, and this may be why Nephi made them the opening sequence of "the more sacred things" in 2 Nephi 6–30. We certainly noticed a number of differences between Nephi and Jacob when it comes to interpreting Isaiah 49:22–23. For Nephi, these verses are wholly positive and affirming, as concerns the Gentiles, and they seem to be focused in their unlikened state just on the return of Judah from Babylon. For Jacob, on the other hand, these verses express important ambivalence regarding the Gentiles—some repent, but many or even most rebel—and they seem to focus in their unlikened state on the *long* history of Judah, anticipating eschatological redemption. Nephi seems to have taken all this to heart. Where there's little focus on Jewish history in Nephi's reading of Isaiah in *First* Nephi, there's a good deal more in the later parts of *Second* Nephi.

Perhaps we can let that suffice for a summary. It's as full of holes as our treatment of 2 Nephi 6–10 more generally. I can feel Jacob's depth and richness leaking out of our discussions. But I want to make sure we have plenty of time to deal carefully with the so-called "Isaiah chapters" themselves—that massive quotation of Isaiah 2–14 in 2 Nephi 12–24. There's so much to say there, and we'll end up failing to give them due attention if we don't move on.

Let's get started, but let me first explain what we *won't* be doing with Isaiah 2–14 or 2 Nephi 12–24. We *won't* be skipping over these chapters in order to focus all of our attention just on 2 Nephi 25:1–8 while leaving most of the hard work for you to do on your own. Have you ever noticed how often people do that? If you're familiar with Book of Mormon commentary, you'll know that this is the usual move: to cover thirteen chapters of Isaiah in just a couple of pages, and then to follow that with a longer, closer reading of Nephi's so-called "keys" to reading Isaiah. Do you remember that passage at the opening of 2 Nephi 25? It's all the Sunday School lesson on the Isaiah chapters focuses on every four years also. There Nephi says a bit about knowing geography and history, about having the spirit of prophecy, about living in the last days, and so on—and all these things are supposed to help make sense of Isaiah. So teachers and commentators tend to give their attention just to what Nephi says *there*, recommending these "keys" as the way in to Isaiah. Now, I don't know about you, but that always rubs me the wrong way. If someone can't provide me with some solid commentary on Isaiah's *actual* writings, why should I trust his or her commentary on Nephi's *keys* for understanding Isaiah? If you really *can* tell me what those keys are, and therefore can tell me how I should go about interpreting *Isaiah*, why don't you yourself tell me something about what Isaiah's writings mean? The preference for discussing *how to read* Isaiah over *actually reading* Isaiah makes me more than a bit suspicious.

I get especially suspicious when I hear—I've heard this a couple of times over the years—that those who *do* understand Isaiah thanks to Nephi's keys shouldn't share what they've learned with others, since we're supposed to struggle individually to develop the right understanding. That not only strikes me as remarkably arrogant and uncharitable, it also seems to go directly against what Nephi actually says in 2 Nephi 25. We'll spend some time on Nephi's so-called "keys" in a later lecture, but only *after* we've done some work on Isaiah's actual writings. And I think we'll see that they don't say much at all of what we usually assume they say. There's something rather different going on there, I think. We'll get to that.

For now, let's turn our attention directly to the so-called "Isaiah chapters."

Chapter Breaks in 2 Nephi 11–24

We can't take even a first step here without making a few general observations. And the first one concerns chaptering. We've noticed along the way of our discussions that the original chapter breaks in the Book of Mormon are really important. You'll remember that they seem to be key to making any real sense of First Nephi. So let's take note of the original chapter breaks in 2 Nephi 11–24. It turns out they're quite instructive. When Orson Pratt redid the chapter breaks in the 1870s, he reproduced in this part of the text the chapter breaks of the King James Version of the Bible. Where Isaiah 2 ends in the biblical text, 2 Nephi 12 ends in the Book of Mormon. Where Isaiah 3 ends in the biblical text, 2 Nephi 13 ends in the Book of Mormon. And so on. But as the Prophet Joseph originally dictated this larger block of Isaiah, it came in only *three* chapters—not at all today's *thirteen*. Here's how they work out:

> Chapter VIII   2 Nephi 11–15 (Isaiah 2–5)
>
> Chapter IX   2 Nephi 16–22 (Isaiah 6–12)
>
> Chapter X   2 Nephi 23–24 (Isaiah 13–14)

Note here that we're getting in 2 Nephi 11–24 what in the Bible comes as thirteen chapters, but we're to read them as coming in three sequences. We're to take Isaiah 2–5, Isaiah 6–12, and Isaiah 13–14 as three distinct chunks.

Why should that be important? Well, at the very least because what Joseph originally dictated follows relatively close to the structure recognized by modern scholars. For a century at least, Isaiah scholars have understood Isaiah 6–12 to form a coherent whole, at least in its final form, opening with the so-called *Denkschrift* or "memoir" of Isaiah (Isa. 6:1–9:6) and continuing with a series of related oracles that culminate in the deliverance of Judah from the Assyrian threat (Isa. 9:7–12:6). Apparently, we're to understand that Nephi saw the same seven chapters holistically, recognizing the totality they form. Further, there's no question that Isaiah 13–14 form a coherent whole, together making up the burden of Babylon. It's entirely unsurprising that Nephi lumps these two chapters of Isaiah together. The only slightly puzzling move—here's why I said a moment ago that the original chapters follow today's interpreters of Isaiah only "relatively closely"—the only slightly puzzling move is the weaving together of Isaiah 2–4 and Isaiah 5 as a single, coherent totality in Second Nephi's original Chapter VIII. Today, more or less all interpreters of Isaiah regard these chapters (Isa. 2–5) as containing, in final form, two distinct textual units: chapters 2–4 and chapter 5. But Nephi treats them as one. But then let's note already that there are certain textual variants in the opening verse of Isaiah 5 as quoted in the Book of Mormon that bridges what in the biblical text is a transition-less break. The reader of the Book of Mormon is apparently to understand that Isaiah 2–5 was a single textual unit, a single prophecy, in Nephi's source text—in the brass plates, that is.

So it's clear we've got to give some credence to the original chapter breaks here. We won't get far in the "Isaiah chapters" if we don't have an eye on the fact that Nephi seems to want us to see these chapters of Isaiah as telling us three successive stories. And we can say something about what's to be found in each of these three stories. First, Isaiah 2–5 tells of Israel's waywardness, of a general abandonment on Israel's part of their covenantal responsibility, and the consequence of all this is announced to be chaos within and oppression from without. Second, Isaiah 6–12 tells of how God plans to do something with this situation, aiming to use Israel's ill-timed waywardness to reduce the covenant people to just a remnant—a people within the people who will be prepared to pursue righteousness and the fulfillment of Israel's covenant obligation. Third, Isaiah 13–14 tells of the subsequent fall of Israel's enemies, an event that makes way for the full redemption of the covenant people. Together, these three sequences tell a coherent story: (1) Israel goes wildly astray and ends up in serious trouble, but (2) God uses that trouble to purify Israel and prepare them for full redemption through (3) the eventual destruction of their enemies. Nephi seems to have chosen out these thirteen chapters of Isaiah and divided them into three sequences in order to tell this three-part story. In fact, we'll see that he himself makes this three-part story perfectly clear in 2 Nephi 25. All this is clearly intentional.

In light of all this, it's relatively clear where we need to go with our next handful of lectures. We'll want to work through these three sequences. We can't tackle whole sequences in single lectures, for the most part. Certainly, it would be impossible to handle the whole of the massively complex second sequence, Isaiah 6–12 or 2 Nephi 16–22, in one meeting. So we'll have to work our way through the three sequences somewhat more slowly than that. Here's what I propose. I'd like to spend the remainder of our discussion today just on 2 Nephi 11 and the first few verses of 2 Nephi 12—that is, on Nephi's few words of introduction to the "Isaiah chapters" as such, and then on the opening prophecy of the first sequence. That should set us up well for next time. We'll see if we can't get all the way through the rest of the first sequence in our next lecture. And then we'll have to slow down a bit when we come to the second sequence. We'll be able to speed up again when we come to the third sequence, since it's only two chapters long and it's relatively straightforward, at least in comparison to the rest of this material.

If we're all okay to proceed as I've just laid things out, let's get to work.

Notes on 2 Nephi 11

The first sequence of the "Isaiah chapters" consists of 2 Nephi 11–15, where you can find Isaiah 2–5. But notice that you find there a little bit more than Isaiah 2–5, since 2 Nephi 11 consists of Nephi's words, a kind of introduction to the lengthy quotation of Isaiah. I don't want to dwell too terribly long on what Nephi says there—at least in part because I've commented on it at some length elsewhere (take a look at *An Other Testament*, if you dare). So let's move quickly here for a few minutes.

2 Nephi 11 opens with Nephi explaining the motivation behind the triadic structure of "the more sacred things." He and Jacob saw the Redeemer that makes up the focus of Isaiah's prophecy, and so they're prepared to provide plain and precious explanations of the Old-World prophet's writings. That's simple enough, and "by the words of three" God "will establish [his] word," as Nephi familiarly explains (2 Ne. 11:3). With this preliminary point made, Nephi goes on to provide a few words about the typological nature of the Law of Moses. These verses are, I think, theologically quite complex. We're accustomed to saying that the Law served as the repository of a whole host of symbolic rituals, all meant to point to the coming Christ. And you can find passages in Abinadi's and Benjamin's speeches in Mosiah that make that claim very clearly. But Nephi seems to mean something different with his talk of typology. This is signaled at the very least by his curious wording. He says that the Law, and in fact "all things which have been given of God," are—here's the odd wording—"the typifying of him" (v. 4). That's a weird formulation, and it's one that has pretty large implications. The fact that he says that this holds not only of the Law, but also of every God-given gift, is significant also. It suggests that Nephi's interested in a much broader or more general concept of the typological than other Book of Mormon figures. Again, I'll forbear from getting into this in any detail. Let's leave it at this: Nephi wants to get clear, theologically, about the status of the Law of Moses before he turns his attention directly to the quotation of Isaiah. The Law has to be read typologically, but the Prophets should be read in a different way. It's this he makes clear in the last verse of 2 Nephi 11.

How to read Isaiah, then, if not typologically—meaning, christologically? Nephi uses a word we're more than used to by now: *likening*. Here is 2 Nephi 11:8: "And now I write some of the words of Isaiah that whoso of my people which shall see these words may lift up their hearts and rejoice for all men. Now, these are the words, and ye may liken them unto you and unto all men." Isaiah is to be likened. We've seen that a half-dozen times by now. But let's notice immediately that there's something a bit odd about what Nephi says here about likening. Remember how this works everywhere else in Nephi's writings so far—including in Jacob's contribution to "the more sacred things." Likening has so far been a matter of taking prophetic words addressed to the whole of Israel and applying or adapting them quite specifically just to a remnant or a branch of Israel. The idea seems to have been that what's addressed to Israel in general can, without much violence, be adapted to Israel in rather specific circumstances. But here in 2 Nephi 11, Nephi seems to be broadening the concept of likening. There's no real talk of Israel here. Instead, it's about "all men." What are we to make of that?

Well, notice that Nephi *twice* mentions "all men." First, he says that his own people, Israelites all of them, might "lift up their hearts and rejoice for all men" when they read Isaiah 2–14. Second, he says directly to his own people, still Israelites, that they're certainly free to liken Isaiah 2–14 to themselves, but they might also "liken them . . . unto all men." So maybe we spoke a little too soon a moment ago. There *is* real talk of Israel here, since Nephi's talking about his own people. Nonetheless, the only bit of Israel that comes into the story at this point is a branch or a remnant of Israel—not the whole of Israel, and apparently nothing of Old-World Israel. And of course Israel comes into this passage only as the people who can rejoice "for all men" and liken the text to themselves inasmuch as they're among "all men." It seems that Nephi wants his people to keep their eyes on the way these particular chapters of Isaiah, about to be quoted, focus in a peculiar way on *everyone*, Israel and Gentiles alike.

Perhaps there's something to be said here about the focus and applicability of different parts of the Book of Isaiah, then? We noted a few lectures back that once Jacob's sermon is over we shift pretty definitively from a consistent focus on materials from Second Isaiah (from Isaiah 40–55) to a consistent focus on materials from First Isaiah (from Isaiah 2–39). Perhaps we're to understand at this point that the program of likening we traced in First Nephi and in Jacob's contribution to Second Nephi applies *uniquely* to Second Isaiah materials. That is, perhaps we're to understand that it's specifically Isaiah 40–55 (or really, given what Nephi and Jacob actually quote from Second Isaiah, Isaiah 48–55) that's addressed to all of Israel and therefore can be likened to remnants or branches of Israel. And then perhaps we're to understand that once we turn our attention to First Isaiah materials, we have to outline a somewhat distinct program of likening, one that finds Isaianic prophecy to apply to *all* nations, with Israel simply ranked among them. That is, perhaps we're to understand that Isaiah 2–39 (or really, given what Nephi actually quotes from First Isaiah, Isaiah 2–33) has a good deal larger scope than the later parts of the book.

There may be good reasons to think this is the case. Let's note, for instance, that a major portion of First Isaiah—today's chapters 13–23—constitute a set of oracles against the nations, and that Judah and Israel are simply ranked among the nations that come in for prophetic criticism. It's a bit difficult in reading those chapters to think that Israel has anything like a unique status among the nations. That's intriguing, to say the least. But the same can't be said of much of the rest of First Isaiah, and especially of the chapters Nephi focuses on: Isaiah 2–14 and Isaiah 28–29. In these chapters, there's a story to be told about Israel's peculiar role among the nations, among all peoples. So I don't think we've quite got the picture right yet.

Here, instead, is what I think is going on here. Note that the remnant of Israel that Nephi addresses in 2 Nephi 11 is to "rejoice for all men." That's important, I think. The point isn't that Israel is just one among so many nations. Instead, it seems the point is that Israel is to develop a certain attitude toward the nations, an attitude of joy at their repentance and redemption. The nations that deal with Israel in Isaiah 2–14 are effectively presented with a choice. They can work against God's people and God's purposes, and the result will be destruction. Or they can work for and with God's people and God's purposes, and the result will be their inclusion among those who worship God at Mount Zion. And the fact of the matter is that Isaiah 2–14 begins with a prophecy of the nations doing precisely that, joining Israel in the worship of the true God. Moreover, Isaiah 2–14 ends with a prophecy of the nations rejoicing at the collapse of Israel's most serious enemies, aligning themselves with Israel as so many servants. So *here's* the picture I think we're getting with Nephi's talk of "all men." There's a story in Isaiah 2–14 about how the nations find themselves freed alongside Israel from massive political oppression, and, because they recognize that Israel's God produced their freedom through his peculiar work with Israel, they join in the worship of Israel's God.

Why is this a matter of *likening*, in Nephi's words? That, I think, can be answered rather straightforwardly. Isaiah 2–14 tells this story in terms of very specific historical sequences—the rise and subsequent fall of two successive imperial powers from ancient times, Assyria and Babylon. But it seems Nephi wants to read this story as typical of the whole history of the world. These are nations that, on Nephi's reading, stand in for much larger historical forces. And so it's not just the nations of Isaiah's day or thereabouts who can join with Israel in the worship of the true God. It's "all men," eventually, who can and will do so. That's reason to rejoice, no? And it's certainly reason to liken this text to everyone.

The Covenant's Fulfillment

Now, with what time we've got left today, let's turn to the opening of Isaiah 2, the first oracle quoted in the first sequence of Nephi's three-sequence quotation of Isaiah 2–14. We just mentioned it a moment ago. Isaiah 2–14 begins, we said, with a prophecy of the nations joining Israel in the worship of the true God at Mount Zion. Let's take a look at that prophecy, and we'll see that Nephi says something about likening Isaiah 2–14 to "all men" for a pretty clear reason, and it's significant that he does so *immediately* before he quotes this opening oracle.

You're all familiar with the passage, I'm sure. But let's quote it in full. I'll quote it in the Book of Mormon's rendering, because it appears there with a variant or two we'll want to keep an eye on. Here it is:

> The word that Isaiah the son of Amoz saw concerning Judah and Jerusalem, and it shall come to pass in the last days, when the mountain of the Lord's house shall be established in the top of the mountains and shall be exalted above the hills, and all nations shall flow unto it and many people shall go and say, "Come ye, and let us go up to the mountain of the Lord, to the house of the God of Jacob! And he will teach us of his ways, and we will walk in his paths!"—for out of Zion shall go forth the law, and the word of the Lord from Jerusalem—and he shall judge among the nations and shall rebuke many people, and they shall beat their swords into plowshares and their spears into pruning hooks, nation shall not lift up sword against nation; neither shall they learn war anymore. (2 Ne. 12:1–4)

Getting the grammar and punctuation right for the Book of Mormon version of this passage is difficult, but let's leave that question to one side for a moment, since the general theme of the passage is clear enough. Clearly, Isaiah is seeing something "concerning Judah and Jerusalem," and it's what "shall come to pass in the last days." And what's that "something"? He's clear about that as well. The Lord's house is to be "established in the top of the mountains," exalted above every other form of worship and towering over all nations. And then we find "all nations" flowing to it, like rivers inexplicably running uphill—so many Gentile nations urging each other to seek out the true God worshiped by Israel. As they arrive at the temple, they let God adjudicate their differences and so give up their constant warfare with one another. According to Isaiah's *beautiful* image, "they shall beat their swords into plowshares and their spears into pruning hooks." At last, there's peace among the nations: "nation shall not lift up sword against nation; neither shall they learn war anymore." (On one reading of the grammar and punctuation, it's only those last two lines that function as independent clauses in the whole passage. And anyway, there's a clear emphasis on them.)

But what to say of this prophecy? I think if we were to put its thrust in the simplest possible way, it would be this: *Isaiah 2–14 opens with a clear anticipation of the fulfillment of the Abrahamic covenant.* And *that* is reason for Israel, as Nephi puts it, to "rejoice for all men." Remember the focus of the Abrahamic covenant, something we discussed a bit some lectures back. In response to proliferating violence—violence that results either from private selfish desires or from self-definition in terms of national identity— God called Abraham to launch a two-faceted program: the first of direct or even private hospitality for individuals, and the second of a more general pursuit of peace through the redefinition of human beings as part of one universal family. Abraham's children, Israel, would have the responsibility of reconciling all the nations (the Gentiles) to each other by inviting them to worship the true God. And Isaiah opens his prophecy with a clear anticipation of that program finally coming to full fruition. The nations at peace, subjecting themselves to God's righteous judgment as they come up to the temple where Israel worships the only God that *is* God.

That seems terribly important to me—that Isaiah, as Nephi copies him down, begins with this vision of the future. Everything we'll be looking at after this oracle in Isaiah 2–14 must be seen in its bright light. Indeed, we can tell the triple story of Isaiah 2–14 quite precisely in terms of what Isaiah here anticipates. Let's take a minute to do just that.

In the first sequence of Nephi's quotation—that is, in Isaiah 2–5 (or 2 Nephi 12–15)—we get a clear contrast between what's to come and where things are at presently. Israel and all nations will gather together in peace to worship the true God someday, but for the moment Israel is entirely flouting its responsibility to the nations, with the result that Israel is largely indistinguishable from them. The nations aren't joining Israel in offering hospitality to those in need; instead, Israel is joining the nations in the systematic oppression of the poor. The nations aren't reconciling themselves one to another as Israel invites them to recognize their fraternal identity; instead, Israel seeks to define itself in terms of military might in full imitation of what the Gentile nations. The result, horrifically, is that the nations *do* indeed come swarming to Israel, but only to lay her in ruins. There's a promise already of a remnant who'll escape, but the emphasis is unmistakably on the perfect inversion in the present of what's to be anticipated in the future.

Then in the second sequence of Nephi's quotation—now in Isaiah 6–12 (or 2 Nephi 16–22)—our attention is turned to the process of producing the remnant that's only mentioned in passing in the first sequence. The task of the surviving remnant will of course be to accomplish the work of the Abrahamic covenant, to see to the work of converting the nations to peace and to the worship of the true God. Isaiah himself is key to this story, since he's commissioned at the outset of this second sequence to preach a message that will be entirely rejected—circumstances that then lead him to recognize that his message is directed primarily to a later age. The people of that later age is, of course, precisely the remnant that's being produced through the difficult events of Isaiah's own day, through the devastation of Israel due to its complete abandonment of its covenant responsibility to the nations. The whole of the second sequence of Isaianic text works through the devastating process of winnowing Israel down to the remnant that will be prepared to make real sense of Isaiah's message. And it culminates with the announcement of divinely appointed leaders—perhaps actually *divine* leaders—who will arise to lead the remnant as they turn their attention to their true task. Thus where the first sequence marks the complete inversion of the inaugural vision of the fulfillment of the Abrahamic covenant, the second sequence marks the beginnings of a conversion to that possibility. The slow production or emergence of the righteous remnant, ready with Isaiah's prophecies in hand and a divine or divinely appointed leader to guide them, makes possible the ultimate fulfillment of Isaiah's opening anticipation.

Finally, in the third sequence—in Isaiah 13–14 (or 2 Nephi 23–24)—the last obstacle for fulfillment of Isaiah's inaugural vision is removed. The imperial power that ruins all nations and closes the door on all things Abrahamic finally collapses. The former rulers of the nations that are now free to join the righteous Israelite remnant in the building of a new Jerusalem join together in the realm of the dead in mocking the fallen imperial power. They recognize in song the removal of the last obstacle to peace. That imperial power, Isaiah is careful to note, will be without any remnant, and its final ruler's corpse will be left to rot "like an abominable branch" (2 Ne.

24:19). In strict antithetical parallel to the Israelite branch or remnant that celebrates God in conjunction with the nations finally at peace, oppressive powers are left at the end without remnant or branch, condemned to an eternity in hell. And the whole thing ends with messengers arriving from all the nations who announce "that the Lord hath founded Zion, and the poor of his people shall trust in it" (v. 32). With the last obstacle out of the way, Isaiah's opening vision comes to perfect fulfillment.

All this couldn't be much clearer, no? There's a straightforward story to be told in "the Isaiah chapters," and it takes all of its orientation from this opening vision of Israelites and Gentiles worshiping together in Zion. It's no surprise whatsoever that Nephi sees *this* triple sequence of Isaianic texts to be likenable to "all men" and to give reasons to rejoice for "all men." What we're looking at here is the way that the eventual redemption of Israel is inseparable from the ultimate redemption of the whole world. This is good news for all.

And now we've got a basic picture, I think, of what we're to expect going forward in Nephi's long quotation of Isaiah. I hope you're already thinking to yourself that this stuff isn't nearly so hard as you've always thought. It's of course plenty difficult. And we'll look at passages that become clear only after careful analysis, certainly. But the overarching picture isn't too terribly difficult, I think. You can get a basic sense for what's going on without a lot of trouble. And that basic sense will be crucial going forward. Keep a close eye on this really big picture we've sketched. Every detail fits into this larger picture, and we'll only hurt ourselves by losing sight of it. At every step along the way, keep an eye on where we are in this larger story, and everything will make a good deal of sense. I promise.

Well, we're about out of time, and we're actually not racing the clock for once! Next time, let's turn our attention to the whole of the first sequence of the "Isaiah chapters"—that is, to Isaiah 2–5 as Nephi quotes them. Our first aim will be just to get a decent sense for what's going on in these first chapters. And I think we'll find that we're successful. Of everything we'll be reading in Isaiah, these are probably the easiest to get our minds around. It's only when we get beyond them to Isaiah 6–12 that things will get pretty difficult. So let's enjoy things while they remain relatively simple!

Lecture XIV

Isaiah 2–5

So, our task today is just to get a decent, general sense for Isaiah 2–5, recorded in 2 Nephi 12–15. And today's the only day we'll spend on these chapters. We can get away with that because Nephi seldom refers back to Isaiah 2–5 later. It's really the material to be found in Isaiah 6–12 (recorded in 2 Nephi 16–22) that seems to get him excited. So we can move kind of quickly here. And we've already covered some of the material, since we gave our attention last time to the opening verses of Isaiah 2, the vision of the fulfillment of the Abrahamic covenant that sets the stage for everything Nephi finds in Isaiah.

Isaiah's Present and Future

Here's the place to start, then: with the contrast Isaiah draws between that remarkable day of fulfillment and the terribly depressing situation of Israel during Isaiah's own time. Immediately after the vision of the nations streaming up Zion's hill to join Israel in peaceful submission to God, Isaiah says this: "O house of Jacob! Come *ye*, and let us walk in the light of the Lord. Yea, come! For ye have all gone astray—every one to his wicked ways!" (2 Ne. 12:5). You hear what I'm emphasizing in that quotation. It's one thing to reflect on the day when the Gentile nations will seek to walk in the Lord's paths. It's another thing, though, to realize that in the meanwhile *even Israel* isn't on the right path, isn't "walking in the light of the Lord." And Isaiah calls them out for it. You should be aware that this is clearer in the Book of Mormon version of the text. Nephi either himself adds, or at least finds in the brass plates text he has in his possession, words that don't appear in your King James Bible: "Yea, come! For ye have all gone astray—every one to his wicked ways!" This makes starkly clear the transition from the vision of fulfillment to the bitter reality of Isaiah's own rather unfulfilling circumstances.

The distinct text of Book of Mormon Isaiah here is interesting in another regard, though. Do you recognize the language of the additional line, its talk of going astray, every one to his wicked ways? It's the language of Isaiah 53, that Isaiah chapter of Isaiah chapters that describes the suffering of God's servant, by whose stripes others are healed. You know the prophecy. (It's likely the only chapter of Isaiah you're terribly comfortable with, right?) In the course of describing the suffering of the servant, the plural speakers of that prophecy say this: "All we like sheep have gone astray; we have turned every one to his own way; and the Lord hath laid on him the iniquity of us all" (Isa. 53:6). There's the apparent source for the language of Isaiah 2:5 in Nephi's version. Nephi's Isaiah opens his excoriation of Israel by telling them that they've gone astray, every one to his own wicked way. They're the people of Isaiah 53, the very ones who will later collectively confess to having gone astray, to having turned every one to his own way, while the Lord laid their iniquity on his suffering servant. That's a remarkable connection, I think. Remember that the Book of Isaiah as Nephi had it seems to have begun with Isaiah 2 and to have ended shortly after Isaiah 53, so that it opens and closes with parallel descriptions of Israel's waywardness. Nephi's Book of Isaiah traces the path of Israel's shift from having to be told that they're off God's path to willfully confessing that they've been off that path. When they finally make that confession, perhaps the fulfillment of the vision that contrasts with their apostate condition can finally come to pass.

That's really fun stuff, I think. But I'm already going far, far too slowly if we're going to get through Isaiah 2–5 today! After marking the transition from the vision of the covenant's fulfillment to the excoriation of Israel's apostate condition, Isaiah gives us a series of accusations. Really, we get several series of accusations over the course of these four chapters, divided up by bits of prophecy about Israel's disastrous future. The first of them should perhaps command our attention most sustainedly, since it's what Isaiah gives us first. It's relatively simple, even if you have to riddle your way through some of Isaiah's cultural references. There are, he says, several things their land is "full" of (or, in one odd case, "replenished" with). First and last, he mentions idolatrous religion—"soothsayers like the Philistines" (2 Ne. 12:6) and the "worship" of "the work of their own hands" (v. 8). Sandwiched between these two mentions of idols, however, he tells us what else fills up their land, and it's perhaps this that helps to clarify their interest in idolatrous cults: "Their land also is full of silver and gold, neither is there any end of their treasures. Their land is also full of horses, neither is there any end of their chariots" (v. 7). What's at issue here? It's easy enough to understand the references to "silver and gold" and "treasures." Israel's after wealth, like all the other idolatrous nations. But what of the reference to "horses" and "chariots"? Horses and chariots were used for one thing, and one thing only, in the world of Isaiah's day: war. Israel had become a warmongering people, seeking not only wealth but also military might.

I can't resist the temptation to insert a reference here to Spencer W. Kimball's beautiful talk, "The False Gods We Worship," given in 1976. Hugh Nibley used to refer to it often. In the course of the talk, President Kimball said that Latter-day Saints are given to two forms of idolatry in particular: selfishly seeking wealth and trusting in military power. Perhaps Israel hasn't changed much. But I don't want to get distracted with questions of application. Let's be clear about this: Isaiah claims that Israel goes astray by seeking out abundant wealth and military might. And it's apparently these desires that draw them into the ancient idolatrous cults they could find all around them. At the very time Isaiah sees in vision that the nations who sponsor those idolatrous cults will eventually abandon their idols in order to promote universal peace, Israel is abandoning their responsibility to sue for peace and joining in the idolatrous lust for economic and military control over the world. The Gentile nations will turn from their idolatry and warmongering to seek out the true God. Israel at the time is turning from the true God to seek out idolatry and warmongering. The contrast between the covenant's future and its present is pretty sad.

Consequent Judgment

And so Isaiah turns from listing particular sins to describing where things are going to go for Israel: "O ye wicked ones! Enter into the rock, and hide thee in the dust! For the fear of the Lord and the glory of his majesty shall smite thee!" (2 Ne. 12:10). Over the course of several verses, Isaiah confirms this picture by describing the fall of everything high and lifted up—"the lofty looks of man" (v. 11), "the cedars of Lebanon" (v. 13), "every high tower" (v. 15), "all the ships of the sea" with their towering masts (v. 16), and so on. All high things will be brought low—all, of course, except the Lord himself: "And the Lord alone shall be exalted in that day" (v. 17). What apparently lay behind the process of accumulation that resulted in so many exalted human productions—every one eventually razed to the ground—is idolatry. And as everything but the Lord's highness comes crashing down, Israel finally relinquishes its worship of idols. They run for cover, seeking out "the holes of the rocks" and "the caves of the earth" (v. 19), throwing their idols "to the moles and to the bats" (v. 20)—those blind and ritually unclean cave-dwellers—hoping they won't be found in possession of the very gods who have ruined them.

But what does this event of social collapse look like in more concrete terms? In Isaiah 2 (2 Ne. 12), we get classically Isaianic images: cedars of Lebanon and oaks of Bashan, the ships of Tarshish and other now-obscure cultural references. But in Isaiah 3, the prophet gets a good deal more explicit, setting aside evocative but now-dated imagery for direct description of what collapse would look like for the covenant people. First, basic staples run out as drought and famine prevail: "The Lord of Hosts doth take away from Jerusalem and from Judah . . . the whole staff of bread and the whole stay of water" (2 Ne. 13:1). Established authorities—Isaiah gives a whole list of them (vv. 2–3)—lose control over the people, while "children" becomes "princes" (v. 4). The social chaos causes a general panic as viable leadership can't be found. Any would-be savior, though, responds to repeated requests for help with "Make me not a ruler of the people!" (v. 7). And it's just as well, since everything that's gone wrong—"Jerusalem is ruined! And Judah is fallen!" (v. 8)—is ultimately to be traced back to corrupt leaders. "O my people," the Lord says, "they which lead thee cause thee to err" (v. 12).

At this point we get a second specific accusation, a second identification of Israel's sin. It's perhaps a bit tricky, thanks to the complications of historical interpretation. Isaiah says that the people's "countenance . . . doth declare their sin to be even as Sodom" (2 Ne. 13:9), but don't assume you know exactly what that means. The ancients understood the sin of Sodom to be lack of hospitality and mistreatment of the poor. This is clear in Ezekiel: "Behold, this was the iniquity of thy sister Sodom, pride, fulness of bread, and abundance of idleness was in her and in her daughters, neither did she strengthen the hand of the poor and needy" (Ezek. 16:49). And it's also clear, despite our obfuscations, right in the story of Sodom and Gomorrah in Genesis, where the people of Sodom, unlike Abraham, refuse to house wandering strangers and then respond with violence when Lot actually bothers to feed them (see Gen. 19). So let's be clear about this: Israel's sin is Sodom's sin, and that means that they oppress the poor. Isaiah himself makes this perfectly clear. When he expands on Israel's specific sin, this is what he says: "Ye have eaten up the vineyard and the spoil of the poor in your houses. . . . Ye beat my people to pieces and grind the faces of the poor" (2 Ne. 13:14–15). What lies behind Israel's social catastrophe is their consistent support for leaders who create an opulent life for the wealthy through systematic exploitation of the many poor.

War and Women

And following immediately on the collapse of social order within Israel, according to Isaiah, is violence against Israel from without. There's a cry of war. And it's not going to go well. Israel of course tries to get out of danger by using a classic strategy, one you can find used in desperate situations of violence throughout the Old Testament and the Book of Mormon. They send out the women of the city, dressed to the nines, offering their charms to the invading army in the hopes of delivering the city from violence and destruction. They come out "with stretched forth necks and wanton eyes, walking and mincing as they go" (2 Ne. 13:16), covered in jewelry. But the Lord's apparently less than impressed with this sort of thing, stripping the women bare—"the Lord will discover their secret parts," Isaiah says (v. 17)—and sending them off into slavery—"instead of a girdle a rent" or a rope (v. 24). And then, with the women hauled off by the invading army, the men face their doom: "Thy men shall fall by the sword, and thy mighty in the war, and her gates shall lament and mourn" (vv. 25–26).

I have to add a couple of words about the reading I've just given you of the last part of Isaiah 3. Latter-day Saints tend to read that passage as a divine condemnation of fashion and fine apparel. It's certainly in part that, since there's so much in the surrounding context concerning the evils of hoarded wealth and oppression of the poor. But there's a historical context that's crucial for understanding Isaiah's discussion of "the daughters of Zion" who "are haughty" (2 Ne. 13:16). There's a pretty clear reference here to that ancient practice of offering women to invading warriors in the hopes of securing escape for the men. You might remember, in fact, that this is something Lot tries in Sodom, when violence and lack of hospitality make themselves manifest in Genesis 19. This move comprises Lot's complicity in Sodom's sinfulness, in fact. Is it any surprise that we get the same from Israel in Isaiah 3? Facing the violence of a war they can't hope to win—a war, moreover, they've brought on themselves through their systematic mistreatment of society's most vulnerable—they send out the women in the hopes of transforming violence toward men into violence toward women, warriors taking advantage of the lawlessness of battle to claim whatever (violently executed) pleasures they desire. The Lord will have none of it, though, thank heaven. In the place of satiated lust and violence on the women's persons, the warriors execute the Lord's warning or promise that bondage is coming to Israel. And then the Israelite men suffer for their abuses.

So there's the rather clearer story Isaiah wishes to tell about all high things being brought low. Leaving off images for direct description, he tells us of Israel's social collapse, a time when drought and famine force the illusion of prosperity to reveal itself for what it is: a cover for Israel's systematic mistreatment of the poor. And this is followed quickly by an opportunist war (what better time to attack than when the enemy is already weakened?), a war that results in slavery for Israel's women and death for Israel's men. Things are bad, and Israel is ruined.

A Remnant Delivered

Well, not entirely ruined. Here's the weird thing. After all this talk of devastation and death and horror, there's a word of promise that gets slipped into Isaiah's prophecy. It's only a few verses long, and it's immediately followed by predictions of more misfortune. But it's an important word of promise, a first hint at a major theme in subsequent chapters of Isaiah's book. So let's give at least a minute or two to this intervening word concerning possible redemption. It concerns, oddly, "that day" (2 Ne. 14:2)—that is, the day when Israel's collapse is complete and Jerusalem "shall be desolate and shall sit upon the ground" (2 Ne. 13:26). But here's the word of promise Isaiah gives: "In that day shall the branch of the Lord be beautiful and glorious, the fruit of the earth excellent and comely, to them that are escaped of Israel" (2 Ne. 14:2). Let's note first that the focus here is on "them that are escaped of Israel," the war's survivors. This is the group Isaiah usually calls *the remnant*, a theme we'll be highlighting often. So already here we have a clear indication that any dark days Israel is called to pass through serve a kind of purpose. So much internal strife, followed by devastating war, but all this is supposed to produce from among Israel a righteous remnant.

And what's the remnant doing in this word of promise? Apparently, they're admiring "the branch of the Lord," which finally bears fruit both "excellent and comely." It might not be obvious if you aren't familiar with Hebrew prophecy, but this is most likely to be understood as a messianic reference. Jeremiah twice uses the image of a branch as a title of sorts for the Davidic king who would "reign and prosper" and then "execute judgment and justice in the earth" (Jer. 23:5; 33:15). You can find the same thing in Zechariah, where the King James Version of the Bible even uses all capitals in rendering the word (see Zech. 3:8; 6:12). Importantly, another passage from Isaiah also calls a promised Davidic king the branch—a passage we'll be looking at closely later (see Isaiah 11:1). So it seems likely we're to understand the word of promise in Isaiah 4 as linking Israel's remnant to the appearance of some kind of messianic figure, a royal Davidic ruler who dwells with redeemed Israel. And of course we've already seen that all the devastation preceding the fulfillment of this word of promise comes in connection with the moment when the Lord "shall be exalted" and "the glory of his majesty shall smite" the wicked (2 Ne. 12:10–11).

So there's a remnant, purified and delivered. They're led to lands of promise in a kind of second exodus (see 2 Ne. 14:5–6). And we're told this of them: "them that are left in Zion and remaineth in Jerusalem shall be called holy—every one that is written among the living in Jerusalem" (2 Ne. 14:3). The surviving remnant is holy, and their names are "written among the living"—or, as the underlying Hebrew is often translated today, their names are "written for life." Interpreters generally agree that there lies behind this reference the ancient belief, still very much alive among Latter-day Saints, that there is a book of life that's kept in heaven, in which the names of the righteous are recorded. The remnant, dwelling together with a messianic deliverer, makes up the saints whose names are found in the book of life. That's a beautiful word of promise, perhaps well needed in the middle of so much talk of devastation and destruction.

The Song of the Vineyard

But the word of promise doesn't last long. It gives us just a short respite, because Isaiah 5 (or 2 Nephi 15) takes us right back to prophecies of judgment, and it especially refocuses us on specifiable sins associated with Israel's waywardness. Isaiah 5 opens with the famous song of the vineyard. You'll likely remember it. Isaiah sings a song about a vineyard to his beloved—a song about "a vineyard in a very fruitful hill" (2 Ne. 15:1), properly prepared by its owner to produce the best fruit possible. What does it do, though? "It brought forth wild grapes" (v. 4), and so Isaiah announces his beloved's intention to lay the vineyard waste. At the song's conclusion, we get this: "The vineyard of the Lord of Hosts is the house of Israel, and the men of Judah his pleasant plant" (v. 7). It's a pretty transparent allegory. And in fact, in a beautiful play on words in Hebrew, Isaiah decodes the whole thing. The owner of the vineyard looked for grapes and found only wild grapes. Isaiah explains: "He looked for judgment—and behold, oppression! For righteousness—but behold, a cry!" (v. 7). The English translation doesn't capture what Isaiah's doing there. In Hebrew, "he looked for *mishpat*," for upright judgment in behalf of the vulnerable, "and behold, *mispakh*," violence and bloodshed. You see the play on words? Followed by, he looked "for *tsedaqah*," for justice and covenantal fidelity, "but behold, *tse'aqah*," a cry due to oppression. There's the meaning of the song. Israel was carefully established by the Lord, and he looked to see them repeat Abrahamic behavior. All he could see, though, was their imitation of wrongdoing by the nations Abraham was called to minister to.

Interestingly, in the Book of Mormon version of the Isaiah text, this song is presented as something sung "*then*" (2 Ne. 15:1)—that is, at that day when the word of promise from Isaiah 4 is fulfilled. (This is a consequence of the way the Book of Mormon makes Isaiah 2–4 and Isaiah 5 into a single chapter.) The projection of the song of the vineyard into the future is a peculiar thing. In the biblical presentation of Isaiah, one understands that the song of the vineyard is utilized as a kind of sneak-attack form of prophecy. Love songs that began in much the way the song of the vineyard begins were often sung at harvest festivals in Israel—when wine was flowing and everyone was happy. Interpreters of Isaiah suggest that the prophet showed up at such a festival and offered to add a song to those being sung by others. After starting in a way everyone would recognize, though, his song took a critical turn, and it suddenly became clear that Isaiah was taking advantage of the occasion to call Israel out for the sins we've already seen him criticize. The Book of Mormon doesn't deny that the song had its origins in that sort of context, but it curiously projects the song into the future, making it something that will need to be sung once Israel has been reduced to just a remnant.

In the end, though, perhaps that makes good sense. It's as the remnant beholds the branch and its excellent, comely fruit—grapes, perhaps?—that the song of the vineyard is finally sung. Isaiah 4 gives us a word of promise that's not without its connection to the harvest. And perhaps it's only possible from that eschatological setting to make any real sense of the Lord's complex handling of Israel's history. Maybe the remnant will feel like there's some explaining to do regarding the devastations they've uniquely escaped. At any rate, Nephi's Isaiah places the song of the vineyard at the end of Israel's complicated history, and the song retroactively explains the history of Israel's waywardness. Perhaps it's no surprise, then, that the remainder of Isaiah 5 focuses first on the various sins for which Israel is guilty and then on the consequent destructions Israel will face. A word of promise is followed by an accusation regarding Israel's problematic history, which, once reviewed, is seen to lead to dire consequences. That's exactly what we saw in Isaiah 2–3 just a few minutes ago. So let's work our way through what Isaiah has to say about Israel's sins and their consequences in the rest of Isaiah 5.

Israel's Sin

Occupying the center of Isaiah 5 is a series of so-called woe-oracles, prophetic words of condemnation that organize themselves into a series through the repetition of the word "woe." We get six of them here, of drastically varying length. The first three are all a few verses long each, and they're interrupted, moreover, by a five-verse-long aside about how all these sins justify Israel's going into captivity. The final three woes are all quite short, offered collectively in the course of just four verses. Interestingly, two of the woes—one of the longer ones, and one of the shorter ones—focus on the same sin, and it's closely connected to the song of the vineyard. Moreover, they together help to highlight the basic theme of all the woes. These two concern those who "rise up early in the morning that they may follow strong drink" (2 Ne. 15:11), those who are "mighty to drink wine" and "to mingle strong drink" (v. 22). Now, remember that the Word of Wisdom is a modern revelation, that nothing in the Law of Moses proscribed drinking wine. Yet Isaiah sees something symptomatic in the persistent drunkenness of Israel's elite. As he says in the first woe that focuses on wine, their revelry occupies them all the time, from "early in the morning" and "continu[ing] until night" (v. 11). It's wine and music all the time—"the harp and the viol, the tabret and pipe," and so on (v. 12)—and this distracts them from what's essential: "They regard not the work of the Lord, neither consider the operation of his hands" (v. 12). We talked about this theme way back, early in this lecture series. Running through Isaiah is an emphasis on the Lord's work, his large-scale historical plan with Israel. And here we're told that alcohol has become for Israel's rulers a way to forget, a way systematically to ignore that work. And according to the other woe-oracle focused on wine, they do this as they pursue their everyday corruption, "justify[ing] the wicked for reward and tak[ing] away the righteousness of the righteous from him" (v. 23).

We've got a sense for the theme of the woe-oracles? Israel has given itself to be ruled by corrupt officials who glut themselves on the labor of the poor, taking their positions of power and authority to license riotous behavior. And what they ignore, as a result, is quite precisely Isaiah's message concerning God's work, the Lord's massive project in history. The other woes, unsurprisingly, circulate around the same theme. The opening woe-oracle calls out the wealthy in Israel for buying up all the land—"them that join house to house till there can be no place" (2 Ne. 15:8)—so that the poor have to pay exorbitant rent. Isaiah promises famine for those causing such oppression. The third woe-oracle compares Israel's elite to work animals, yoked to heavy loads of sin they drag about, and the manifestation of their wickedness is the taunt with which they torment the prophet: "Let [the Lord] make speed," Isaiah! "Hasten his work that we may see it! And let the counsel"—that's one of Isaiah's words for the Lord's global-historical work—"let the counsel of the Holy One of Israel draw nigh and come that we may know it!" (v. 19). They demand immediate fulfillment of the Lord's whole plan for history, failing which they refuse to pay any further attention to Isaiah. In the other two of the shorter woe-oracles, we find Isaiah describing these people as those who "call evil good and good evil" (v. 20) and as "the wise in their own eyes and prudent in their own sight" (v. 21)—two rather self-explanatory words of condemnation.

So here's another set of accusations. And in the course of his aside at the heart of the woe-oracles, Isaiah announces that all this justifies the Lord's sending Israel into captivity. The realm of the dead—*sheol*, translated "hell" in the King James Version and the Book of Mormon—opens up to receive them, along with "their glory and . . . their pomp" (2 Ne. 15:14). All the high things are again brought down (we even get a repetition of Isaiah 2:9 in Isaiah 5:15, though the Book of Mormon complicates that repetition in certain ways), while God alone is exalted: "The eyes of the lofty shall be humbled, but the Lord of Hosts shall be exalted in judgment" (2 Ne. 5:15–16). Israel will become only a pasture for grazing animals. Here we have a kind of restatement of Isaiah 2—the exaltation of the Lord and the razing of Israel to the ground. So perhaps it's no surprise that the chapter concludes with a kind of restatement of Isaiah 3, and especially of the prophecy there of war.

That's how Isaiah 5 ends, then, with a prophecy of war against Israel. Oddly, there's a longstanding tradition among Latter-day Saints of reading this concluding prophecy here as about missionary work, but it's about war. You'll hear people refer to the bent bows and sharp arrows of Isaiah's prophecy, the whirlwind of wheels and the flinty hooves of horses, and they'll say that Isaiah's struggling here to describe trains or planes or whatever other modern means of transportation, carrying missionaries out to the world to preach the gospel. Missionaries, such argue, are those who "lay hold of the prey" and "carry away safe" (2 Ne. 15:29). We can grant that this sort of interpretation is imaginative and inventive, but it makes very little sense of the passage. Isaiah concludes this chapter with a prophecy of war and destruction. It opens with devouring fire and consuming flame, a response to those who "have cast away the law of the Lord of Hosts" (v. 24). And we're then told that "the anger of the Lord" is "kindled against his people," such that "their carcasses were torn in the midst of the streets" (v. 25). It's to accomplish this that the Lord here "will lift up an ensign to the nations from far" (v. 26). He's waving a banner to invite the armies of the nations to come and devastate Israel. This isn't the ensign you find elsewhere in scripture—elsewhere, in fact, in Isaiah—that signals a gathering place for Israel. It's a flag that's meant to signal the start of a war.

And so Isaiah prophesies destruction. Armies "come with speed swiftly" (2 Ne. 15:26). Their bows are bent with sharp arrows on the string. They come in their chariots (used only for war, remember), pulled by tireless horses (see 2 Ne. 15:28). And as they come to the battle, they do what all ancient armies did; they "roar like young lions" (2 Ne. 15:29). Sadly for Israel, they "lay hold of the prey . . . , and none shall deliver" (v. 29). The whole prophecy ends on an unmistakably dour note: "If they look unto the land, behold, darkness and sorrow, and the light is darkened in the heavens thereof" (v. 30). War and destruction, devastation and death, and all that's left at the end is darkness.

There's Isaiah 2–5 as presented in 2 Nephi 12–15. It's one simple story, told twice over. Each half of it opens with an anticipation of glorious things to come—a time when the nations come to the temple to worship the true God, giving up war at last (2 Ne. 12:1–4); a time when Israel's remnant is holy and ready to receive their messianic ruler (2 Ne. 14:2–6). This vision of things is then contrasted with Israel's condition at Isaiah's time, when they've given themselves over to rulers who systematically oppress the poor so that they can live the high life (2 Ne. 12:5–11; 13:8–15; 15:1–12, 18–23). In each half of Isaiah 2–5, we're then told that all this leads to collapse within Israel and attack from without Israel, culminating in a war that leaves Israel in ruins (2 Ne. 12:12–13:7; 13:16–14:1;

15:13–17, 24–30). But all this is the work of the Lord, with the possibility that a remnant will remain (2 Ne. 14:2–6 again), ready to return to the Lord (2 Ne. 12:1–4 again).

There's hope, then. But why and how? That's the subject of the next sequence of "the Isaiah chapters."

Lecture XV

Isaiah's Vision of God

The Place of Isaiah 6

Since we last met, I sat down to look at what we need to cover still. I think we can pull this off without having to skip over anything essential. I've decided to aim at focusing this and our next three meetings on Isaiah 6–12, reproduced in 2 Nephi 16–22. And my plan is to focus just on Isaiah 6 today *and* next time—unless, of course, we end up feeling like we can move more quickly. Isaiah 6 is especially important, I think, and it's rather complicated at the same time. So we need to give it close attention.

To see what's at stake here, we need to step back from Nephi's record to take in the whole scope of the project again. It's now been awhile since we last looked at questions of structure and such, so I hope you haven't forgotten the basics. Maybe you'll readily remember the richness of the structure we uncovered in First Nephi, which aims at training readers to understand Isaiah. Do you remember the basic structure of Second Nephi? It has an introduction of sorts (Lehi's final words to his sons) and a conclusion of sorts (Nephi's final exhortations regarding the gospel of Christ), but the body of it (Nephi's "more sacred things") consists of three successive prophetic sermons of sorts—one by Jacob, one by Isaiah, and one by Nephi. At the heart of things here is Isaiah, not just because the very chapters we're considering now make up the central stretch of this most privileged portion of Nephi's record, but also because Jacob and Nephi dedicate their contributions to quoting and explaining other Isaianic texts.

One way we might think of all this is to envision Second Nephi as a series of concentric circles. The outermost circle takes in the introductory and concluding material of the book, those bits that lie beyond the scope of Nephi's "more sacred things." The next circle inward consists of Jacob's and Nephi's treatments of Isaiah, preceding and following the long quotation of Isaiah we're now in the middle of. The innermost circle, of course, consists simply of these very "Isaiah chapters" in 2 Nephi 11–24.

So far, so good? But now let's note that we might well see *two* circles in this most central part of the text. There's a circle that takes in the first and third blocks of Isaiah text, Isaiah 2–5 (which we covered last time) and Isaiah 13–14 (which we'll cover a few lectures down the road). And then there's an innermost circle that covers just this block of Isaianic text we'll be looking at now, Isaiah 6–12. It's Nephi's record's heart of hearts, and it concerns the production of Israel's remnant, as we've already noted:

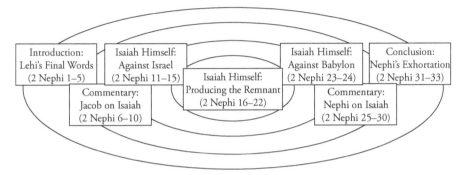

In tackling Isaiah 6 and what follows it, then, we're coming up against the very center of Nephi's writings.

A Remnant Story

We've already anticipated in previous lectures the basic topic we'll be dealing with here. The point of Isaiah 6–12, as Nephi sees it and as most good readers today see it, is to trace the Lord's production of an Israelite remnant. We mentioned this theme last time, since the remnant makes a brief appearance in Isaiah 4. Here, though, we leave off allusions and anticipations for systematic exposition. In Isaiah 6–12, we'll watch as the remnant comes into existence. As you might guess, the process is anything but simple. We've got seven chapters to cover, and they're notoriously difficult to interpret. These are, after all, the chapters that have most often left *you* scratching your head when you've read Nephi. And our job is to get quite clear about what they're saying as they track the production of the remnant.

To get started, remember where we left off last time. In Nephi's re-production of Isaiah 2–5 we get the same story told twice over. It's a relatively simple story. Isaiah looks with a prophetic eye to the day when the Abrahamic covenant is fulfilled, the vision of which gives reason to rejoice and to despair. The emphasis in those chapters is on the reasons we have to despair. Knowing what's coming, knowing what *could* be, Isaiah's forced to recognize how devastatingly far off from their destiny Israel is during his time (and maybe at all times!). So he turns in each telling of the story from prophetic anticipation of redemption to prophetic condemnation of corruption. The Israel of Isaiah's day has given itself to wickedness, and wickedness of a very specific sort. They oppress the poor in their support for corrupt leaders, hoping selfishly just to benefit materially from their support for the wealthy elite. And Isaiah doesn't hesitate to announce what the result of such corruption will be. It's internal calamity first (famine and social chaos), and this is to be followed by danger from without (war and devastation). But all this—here's the promise!—will result in the production of the remnant.

As we finish Isaiah 2–5, then, we're primed for Isaiah 6–12. We're ready—do you see it?—to learn how the remnant is actually to be produced. And we're soberly aware as we prepare for our lesson that the process of production will involve war and destruction, following pretty quickly on a time of apparent prosperity. And that's exactly what we find in Isaiah 6–12. These chapters open "in the year that King Uzziah died" (2 Ne. 16:1). Uzziah (or Azariah, as he's sometimes called in scripture) ruled for five decades, and he oversaw a time of rare peace and consequent wealth and abundance both for his kingdom of Judah and for the kingdom of Israel to the north (under King Jeroboam). But as Isaiah's prophecy begins, that time of peace and prosperity is basically over. Uzziah is dead. And anyway, we've already seen how Isaiah prophetically understood the social structures that made for prosperity under Uzziah. He saw it not as a time of blessing, but as a time of systematic oppression of the poor through the enrichment of the already-wealthy, accomplished only through of a series of expansions of Judah's military control over nearby trade routes. And military expansion wasn't the best game to be playing. In the very year of Uzziah's death, Tiglath-pileser III came to power in Assyria; he'd cause endless trouble for both Judah and Israel.

So our text opens at a crucial historical moment. As Isaiah 6 begins, what's over is an era of prosperity obtained through corruption and warmongering, and what's on the horizon is a time of terror at the rise of the first major world empire. Isaiah 7–10 will move us forward a decade to the Syro-Ephraimite crisis, which we'll deal with in a later lecture. By that point, the good old days are unquestionably over, and Isaiah finds himself saddled with the task of explaining the situation to an unwilling audience. And what he'll try to explain is how all the bad Judah passes through in that difficult time serves the Lord's purposes, since he wishes to make of Israel a holy remnant. We'll come to all this, but we've got to begin with Isaiah 6, where the prophet receives his anticipatory commission. So let's hover in that crucial historical moment, the year of Uzziah's death, for a while longer, when only the prophet sees what's really going on.

Paradigmatic Experience

I already noted that I plan only to get through part of Isaiah 6 today. Our focus will be just on verses 1–8, the text leading up to Isaiah's odd commission. We'll look at the commission itself next time. What we'll be looking at here is really just Isaiah's encounter with the Lord in the temple, the *occasion* of Isaiah's receiving a prophetic commission.

Now, we've already spent a little time today showing that the block of Isaiah beginning with this story is structurally privileged in Second Nephi. Isaiah 6–12 is, we've said, Second Nephi's heart of hearts. But now let's note that there's another structural feature of Nephi's record that privileges Isaiah 6 still further. I have a discussion of this in *An Other Testament*, but I think it's worth reviewing here in some detail. The basic picture is just this: at two structurally privileged points in Nephi's larger record, we find stories with startling parallels to Isaiah's encounter with the Lord in the temple. One of these can be found in 1 Nephi 1, in the course of Lehi's first visions at the outset of the story Nephi wants to tell. The other can be found in 2 Nephi 31, in Nephi's final exhortation to his readers, right as he finishes his project. We've thus got Nephi telling us the same story three times over—once right at the beginning of the record, once at the privileged center point of the "more sacred things," and once right at the conclusion of the record. That's clearly significant.

And what's the story we're told on all three occasions? In each case, we have someone who encounters the Lord: Lehi in 1 Nephi 1, Isaiah in 2 Nephi 16, and every reader in 2 Nephi 31. In each story, the one seeing God ends up overwhelmed, with Lehi "quak[ing] and trembl[ing]" (1 Ne. 1:6) and then "cast[ing] himself upon his bed" (1 Ne. 1:7), with Isaiah crying out "Woe is unto me!" (2 Ne. 16:5), and with Nephi expressing his amazement at "how much more need" we have "to be baptized" than did Christ (2 Ne. 31:5). On all three occasions, there's a divine response to the individual's being overcome: some kind of angel or even more divine figure comes to Lehi (1 Ne. 1:11), "one of the seraphim" flies over to Isaiah (2 Ne. 16:6), and the Holy Ghost comes upon those who follow Christ's example in being baptized (2 Ne. 31:12). In each case, interestingly, there's some kind of implement that's used by the divine comforter in question to reassure the person encountering God: Lehi receives "a book" (1 Ne. 1:11), Isaiah "a live coal . . . taken with the tongs from off the altar" (2 Ne. 16:6), and Nephi's readers a "baptism of fire" (2 Ne. 31:13). Finally, each story ends with the individual in question coming into the presence of God fully enabled to speak and to hear the language of heaven. Lehi "was filled with the Spirit of the Lord" and "did exclaim many things unto the Lord . . . , praising . . . his God" (1 Ne. 1:12, 14–15); Isaiah had his "lips" cleansed and his "sin purged" so that he could hear the Lord's commission and answer with the divine words, "Here am I; send me" (2 Ne. 16:7–8); and Nephi's readers are promised the ability to "speak with the tongue of angels, and shout praises unto the Holy One of Israel" (2 Ne. 31:13).

There's the story that's told three times over. An overwhelming encounter with the Lord, to which some divine figure responds with a gesture of compassion that ultimately inducts the individual in question into the heavenly presence, fully prepared to engage with the Lord as one of his called. Lehi launches the Nephite prophetic tradition by having such an experience. And in doing so, he really only echoes the pre-Nephite prophetic tradition as it's exemplified by Isaiah's experience. Finally, Nephi goes beyond the prophetic tradition by inviting every one of his readers to experience the same sort of thing. *All* of Nephi's readers are to become prophets, in a way, imitating the experiences of Lehi and Isaiah, paradigmatic prophets from both the Old- and the New-World traditions. Of course, for our purposes, we want to hover just on the way this story, told several times over, functions in its Isaianic form. Our little digression of the past couple of minutes has been aimed just at making clear how much Nephi seems to have invested in Isaiah's experience. He sees in it the model for every right encounter with the Lord.

The Throne Room

So what do we find in Isaiah 6:1–8, then? Some of it we've already mentioned, but let's get down to details. We noted a couple of minutes ago that the experience takes place "in the year that King Uzziah died" (2 Ne. 16:1), but significantly, there's a deliberate contrast being set up in the text by that notice. At the very time the earthly king dies, Isaiah sees this: "I saw also the Lord sitting upon a throne, high and lifted up, and his train filled the temple" (2 Ne. 16:1). You see the contrast? Every earthly ruler dies, but the vision opens with the everlasting king enthroned. At the very time Isaiah might have expected to witness the enthronement of another earthly king, Uzziah's successor, he sees instead the Lord exalted on the throne. The description of the Lord enthroned is interesting. He's said to be "high and lifted up," which echoes—but by way of contrast—the descriptions of everything leveled to the ground in Isaiah 2. There "everyone which is lifted up . . . shall be brought low" (v. 12), everything "high and lifted up" (v. 13) will be "bowed down" and "made low," while "the Lord alone shall be exalted" (v. 17). It would seem we're here to understand that we're witnessing the fulfillment of what Isaiah's been talking about in the preceding several chapters, the ones we covered last time. As King Uzziah, a kind of symbol of earthly pomp and prosperity, is laid low in the earth, the King of Heaven is exalted on a throne, "high and lifted up."

We're told further that the Lord's "train filled the temple." Don't let the word "train" trip you up here. The word in Hebrew refers to the hem of a garment. Think of the train on a bride's gown. That's the sort of thing we've got in mind. The sumptuous robes of the enthroned King of Heaven fill up the whole of his palace on earth, the temple. So perhaps it's no surprise that he's surrounded, like any king would be, by his attendants. Isaiah calls them "seraphims" (2 Ne. 16:2), as the Book of Mormon, following the King James Version, somewhat clumsily puts it. (It's clumsy because "seraph" is the Hebrew singular and "seraphim" the Hebrew plural. There's a double plural in "seraphims.") What are these things? There's a long theological tradition that attempts to fit the seraphim into an ordered hierarchy of divine beings, but it's entirely unlikely that Isaiah would have had any such thing in mind. Those traditions seem to have grown up among Jews thanks to Persian influence during the last part of the exile, but Isaiah's experience took place centuries earlier. The Hebrew word suggests fiery divine beings (the same word lies behind the fiery flying serpents who poison Moses' people in the desert). But that doesn't give us too much to go on.

And anyway, the emphasis in Isaiah's account isn't so much on the fiery nature of the seraphim as it's on their gestures of praise and self-humiliation. "Each one," Isaiah says, "had six wings. With twain he covered his face, and with twain he covered his feet, and with twain he did fly" (2 Ne. 16:2). Perhaps we don't need to say much about flying here—apart from the obligatory notice in Latter-day Saint contexts that angels apparently don't *actually* have wings. But let's note what's going on with the seraphim's other wings. Two serve as a sort of veil, covering the face.

And two serve as a sort of apron, covering the groin. ("Feet" was a euphemism for genitalia in ancient Israelite culture. We'll have occasion to note this again in other Isaiah texts.) These seraphs, then, doubly mark their humility before the Lord, veiling their faces and covering their shame. Appropriately clothed and veiled, they encircle the Lord's throne and cry in unison: "Holy! Holy! Holy is the Lord of Hosts! The whole earth is full of his glory!" (2 Ne. 16:3). An angelic chorus of sorts, gathered about the throne and offering up prayers of praise—it's a familiar scene. You can find it, as we've already said, in 1 Nephi 1. You can find it in a number of places in the Bible as well. It's a classic vision of the heavenly throne room, figured by the ancient Israelite temple's so-called holy of holies, where the Lord sits enthroned on the Ark of the Covenant.

Day of Atonement

So far, so relatively clear. But then we get this detail: "And the posts of the door moved at the voice of him that cried, and the house was filled with smoke" (2 Ne. 16:4). This is pretty weird. Commentators routinely point out that earthquakes and fire and the like tend to accompany appearances of the Lord, as at Sinai or Horeb for Moses and Elijah, for instance. But the filling of the house—of the temple—with smoke suggests something more specific: the Day of Atonement, *Yom Kippur*. Are you familiar with this? If not, spend some time with Leviticus 16 and a decent commentary. Only once a year in ancient Israel was anyone permitted into the most holy place, the temple's holy of holies, and that was on the Day of Atonement. The priests attended regularly to the services of the holy place, one room removed from the holy of holies. They kept the seven-branched lampstand burning, replaced the bread and wine kept there in perpetuity, made sure that the altar of incense was going. But only the high priest, the oldest direct descendant of Aaron, could pass from that room through the veil and into the holy of holies, where the ark of the covenant stood. And he could do that only on that one day a year, the Day of Atonement.

To approach God's throne was, of course, a terrible thing. The rabbis describe the practice of tying a rope around the ankle of the high priest, so that, if the appearance of the Lord should strike him dead, the priests could drag his corpse from the holy of holies without having to enter that most sacred space themselves. In part to prevent such a thing happening, a major feature of the Day of Atonement consisted of the high priest preemptively placing a shovel full of incense through the veil, filling the holy of holies with smoke before passing into the presence of the Lord. Here's how it's put in Leviticus: "And he shall put the incense upon the fire before the Lord, that the cloud of the incense may cover the mercy seat that is upon the testimony [that is, the ark of the covenant], that he die not" (Lev. 16:13). The high priest fully expected the Lord to appear, and so every precaution had to be taken so that he wouldn't actually be able to see the Lord, whose glory would strike him down. Now bring all this back to Isaiah 6. As Isaiah watches the heavenly scene, the house fills with smoke. It's the Day of Atonement, and he seems to be the high priest. Yet *before* the incense can fill the holy of holies, Isaiah sees the Lord seated on the ark of the covenant. The thunderous praise of the seraphim has drawn Isaiah's eyes to God before he's ready to see him.

Now, we might pause here to note that there are a few oddities about all this. Why is Isaiah in the temple? Is he a priest? Or even a high priest? Why should he be the one holding the incense shovel on the Day of Atonement? And what of the earthquake we've skipped over rather too quickly? Is all the odd talk about "the posts of the door" supposed to indicate a kind of parting of the veil, a shaking down of the uprights that hold the veil in place? Are we witnessing a kind of Day of Atonement to end all Days of Atonement? And again, why is Isaiah there? Is this supposed to be something he just sees in the nighttime, a dream in which he's for some reason serving as high priest? Or what?

Isaiah's Lips

These are good and important questions. For now, let's let them go to focus on Isaiah's entirely predictable response. He's seen God! Even the angelic beings gathered about the throne are covering their faces, but Isaiah's looked on the Lord with his own eyes! There wasn't any smoke yet to obscure the Lord's presence, and it's entirely unclear whether all the processes of purification that take place on the Day of Atonement are supposed to have been completed by this point. So what do we see Isaiah do next? He tells us: "Then said I, 'Woe me! For I am undone! Because I, a man of unclean lips—and I dwell in the midst of a people of unclean lips—for mine eyes have seen the King, the Lord of Hosts!'" (2 Ne. 16:5). You might note how much more fragmentary or how much more halting those words read in the Book of Mormon. Isaiah's at a complete loss, tripping over his words as he announces what he takes to be his inevitable swift demise. He's seen God face to face, and he fully expects to be annihilated.

Notice, though, that Isaiah gives us a *reason* for his expectation. It's not simply that he's seen God. It's that he's seen God when he's himself "a man of unclean lips" and "dwells in the midst of a people of unclean lips." And what's that supposed to mean? Let's note that there isn't much agreement among commentators about exactly what to say about this. It was already something of a puzzle to interpreters two thousand years ago. Ancient legends about Isaiah's life and death focused in curious ways on Isaiah's words here. (I wish we had time to go into that. We don't.) Modern commentators are still puzzled, and you can go read through the literature and see the variety of opinions. I'd like to take a stab myself, going in a direction I've not found in the available commentaries—but one that's perhaps worth exploring.

The key here would be to note that the Hebrew word translated "lips"—that's a literal translation, of course—is one of two that Israelites used to refer to language, the other being "tongue." Thus when you read the story of the tower at Babel, for instance, the several instances of the word "language" there actually translate the word "lip" or "lips" in the original. What if we read Isaiah 6 in this light? That is, what if we read Isaiah as attributing his fear before the appearance of the Lord in major part to his inability to speak the divine language? He's seen God, but he lacks the ability to shout forth articulate anthems of praise like the seraphs arranged about God's throne. A speaker only of human languages, of what the Apostle Paul calls "the tongues of men" as opposed to "the tongue of angels" (1 Cor. 13:1), Isaiah's alarmed at having come into the presence of the divine council. And his language is his people's language. He has "unclean lips," and he dwells among "a people of unclean lips." God's divine language is shared with the seraphim, but Isaiah's human language is shared with his too-human neighbors.

You know what happens next. A seraph flies to Isaiah, "having a live coal in his hand, which he had taken with the tongs from off the altar" (2 Ne. 16:6). Note two things here. First, what the angel figure brings to Isaiah is a glowing coal, a kind of white stone. It's more than doubtful that Isaiah or Nephi had anything like this in mind, but Latter-day Saints might well be reminded of the Book of Revelation, with its talk of a white stone with a new name written on it (see Rev. 2:17; D&C 130:9–11). Such a thing, apparently, is brought to Isaiah as a kind of cleansing agent. Second, the stone was taken "from off the altar." What altar? There are only two options, since there were only two altars adjoined to the Israelite temple: the altar of sacrifice, located outside the temple building in the courtyard, and the altar of incense, located in the holy place and positioned immediately before the veil. Since everything we're witnessing so far takes place within the building of the temple, and because we've already seen that there is reason to think Isaiah's handling the incense already, it seems pretty obvious that the stone the seraph brings comes from the altar of incense. So remember what the altar represents. It stands immediately before the veil, and the smoke constantly going up from it represents a kind of truer form of prayer. Let's say that more clearly. There's an altar that stood immediately before the veil, and there went up from it—as it were through the veil and into the presence of the Lord—a true (temple) order of prayer. Here again we're offering a more strictly Latter-day Saint interpretation of the text, one that Isaiah or Nephi would well have wondered at. But pressing forward nonetheless, we might note that what's brought to Isaiah and pressed to his lips is a white stone of sorts, perhaps with a new name written on it, brought from the altar that stands at the center of every temple prayer. It is this that the seraph lays on Isaiah's mouth and says, "Lo, this hath touched thy lips, and thine iniquity is taken away, and thy sin purged" (2 Ne. 16:7).

What's happened here? Well, the *next* thing that happens is that Isaiah finds himself ranked among the seraphim. He'll hear the voice of the Lord over the angelic songs of praise, and he'll end up commissioned like an angel. He'll have a divine task to perform, and you can bet he'll go forth—as Nephi puts it in his exhortation set in parallel to this story—with the ability to speak the tongue of angels, shouting praises to the Holy One of Israel. So what's happened with the seraph's placing the coal from the altar on Isaiah's mouth? It seems the purpose of the stone is to cleanse Isaiah lips, his language, granting him the ability to speak like the angels, providing him with the divine language he recognizes he otherwise lacks. Branded with a new name, perhaps, or initiated into the temple order of prayer, perhaps, Isaiah can join the angelic throng, can pass through the veil into the Lord's presence, and can receive there a specific mission he's to perform in Israel. And he'll have the divine word on his lips at last, because his response to the Lord's question about whether there might be someone to fulfill the mission will be the most divine words of all: "Here! I! Send me!" (2 Ne. 16:8), a clear echo of Christ's own "Here am I, send me!" (Moses 4:1; Abr. 3:27).

There's a picture taking shape here, no? To flesh it out, especially with a theological eye, we've had to go beyond the strict resources of Isaiah 6 alone. So let's be clear that the interpretation we've worked up of the cleansing of Isaiah's lips should probably be called a strictly Latter-day Saint interpretation. I doubt any non-Mormon biblical scholar would want to go too far with it. Be that as it may, I think we've begun to get a sense for the meaning of Isaiah's encounter with the Lord, and at least for the way that Nephi wishes to set it in parallel to other prophetic experiences—that of his father, to be sure, but also that of every reader of Nephi's record. What we have here is a kind of paradigm for prophetic commission. Nephi has got all kinds of larger purposes with it (and we, theologically speaking, even more!), though Isaiah's aims or intentions with recounting the experience might be said to be somewhat narrower, more local, less grandiose. So let's leave off the spirit of theological expansion to return just to what Nephi's text seems to be doing in the development of Isaiah 2–14.

Remember where we're at in the larger story Nephi sees Isaiah telling in these chapters. We're watching the very beginnings of the transition toward an actual historical sequence during which the Lord, according to Isaiah, produced a remnant of Israel. And here we're seeing that process of production beginning with an encounter between Isaiah and the Lord. It turns out that the Lord's big historical plans can't move forward without the work of a commissioned prophet. Interestingly, this'll be the first thing Nephi has to say about these chapters when he provides us with a few verses of commentary. He'll speak of destruction for Judah, but he'll assert that "never hath any of them been destroyed save it were foretold them by the prophets of the Lord" (2 Ne. 25:9). Here we're watching the beginnings of that pattern unfold. That Isaiah's commission has everything to do with the production of an Israelite remnant will become clear when we turn, next time, to the actual words of commission given.

For the moment, it's enough to rejoice in Isaiah's temple vision, and to recognize the emphasis Isaiah himself wants to place on the beginnings of the Lord's intervention in Israel. We're to understand that God's work is intentional, planned out, and carefully executed. It is not a kind of retroactive reinterpretation of history, a "Whoops! Um. I *meant* to do that . . ." sort of thing. We're to assume that we're looking at a deliberate effort on the Lord's part, and that Isaiah is at the very heart of it. There needs to be a commissioned prophet intervening so that the right sort of history can unfold.

And perhaps—*just* perhaps—we might hear in all this something that inspires us to take more seriously our own encounters in the temple, our own (at least symbolic) contact with angels there, our own hymns of praise and prayers around the altar. Perhaps we can find in Isaiah's experience an ancient outline of our own experience, which would suggest that we're also being commissioned. We pass through the veil into the celestial room so that we can be sent out, chaste and consecrated, to do the work of building up a covenant people. Or else we make our way from the celestial room into a sealing room where we're welded into the Abrahamic family and taught of the meaning of the Abrahamic covenant so that we'll go about that same work. In a crucial way, Isaiah's experience is our own.

Just be glad your commission is a little different from Isaiah's! You get to do the pleasant work of the covenant. We'll see next time that he gets to do anything but that.

Lecture XVI

Isaiah's Commission

With our discussion last time, we only began to work on Isaiah 6, reproduced in 2 Nephi 16. As we press our way toward the end of the chapter, we'll begin to see that it opens quite deliberately onto everything that follows in Isaiah 7–12. And let's not forget that all seven of these chapters, Isaiah 6–12, are treated as one solid block of text in the original dictation of the Book of Mormon. We saw at the end of our discussion last time that Isaiah 6 opens this sequence in large part by showing that the Lord's intervention in Israel begins with him sending a prophet. But today we've got to turn our attention to what the Lord actually commissions that prophet to do.

We concluded, more or less, with the Lord asking the heavenly council a simple double question: "Whom shall I send? And who will go for us?" (2 Ne. 16:8). And we've already dealt with Isaiah's exemplary and even divine response, evidence that he'd acquired the tongue of angels: "Here! I! Send me!" (v. 8). You'll soon be wondering whether Isaiah felt so excited or confident, however, once he learned the task the Lord was sending him to accomplish. Without further ado, then, let's get right to the text of Isaiah's commission. And I'm going to begin from the King James Version, rather than from the Book of Mormon in order to see how Nephi's text alters what you find in the Bible.

A Paradoxical Task

Here's Isaiah's commission as it's reported in your King James Bible: "Go, and tell this people, 'Hear ye indeed, but understand not'; and 'see ye indeed, but perceive not.' Make the heart of this people fat, and make their ears heavy, and shut their eyes; lest they see with their eyes, and hear with their ears, and understand with their heart, and convert, and be healed" (Isa. 6:9–10). Do you feel the impact of that commission? Let's say it straight. It seems pretty clear here that Isaiah is being commanded to preach and prophesy in a way that will ensure Israel's destruction. God, it seems, sends Isaiah out to *prevent* rather than to *procure* Israel's repentance. Isn't that how the text reads? Isaiah's to command the people to hear and to see, but they're to do so without understanding or perceiving. Further, he is to ensure that the people can't "see with their eyes" or "hear with their ears" or "understand with their heart"—all this so that they won't "convert and be healed"! That's a pretty shocking commission, isn't it?

Now, you might well be asking yourself at this point whether there's not some way to get around the objectionable implications of the text. Perhaps the King James translators took some horrific liberties here? Unfortunately, no. We're here up against a theologically difficult text, one that's plagued interpreters for twenty-five hundred years. Craig Evans has written a nice little book, *To See and Not Perceive*, that tracks attempts to grapple with this passage between about 300 B.C. and 300 A.D. More or less every ancient reader we know of tried to finesse the text to make it say something different. But the Hebrew straightforwardly says what the King James Version translates, and readers haven't liked its implications for a *very* long time. Sickeningly, it seems the only interpreters through much of Christian history who were fine with the text as it stands in the Hebrew were those who read it in strictly anti-Semitic terms. They saw the Lord's commission to Isaiah as an indication of the Lord's intentional punishment of a cursed race. That's not at all the right direction to go. And yet we've got to grapple with this commission.

The past century or so has seen the development of an interpretation of Isaiah's difficult commission that, finally, doesn't have to get around the text and yet makes a good deal of theological sense. It was laid out first, so far as I'm aware, by Gerhard von Rad in his two-volume *Old Testament Theology*. The idea is basically that there lies behind Isaiah's commission a theological conception of divine sovereignty. Israel's God is a God whose sovereignty is so radical that he occasionally hardens hearts against his message in order to accomplish larger aims. The Hebrew Bible actually shows this happening on other occasions—you'll remember that the biblical text has God harden Pharaoh's heart against Moses's message, with the intention to show his marvelous works before the whole world. We tend to be a bit more okay with those other occasions, though, because it's the bad guys there who get hardened. We're less comfortable with the idea that God deliberately hardened *Israel* against his message. But that's what we've got right here in Isaiah 6.

Von Rad went further. He suggested that the hardening of Israel against Isaiah's message was bound up with a larger historical transformation of the institution of prophecy during the eighth century. Before Isaiah's time—think here of the stories of Elijah and Elisha—prophets didn't write; they simply went about performing miracles and delivering oracles. But during Isaiah's generation, there's suddenly this phenomenon of "writing prophets": Amos, Hosea, Micah, Isaiah. Von Rad argued that this turn to *written* prophecy went hand in hand with the idea of a divinely hardened people. When Isaiah is forced through his commission to recognize that his contemporaries won't listen to a word he has to say, he (along with other prophets from his generation) begins to realize that his message is for a people to come only after his death. Hence von Rad marked a connection between Isaiah's commission in Isaiah 6 and a crucial passage in Isaiah 8. In the latter chapter, Isaiah commands his few followers to "bind up the testimony" he's been offering, to "seal the law" among his disciples (2 Ne. 18:16). And Isaiah announces his intention to "wait upon the Lord, that hideth his face from the house of Jacob" (v. 17). God has done something mysterious in Israel, hardening his people's hearts against the prophet's message, but Isaiah recognizes that this calls for an orientation to the future, as well as for trust in the paradoxical God who hides his face from his people.

I think we ought to go pretty far down the trail von Rad has blazed for us. He finds in Isaiah's theologically difficult commission a kind of basic motivation for the prophet's larger purpose in writing. Because of his divinely appointed task, Isaiah was provided with the unique responsibility to focus his prophetic efforts on writing a record that would be sealed up and kept for a later generation that is to approach prophecy *in precisely the way that Nephite prophets would be forced to approach it.* In other words, Isaiah is a proto-Nephite prophet. He knows in advance that his people won't receive his teachings, and so he writes for a "latter-day" audience, for a people still to come. He prophesies and he writes, but then he seals up his prophecies and his writings so that they can be read by a people finally ready to receive the message.

Now, hopefully you'll remember that we talked about some of this stuff before. Now we're focused on the text where it first emerges. What seems to lie behind Isaiah's project is this weird commission in Isaiah 6. So we can't get around it. Or perhaps we can in certain ways, but only slightly. The Book of Mormon version of Isaiah 6 is slightly different from what you find in the King James Version. It's not different enough to get us entirely off the hook, though you can be sure you can find Latter-day Saint authors claiming that the Book of Mormon gets us entirely out of the theological difficulty of the biblical version of the text. That's going too far. And anyway, we've already seen today that there may be reasons we actually might *want* Isaiah's commission to read as it does in the biblical text. It might play into the Book of Mormon's larger theology of writing.

Let's now leave off the King James Version to turn directly to the Book of Mormon. What does Isaiah's commission look like there? And what might it suggest regarding these larger questions we've already begun asking?

Reconstructing the Text in the Book of Mormon

We can't quote Isaiah's commission as it's recorded in the Book of Mormon without providing a few notes about some complications with the transmission of the text. What do I mean by that? I mean that 2 Nephi 16:9–10 hasn't come down to us in a straightforward way from the time of the original dictation. And while I've usually contented myself with quoting from Royal Skousen's reconstruction of the dictated text as we've worked through things here, I can't do so uncritically this time. The situation with the manuscript and print sources on this passage forced Skousen to take a couple of guesses here, and we can't be sure he's guessed right without going over things. We've got to look at all the evidence ourselves. Does that make sense? Well, let's get into the details, and it'll begin to make sense if it doesn't already.

The basic source of the problem is that there's an important difference in this passage between the 1830 (or first) edition of the Book of Mormon and the 1837 (or second) edition of the Book of Mormon, and there's an obvious problem in the 1830 version and therefore a clear motivation for the change found in the 1837 version. So here's just verse 9 of the commission as it's found in the 1830 text, which I'm intentionally leaving unpunctuated because of a set of interpretive difficulties: "and he said go and tell this people hear ye indeed but they understand not and see ye indeed but they perceived not." Do you see the problem? If we compare this with the King James Version, maybe it gets clearer. Here's the biblical text and the 1830 Book of Mormon text set in parallel (I've italicized the changes):

King James Version	1830 Book of Mormon
go and tell this people	go and tell this people
hear ye indeed	hear ye indeed
but understand not	but *they* understand not
and see ye indeed	and see ye indeed
but perceive not	but *they perceived* not

Note that in each of the "but . . . not" clauses, the Book of Mormon version adds the pronoun "they." This changes the verbs in those clauses from imperatives or commands to indicatives or simple descriptions. In the Book of Mormon version of the text, no one's being told not to understand or not to perceive. We're simply being told that someone doesn't understand or perceive. But then notice that while both verbs become indicative rather than imperative, just one of them gets a change in tense. The word "understand" doesn't change from what's found in the King James Version, even if the word "they" gets tacked on to it. But the word "perceive" *does* change, becoming "perceived." So we get "they understand not," apparently in the present tense, but "they perceived not," clearly in the past tense. That seems odd, doesn't it?

We're not the only ones who think that's odd. When preparing the 1837 (second) edition of the Book of Mormon, someone—we're not sure whether it was Joseph Smith himself, or someone else working on the printing—*someone* thought this didn't make any sense. And so the 1837 edition changed "understand" to "understood," rendering both verbs in the past tense. And every printed edition of the Book of Mormon since then has read like the 1837 edition, with "understood" in the place of "understand." This smooths out the text, since both verbs are in the same tense, but we're left with the question of whether that's what Joseph Smith originally dictated or not. And it turns out that turning from printed editions to manuscript sources doesn't help us any here. The printer's manuscript, a copy of the original that was used for setting the print of the first several editions of the Book of Mormon, reads exactly like the 1830 text, with the inserted pronouns and just the one verb in the past tense. And the original manuscript itself is unfortunately non-existent for this part of the Book of Mormon. (That manuscript suffered water damage at one point, and major parts of it were destroyed.) So the only manuscript source we have agrees with the odd 1830 reading.

Royal Skousen, in his work on producing a critical edition of the Book of Mormon, has suggested an emendation here. Basically, he suggests that the original manuscript probably read just like the printer's manuscript, but he argues for the possibility that "perceived," in the past tense, was the result of Oliver Cowdery's mishearing what Joseph said in the course of dictation. He points out that "perceive not" and "perceived not" can sound more or less identical when spoken aloud, making it possible that Oliver *heard* and therefore *wrote* "perceived not" when Joseph actually *said* "perceive not." It should be added that "understood not" would be hard to mishear as "understand not," so Skousen argues that the 1837 solution to the problem got things exactly backwards. Whoever made that change, on Skousen's account, rightly saw that the two verbs should have the same tense but set them both in the past when they should have been set both in the present. Hence Skousen reconstructs the originally dictated text as follows, once again without punctuation: "and he said go and tell this people hear ye indeed but they understand not and see ye indeed but they perceive not."

At this point, we've got *three* different possible readings of Isaiah's commission provided to us by the Book of Mormon. There's Skousen's reconstruction of the supposed earliest text: "they understand not" and "they perceive not." And then there's the uneven 1830 text, found in the printer's manuscript and perhaps even in the original manuscript: "they understand not" and "they perceived not." Finally, there's the text as it's consistently appeared since 1837: "they understood not" and "they perceived not." What do we do with this mess? And why have I bothered to go through all this mess of details instead of just moving on with whatever I take to be the best interpretation? Well, let me answer this last question really quickly, because I think it's important to recognize why we're bothering to dwell on all this. I've subjected you to this long tangent of sorts in order to make clear that it's not always obvious *what* the differences are between the biblical text of Isaiah and the Book of Mormon text. To look carefully at how Nephi puts Isaiah to use, it sometimes requires attention to documentary sources and the print history of the Book of Mormon. As Skousen's reconstruction makes clear also, it's sometimes necessary to draw on the resources of linguistics to make educated guesses about the text actually dictated by Joseph Smith. Although I *can* give you my conclusions and just move on from there, it's hopefully useful to you to see how much work needs to be done on the texts if we're to proceed responsibly.

But now what are we to do with Isaiah's commission? Is one of the three versions of the Book of Mormon text to be preferred above the others? And then, whichever text we decide is best, we have to ask what the changes in the Book of Mormon tell us about the nature of Isaiah's commission as it's understood in the Book of Mormon. Might one of these help us to view with new eyes the set of theological difficulties that attend the biblical version of the commission?

Variants in Isaiah 6

Of the three options, I think it's relatively clear that Skousen's reconstruction is the best. His reasoning seems solid, at any rate, and it does away with the apparent unevenness of the earliest print and manuscript sources. So perhaps we can just go along with Skousen's conclusions and work with his text as we've been doing all along. So once more, let's quote Isaiah's commission as the Book of Mormon gives it to us. We still can't yet punctuate it, though, because there's some difficulty about deciding what the changes made to the commission's wording in the Book of Mormon mean. But here are the words, anyway, still quoting just verse 9: "and he said go and tell this people hear ye indeed but they understand not and see ye indeed but they perceive not." How might we punctuate these words and thereby make sense of what's going on here? It's clear that "and he said" is supposed to be understood as Isaiah's own words narrating Lord's response to the prophet. And it's equally clear that "go and tell this people" are the Lord's words to Isaiah, while "hear ye indeed" are certainly the words the Lord wants Isaiah to "tell this people." All that causes no trouble. The question is what should be done with the next words, "but they understand not."

So, remember back to the King James Version we quoted before. It's clear there that the prophet is told to command the people both to "hear . . . indeed" and to "understand not." But with the insertion of "they" before "understand not" in the Book of Mormon version, "understand" becomes indicative rather than imperative, and it becomes entirely unclear whether we're to see these words as among those Isaiah is supposed to tell the people, or whether we're to see these words as a kind of aside to Isaiah by the Lord regarding the way the prophet's words will be received. Let's see if we can't make this clearer by punctuating the verse as it appears in the Book of Mormon in two distinct ways. First, let's punctuate it as if "but they understand not" were part of the message Isaiah's supposed to deliver to the people. And then let's punctuate it as if "but they understand not" were instead an aside spoken by the Lord by way of explanation to Isaiah. Here are the two pointings of the text, one after another:

> And he said, "Go and tell this people, 'Hear ye indeed, but they understand not.'"

> And he said, "Go and tell this people, 'Hear ye indeed,' but they understand not."

Do you see the difference? I hope that's relatively clear.

So now the question is this: Which of these makes more sense? I think it's difficult to make a whole lot of sense of the first one. What would it mean for Isaiah to say "Hear ye indeed, but they understand not"? Who would "they" refer to? Would we have to imagine Isaiah speaking the second part of his message as a kind of soliloquy that interrupts his preaching? "Hear ye indeed!" he shouts, but when he sees the people's response, he says to himself, "But they understand not"? All that seems rather complicated if we're going to get it to work. So perhaps we should prefer the second pointing of the text. If we've got the Lord here explaining to Isaiah that, despite his message ("Hear ye indeed!"), "they"—clearly "this people"—"understand not," then we've got the Lord giving the prophet a kind of heads up about how his message is going to be rejected. That shows a bit of kindness on the Lord's part, doesn't it? And it maybe makes better sense of the text in its revised form. Isaiah's to call out "Hear ye indeed!" and "See ye indeed!" to a people who, nonetheless, don't "understand" and don't "perceive." That makes decent sense, I think.

If we can satisfy ourselves with this interpretation (and I'll note that I'm not myself fully satisfied), then we can begin to ask whether the Book of Mormon softens the blow of Isaiah's commission. And, let's be clear about this, it certainly *does* to some extent. We don't have the Lord telling Isaiah to command the people not to understand, not to perceive. It's just a kind of fact that they don't understand or perceive. And we've even got a kindly God here, letting Isaiah know in advance that people will be disposed against his message. From all this, it might well seem that the Book of Mormon text in fact does get us around the theological difficulties of the commission as it stands in the original Hebrew, reflected in the King James rendering. But then there's this difficulty that we can't ignore. The Book of Mormon in no way revises verse 10. It stands in the Book of Mormon exactly as it does in the King James Bible: "Make the heart of this people fat, and make their ears heavy, and shut their eyes—lest they see with their eyes, and hear with their ears, and understand with their heart, and convert and be healed." Although some changes in verse 9 soften the impact of Isaiah's commission in certain ways, there's a parallel *lack* of changes in verse 10 that restores a good deal of the impact softened through the revisions of the previous verse. Perhaps we don't have Isaiah being told to command the people not to understand or to perceive, but we do have Isaiah being told to do what's necessary to prevent Israel from seeing, hearing, understanding, converting, and being healed.

How to make sense of this? We've still got to deal with a God who deliberately thwarts his people's repentance ("repent" would be a better translation of the Hebrew behind the word "convert," by the way). The God of Nephi's Isaiah, as much as the God of the Bible's Isaiah, commissions this particular prophet to prevent Israel's repentance. They don't understand, and they don't perceive—perhaps that's their own doing, in light of the revisions in verse 9—but God here sends out a prophet whose task is to make sure that doesn't change. They're to remain in their hardened state; God wishes that nothing be done to recover them. And that's something that's hard to feel terribly comfortable about, no? This isn't the God we like to talk about in the twenty-first century. Yet this is the God of Isaiah, the God who hides his face from Israel to accomplish his own purpose. And what's that purpose? We've already stated it a dozen times: the production of a remnant, sanctified and prepared to receive the Lord's word. Isaiah's commission is to help see to it that the remnant is produced, even as he records the prophecies that must be sealed up and saved for that remnant's eventual perusal.

The Holy Seed

That's the picture. But note that Isaiah himself doesn't yet know anything of the remnant at the time he receives his commission. He's just hearing the Lord's odd requirement that he keep Israel from repenting and being healed. So there's no real surprise when we hear Isaiah's mournful response to the commission: "Lord, how long?" (2 Ne. 16:11). But in reply to that plaintive question, the Lord lays out the whole story of the remnant in outline. And we've got to conclude our discussion today by looking carefully at this clarification of Isaiah's commission. It probably won't make us any more comfortable with what we've been looking at, but perhaps it'll help us to understand what's going on here anyway.

Here's the first part of the Lord's response to Isaiah's "How long?":
"Until the cities be wasted without inhabitant, and the houses without
man, and the land be utterly desolate, and the Lord have removed men
far away—for there shall be a great forsaking in the midst of the land" (2
Ne. 16:11–12). This first part of the Lord's response is relatively clear, isn't
it? It has two parts, it seems to me. First, it seems to refer to destruction
and conquest (cities wasted, houses empty, the land desolate). And then
second, it seems to refer to exile and dispersion (people removed far away,
a great forsaking in the middle of the land). So the Lord's response to
Isaiah's "How long?" isn't a measure of time ("You'll be accomplishing this
task for forty years") but an orientation to a purpose, to a situation or a
state that's on the horizon. Isaiah is to shepherd Israel away from deliverance until the possibility of deliverance is past and devastation and ruin
have come on the people.

All that's not terribly surprising at this point. It's more or less what we
already expected given what we've seen from Isaiah's commission. But it's
what the Lord says next that's really interesting, because it makes all this
talk of destruction and exile into just a part of a larger historical scheme.
So let's get the rest of the Lord's response on the table. There's to be "a great
forsaking in the midst of the land," yes; "but," the Lord goes on, "yet in it
there shall be a tenth, and they shall return—and shall be eaten, as a teil
tree and as an oak, whose substance is in them when they cast their leaves.
So the holy seed shall be the substance thereof" (2 Ne. 16:13). Now, how's
that for an Isaiah passage that'll drive you up the wall? A tenth? Eaten?
Teil trees and oaks? Substance? Holy seed? What in the name of heaven is
going on here?

I find it fascinating that the Book of Mormon doesn't offer any interpretive help on this passage. It doesn't tweak the translation of Isaiah
in this notoriously difficult verse, but rather it leaves us with the stilted,
awkward rendering of the King James Version. But perhaps we're then
free to look at other translations of the same Hebrew text that underlies
the King James Version. The Book of Mormon doesn't suggest that there's
any different Hebrew text, right? So can we make sense of the underlying
Hebrew more directly, sidestepping the terribly awkward rendering shared
by the King James Bible and the Book of Mormon? Definitely. But part of
the difficulty in the King James rendering is that the underlying Hebrew
is itself pretty tortured.

Let me illustrate by quoting a couple of different recent translations
of the passage. Here, for instance, is Joseph Blenkinsopp's rendering in

his commentary: "If but a tenth of the land is left it will revert to pasture. It will be like the oak and the terebinth which, when felled, have only a stump left. Its stump is the holy seed." That's a good deal clearer than the King James rendering, but now set it side by side with Gary Smith's translation, to be found in his commentary: "And though a tenth remains in the land, it will again be laid waste. But as the terebinth and oak leave stumps when they are cut down, so the holy seed will be the stump in the land." A little different, no? Or really, a lot different. Then here's Hans Wildberger's rendering, found in his commentary: "And if there is still a tenth there, it will serve as pasture until grazed bare as the oaks and terebinths, which, if someone fells them, shoots are still there. The shoots upon it are holy seed." We're getting quite a range. Let's quote one more, this time John Oswalt's rendering in his commentary: "If there is still a tenth in it, it will be burned again. Like the terebinth and the oak which leave a stump when they are cut down, the holy seed is its stump." Are you getting a feel for the difficulty?

Obviously, we're not going to get to the bottom of this today. But let's note what all these translations share. All translations recognize that there's some fraction ("a tenth") of something left over after destruction and exile. And the Lord tells Isaiah that that fraction—that remnant—will return in some way. The King James Version and the Book of Mormon leave us with the possibility that we're speaking of a people returning from exile, while most of the translations we've quoted suggest rather that the return in question is a return of a certain condition (it's usually translated "again" in these renderings). Whatever that difference amounts to, there's some kind of returning of a remnant or a fraction of what was there before destruction and exile. And then it's clear that the return or repetition in question can be compared to oaks and terebinths, trees that, even after being cut down, sometimes retain life in them. These are trees whose apparently-dead stumps sometimes sprout again, new shoots coming up out of the still-living roots. And all renderings agree that the Lord's saying something about the holiness of the new shoots or "seed" that's springing from what otherwise appears to be dead.

So, despite certain interpretive difficulties, we've got a relatively clear picture here. There will be destruction and exile, but there will also be a remnant left over. Israel—or perhaps its land—looks like an old, dead tree stump, but there's a promise that something's going to spring out of its still-living roots, hidden beneath the ground. The remnant, barely surviving the devastation to come, is going to grow into a brand new tree. And the tree will be holy. What we have here, however awkwardly worded it is in Hebrew or even in English translation, is a prediction of the remnant that the whole process of destruction and exile is meant to produce. Here we get the aim or purpose of the Lord's odd commission for Isaiah. His preaching is meant to trigger the events that will result in the production of Israel's remnant, and then his preaching is meant to serve as the scriptures to which that remnant will turn in faith.

We're quickly running out of time today, so let's wrap this up. Isaiah's commission, difficult as it might be for us to swallow, fits into his larger theology. We spent a bit of time some lectures back looking at Isaiah 10:22. It's part of the larger sequence Isaiah 6 opens in Nephi's quotation. Here's what it says again: "The consumption decreed shall overflow with righteousness," and that because "a remnant of [Israel] shall return." That's Isaiah's message. In fact, *everything* about Isaiah focuses on this remnant. He is given the divine responsibility to help see to the production of the remnant, pressing Israel toward its fate. In the meanwhile, he lays out a complicated theology of the remnant, outlining the process of its production and anticipating its future. And finally, his prophecies are written and sealed up so that they can be read by that remnant once it's finally produced.

And all this is there, at least in outline, in Isaiah's commission. You can see, hopefully, how this experience of Isaiah's in the temple serves as a fitting introduction to Isaiah 7–12, that is, to the six chapters of Isaiah where the detailed story of the remnant's emergence is told. And that's what we've got to look at next. We'll spend our next two lectures laying this out as best we can. We've got a lot of work to do.

Lecture XVII

The Production of the Remnant

Wow, we've got a lot to cover today. We want to see if we can't make general sense of what's going on in Isaiah 7–12. I plan on giving my next lecture to these same chapters, but I want to be able to focus in next time on what we might call "the messianic question"—the question of what, if anything, passages in Isaiah 7, 9, and 11 have to say about the coming of a messiah. So we've really got to cover Isaiah 7–12 as fully as possible this time. It's a daunting task, but we'll just have to see what we can do.

The Syro-Ephraimite Crisis

We've made clear already that these chapters tell a kind of story, the story of the emergence or the production of an Israelite remnant, a people prepared to receive Isaiah's untimely meditations. But now we've got to do a bit of history, because Isaiah tells this story by setting it in the context of a very specific historical event, one that took place during his intensely difficult days. How many of you have heard of the Syro-Ephraimite crisis? That's the key to making sense of Isaiah 7–12, even in a preliminary way. It's a kind of minor episode within the larger Assyrian crisis of the eighth century before Christ, about which we've said a bit along the way in these lectures. It's a minor episode from the global—or certainly from the Assyrian—perspective, but Isaiah blows it up into an event of massive importance, a turning point in Israelite—and therefore in world—history. Let's see if we can't make it clear in relatively short order.

Here's the situation. Assyria's on the rise, quickly becoming the greatest power in the world known to the Bible. And Assyria is devastatingly brutal, making our modern forms of warfare or torture—may they all come to an end!—look like child's play. As they expand their borders and try to conquer the world, they've especially got to do everything possible to take out the most venerable among their potential enemies: Egypt. So their campaign trail leads them along the curve of the Fertile Crescent, as we call it, first heading north and west from their headquarters on the Tigris River into what we call Asia Minor, and then moving directly southward to pass through Syria and Palestine on their way to Egypt. Along the way, they've got to contend with a great number of little nations, largish tribes most of them, who haven't got a hope against the massive Assyrian armies. Each little nation has to decide how to deal with the Assyrian threat—little nations whose names you'll remember from the Old Testament: Edom and Moab and Ammon and so on. If you're one of these nations, would you attempt a standoff? That's suicide. So your best bet is simply to submit to Assyria before there's any violence, pledging yourself to the new imperial power's support, which of course involves heavy tribute and a lot of other annoyances. But hey, it's better than massacre, isn't it? And Assyria doesn't just kill in order to subjugate. Once they've conquered a people, they scatter their population to ensure that there won't be any sense of ethnic or religious identity left that might help to spur a movement of rebellion. Keep people divided once you've conquered them—that's their rule.

It seems hopeless, doesn't it? Well, before Assyria makes its southward turn that will lead it through the lands in and around Israel, the little nations and tribes dwelling there come up with a plan. They find some hope in the possibility of a successful alliance, a coalition of smaller nations that together can stand against the imperial threat. This is, of course, a desperate and dangerous plan. The second it looks like resistance will fail, weaker or more opportunistic members of the coalition will inevitably try to cut their losses, defecting to Assyria's side to avoid being eradicated when Assyria wins. And every such defection will mean all the harsher consequences for those who remain a part of the effort at resistance. How do you keep the alliance together? The stakes are too high to be terribly confident about anything working out in the right way. And then even before any of that becomes a worry, how do you get people to join the coalition in the first place? Any king who has more confidence in Assyria's reputation than in the strength of any local alliance simply won't join in the first place, and that means that Assyria will itself have local allies. As you can imagine, that'll make things difficult long before there's any question of holding the coalition together in the actual event of battle with Assyria.

Well, there's the situation in the 730s B.C., where we pick up in Isaiah 7. The two nations heading up the anti-Assyrian coalition are Syria or Aram (to be distinguished from Assyria) and Israel or Ephraim (the northern kingdom that divorced itself from Judah almost two centuries earlier). And Judah, the southern kingdom with Jerusalem as its chief city, has refused to join the alliance, preferring to throw its lot in with Assyria. Already, then, the plan of launching an alliance of nations against Assyria is faltering. But Syria and Ephraim have a plan. They've apparently decided that they have enough time before Assyria's arrival to see if they can't use military force to secure Judah's support. They're planning an assassination of Judah's king, basically, and their plan is then to put someone else on the throne in favor of the coalition ("the son of Tabeal," according to Isaiah 7:6). That would allow the alliance to go forward with greater strength and without local opposition. As you can imagine, this causes more than a bit of consternation in Jerusalem, since they had already decided to submit to Assyria in order to keep *out* of war, but now their decision is bringing on a war in advance of the actual arrival of Assyria.

That's the Syro-Ephraimite crisis. You can see how it's really a minor episode from the larger perspective of ancient history. It's a local skirmish by minor nations who hope, vainly, to stand against the Assyrian threat, something that's over in just a couple of years. But Isaiah makes this into an episode of great importance, asking his readers to reflect deeply on what this situation ends up doing to Judah. When the danger from Syria and Ephraim is reported to the leaders in Jerusalem, they're understand-ably scared, but the Lord sends the prophet Isaiah to talk to the king. They meet up just outside the city, where the king is inspecting Jerusalem's water supply in preparation for battle. (He's clearly expecting a siege.) And Isaiah's message is this simple: "Don't bother. And don't worry. Syria and Ephraim will fall before Assyria before they can do you any harm. Just relax." The king doesn't take that very well. The danger's too much for him, apparently, so he doesn't buy in. And so Isaiah announces the consequence: Assyria will not only lay waste Syria and Ephraim, but will also cause a lot of trouble for Judah.

A lot of trouble, but Judah will survive, according to Isaiah. After the present Judean king's gone (Isaiah's confronting Ahaz, grandson of Uzziah), he'll be replaced by a king, the famed Hezekiah, who'll be able to survive the Assyrian onslaught. Only at that point will Assyria discover its limits. Arrogant Assyria will begin to collapse, and Judah will be left with a righteous remnant ready for a time of restoration and peace. In fact, the fall of Judah's enemies will usher in a time of such remarkable peace that Isaiah predicts lions and lambs lying down together! Things will be good, but only after all the consequences of Judah's unfaithfulness during the

Syro-Ephraimite crisis. In other words, things will be good but only for the remnant of Judah.

Is that enough historical background? We've basically just outlined the story of Isaiah 7–12, and maybe it's enough by way of general picture that we can now turn our attention to some of the details of the text. I've already said that we'll be leaving the so-called "messianic" texts for next time—passages in Isaiah 7, Isaiah 9, and Isaiah 11. I'll nonetheless have to say a little about them as we go along.

Isaiah's Faithless Contemporaries

Isaiah 7 opens in the middle of the Syro-Ephraimite crisis we've been discussing. It's "the days of Ahaz" of Judah (2 Ne. 17:1), and the kings of Syria and Ephraim, Rezin and Pekah by name, are trying to force Ahaz into joining the coalition. It's disturbing, of course, and the people of Judah's hearts were "moved . . . as the trees of the wood are moved with the wind," says Isaiah the poet (v. 2). And so Isaiah's sent to meet the king at the city's water supply, as we already said. He's told to take his son with him, a kid named Shear-jashub—literally (in Hebrew), "a remnant will return." It's not hard to see the significance in that, no? He tells the king to hush his fears. Why? Because the two kings can be compared to "two tails of . . . smoking firebrands," once-burning sticks that are now just giving off smoke (v. 4). They're matches that have already gone out; any damage they might have done is now beyond their capacity. So Ahaz isn't to worry about the two kings' confederacy, their plan to put "the son of Tabeal" on the Judean throne (v. 6). Here's the Lord's word through Isaiah, simply put: "It shall not stand, neither shall it come to pass" (v. 7). And then Isaiah makes a clear prediction that it won't be long before both enemy nations are eradicated, with the northern kingdom of Israel "broken" in such a way that it won't even be "a people" anymore (v. 8). Then here's the word of Ahaz: "If ye will not believe, surely ye shall not be established" (v. 9). There's a beautiful play on words in that prophetic word, with "believe" and "be established" translating two versions of the same word. If Ahaz doesn't trust God, the king won't himself be trustworthy. That maybe catches the spirit of the Hebrew.

Here's the weird thing, though. The Lord has Isaiah tell the king next to ask for a sign that this is really a divine word. The king, apparently in a disingenuous act of affected piety, refuses. So the Lord gives him a sign anyway. We'll dwell on the meaning of this sign next time, but the immediate upshot is that within just a couple of years, Ephraim and Syria will be "forsaken of both [their] kings" (2 Ne. 17:16). But there's the matter of Ahaz's failing, in the meanwhile, to trust the word delivered through Isaiah. So this good news gets doubled with some not-so-good news: "The Lord shall bring upon thee and upon thy people . . . the king of Assyria" (v. 17). Well, not just that. The Lord will summon both Assyria, presented as a trained bee, and Egypt, presented as a trained fly. (Did you know you can train these insects? You can!) These world powers will be clashing in Judah's backyard. But for the moment, Ahaz can forget Egypt, because it's really Assyria he should worry about. Isaiah tells him to expect his people to be shaved by Assyria, which the prophet describes as "a razor that is hired" (v. 20). In the ancient world, you shave those captured in war. It's an act of humiliation. And Isaiah mentions not only the shaving of heads and beards, but also "the hair of the feet" (v. 20). Remember that "feet" is a euphemism for Israelites. Judah's men will be forcibly shaved bare in the most humiliating way possible. And this is to be done by a hired razor, the king of Assyria as a tool in someone else's hands. You can guess who's using the razor from Isaiah's perspective. The Lord.

And the result is that things aren't good in Judah. The last part of Isaiah 7 describes the conditions using a bunch of imagery foreign to us today. Take a look at a good commentary sometime to work your way through it. But for the moment, just realize that we're being told that things will be bad.

Isaiah 8 now describes everything we've just covered all over again. Just as in Isaiah 7, there's here a prophetic word announced to the people of Judah, making clear that it won't be but a couple of years "before the riches of Damascus [Syria's capital] and the spoil of Samaria [Ephraim's capital] shall be taken away before the king of Assyria" (2 Ne. 18:4). But here again the people in Judah don't buy the prophet's word, just as we've come to expect. This time their resistance is described in a striking image. Judah "refuseth the waters of Shiloah that go softly" (v. 6); they don't like the gentle brook that provides their city with life-sustaining water. And the result is that "the Lord bringeth upon them the waters of the river, strong and many"—a symbol of "the king of Assyria" with all his military force (v. 7). In the place of a trustworthy spring, they'll get a flood, "reach[ing] even to the neck" (v. 8). See, the difficulty is that Judah's seriously considering giving in to Syria and Ephraim; they collectively want to join the coalition or confederacy. So Isaiah tells them to go right ahead and see whether their lack of faith gets them anywhere: "Associate yourselves, O ye people!" he says. Join the coalition, "and ye shall be broken in pieces" (v. 9). They're free to pursue their plans, but "it shall come to naught" (v. 10).

It's at this point that Isaiah decides to lay out what the Lord has told him about this whole affair. He explains that the Lord's guided him "with a strong hand" (2 Ne. 18:11) and guided him away from supporting the confederacy of nations: "Say ye not 'A confederacy!' to all to whom this people shall say 'A confederacy!'" (v. 12). While the people "stumble and fall," then (v. 15), Isaiah's to let God be his "fear" and his "dread" (v. 13). And because Isaiah's people won't hear any of this, he's now told—we've talked about this passage already several times—to "bind up the testimony" he's offered, to "seal the law" for a later people that'll finally be ready to receive his message (v. 16). In the meanwhile, Isaiah himself is content just to "wait upon the Lord," that paradoxical God who "hideth his face from the house of Jacob" (v. 17). Isaiah gathers his "disciples" (v. 16) and his "children" (v. 18) about him as they look to a future of redemption and renewed possibility.

Interestingly, Isaiah sees an intervening series of events happening between his own time and that future of redemption and renewed possibility. He anticipates there being some who recognize too late that the prophet was right. Remembering Isaiah only when his prophecies of destruction are fulfilled—that is, after the prophet's death but before the time of the remnant's redemption—these people decide to stage a séance! They seek out "familiar spirits" and "wizards that peep and mutter," hoping "for the living to hear from the dead" (2 Ne. 18:19). But Isaiah's anticipatory response to this nonsense is simple: "To the law and to the testimony!" (v. 20). He hopes such fools will recognize that the answers they seek are to be found in the sealed writings of Isaiah, in a text directed to the surviving remnant. Unfortunately, such misguided people will "curse . . . their God" (v. 21) and then "be driven to darkness" (v. 22). They won't seek out Isaiah's writings or join those who will be preserved to read them when they can be opened again.

The darkness to be experienced by these people who, as Isaiah puts it, have "no light in them" (2 Ne. 18:20), won't last forever, however. "The people that walked in darkness" will instead "have seen a great light . . . ; upon them hath the light shined" (2 Ne. 19:2). This is because Assyria will finally be off their backs. God will have "broken the yoke" that weighs so heavily on Israel (v. 4). How? With the rise of a new king. There's a prediction at the outset of Isaiah 9 of a "child" to be "born" with "the government . . . upon his shoulder" (v. 6). You know—you can *sing*—the text. We'll be looking at it in more detail next time, since it's messianic. For now let's just put it this way: Isaiah imagines a time to come when those who have struggled under Assyria's weight will be delivered by a righteous king.

But no sooner does Isaiah announce that good news than he goes back to the problems Israel's to face in the meanwhile. There's a "word unto Jacob" that has to be reviewed (2 Ne. 19:8). The northern kingdom proves arrogant in its defiance of Assyria, despite the obvious gains the enemy makes against its little coalition of local nations. They ridiculously claim that their losses—"the bricks are fallen down," and "the sycamores are cut down"—will be followed by gains: "We will build with hewn stones" instead of mere bricks! "We will change [lowly sycamores] into cedars!" (v. 10). But of course they'll fall before Assyria, destroyed and scattered. Their own allies will in fact turn against them, "the Syrians before and the Philistines behind" (v. 12). Ephraim will be cut down to size, misled (like Judah!) by their "leaders"—wayward elders and "the prophet that teacheth lies" (vv. 15–16). The devastation predicted for Ephraim is disastrous, with no "mercy on their fatherless and widows" (v. 17). Their "briars and thorns" will be burned up, but by their own folly, since their "wickedness burneth as the fire" (v. 18). They themselves will be "the fuel of the fire" (v. 19). The northern kingdom will end up destroying itself, "Manasseh Ephraim, and Ephraim Manasseh," both set against Judah (v. 21).

As you might guess, all this is supposed to serve as a warning to the southern kingdom, to Judah. They watch as their Israelite brothers to the north are crushed by the imperial foe. They see the reality of the threat, and yet they fail to trust in God as well! Well, Isaiah calls on them to turn around, echoing the woes we talked about back in Isaiah 5: "Woe unto them that decree unrighteous decrees" (2 Ne. 20:1), people writing laws "to turn aside the needy" from justice and "to take away the right from the poor" (v. 2). Here's Isaiah's poignant question to such a people: "What will ye do in the day of visitation? . . . To whom will ye flee for help?" (v. 3). Things can't look good for Judah.

Survival of the Remnant

And yet Isaiah quickly turns back to his theme of a promised redemption. Actually, "redemption" is too strong a word at this point, isn't it? Isaiah turns back to his theme of deliverance. A remnant will escape the devastation. But how? Here there's no more allusive talk of a coming king.

Instead, as Isaiah 10 goes on, we get a story about God himself placing a limit on Assyria's advance. As before, Isaiah calls Assyria a mere "rod" or a "staff," a tool in God's hand to accomplish divine purposes (2 Ne. 20:5). The empire has been sent "against a hypocritical nation" with the task of "tread[ing] them down like the mire of the streets" (v. 6). But Assyria has interpreted this all rather differently—and rather self-servingly. The king of Assyria "meaneth not so . . . , but in his heart it is to destroy and cut off nations not a few" (v. 7). Reflecting on his military successes—and in particular those over the northern kingdom of Ephraim—he assumes he has the power to do anything he wants to Judah: "Shall I not, as I have done unto Samaria and her idols, so do to Jerusalem and to her idols?" (v. 11). But here's Isaiah: "When the Lord hath performed his whole work upon mount Zion and upon Jerusalem," producing a remnant ready to be holy, the Lord "will punish the fruit of the stout heart of the king of Assyria, and the glory of his high looks" (v. 12). The ax won't "boast itself against him that heweth therewith" (v. 15).

The Lord's plan of action? We saw a moment ago that Ephraim's briars and thorns burned up, set on fire by their own wickedness. Now Isaiah says this of Assyria: "The light of Israel shall be for a fire and his Holy One for a flame, and shall burn and shall devour [Assyria's] thorns, and his briars, in one day" (2 Ne. 20:17). What's left of Assyria at the end of this is a few trees, few enough "that a child may write them" (v. 19). And there emerges from the wreckage "the remnant of Israel," those "escaped of the house of Jacob" (v. 20). They no longer trust in Assyria but instead in the Lord. And "the remnant shall return—yea, even the remnant of Jacob—unto the mighty God" (v. 21). There's been "a consumption, even determined in all the land" (v. 23), but this consumption "shall overflow with righteousness" (v. 22), since there's a righteous remnant that's left over at the end. And so Assyria's threat has lasted only "a very little while," Isaiah says (v. 25).

Isaiah 10 ends with a bit of theater meant to dramatize Assyria's failure to conquer Judah according to its plans. The prophet describes the Assyrian army marching from Ephraim toward Judah, listing the cities one by one as they get closer and closer. For ancient readers and listeners, the tension builds as the danger gets nearer and nearer—and nearer. But then, just a short distance from Jerusalem, the army is stopped. Assyria will "remain at Nob that day. He shall shake his hand against the mount of the daughter of Zion" (2 Ne. 20:32), but he'll do no more than that. And as Assyria, frustrated, shakes his angry fist at Jerusalem, "the Lord—the

Lord of hosts!—shall lop the bough with terror" (v. 33), cutting down the Assyrian tree in spectacular fashion. Where once there was a towering cedar, there's now nothing but a stump.

Which leaves us with *two* stumps, if you'll remember. Isaiah's commission, which we talked about last time, ends with a prediction that Judah's difficulties with gigantic imperial powers will reduce it to a stump, dead in all appearances. But now we've got two stumps, a Judean and an Assyrian stump. Both look dead, of course. Each reminds us of a once-glorious tree that's now gone. But only one of those once-glorious trees is gone *forever*. You remember the promise at the end of Isaiah's commission. Judah leaves only a stump behind, but that stump is also, curiously, a "holy seed" (2 Ne. 16:13). The stump of Judah, unlike the stump of Assyria, should sprout again and start growing. Perhaps it's no surprise, then, that this is what Isaiah describes next. Immediately after he tells us that the Assyrian tree has been cut down, he brings our attention back to the apparently-dead stump of Judah, and he asks us to watch new life spring out of its roots.

You may be familiar with this text, since it gets attention in the Doctrine and Covenants—in section 113, that is. There, Joseph Smith recounts Moroni reciting this text to him during his visitation in 1823. At any rate, Isaiah 11 opens with "a rod" coming "out of the stem of Jesse" (2 Ne. 21:1). Stem? A more straightforward translation of the Hebrew would just be "stump." There's something growing out of the Judean stump, the one described back in Isaiah 6. Perhaps this is more straightforward in the next line: "A branch shall grow out of his roots" (v. 1). Assyria came through Judah like a lumberjack, felling Judah's tree. But now Assyria has in turn been cut to the ground, and the stump of Judah—or really, of Jesse, or of the royal house in Jerusalem—that stump begins to sprout again. There's a new branch to be seen there.

That's a rich image. The Book of Mormon makes a whole lot of this image, with all its talk of the "branch of Israel"—a phrase it uses to refer to the Israelite remnant. But forget the Book of Mormon for a moment. We've already seen this image being used just within Isaiah. Back in Isaiah 4, in the second oracle of promise offered in the Book of Isaiah, we were told that "the branch of the Lord" would be "beautiful and glorious" (2 Ne. 14:2). We noted when we looked at that text that this image of the branch was regarded by Nephi's time—as evidenced in Jeremiah's prophecies—as messianic in nature. And we'll be coming back to this image of the branch when we look at Isaiah 13–14 as well. So don't miss the significance of this branch coming out of the roots of the supposedly dead tree.

But also recognize that the significance we've just highlighted means that we're going to leave detailed discussion of much of Isaiah 11 for next time, since we've promised to address the question of the messianic in Isaiah 7–12 all at once in our next lecture. For the moment, it's enough just to recognize that we've got more that needs saying about all this.

Moving along in Isaiah 11, then, here's what we find next. Assyria's fall, coupled with the rise of a good Judean king, results in a time of remarkable peace. Isaiah famously talks here about the wolf dwelling with the lamb, the leopard lying down with the kid, the calf and the young lion and the fatling together, "and a little child shall lead them" (2 Ne. 21:6). We pretty consistently jump straight from Isaiah's words to the idea that there's a millennium of peace coming someday soon. But let's stick with Isaiah himself a while longer. From his own immediate historical and political point of view, he's been talking about the retreat of Assyria from its attempt at domination. And he's been talking about there being a remnant of Judah present and prepared at that point to receive the prophet's message. The peace he describes, with even the animals participating, is supposed to give us a sense of how utopian the era of the remnant is supposed to be. Things will finally turn around for Judah. Gentile nations will come seeking out the God of Israel—just as promised back in Isaiah 2—and "the Lord shall set his hand again the second time to recover the remnant of his people" (2 Ne. 21:11). They're returning "from Assyria and from Egypt and from Pathros and from Cush and from Elam and from Shinar and from Hamath and from the islands of the sea" (v. 11). In short, the survivors come from "the four corners of the earth" and "gather together" again in Judah (v. 12). There's finally a remnant fully constituted and ready to understand the prophet's message. Assyria, it turns out, has been rather useful, an effective tool that could be dispensed with at the end of the process. The remnant's there, and Assyria's out of the way.

But there's an even greater promise from Isaiah here. With the remnant in place, much bigger things can be accomplished. In fact, the whole of Israel can be redeemed by the remnant. Here's what Isaiah says along these lines: "The envy of Ephraim also shall depart . . . . Ephraim shall not envy Judah, and Judah shall not vex Ephraim" (2 Ne. 21:13). The two rival kingdoms of Israel, north and south, are to be reunited after a long period of strife. The sort of thing, for instance, that happened with the Syro-Ephraimite crisis won't happen again. Instead, a reunited Israel, developing out of the seed or remnant, will finally gain dominance over its foes—hopefully opening onto a time of worldwide peace and worship of the true God. At any rate, together the two houses of Israel "shall fly" against any remaining enemies (v. 14). And then all of Israel will sing a song of praise to the Lord, which makes up Isaiah 12. It's short, and perhaps we should just quote it in its entirety: "O Lord, I will praise thee. Though thou wast angry with me, thine anger is turned away, and thou comfortedst me. Behold, God is my salvation. I will trust and not be afraid. For the Lord Jehovah is my strength and my song. He also is become my salvation" (2 Ne. 22:1–2). There's verse one, as it were, of the song. Here's verse two: "Praise the Lord! Call upon his name! Declare his doings among the people! Make mention that his name is exalted! Sing unto the Lord, for he hath done excellent things! This is known in all the earth. Cry out and shout, thou inhabitant of Zion! For great is the Holy One of Israel in the midst of thee!" (vv. 4–6). There's the song. And Isaiah uses an interesting metaphor to describe the people singing it. They "draw water out of the wells of salvation" as they sing (v. 3).

There. There's the story of the production of the remnant. It's a beautiful story, I think. And it's not *nearly* so difficult as we tend to make it as readers. It's complex, certainly. But it's relatively clear. Of course, there's a little more we've got to do with these chapters. We've conveniently avoided dealing with the difficult texts so often regarded as messianic in Isaiah 7, 9, and 11. But we can leave that for next time.

Lecture XVIII

Isaiah and the Messiah

The Question of Messianic Texts

Today we're going to talk about so-called "messianic" texts in Isaiah 6–12. There are three of them we need to consider, and we've got to look at them carefully. Not only do we want to ask about how they fit into the story Nephi's Isaiah has to tell about the production of an Israelite remnant—that's crucial, of course—but we also want to ask just what they mean on their own terms. *Do* these chapters of Isaiah anticipate the coming of the Messiah?

That question might—and perhaps it *should*—make you feel a bit apprehensive about where we're headed. How can I get away with attaching the words "so-called" to the words "messianic prophecies"? If you're a reader of chapter headings, you can't help but know how often the official LDS edition of the Bible says that the prophets speak messianically. And if you've read the Gospels, you know how often you can find statements there about how this or that event in the life of Christ fulfilled this or that Old Testament prophecy. Besides, the Book of Mormon is pretty clear that "all the holy prophets" had "a hope of [Christ's] glory many hundred years before his coming" (Jacob 4:4). What good reason could any believing Latter-day Saint have for raising a question about whether Isaiah prophesied of the coming of a messiah?

Well, actually, *some* of you might have suspicions. Perhaps you've read or heard that a great many biblical scholars these days have all kinds of doubts about whether the Hebrew prophets genuinely anticipated the coming of Christ. Perhaps you're aware that the great majority of working interpreters of the Hebrew Bible think that most of the texts that average Christians regard as clearly predicting Jesus's ministry and atonement have little or nothing to do with the New Testament. And perhaps you've wondered whether—or angrily concluded that—all these scholars are simply tools of secularism and irreligion. How could such scholars *not* be perfect examples of what Jacob in the Book of Mormon warns against: the "learned" who "think they are wise" and so "hearken not unto the counsel of God—for they set it aside, supposing they know of themselves." Such actions, Jacob tells us, make the scholarly world's wisdom into "foolishness"; he not only says that "it profiteth them not," but also that "they shall perish" (2 Ne. 9:28). Can't we simply write off much or most of biblical studies as a gathering of such wise fools, too committed to pandering to secular humanism to read the scriptures honestly?

Fortunately or unfortunately, I don't think things are as simple as that. Biblical scholars make arguments for their conclusions, and their arguments about the relatively un-Christian scope of much of the Hebrew Bible are generally good ones. We commit a logical fallacy when we dismiss these arguments simply on the grounds that the people who have written them up work within the secular academy—that's the logical fallacy called "ad hominem attack." (And besides, we ought to get to know some of these scholars. It turns out that very few of them are warriors for the secular.) So we've actually got to take a look at what interpreters of, for instance, Isaiah 6–12 have to say about whether these are messianic prophecies. And it turns out that this is a *really* complicated question.

Let me begin by noting that there's no full-blooded scholarly consensus on whether Isaiah 6–12 contains messianic prophecies. This is a point of debate. Much depends on exactly how the term "messianic" is understood. But much more depends on exactly how we understand the process through which these chapters came to have their present form. So that's where we've got to start, it seems to me. Let's say a few things about the meaning of the term "messianic," and let's say at least a little bit about the debate concerning the formation of Isaiah 6–12.

What Is a Messiah?

Average Latter-day Saints probably hear the word "messianic" and think simply of Jesus Christ. That's entirely appropriate, of course, but we need to be clear that that's not exactly what the term means. Note that the word "messianic" is a bit more general, suggestive of a *concept* or a *category* rather than an *individual* or a *person*. Messianic prophecy would be prophecy that anticipates *a* messiah, however that messiah figure is understood. Early Christians don't seem to have claimed that the prophets of the Old Testament anticipated *Jesus*, but rather that they anticipated *a messiah who turned out to be Jesus.* Messianic prophecy focuses on a figure still to come whose work is that of deliverance for God's people.

So what's a messiah? You may know that our English word "messiah" is just a transliteration of a Hebrew word that means "anointed." A messiah is simply an anointed person. So think for a moment of those passages in the story of David where he has a chance to kill Saul but doesn't. You remember his reason for restraint? He says he wouldn't dare to harm the Lord's anointed. You can probably guess, now, what Hebrew word you can find in those passages. David says he wouldn't dare to harm the Lord's messiah. And this means that the Hebrew Bible is *filled* with messiahs. It's filled with anointed people: kings, at the very least. But not only kings. Priests were anointed by way of preparing them to serve at the temple. And there were a great many priests in pre-Christian times. As you read through the Old Testament, then, recognize that you're *constantly* reading about messiahs.

Now, the fact that you can find references to messiahs all through the legal and historical books of the Old Testament doesn't make those books into messianic prophecies. Why not? Well, they're not prophecies. They're stories, for the most part. They tell us about people who were anointed, but they don't prophesy of some *other* anointed figure, some *other* king or priest, still to come. What makes messianic prophecy messianic prophecy is the way it looks *beyond* these "everyday" messiahs, who were all over ancient Israel, to a messiah you couldn't find in Israel's midst. Messianic prophecy essentially looks at all the available messiahs and finds only reason to despair, but then it looks to a future in which some messiah of messiahs will show up and set things right. We do this sort of thing all the time ourselves, don't we? You're in college, taking class after class from boring professors. At some point, you begin to daydream about a class where the professor is genuinely interesting, genuinely engaging. You might find yourself working up a kind of description of this ideal professor, waiting for her or his arrival in the classroom. You're looking for what you're already experiencing—a professor—but one who finally gets things right. That's something very like messianic prophecy.

So to ask whether this or that biblical text is a messianic prophecy is most basically to ask whether it anticipates someone coming along eventually, occupying more or less an already-established institutional position, but finally doing so in a way that makes the institution work. And there's a rather specific set of institutions that messianic prophecy would have in mind: Israel's monarchical government—a king who finally does things right, delivering the people—or Israel's temple cult—a priest who finally mediates between people and God in a way that redeems. The focus of most supposedly messianic prophecies you can find in the Old Testament is the monarchy. These prophecies look to the possibility of a good king finally occupying the throne of David.

Okay, we've got a general picture here. But as you might imagine, there's a good deal of disagreement among biblical scholars about any further specifics. If you read Joseph Fitzmyer's *The One Who Is To Come* for instance, you'll find him defining the messianic a good deal more strictly than we've done here, with the result that he finds more or less no messianic prophecies in the Old Testament. On the other hand, you can read someone like Antti Laato—his *A Star Is Rising*, for example—and there you find a definition of the messianic that allows for a careful historical reconstruction of the development of messianic anticipation in pre-exilic Israel. So whether one reads Isaiah 6–12 as containing messianic prophecies or not will largely depend on how narrowly or broadly one defines the term "messianic." And let's make clear right away that you can find a good many scholars arguing both positions as regards these chapters specifically. There are those who think it's entirely inappropriate to speak of messianic prophecy in connection with Isaiah, and there are those who think it's perfectly clear that messianic prophecy had its crucial beginnings in precisely these chapters of Isaiah.

But there's more to the debate and disagreement here than just questions of definition. A major part of the difficulty springs from the fact that there's no consensus about exactly how to read these chapters with a historical-critical eye. You see, at the height of textual-critical studies of the Bible—around a century ago now—people working on Isaiah saw as their task to nail down exactly which parts of the present Book of Isaiah were actually original to the eighth-century prophet. And one chunk of the Book of Isaiah came to be pretty widely recognized as among the earliest kernels of the Isaianic corpus: chapters 6, 7, and 8, along with the first several verses of chapter 9. This stretch of the text scholars generally referred to (biblical studies was dominated at the time by German scholarship) as Isaiah's *Denkschrift*, his "memoir." The idea was that the text reporting Isaiah's experience in the temple, his subsequent encounter with Ahaz, his testimony regarding the threat from Assyria, and his anticipation of a Davidic king who would deliver Judah from that threat—in short, Isaiah 6:1–9:6—formed the earliest prophetic word Isaiah had to offer. This general point of consensus inevitably raised the stakes of the question of whether anything messianic can be found in Isaiah, since some of the supposedly messianic texts were at that point widely regarded as having certainly originated a century and a half before the exile in Babylon. That'd be *really* early messianic anticipation!

That gives you a sense for where the debate got started, basically. But then things have become a great deal more complicated in the past half-century or so. Not only have most Isaiah scholars long since ceased to aim at discovering just the Isaianic original, but a host of difficulties with the old *Denkschrift* thesis have been identified. There's now relatively little agreement about exactly when and by what process Isaiah 6:1–9:6 took shape, or even whether it's advisable to draw such tight boundaries around that text. There's a good deal of discussion going on regarding a whole variety of ways one might make sense of the internal structure and shape of Isaiah 1–12. In a way, this means that the high-stakes debate regarding the presence of messianic prophecy in Isaiah 6–12 has both been put on hold and been rendered even more important than before. Before any one scholar can make a contribution to the question of the messianic here, she first has to establish what she takes to be the basic textual history of these chapters, and that will always be a rather controversial position. So opinions aren't converging, and there's no evidence that they'll be converging any time soon.

Nephi and the Messiah

Where does all this complexity leave us? Well, let's mark out a few points of orientation to see if we can get our bearings. First, let's note that Nephi seems to find *something* messianic in these chapters. He doesn't tell us *which* texts he reads messianically—is it Isaiah 7? Isaiah 9? Isaiah 11?— but he pretty clearly finds *something* messianic there. Second, though, it's worth noting that the way Nephi talks about his father's prophecies suggests that the Lehites understood themselves to be launching a more explicitly messianic—perhaps a uniquely explicitly messianic—prophetic tradition. Remember that Lehi was driven out of Jerusalem precisely because he had things to say about "the coming of a messiah" (1 Ne. 1:19), and remember that Nephi and his brother only eventually received clear and specific revelations concerning Jesus Christ, which allowed them to make sense of Old-World scripture in a way they couldn't have done back in Jerusalem.

Taking these two points together, it seems that Nephi reads certain parts of Isaiah messianically even as he recognizes that his predecessors may seldom, if ever, have been able to do that. This puts us in a funny position, doesn't it? It'd seem like we're free to see in Isaiah 6–12 *two* rival interpretations of the text—one non-messianic (or at least not messianic in any strong sense), and one messianic (in a strong sense). We've got something like Jesus's parables here, stories that carry both a straightforward meaning that anyone can understand and a mysterious meaning that only those with ears to hear can riddle out. Nephi has ears to hear, but he seems to be fully aware that these text can be read in another way as well. And remember that we've already seen Nephi using a kind of technical term to describe the tension between these two sorts of things, haven't we? "Likening." Isaiah 6–12 should probably be understood to fall under the same paradigm. These are texts that can be read without an eye to likening, and they're texts that can be read with an eye to likening as well. And in this case, likening seems to have something to do with reading messianically.

So here's what I propose to do with the time we've got today. Let's take a look at the three prophecies in Isaiah 6–12 that sometimes get called messianic, and let's see how they might be read both non-messianically and messianically, both without an eye to likening and with an eye to likening. We don't yet want to try to nail down exactly how Nephi himself would have read these chapters, but perhaps we can find ourselves exploring the tension between a relatively naturalistic interpretation of the texts and a more emphatically theological reading of them. And before we do so, let me add this further point, just for fun. The shape of Isaiah scholarship *right now*, with the rise of the so-called "Formation of Isaiah" school, is such that there's increasing recognition that you can find a transition from the naturalistic to the theological, from the non-messianic to the messianic, going on right in the formation of the text. That's way too quick a way of summarizing a remarkable development in Isaiah scholarship, but hopefully some of you will go look at some of the work being done (I highly recommend the work of Hugh Williamson). The rest of you can feel quite free to ignore my little aside here.

The Virgin's Son

Okay, what do we find in Isaiah 6–12 that looks messianic? Well, we flagged the relevant passages as we went along last time, but let's focus in on things in more detail now. Perhaps we can start with the most famous of the prophecies: the virgin conceiving and bearing a son. Let's turn to Isaiah 7.

Remember the context we established last time. We're in the thick of the Syro-Ephraimite crisis, and Isaiah has just come to see Ahaz at Jerusalem's water supply with a message about trusting in God rather than in military strategy. But Isaiah doesn't just tell Ahaz that his enemies will soon be gone; he says also—apparently in the Lord's voice—that Ahaz is free to ask for a divine sign that would confirm the truth of such a remarkable prophecy. Ahaz demurs, contrary to God's will, and so, as Isaiah says, "the Lord himself shall give you a sign" (2 Ne. 17:14). What is it? You know the verse well: "Behold, a virgin shall conceive, and shall bear a son, and shall call his name 'Immanuel'" (v. 14). Thanks especially to the Gospel of Matthew, Christians hear these words and can't help but think of Jesus. A virgin birth! And what a name—"Immanuel," God with us! What else *could* this mean?

Perhaps you're aware, though, that scholars routinely dismiss the messianic interpretation of this text. In fact, if there *is* consensus about anything regarding the messianic in Isaiah 6–12, it's that *this* text isn't messianic. Why? Well, for one, the King James rendering of the text is misleading in an important way. The Hebrew word translated as "virgin" doesn't, strictly speaking, mean "virgin"; it means "young woman." Of course, plenty of young women are virgins, and there are contexts in which the word *is* used to refer to virgins, but no one would translate the passage in this narrow way without an eye to Matthew's use of the passage. And in context—both textual and historical—there's very little reason for seeing Isaiah's prophetic sign as referring to Jesus. Let's make this clear by reading the continuation of the sign. Yes, "a virgin shall conceive, and bear a son," but the text goes on to explain this: "Before the child shall know to refuse the evil and choose the good, the land that thou abhorrest shall be forsaken of both her kings" (2 Ne. 17:16). You see what the sign's supposed to do, right? Let's paraphrase: "Look, Ahaz, God himself will give you a sign. A young woman here in the city will get pregnant soon and then give birth, naming her child 'God is with us!' as a gesture of the trust you lack. And then before that kid's old enough to know the difference between right and wrong, the Syrian and Ephraimite kings you think are so threatening will both be dead!" *That's* Isaiah's message. You can see immediately why it makes little sense in context to understand it as a reference to Jesus. How would the birth of Jesus, seven and a half centuries away, serve as a sign to Ahaz regarding the imminent demise of his enemies?

Hopefully you can see why scholars aren't terribly convinced that there's much of anything messianic going on in Isaiah 7. And they aren't driven to their conclusions by some kind of secular zeal. They're just asking us to read the passage in context. And the context doesn't suggest much of anything by way of the messianic. That said, let's note this: it's entirely possible that Nephi read the passage messianically. He'd seen the Virgin in a vision, and he might well have come to read Isaiah's words in the way Matthew would much later, or the way Christians have quite generally read the passage. Let's be clear that, even if Isaiah himself didn't have Jesus in mind here—even if, in fact, it doesn't make much sense at all to see Jesus as the focus of this prophecy—there's still something legitimate about the Christian interpretation. One can certainly claim that the Holy Spirit intended something in Isaiah's words that neither he nor Ahaz could have recognized. And one can certainly claim that the Christian is free to find here a kind of trace—a type or shadow—of Jesus Christ. That seems to me quite legitimate, really. But the most honest way of doing this is to make that claim *while at the same time* recognizing how those without belief in Christ responsibly and legitimately read the text in another way.

A Child Is Born

That's enough on Isaiah 7, I hope, because we don't have any more time to spend on it. Let's turn to Isaiah 9, where we come to a passage that's more *objectively* messianic in nature. Again, remember the context we developed last time: Isaiah's been talking about the difficulties Assyria will force on Judah due to the king's lack of trust in God. But at the beginning of this chapter, the prophet begins to lighten the burden of his prophecy, announcing that things won't be quite so bad as they might have been. Why? Because a new king will arise to deliver Judah from the Assyrian yoke. You can sing the words, I'm guessing: "For unto us a child is born! Unto us a son is given! And the government shall be upon his shoulder! And his name shall be called Wonderful Counselor, the Mighty God, the Everlasting Father, the Prince of Peace!" (2 Ne. 19:6). The prophecy continues, of course, with a reference to "the throne of David" and the continuation of an increase in the influence and power of the enthroned (v. 7). Notice that here we're already closer to the question of the messianic, because we're clearly dealing with a king—an anointed figure—who's associated with the throne of David. And what's predicted here is a Davidic king who will finally get some things right.

At this point, then, stricter and looser definitions of the messianic will decide whether the text actually fits the label. If we think the prediction of any decent Davidic king amounts to a messianic prophecy, then we've got a messianic prophecy here. If we think messianic prophecy must include something bigger than that—an anticipation of a figure who will bring history to a kind of end, suspend the law in fulfilled righteousness, and usher in an era of unending peace—then we're arguably not yet dealing with messianic prophecy. You see, it seems pretty clear in context that Isaiah's prophecy here is focused primarily on Ahaz's son Hezekiah. Ahaz has proven himself untrustworthy, since he refuses to trust the Lord. But there's a royal baby, heir to the throne, whose destiny is to turn the situation in Judah around. If you look at Israelite history, that's just what Hezekiah does. Isaiah himself tells the story in Isaiah 36–37. Hezekiah will repel the Assyrian forces and deliver Jerusalem, just barely. And it seems that *this* is what Isaiah's anticipating at this point. As before, it's context that makes this clear. Isaiah's trying to talk about the reversal of Judah's bad fortune in its confrontation with Assyria. It'd be a strange thing to predict the coming of Jesus, some seven centuries after Assyria's failure to capture Jerusalem, if he wished to provide any comfort in the immediate historical setting. It seems pretty clear he's got Hezekiah in mind.

What of those titles, though? "The Mighty God"? "The Everlasting Father?" "The Prince of Peace"? Don't they pretty clearly point to a divine figure rather than some merely earthly king like Hezekiah? Well, actually, these are throne names that would be applied to the newly crowned king. There's nothing terribly surprising about any ancient society calling the king a "wonderful counselor" or an "everlasting father" or a "prince of peace." Maybe calling a king "the mighty god" seems a bit more extreme, though it certainly wouldn't have been out of place in every one of Israel's ancient neighbors. You might be aware of how the Egyptians viewed the divine status of their kings, for instance. But perhaps we'd naturally balk at the claim that a prophet like Isaiah would concede to calling a merely earthly king like Hezekiah "the mighty god." And I think we're right to balk at that idea. But it might be argued that this is just a translation issue. Recent translations don't render the Hebrew there as "the Mighty God." Here's Joseph Blenkinsopp's translation from the *Anchor Bible*: "His titles will be: Marvelous Counselor, Hero Warrior, Eternal Father, Prince of Peace." Not dissimilar is the translation offered by Mormonism's own Avraham Gileadi: "He will be called Wonderful Counsellor, one Mighty in Valor, a Father for Ever, a Prince of Peace." That these are possibilities perhaps gets us out of trouble, showing that Isaiah may not exactly have meant to indicate that anyone about to be enthroned was fully divine.

Now, someone could of course object that, whatever recent translations might suggest, the Book of Mormon still renders the title as "the Mighty God." That's entirely fair. But perhaps there we're getting a sense for how Nephi interpreted or at least likened the verse, and we'll see in a later lecture that we've got some reason to think that Nephi interpreted this passage in terms of the coming Christ.

So here in Isaiah 9 we're clearly a good deal closer to the messianic than in Isaiah 7, but we might begin to see why some interpreters would hesitate even here to speak too strictly of the messianic. It seems relatively clear in context that Isaiah was looking at the already-born heir to Ahaz's throne, an up-and-coming king who would stand against Assyria and deliver Judah after a great deal of trouble. He was apparently looking forward to the possibility that the monarchy might get on the right foot, and that's certainly a messianic concern in a certain limited sense. But he doesn't seem to have been looking out from the Assyrian situation onto the much-later birth of Jesus. We're free to sing along to Handel's *Messiah*, finding shadows of New Testament events in the birth of Hezekiah. And perhaps we're even *expected* as Christians to see such shadows in the events of Isaiah's day. But I suspect we're also to see with real clarity how people in Isaiah's days themselves— Isaiah included—likely wouldn't have understood any of this to point to Jesus. Rather, the message they'd have heard in Isaiah's words concerned the immediate Assyrian threat and the way that could yield the production of an Israelite remnant, ready to hear the word of God.

The Branch

Let's turn, then, to the third and final of the three supposedly messianic texts in Isaiah 6–12. It's found in Isaiah 11, and it's a text we as Latter-day Saints have a great deal to say about. We talked last time about the apparently-dead stump of Judah sprouting new life, with a young and tender branch growing out of its roots. This "rod . . . of Jesse" (2 Ne. 21:1) has often in the Christian tradition been interpreted as Jesus Christ, at the very least because Isaiah goes on to say that "the Spirit of the Lord shall rest upon him . . . and shall make him of quick understanding" (vv. 2–3). That's the kind of language Jesus uses in the Gospel of Luke to describe himself, though he draws that language in large part from a much later Isaianic text—the opening verses of Isaiah 61. You can see how this has come rather generally to be regarded as a messianic prophecy in the Christian tradition.

Are we here in the vicinity of the messianic? Well, by the standard academic criteria, we're now even closer to the messianic than in Isaiah 9. We've got here a reference to the monarchy, and specifically to a coming king who'll finally get things right. That's pretty clear. It could of course again be that it's just Hezekiah that's in question, but that's less clear here in Isaiah 11 than in Isaiah 9. Why? Well, because we get here in Isaiah 11 a good deal more end-of-times talk. The dead stump sprouts a new branch, endowed with a divine spirit. And then we're told that this branch will "smite the earth with the rod of his mouth" and "with the breath of his lips" will "slay the wicked" (2 Ne. 21:4). That's the sort of talk the prophets associated with the eschatological (end times) Day of the Lord, when judgment would be meted out against the proud. Further, the prophecy rather famously goes on to describe a time of universal peace, with lambs and lions lying down together. You know the passage. So if we're dealing with Hezekiah still, we're getting a good deal more elevated language in the description. Here it seems we're beginning to move beyond mere anticipation of imminent deliverance through a human king to eschatological anticipation of final deliverance through a divine figure.

So here perhaps we're finally relatively securely in the realm of the messianic. More or less precisely for that reason, many Isaiah scholars regard this passage as a late addition to Isaiah, the kind of thing that could only have been inserted into the text after the rise of certain messianic hopes. Basically, the view is that certain disappointments concerning Hezekiah's anticipated deliverance led to an attempt, found here in Isaiah 11, to reinterpret Isaiah's word concerning Hezekiah as a word concerning a king still further off in history, one who would more drastically serve to fulfill Israel's most desperate desires. Whatever must be decided about the dating and authorship of Isaiah 11, however, things seem to indicate that we certainly *have* come to a more strictly messianic text here.

There's a terrible oddity here for Latter-day Saints, though. We have Section 113 of the Doctrine and Covenants, where the Lord himself declares that the rod of Jesse emphatically *isn't* Christ, but rather "a servant in the hands of Christ, who is partly a descendant of Jesse as well as of Ephraim, or of the house of Joseph, on whom there is laid much power" (D&C 113:4). We haven't anything like the time to go into all the complications that come with *that* interpretation. Let's just note that at the point in Isaiah 6–12 where it seems to biblical scholars that we're most likely in messianic territory, there are uniquely Mormon scriptural resources that suggest that we've moved right past the messianic into a strictly postmessianic eschatological context. Perhaps as Latter-day Saints, we have unique reason to doubt that we're dealing with the messianic in Isaiah 11—though let's be clear that Nephi hadn't read D&C 113, and he may well have interpreted this text messianically. Perhaps. We'll be raising this question again after next time's lecture, when we come to 2 Nephi 25.

Where does all this leave us? Presumably in a good deal of confusion. My aim today has largely been just to complicate matters. I want us to be aware that we're *far* too quick to find Jesus in Isaiah, privileging traditionally messianic passages over everything else because we think we can see Christian themes in the prophet. But let's be clear that there are other ways to read these texts, and that any interpretation of these texts is highly debatable. We're on the safest ground when we simply recognize that there's a lot more work to do if we're interested in really coming to an understanding of what's going on here.

But perhaps we've also come to this. I know we're out of time, but let me throw one last point of conclusion at you: We've perhaps come to see also that by far the *surest* thing going on in Isaiah 6–12 concerns the production of the remnant, something Isaiah sees as having happened primarily (but symbolically) in the wake of the Syro-Ephraimite crisis. That's where we should probably focus our attention when reading these chapters. We'll get back to this.

Lecture XIX

Isaiah 13–14

A Focus on Babylon

We've taken quite a while to absorb Isaiah 6–12, but we want to move more quickly through Isaiah 13–14. My hope is to be done with it after today's lecture, so that we have sufficient time to deal with 2 Nephi 25–30 before this lecture series has to wrap up. So let's see what we can say, relatively briefly, about Nephi's quotation of Isaiah 13–14 in 2 Nephi 23–24.

We said some lectures back that these two chapters were originally—that is, when Joseph Smith dictated the text of the Book of Mormon—just one chapter. And it turns out that more or less all scholars working on Isaiah agree that they should be considered a single oracle. Really, Isaiah 13–14 opens a longer sequence of text in the Book of Isaiah, often called the oracles against the nations, stretching through Isaiah 23. What characterizes these eleven chapters is a consistent focus on the doom facing all the nations round about Judah (and sometimes Judah as well!). Moreover, each individual oracle inserted into this larger sequence is introduced in the same way, that is, with the same repeating formula: "the burden of X," the burden of whatever nation's being prophetically confronted with its doom. The first and the longest entry in the whole collection of burdens is that of Babylon, and that's what Nephi quotes in 2 Nephi 23–24.

Some interpreters find significant patterns in the larger ordering of the oracles against the nations. For instance, it begins with Babylon, the center of commerce, and it ends with Tyre, the center of trade. Such insights are interesting, but they don't seem to have interested Nephi much. He's happy just to copy over into his record the oracle concerning Babylon's doom, leaving the remainder of the oracles against the nations in the brass plates. He's clearly interested only in what this larger sequence of oracles has to say about the fate of the imperial threat of his own day. It's important to note also that he copies the last part of Isaiah 14. It's not uncommon for interpreters of Isaiah to assign the last few verses of that chapter to a distinct oracle against a distinct nation. But we'll see as we go along that there's a logic to Nephi's inclusion of this material in Babylon's demise, at the very least because it brings Babylon's demise into a kind of relationship with the Assyrian situation of Isaiah's day. We'll have to clarify all this as we go along.

We're being too preliminary and therefore too abstract. Let's get into the text itself, and we'll let it work on us more directly.

Babylon's Demise

"The burden of Babylon, which Isaiah the son of Amoz did see" (2 Ne. 23:1)—there's the opening of the two-chapter oracle. We're focused right from the outset, without any sense of suspense, on Babylon. And it's got a burden. What is it? Well, the prophet issues a command to "lift . . . up a banner upon the high mountain," but this isn't a happy occasion (v. 2). Instead, the purpose of the banner is to gather an army together. The prophet reports "the noise of the multitude in the mountains, like as of a great people—a tumultuous noise of the kingdoms of nations gathered together"; and then he clarifies the meaning of all this: "the Lord of Hosts mustereth the host of the battle" (v. 4). An extremely dangerous army prepares to go against Babylon, with the aim of "destroy[ing] the whole land" (v. 5). And this army means business. Unsurprisingly, their approach causes terror: "Every man's heart shall melt, and they shall be afraid" (vv. 7–8). But this fear has to do with more than just merely human danger. Isaiah goes so far as to call this event "the day of the Lord," describing it as "cruel, both with wrath and fierce anger" (v. 9). That's language many of the Hebrew prophets use—"the day of the Lord"—to describe the time of reckoning, a moment when the Lord himself comes to level judgment against the peoples whose rebellion have gotten in the way of the divine purpose. Isaiah speaks in this oracle again and again of the "evil" of the world (v. 11), of its "sinners" (v. 9). And the army gathered is made up of God's "sanctified ones" and "mighty ones"—divine rather than human warriors (v. 3).

The coming desolation is catastrophic, then, and it's described in apocalyptic terms. "The stars of heaven and the constellations thereof shall not give their light, the sun shall be darkened in his going forth, and the moon shall not cause her light to shine" (2 Ne. 23:10). These are classic metaphors for terrifying times—times of frightening heavenly phenomena that ancient peoples had no way of explaining without attributing them to a wrathful god. Isaiah goes on to mention earthquakes and the like as well: "I will shake the heavens," he has God say, "and the earth shall remove out of her place" (v. 13). All of this combines with the army's advance to cause widespread death and destruction. In fact, the population will be so reduced that it will become prohibitively expensive to buy slaves: "I will make a man more precious than fine gold, even a man than the golden wedge of Ophir" (v. 12). The "proud" and the "wicked" are dying right and left, it seems (v. 15). And Isaiah doesn't hesitate to describe the commonplace human-inflicted horrors of war, both ancient and modern: "Their children also shall be dashed to pieces before their eyes. Their houses shall be spoiled and their wives ravished" (v. 16). In case you're not familiar with early modern English, "ravished" means "raped." This is not a pretty scene Isaiah's describing for us.

The opening formula at the outset of the chapter let us know that we're being shown Babylon's burden here, but note that nothing up to this point actually refers to Babylon. Only in its editorial context do we have any sense for where all this is headed. But perhaps it's useful to feel the rhetorical force of the oracle outside of its editorial setting, since that's how it would have been originally delivered. Can you imagine listening to everything we've just been covering—likely shouted and given great rhetorical force in its delivery—*without* the prophet clarifying until quite late in the game exactly *who* is supposed to experience all this? We hear some fifteen to seventeen verses of prophesied doom before we're given any sense for who's in so much trouble! In its original setting, this would have been even more forceful. Certainly, the *last* nation anyone would have expected the prophet to be talking about would have been Babylon. And the oracle relishes that fact. Only after so much horrific description do we get this: "And Babylon! The glory of kingdoms! The beauty of the Chaldees' excellency—shall be as when God overthrew Sodom and Gomorrah!" (2 Ne. 23:19). That would be like predicting England's downfall in the early nineteenth century, or that of the United States in about 1999!

The surprise of the focus on Babylon must have been forceful, then, when this oracle was originally given. Of course, as we've made clear, we were let in on the secret long in advance. We knew what was coming. But perhaps we can feel something of the original power of the prophecy. At any rate, the prediction is absolute. It's not just that Babylon will face difficult times. The text makes clear that they're to be entirely eradicated. Here's the prediction that follows the finally-offered clarification of who's in question: "It shall never be inhabited, neither shall it be dwelt in, from generation to generation—neither shall the Arabian pitch tent there, neither shall the shepherds make their fold there" (2 Ne. 23:20). Instead, "wild beasts of the desert shall lie there" (v. 21). The prophet goes on to provide a whole list of mythical creatures associated with dangerous and forbidden places: "satyrs" and "dragons," for instance (vv. 21–22). So Babylon becomes the kind of spooky place no one dares approach. It's to become a desolate ruin, a ghost town that really seems to be haunted. Who could bear to walk through its forsaken roads alone or at night? That's the sort of thing Isaiah predicts here.

Israel's Redemption

So, things look pretty bad for Babylon. But why all this destruction? Why this divine fury against "the Chaldees' excellency?" The prophet doesn't make this clear until the very end of Isaiah 13 and the beginning of Isaiah 14. The Lord says this: "I will destroy her speedily—yea, for I will be merciful unto my people, but the wicked shall perish" (2 Ne. 23:22). That's nice and simple, isn't it? Babylon has to face the music because the covenant people of Israel need delivering. So we're not just dealing here with a wicked people that finally get their comeuppance. We're dealing here with those who've oppressed Israel—or really, just Judah. You'll remember that after the Assyrian empire finally collapses under its own weight, it's Babylon that moves into its place as the great imperial power. And by the time of Nephi's childhood, Judah's more or less entirely under Babylon's thumb. The Book of Mormon opens in "the first year of the reign of Zedekiah, king of Judah" (1 Ne. 1:4). By that point, Babylon had already made itself into Judah's overlord, controlling who did and didn't come to the throne in Jerusalem. Zedekiah was only placed on the throne because Babylon's Nebuchadnezzar thought he could keep him in line. And Zedekiah's accession to the throne coincided with Babylon's first major deportation of Jerusalemites, even if it'd be ten years before the Exile proper would begin. As you can imagine, things got a whole lot worse than they were at the beginning of Zedekiah's reign. And Isaiah or whoever was writing in his name saw all this coming. Hence, the destruction of Babylon here in Isaiah 13–14 marks the Lord's mercy to Judah.

We actually get several verses describing the mercy to be given to Judah as Babylon falls to the Medes. First, we get a fuller statement of the Lord's favor to the covenant people: "For the Lord will have mercy on Jacob, and will yet choose Israel and set them in their own land" (2 Ne.

24:1). That's already quite a promise. But then we start to hear the sorts of things we usually associate with Second Isaiah's prophecies. "The strangers shall be joined" with Judah, and these Gentiles "shall cleave to the house of Jacob" (v. 1). So the remnant whose production we've been tracing is brought "to their place—yea, from far unto the ends of the earth—and they shall return to their lands of promise" (v. 2). Judah finally assumes the position of the victors. "They shall take them captives unto whom they were captives, and they shall rule over their oppressors" (v. 3). With all this promise on the table, Isaiah speaks directly to Judah: "And it shall come to pass in that day that the Lord shall give thee rest from thy sorrow, and from thy fear, and from the hard bondage wherein thou wast made to serve" (v. 3). Words of comfort for Judah, then, here appended to words of startling discomfort for the violent imperial power of Babylon.

As I just said, all this sounds a good deal like Second Isaiah, where the focus is also on Babylon—on Judah's exile in Babylon and their eventual return through the instrumentality of Gentiles who come to be numbered among the people of the covenant. But notice that here we've got Second-Isaiah themes in the middle of First Isaiah. In the last few chapters of Isaiah, we've watched how the situation of Judah in the eighth century, under the constant threat of Assyria's growing power, leads to the production of a righteous remnant, gathered about a messianic figure of sorts. Rather suddenly, we've jumped to the sixth century, where Babylon has definitely replaced Assyria, and we find the produced remnant being prepared to leave exile in a foreign land. The two settings are *so* distinct and *so* similar. That ought to make us think a bit. What's remained more or less the same is the fact that Judah's up against a massive imperial power from which only a remnant could possibly escape. But what's especially changed is that deliverance for Israel at *this* point means salvation for the Gentiles in some fashion.

It's striking to have these two stories of sorts side by side, isn't it? Isaiah 6–12 tells the story of Judah's experience with Assyria. Isaiah 13–14 tells the story of Judah's experience with Babylon. The one focuses on surviving invasion in one's own land, with a remnant surviving to bear witness of God's fidelity to any Judean king who fulfills God's expectations. The other focuses on being rescued from exile in a foreign land, with a remnant returning to bear witness of God's democratic work among those Gentiles who assist God's covenant people. The two larger sequences of text grow out of radically different contexts—that's the case *even if* both originated in some way with Isaiah of Jerusalem—radically different contexts, but they've been placed side by side in a profoundly suggestive way. Of course, we've already seen that most interpreters of Isaiah today would call that side-by-side-ness an accident at best. Most regard Isaiah 1–12 as one major "section" of Isaiah and Isaiah 13–23 as another major "section" of Isaiah, with in-text headings serving to distinguish them pretty radically. But then along comes Nephi, who excerpts Isaiah 13–14 from Isaiah 13–23 and makes of it a kind of conclusion to Isaiah 2–12. Apparently, he wants us to sense both the profound similarities *and* the important differences between the Assyrian and Babylonian eras of Israel's struggle among the nations. And we'll see soon enough that he seems to think that these are importantly continuous stories—that the Assyrian situation sets up the Babylonian situation, or that the Babylonian situation reprises and works the kinks out of the Assyrian situation.

What's really interesting, though, is that once Nephi's done his own editorial work here, we start to see some remarkable thematic connections between Isaiah 6–12 and Isaiah 13–14. To see those, though, we've got to look at the rest of Isaiah 14, where talk of Babylon's destruction and Judah's redemption gives way to a most fascinating bit of text: a prophetic taunt song. What we get in Isaiah 14, for the most part, is a poem written and sung in order to mock the fallen king of Babylon. It's a good deal of fun (if also a bit grotesque), but even more importantly, it's what ties together the larger chunks of Nephi's quotation of Isaiah. So let's spend some serious time looking at this last part of the text.

The Fallen King

We begin "in that day" (2 Ne. 24:4), that is, in the day when Babylon falls and Judah is restored. And what the prophet predicts "in that day" is this: Judah will "take up this proverb"—really, a taunt song—"against the king of Babylon" (v. 4). It begins with mocking amazement: "How hath the oppressor ceased?! The golden city ceased?!" (v. 4). Soon, though, it turns to simple celebration: "The whole earth is at rest!" (v. 7). The nations that have been dealing with Babylon's brutal military forces, which Isaiah compares to the towering "cedars of Lebanon," rejoice at their foe's demise: "Since thou art laid down, no feller is come up against us!" (v. 8). Things look and feel pretty good.

What follows at this point, though, is far more interesting. "Hell," we're told, "is moved . . . to meet [the king of Babylon] at [his] coming" (2 Ne. 24:9). Now, when we say "hell" here, don't think of fire and brimstones. The Hebrew word translated "hell"—you might be familiar with it from D&C 121:4, where Joseph Smith uses it—is *sheol*, and it just means the realm of the dead, something like what we Mormons call the spirit world. The ancient Hebrews thought of it in similar ways as the Greeks—think Hades, the realm of the shades, where the dead continue in some kind of half-sentient state. It's *this* that's suddenly moving when the king of Babylon shows up there. "It stirreth up the dead," and especially "all the chief ones of the earth," "the kings of the nations," to have a chat with the emperor who's become just like them (v. 9). Here's their question as he shows up at the gates of Sheol: "Art thou also become weak as we?" (v. 10). And this gets them laughing. The taunt song continues, then: "Thy pomp is brought down to the grave! The noise of thy viols is not heard! The worm is spread under thee, and the worms cover thee!" (v. 11). We might note that this round of mockery echoes Isaiah's condemnation of Judah's own leaders back in Isaiah 5 (see 2 Ne. 15:11–14).

But this is just the first bit of mockery the dead kings of the ancient Near East serve up for Babylon's fallen ruler. To go further, they draw on their old mythology, a story about a god who's cast from the heavens because of his rebellion against the chief god. The King James translation, following the Latin rendering, gives us "Lucifer" as the identifying name of the figure in question, and that's tied up with a long tradition of interpreting this passage as a simple reference to Satan. We'll be coming back to that interpretation in a later lecture, and we already said a bit about it in an earlier lecture, didn't we? For the moment, at any rate, let's stick with what Isaiah himself would apparently have meant in context. It's pretty clear that he had in mind a bit of ancient mythology where some upstart of a young god named Helel ("Lucifer") attempts a takeover of the heavenly council. For his rebellion, this "son of Dawn" ("son of the morning," in the King James rendering) is "brought down to hell, to the sides of the pit" (2 Ne. 24:15). It's no surprise, then, to find Isaiah having those dead kings alluding to their mythology as they describe the terrible fall of the once-mighty king of the Babylonian empire. And so they conclude their comparison with some forceful questions: "Is *this* the man that made the earth to tremble? That did shake kingdoms and made the world as a wilderness and destroyed the cities thereof and opened not the house of his prisoners?" (2 Ne. 24:16–17).

All this would be enough to make the fallen king squirm, I'm sure. But now the prophet's voice takes over again, and Isaiah has a bit to say about how *this* king differs, in the end, from *those* kings—about how the king of Babylon differs from the many kings he deposed as he ravaged the earth. Here's what he says, and it's this that ties together the whole of Nephi's long quotation of Isaiah. Actually, before I start the quotation, let me note that I'm changing one word from Skousen's reconstruction. I believe he is wrong in thinking that "remnant" is an error in the transmission of the text and reverting it to the biblical text's "raiment." Here is the text:

> All the kings of the nations—yea, all of them—lie in glory, every one of them in his own house. But thou art cast out of thy grave like an abominable branch! And the remnant of those that are slain, thrust through with a sword, that go down to the stones of the pit as a carcass trodden under feet—thou shalt not be joined with them in burial, because thou hast destroyed thy land and slain thy people! (2 Ne. 24:18–20)

What do we have here? The first two lines draw up a relatively simple contrast between "the kings of the nations" and the king of Babylon. They're buried in honor, so that they all "lie in glory." Babylon's fallen ruler, however, is "cast out of [his] grave like an abominable branch." You're probably aware of what an offense it was in the ancient world to go unburied. You've maybe read *Antigone* or something. So here we're being told that the king of Babylon is being treated with the utmost disrespect at his death. His body is simple thrown into the street to rot before everyone's eyes. He receives no burial, let alone an honorable one.

Three Branches

But that's just the beginning of what's there in those first two lines. The other point we've got to emphasize is this: Babylon's king is cast out of his grave "like an abominable branch." What's going on there? Well, it's weird, to say the least. Most interpreters today turn to the ancient Greek translation of Isaiah, where there's talk not of a "branch" but a "dead body," and they suggest that this betrays a pre-Greek variant in the Hebrew text. Hence most assume that the earliest Isaianic text read "cast out . . . like a loathsome dead fetus," and that this was oddly corrupted at some point to read "cast out . . . like an abominable branch." The Book of Mormon version gives us "branch" rather than "dead fetus," however, and that leaves us to grapple with this so-very-strange image. What would it mean for the king of Babylon to be cast from his grave like an abominable branch?

Well, I can't pretend to answer that question in strictly historical terms. I have no idea how to reconstruct the original meaning of such a metaphor. But it's not terribly difficult to see what Nephi would have heard in the reference. We've already seen that these Isaianic prophecies speak of an eschatological branch, a kind of messianic figure, as well as of a remnant-branch that sprouts out of the apparently dead tree to be identified as Judah after Assyria's onslaught. Isn't that what we're looking at here? There's Israel's Branch, the messianic or royal figure who'll join Israel's remnant in their eventual deliverance. And then there's Babylon's abominable branch, another royal figure—never so messianic—who's cast out from his grave to be stared at as he decomposes. There's an apparently deliberate contrast being drawn here. And this brings the whole of Nephi's quotation of Isaiah into a larger consistent configuration.

Let's take a quick step back here to take in the whole picture. You'll remember that Nephi is divided the three parts of his lengthy quotation of Isaiah 2–14 into three sequences: Isaiah 2–5, Isaiah 6–12, and Isaiah 13–14. At this point, we can finally see that all three chunks of text work their way toward some kind of statement about a branch, but it seems we're dealing with a different branch in each case. In Isaiah 2–5, we saw a focus on a "beautiful and glorious" branch that's providing fruit both "excellent and comely" to those "escaped of Israel" (2 Ne. 14:2). There, it seems, we're probably supposed to understand the branch in question to be a messianic figure, raised up to accompany the Israelite remnant that's been prepared to hear the prophet's word. Then in Isaiah 6–12, we saw a focus on a branch "grow[ing] out of [the] roots" of the otherwise dead stump of Judah, on which "the Spirit of the Lord" rests in power (2 Ne. 21:1–2). There it's a little more difficult to know exactly how we should interpret the branch in question. It might be the same messianic figure from before, or it might be the remnant of Judah itself. At any rate, we now come to Isaiah 13–14, where we're seeing a focus on "an abominable branch" that's thrown out to rot, while "the remnant," barely surviving, thrives elsewhere (2 Ne. 24:19). Here it's clear that the branch in question is the ruler of Babylon, facing his demise.

Babylon's Remnant

Okay, so we've only looked at the first two lines of the chunk of text we quoted a minute ago. What of the rest of it? After we get the reference to the "abominable branch," we get this: "And the remnant of those that are slain, thrust through with a sword, that go down to the stones of the pit as a carcass trodden under feet—thou shalt not be joined with them in burial, because thou hast destroyed thy land and slain thy people!" I already mentioned that the Book of Mormon rendering of this passage is a bit peculiar, since the biblical text reads not "remnant" but "raiment." But I think it's important to take quite seriously the variant "remnant" reading that's there in the Book of Mormon text. It looks like we're being told something, as in the earlier Isaiah sequences in Nephi, about the link between the branch and the remnant. What we're told this time is that the branch in question—the dead ruler of Babylon—won't be "joined with" the remnant. That's a bit odd. But it's suggestive nonetheless. The abominable branch is cut off from the remnant—cut off from them in that they survive, perhaps, but apparently cut off here even in their death.

Note this also. The text goes on to mention a remnant again. Isaiah next commands that the Babylonian king's family be killed: "Prepare slaughter for his children for the iniquities of their fathers, that they do not rise, nor possess the land, nor fill the face of the world with cities" (2 Ne. 24:21). That sort of talk doesn't settle well with us in the twenty-first century, to be sure. We're pretty uncomfortable with the idea of punishing children for the iniquities of their parents—especially when it comes to capital punishment! Yet you see the point, however uncomfortable it makes you, yes? Think of the Book of Ether, where the civil war never seems to end because the children of the conquered eventually rise up against their fathers' captors. Here the point is to ensure that this doesn't happen by killing off the whole family, "that they do not rise." The Babylonian heritage is to be completely eradicated.

Now notice that Isaiah puts this eradication in terms of a remnant: "'I will rise up against them,' saith the Lord of Hosts, 'and cut off from Babylon the name and remnant and son and nephew,' saith the Lord" (2 Ne. 24:22). A number of things are "cut off" here, all in an attempt to make sure the ashes of the Babylonian empire are cold, to make sure there's no spark left over that might be used to start up the fire again. The very family name of the king is to be obliterated, with "son and nephew" being cut off. But then note that we're also told that the "remnant" will be cut off. At the same moment that Isaiah tells us that the Babylonian king will be without any connection to the true remnant—that is, it seems, to the Israelite remnant—he tells us also that the Babylonian king will be left without any remnant of his own. Babylon, a great Gentile nation, is to be remnant-less in two senses: without access to the remnant of the covenant people, and then without any remnant himself.

This is a pattern that's significant elsewhere in the Book of Mormon, by the way. The Book of Ether, which we just mentioned, tells a similar story. After we finish reading the history of the Lehites, which concludes with the preservation of a remnant of this covenant people, Moroni tells us a story about a non-Israelite or non-covenant people, the Jaredites, who came out from, quite precisely, *Babel*, Babylon. They travel to the New World, but since they came from the great tower, they left before the Abrahamic covenant was given. They are a non-Abrahamic, non-Israelite, non-covenant people. In a word, they're Gentiles of a sort. And Moroni sets their story side by side with the story of Lehi's children. The covenant people have a remnant left at the end. The Jaredites, you'll remember, are entirely eradicated. Moroni highlights this point several times, and he's clear about the fact that he's writing the Jaredite story as a kind of warning to the Gentiles of the last days. "Hey! Listen up! You've got no promise unless you join with the covenant people!" So the Book of Ether reproduces Isaiah 13–14. After the story of the covenant people and their remnant, we get the story of a Babylonian Gentile people who have no remnant. And their only hope would be somehow to be "joined with" the remnant of Israel (2 Ne. 24:20). That's, I think, quite striking.

And we're running out of time. We should say a word or two about how Isaiah 13–14 ends. Let's just note this. It ends with some "messengers"—Isaiah calls them "the messengers of the nations"—and they've got one message and one message only: "The Lord hath founded Zion, and the poor of his people shall trust in it" (2 Ne. 24:32). That's what all this remnant-building and messianic redemption and destruction of the wicked and so on—that's what this all comes to. We're left in the end with a promise regarding the poor in Zion. And that's a beautiful place to conclude.

We'll draw up a summary next time.

Lecture XX

Nephi's Comments
on Reading Isaiah

We've now spent a goodly number of lectures working through the largest block of Isaiah text in the Book of Mormon. It's been fast and furious. We gave a lecture to some general points of introduction. Do you remember? We looked at how Nephi divides this large block of Isaiah into three distinct sequences (we'll be coming back to this point next time), and we looked at the opening verses of Isaiah 2 with their focus on the fulfillment of the Abrahamic covenant. With preliminaries out of the way, we then turned in our next lecture to a kind of summary treatment of Isaiah 2–5. Our aim was really just to get a decent sense for what's going on there with Isaiah's condemnation of Israel. Then we gave two lectures in a row to Isaiah 6. First, we focused on the temple scene of Isaiah's commission, which is clearly related to Lehi's inaugural visions and to some kind of experience Nephi expects all of his readers to have in connection with baptism. And then we focused on Isaiah's theologically difficult commission, which involved in a good deal of textual complexity. We then dedicated two further lectures to Isaiah 6–12, one mostly a summary of Isaiah's account of the production of Judah's remnant, and the other an overly abstract discussion of the messianic texts distributed throughout that account. With those two lectures, our hope was really just to get a general sense for what's going on in Isaiah 6–12 in general terms. I can only hope we succeeded. Finally, the lecture you sat through last time focused on Isaiah 13–14, the burden of Babylon. And there our aim was just to make basically clear what's going on in these final two chapters of Nephi's long quotation of Isaiah.

That's where we've been lately. And now we're coming to the end of it, it seems. But it only *seems* so. We're actually going to dedicate two *more* lectures to Isaiah 2–14. Here's what I'm planning. You might be aware that 2 Nephi 25, which follows immediately after the lengthy quotation, contains a few words of general advice regarding the interpretation of Isaiah. We'll spend today looking at that. But then 2 Nephi 25 goes on to provide Nephi's own prophetic summary of Isaiah 2–14, in a passage that's usually ignored by people working on Isaiah in the Book of Mormon. That's where we'll focus next time. What we hope to get out of this lecture and the next, then, is a bit of clarity regarding what *Nephi* saw in the chapters we've been reviewing. I think we'll learn a lot.

The roadmap is clear, then? Let's get to work!

What Nephi Doesn't Do

I've mentioned 2 Nephi 25:1–8 before. Here we've got a general statement of sorts on Isaiah. At any rate, it begins this way: "Now I, Nephi, do speak somewhat concerning the words which I have written, which have been spoken by the mouth of Isaiah" (2 Ne. 25:1). And because Nephi goes on to confess that Isaiah's writings are "hard . . . to understand" (v. 1), Latter-day Saints tend to like this passage a lot. We find comfort in Nephi's concession. This has led commentators on the Book of Mormon rather generally to focus their attention on these verses in 2 Nephi 25 much more than on any actual words of Isaiah. For example, in their best-selling commentary, Robert L. Millet and Joseph Fielding McConkie initially hold off any direct commentary on the Isaiah passages in 2 Nephi 12–24. Before engaging the actual text, they provide some reflections on why the Nephites quoted Isaiah, outline a number of "suggestions for better understanding Isaiah" drawn from 2 Nephi 25:1–8, and say a bit about Isaiah's importance more generally. All this takes them five pages. They then provide their actual commentary on the Isaiah chapters, which also takes them five pages. In the end, they write fewer words on what Isaiah actually says than they do their commentary of how one might go about reading Isaiah.

They are not alone. Millet and McConkie do more or less what most other Mormon commentators do. Because it looks like 2 Nephi 25:1–8 provides a few words about *how* to read Isaiah, commentators find it easier to comment extensively on those verses while more or less ignoring *what* Isaiah actually has to say. I think I mentioned this before, but I've deliberately avoided saying much of anything about 2 Nephi 25:1–8 before now. Nephi doesn't begin with hints about reading Isaiah *and only then* go on to quote the prophet. He gives us Isaiah first, often and at length, and only subsequently does he say anything about strategy—if he ever really says anything about strategy at all. He wants us wrestling with Isaiah directly first, it seems. And so we've tried to do just that here. Nonetheless, it's now time to see what we can learn from 2 Nephi 25:1–8. Do these verses help us to see what's at stake in reading Isaiah?

Let me put all my cards on the table right away. I don't find here anything like what's usually found here. I don't find Nephi giving us instruction about how to read Isaiah. It seems to me that there's something rather different going on, in fact. We've got to read these verses carefully, and if we do, I think we find Nephi telling his readers that they're largely *incapable* of reading Isaiah, and then promising them that he's willing to help them nonetheless. Let's see if we can't spell this out.

Words that Aren't Plain

Let's begin at the beginning: "Now I, Nephi, do speak somewhat concerning the words which I have written, which have been spoken by the mouth of Isaiah" (2 Ne. 25:1). Nephi's about to tell us something about Isaiah 2–14. That much is clear, right? He then tells us why he's going to say a bit about these Isaiah chapters. It's because "Isaiah spake many things which were hard for many of my people to understand" (v. 1). We've discussed how Nephi recognizes that Isaiah can be difficult to understand, but we didn't mention what is clearly at issue here in this verse: Nephi recognizes that Isaiah is difficult for *his*—that is, *Nephi's*—people to understand. He doesn't say that Isaiah's just generally hard to make sense of. He says that he's hard for the Nephites to get their heads around. *They* have trouble with Isaiah. He says nothing about us, latter-day Gentile readers. He's only making a concession to his own people, those who've left the Old World behind to settle on the other side of the world some twenty-six hundred years ago. And what's his concession? He's clear about this: "they know not concerning the manner of prophesying among the Jews" (v. 1). Nephi recognizes that the Nephites have been cut off from the culture that would help them to contextualize Isaiah's prophecies. Lehi, Nephi, and Jacob have launched their own prophetic tradition, and it's a tradition that's rather distinct from Isaiah's. That can only leave them scratching their heads when they try to read the biblical prophet. And so Nephi recognizes the difficulty they face. We shouldn't ourselves be in any such difficulties, should we?

Well, maybe we should. Nephi explains why his people ended up ignorant of the tradition and context in which Isaiah prophesied: "I,

Nephi, have not taught them many things concerning the manner of the Jews, for their works were works of darkness, and their doings were doings of abomination" (2 Ne. 25:2). These words should probably be read as the words of someone still upset at how things went for his family in Jerusalem. Nephi's antipathy for the city he left behind is pretty clear here, and it apparently led him to remain largely silent about Old-World things when he spoke to his children and his people. He basically tells us that he threw out the baby with the bathwater, failing to teach about the necessary context for understanding Isaiah's prophecies because he didn't want to say much about the people who'd threatened his father's life and effectively driven the whole family into the wilderness. But should that be an excuse for us? We find ourselves in difficulties when we read Isaiah because we're as ignorant as Nephi's people about Israelite history, about Hebrew prophecy, about the interpretive tradition, and so on. But they had only one real resource for learning about these things—Nephi—and he wouldn't really talk about these things with them. *We*, on the other hand, have *many* resources to learn about these things, resources that are happy to tell us more or less everything we wish to know. Our ignorance is largely our own fault.

So the first couple of verses here in 2 Nephi 25 leave us without much of an excuse for our being mystified by Isaiah. At the same time, they leave Nephi's own people with a pretty big excuse for *their* being mystified. And Nephi recognizes it. He states next that, even though he knows they can't make much sense of it all, he copies down Isaiah for them so that "they may know the judgments of God—that they come upon all nations according to the word which he hath spoken" (2 Ne. 25:3). In a certain way, it seems, Nephi hopes that his own people will get just one major message as they struggle their way through Isaiah's writings, and that's the idea that judgment comes only after prophetic warnings have first been given. "The judgments of God" come only "according to the word which he hath spoken." Nephi will make this same point with other words in verse 9: "Never hath any of [the Jews] been destroyed save it were foretold them by the prophets of the Lord." There, it seems, is the most basic message of Isaiah as Nephi sees it.

And we've already seen how that message lies at the foundation of Nephi's three-sequence quotation of Isaiah, haven't we? The first sequence mostly lays out the constitutive wickedness of Judean society during the eighth century. The second sequence then describes the Lord's commissioning of a prophet and the prophet's subsequent intervention in apostate Jerusalem before destruction is meted out. There are, of course, other themes at work there as well—we've been dwelling on them ourselves in the past few lectures—but these other themes are apparently the sorts of things Nephi's people won't catch on a first read. The first time through, Nephi expects them just to get the message that God sends prophets to warn his people before he does anything drastic with them.

The Spirit of Prophecy

Of course, Nephi wants his people to get more than *just* this out of their experience with Isaiah. This he makes clear as he goes on. He directly addresses himself to them, telling them to listen up, and then he explains how they might go deeper into Isaiah: "Because that the words of Isaiah are not plain unto you—nevertheless, they *are* plain unto all they that are filled with the spirit of prophecy" (2 Ne. 25:4). Ouch. Seriously? Nephi's willing to hit his people with *that* one? "Look, Isaiah's writings would be simple enough if you just had the spirit of prophecy!" We've got to be prophets to understand this? Then who'll ever get to the bottom of Isaiah? Just a few people who happen to have received the spiritual gift of prophecy? Sometimes we read this verse and we say that Nephi's encouraging those who wish to understand Isaiah to pray for inspiration, but that's a pretty drastic weakening of Nephi's words. He says that Isaiah's words are *plain*—got that? plain!—to anyone with the spirit of *prophecy*—got that? prophecy! We're not talking here about everyday guidance by the Spirit. We're talking about high-octane prophetic experience. And Nephi expects everyone to have that sort of experience?

Actually, he doesn't. Notice what he says as he goes on: "But *I* give unto you a prophecy according to the spirit which is in *me*" (2 Ne. 25:4). Did you catch the significance of that? Here's what I hear in these words: "Isaiah's perfectly clear to those like me who've been given to experience an apocalyptic vision of the world's history, to those like me who've received in pure grace the prophetic gift of seeing the larger stakes of the Abrahamic covenant. But I know that most of you won't ever have that sort of experience. Perhaps you could, but I recognize that most of you won't. But because I *have* had that sort of experience, I can tell you about what I've seen, and that should give you a kind of foothold. You need the spirit of prophecy to make Isaiah plain, so let me give you a few words deriving from the spirit of prophecy that was given to me. And that should help you to get started, anyway." Is that a fair interpretation? Here are

Nephi's words again: "Because that the words of Isaiah are not plain unto you, nevertheless they are plain unto all they that are filled with the spirit of prophecy, but I give unto you a prophecy according to the spirit which is in me." Isn't that relatively clear? Nephi doesn't expect all of his people—or us, for that matter—to have prophetic experiences like he did. He expects us to listen to him as he lays out his own prophetic experience, and that should help us to get beyond just the basic message of Isaiah.

So Nephi's taking us by the hand and gently leading us through the task of interpretation. Or at least he's rather graciously giving us a kind of starting point, a boost, so that we can then begin to figure out what's going on in Isaiah's prophecies. And he goes on to explain that he's doing his best to make this starting point as gentle and useful as possible: "I shall prophesy according to the plainness which hath been with me from the time that I came out from Jerusalem with my father—for behold, my soul delighteth in plainness unto my people, that they may learn" (2 Ne. 25:4). He's going to lay out a prophecy that's as plain as possible, that's plain in the way that so much of Nephi's writing is plain. This is supposed to help Nephi's people to see clearly the kind of general themes Isaiah's working on, and then they can go back and read Isaiah again, getting a whole lot more out of him than just the idea that God sends prophets to warn his people before he visits them with destruction. Nephi's gracious enough to provide his people with this help. And because we're reading the record he wrote for his people, it turns out he's gracious enough to help us as well. He says in verse 3 that he writes not only to his people, but also to "all they that shall receive hereafter these things." So we get to enjoy the gift too.

Now, naturally, your next question is—or should be—this: *Where's the plain prophecy that's supposed to clear up Isaiah?* It appears to start in verse 9, but right now we're only in verse 4. We still have a bit more ground to cover before we get to what Nephi actually has to say. And I've set aside the whole of our next lecture so that we can work through that prophecy in some detail. So you'll have to be patient with me for the moment. Let's spend the rest of our time just leading up to that prophecy. Nephi's now told us that it's coming, but he has a few other things he wants to say before he actually gets to it. Why? What else should we understand before we try to tackle Nephi's plain prophecy?

Repetition and Expostion

Well, as it turns out, there's not a whole lot *more* that we're supposed to understand before we try to tackle Nephi's prophecy. We're apparently supposed just to understand *better* the same thing we've just covered. Why do I say that? Because, curiously, verses 5–7a more or less repeat, but of course in different words, verses 1–4. In fact, it's a bit startling how *exactly* verses 5–7a repeat verses 1–4. Let's take a look at this.

Verse 1 opens with Nephi telling us his intent to focus further on Isaiah, to "speak somewhat" concerning what he's copied down from Isaiah 2–14. Verse 5 opens with Nephi telling us, in parallel, that his "soul delighteth in the words of Isaiah." That doesn't seem like anything terribly substantial, but then see what comes next. Verse 1 continues as follows: "Isaiah spake many things which were hard for many of my people to understand, for they know not concerning the manner of prophesying among the Jews." How does verse 5 continue? Like this: "I came out from Jerusalem, and mine eyes hath beheld the things of the Jews. And I know that the Jews do understand the things of the prophets, and there is none other people that understand the things which were spoken unto the Jews like unto them—save it be that they are taught after the manner of the things of the Jews." Here the parallel is quite striking, isn't it? What's interesting, of course, is that the restatement of verse 1 in verse 5 is a good deal richer than the original. Where verse 1 just says that Isaiah's "hard . . . to understand" if you don't know "the manner of prophesying among the Jews," verse 5 undertakes to explain all this at greater length. It's because Nephi "came out from Jerusalem," and because his eyes "beheld the things of the Jews," that he can make sense of Isaiah. As he puts it, "the Jews do understand the things of the prophets"—and that uniquely, it seems: "there is none other people that understand the things which were spoken unto the Jews like unto them." Here the heavy emphasis on "the Jews" makes clear that we should read Isaiah (and the Hebrew prophets more generally) always in their original context. And Nephi tells us pretty straightforwardly at the end of verse 5 what we need to do if we're serious about making sense of Isaiah and the prophets. We've got to be "taught after the manner of the things of the Jews."

Let's pause on that last statement for a couple of minutes, if we can. Various interpretive programs for making sense of Mormon scripture— programs that are usually novel and provocative but as often as not overly narrow in important ways—have often been justified by making reference to Nephi's talk of being "taught after the manner of the things of the Jews." Some have insisted that these words point to medieval Jewish mystical interpretation. Others have insisted that they point to early rabbinical reading practices. Still others have insisted that they point to modern Jewish interpretive strategies. While I think there's much to be learned from reading the Book of Mormon (or Mormon scripture more generally) by using all of these historically Jewish interpretive programs, I'm entirely unconvinced that *Nephi* has any of them in mind. The Jews Nephi seems pretty clearly to be thinking of are those he left behind in Jerusalem, those to whom the prophets originally addressed their messages. And all of the various Jewish interpretive strategies that get read into Nephi's words here had their origins much, much later in history. Even ancient rabbinical interpretation, the earliest of these interpretive traditions, seems only to have come into existence a century or so before Christ. There's some reason to think that rabbinical interpretation had its roots in the exile in Babylon, but Nephi didn't experience that exile. He seems pretty clearly to have pre-exilic Jews in mind, those who hadn't yet found it necessary to invent novel ways to approach their texts because they hadn't yet been deprived of their land. In short, Nephi seems in verse 5 just to be saying that Isaiah's words were given in a real historical context, and that that context is more than a bit useful for making sense of the prophet's words. Note that he goes on in verse 6 to mention Jerusalem and "the regions round about" as particularly useful for understanding Isaiah.

Besides, a closer reading of what Nephi says suggests that he doesn't at all have reference to reading strategies. He doesn't say, as he often gets quoted as saying, that scripture should be read "after the manner of the Jews." He says that Isaiah's easier to understand when one is "taught after the manner of *the things of* the Jews." The point here isn't to say that there's a specifically Jewish manner of reading or interpreting texts, and that that's the right or privileged way to go about understanding the prophets. It's to say that the prophets become easier to read when one is familiar with *things*, with "the things of the Jews." What things? Well, the things Nephi himself saw when he was growing up in Jerusalem: "I came out from Jerusalem," he says earlier in verse 5, "and mine eyes hath beheld the things of the Jews." Here again it's clear that he has preexilic Jews in mind, the people dwelling in Jerusalem that he and his family left behind. It seems Nephi means only to suggest that Isaiah can be understood more readily if we're familiar with ancient Jewish history and culture, ancient Hebrew language and idioms, ancient Israelite beliefs and practices. We ought to get familiar with all things preexilic and Jewish if we want to get our minds around Isaiah's prophecies.

Okay, that was a bit of tangent, but an important one. There's a lot that can be learned from using traditional Jewish styles of interpretation to read scripture—I've especially learned a lot from rabbinic interpretation (and Bradley Kramer's recent book, *Beholding the Tree of Life*, shows how rich this can be). But Nephi's pretty clearly got something else in mind. At any rate, I think we ought to steer clear of programmatic uses of 2 Nephi 25:5, as well as of interpreters of scripture who claim that they've got access to some kind of special form of Jewish interpretation that can mysteriously get underneath the surface of Isaiah's words, usually to reveal some kind of coded meaning. That sort of thing makes me nervous.

But let's get back to where we were. Verses 5–7a repeat verses 1–4, and apparently in certain cases in a way that expands on and develops what's stated the first time through. We've looked at verses 1 and 5 and seen this happening. What of the rest?

In verses 2 and 6, we find that the first iteration is more detailed than the second. In verse 2, Nephi informs us that he "had not taught" his people "many things concerning the manner of the Jews," apparently because of the "darkness" and "abominations" he saw among them. In verse 6, he tells us simply just that he had "not taught [his] children after the manner of the Jews." Apparently here he feels he's said enough about this subject the first time around. Interestingly, the next item on Nephi's list gets essentially the same attention in each iteration. In verse 3, Nephi identifies what he seems to regard as the basic and most obvious message in Isaiah 2–14, namely that judgment comes upon the nations only after God has announced it in advance. In verse 6, in the parallel text, Nephi says this: "And I have made mention concerning the judgments of God which hath come to pass among the Jews unto my children, according to all that which Isaiah hath spoken—and I do not write them."

By this point, we might start to wonder why Nephi's bothering with this larger repetition of verses 1–4 in verses 5–7a. He seems to have had a good reason to expand on and clarify the material from verse 1, so we're pretty happy to have verse 5. But the rest of this seems largely unnecessary. Is Nephi just repeating for the sake of repeating, giving us structure for the sake of having structure? But maybe we're about to come again to something more expansive? Actually, no. Verse 4, you'll remember, tells us that Nephi's planning to give us a prophecy of his own that'll serve as a interpretive key, a starting point that'll get us moving in our attempt to understand Isaiah. He has a lot to say about this in verse 4. He there explains that because Isaiah *isn't* clear to his people but *is* clear to him because of his prophetic experiences, he's happy to provide them with a prophecy they can use to begin their own work of interpretation. And he there explains that his own prophecy will be plain in nature, following the pattern of his prophesying from the very beginning. Finally, he there says a little bit about how much he himself appreciates plainness. That's a lot of content, all to be found in verse 4. Does this get expanded or contracted in verse 7? The answer, unfortunately, is that it gets drastically contracted. He says only this in the parallel text (in verse 7): "But behold, I proceed with mine own prophecy, according to my plainness, in the which I know that no man can err." That's it. Apparently, he thinks he's said what needs saying already back in verse 4. He has nothing, really, to add.

The Last Days

So we're left wondering all over again why Nephi bothers to repeat verses 1–4 in verses 5–7a. Why state again in such summary terms what's already been said more robustly just a moment before? Actually, the answer to this question comes, I think, in verses 7b–8. Once Nephi's worked back through verses 1–4 in verses 5–7a, you'd expect him to begin laying out his promised plain prophecy. He doesn't do so immediately, however, putting off the prophecy until verse 9. Instead, he uses his repetition of verses 1–4 in verses 5–7a to set up a discussion of Isaiah's relevance in "the last days" (2 Ne. 25:8). His review in verses 6 and 7 of everything he's said at greater length in verses 2–4 sets up Isaiah's relevance in *our* day. This ought to draw our attention.

So what does he say? It comes immediately after he's again stated the necessity of providing his people with his own plain prophecy. And he says this:

> Nevertheless, in the days that the prophecies of Isaiah shall be fulfilled, men shall know of a surety at the times when they shall come to pass—wherefore they are of worth unto the children of men! And he that supposeth that they are not, unto them will I speak particularly and confine the words unto mine own people. For I know that they shall be of great worth unto them in the last days, for in that day shall they understand them—wherefore, for their good have I written them. (2 Ne. 25:7–8)

This is a bit of a shocker, I think. If I understand this right, Nephi's telling us that he's included his lengthy quotation of Isaiah in his record really only because he's become aware that his writings will circulate in the last days. I think we mentioned in one of our first lectures that Nephi writes his record primarily with his children in mind. But here's one of the odd moments in his writings where it's clear that he's also been given to know that his record will get into the hands of many others, specifically in the last days. And here he tells us that that's the only reason he's bothered to make the very heart of his "more sacred things" a long quotation of Isaiah 2–14. He's written it down *for us*, even though we have it already in our bibles. That's peculiar. *Really* peculiar.

Nephi tells us something else rather important here. He lets us know that his own people were pretty skeptical about Isaiah. They didn't just find him difficult; they apparently thought he was something of a lunatic. Nephi's clear here that there are those who suppose that Isaiah's words are "not" of any "worth unto the children of men." And he's equally clear that the people who think this are largely "confine[d]" to "[his] own people." He fully anticipates *our* full recognition of the importance of Isaiah. That's almost funny, I think, since we've generally developed exactly the attitude Nephi says his people had regarding Isaiah. But here's the trick. We seem to have developed that attitude because we *don't* understand Isaiah. Nephi says that those of the last days certainly *will* understand Isaiah's words. But the fact is that we're collectively terrible at making any sense of Isaiah. And so we find ourselves more akin to Nephi's people twenty-five hundred years ago than to ourselves as Nephi describes us. That's puzzling—and fascinating.

Yikes! We've got to wrap up. Here's what all this comes down to, I think. Nephi expects us to be different from his own people. He tells us that he'll confine his attempts at clarifying Isaiah to his own people because he knows they need it. But it turns out that *we* need it also. We're just as hardened against Isaiah as Nephi's people were, and so we find ourselves biting our nails in anticipation of the plain prophecy that's supposed to clear all this up for us. "Please, Nephi! Get us out of having to interpret Isaiah!" I imagine he's now shaking his head at us, wanting to tell us just to open our eyes. We've got the historical resources and the linguistic knowledge to make Isaiah quite plain. And we're living through times to which Isaiah's prophecies are peculiarly relevant. And yet we're scratching our heads.

Well, we'll have to look at Nephi's prophecy, won't we? Next time.

Lecture XXI

Nephi's Plain Prophecy

Our task today is, you'll remember, to look at Nephi's own plain prophecy—his attempt to make Isaiah clear to his people by laying out what he'd himself seen in vision. Isaiah's perfectly clear, he says, to anyone who's had, through the spirit of prophecy, a glimpse of God's larger historical purposes. His people aren't generally gifted in that particular way, but since he's been able to experience such a thing himself, he's more than happy to help them out. Where do we find the prophecy in question? It's in 2 Nephi 25, and specifically in verses 9–19. For just eleven verses, Nephi lays things out quite clearly, and it might be as helpful for us as it was supposed to be for Nephi's own children.

Shall we get started?

Nephi's Summary of Isaiah 2–14

Verse 9 opens, it seems to me, by jumping right into the thick of things. "As one generation hath been destroyed among the Jews because of iniquity, even so have they been destroyed from generation to generation according to their iniquities." That's a pretty nice summary, I think, of Isaiah 2–5. Remember that Nephi divided his long quotation of Isaiah up into three sequences, right? He quoted Isaiah 2–5 in one block, then Isaiah 6–12 in a second block, and finally Isaiah 13–14 in a third block. And hopefully you haven't forgotten the basic themes of each of those. The first block of Isaianic text, Isaiah 2–5, focuses on the contrast between Israel's ultimate destiny—redemption for the whole world, with a messianic figure ruling over the redeemed Israelite remnant, leading all the Gentile nations in the worship of the true God—the contrast, then, between *that* and Israel's iniquitous state during Isaiah's day. And remember that this basic contrast set up, in Isaiah 2–5, a set of prophecies of the doom and the destruction Israel could anticipate. They were going to face all kinds of social and economic calamities, as well as heavy oppression from external enemies. Isn't all of that nicely summarized right here? "The Jews," as Nephi says, "have . . . been destroyed from generation to generation according to their iniquities." This is a kind of general pattern, he says, happening over and over again. We got that sense in Isaiah 2–5 pretty straightforwardly. Those chapters describe Israel's waywardness and consequent destruction, by way of contrast with their ultimate redemption, twice over. "From generation to generation," indeed.

Now Nephi adds this: "And never hath any of them been destroyed save it were foretold them by the prophets of the Lord" (2 Ne. 25:9). That's exactly where the long quotation of Isaiah went next. Once we've got the repeated pattern of wickedness and destruction on the table in Isaiah 2–5, we get the story of Isaiah's commission in Isaiah 6. Destruction won't happen, it seems, until after there's been a messenger sent to warn Israel away from their iniquity. So Isaiah gets commissioned in Isaiah 6, and then we get to watch him intervene in ancient Israelite affairs in Isaiah 7–12. The whole of Isaiah 6–12, that second block of Isaianic text, is thus summarized here in the second half of verse 9. Generation after generation of the covenant people get destroyed because of their iniquities (first half of verse 9, Isaiah 2–5), but God always sends a prophet to warn them earnestly before their doom is sealed (second half of verse 9, Isaiah 6–12). Nephi's just walking us through "the Isaiah chapters" rather straightforwardly here, isn't he?

So we know what to expect next. He should next summarize what we find in Isaiah 13–14, that third and final block of Isaiah text in Nephi's lengthy quotation. But Nephi actually puts that off for just a moment. Why? He seems to think he's got to prepare us for that. Here's what he tells us in verse 10 and the first part of verse 11: "Wherefore, it hath been told them [that is, Judah] concerning the destruction which should come upon them immediately after my father left Jerusalem. Nevertheless, they hardened their hearts. And according to my prophecy, they have been destroyed—save it be those which are carried away captive into Babylon. And now, this I speak because of the spirit which is in me." What's Nephi doing here? Well, for one, he does a bit of likening. He takes the more general pattern he's described as lying behind Isaiah 2–12 and then finds it happening in his own family's experience. His own generation is iniquitous. And God's sent prophets among them. They haven't listened, just as an earlier generation wouldn't listen to Isaiah. And the result is destruction and exile—now in the context of Babylon's growth and spread, rather than that of Assyria. So Nephi sees the Isaianic pattern verified in his own day, according to the spirit that's in him. What spirit is that? The spirit of prophecy that makes Isaiah's overarching meaning and relevance perfectly clear to him. He's seen enough in vision to know how to see what's really at stake in Isaiah.

So Nephi gives us a few words by way of likening. But he's done something else as well. He's brought Babylon into the picture. And that not only allows him to apply the underlying pattern of Isaiah 2–5 and Isaiah 6–12 to his own day and circumstances, it creates a nice bridge between Isaiah 2–12 and Isaiah 13–14. Do you remember that there's a kind of gap between these in the Book of Isaiah itself? Isaiah 6–12 seems especially focused on the situation of Judah facing the threat of Assyrian imperial power. But then Isaiah 13–14 concerns Babylon, the imperial power of a later generation, at least a century after the events described in Isaiah 6–12. There's something awkward about that leap from Assyria to Babylon, even if both empires play similar roles in their oppression of the covenant people. Nephi's insertion of a few words of likening, focusing the pattern from the Assyrian chapters, Isaiah 2–12, on the days of Babylon's ascendency, allows him to bridge the gap between those chapters and the final two chapters of his quotation, Isaiah 13–14, which themselves focus on Babylon. It's a brilliant little move that Nephi makes here, I think.

At any rate, when we come to verse 11, we're ready for a more concrete summary of the third block of Isaiah text Nephi's quoted. Here's what he says: "And notwithstanding that they [once again, Judah] have been carried away, they shall return again and possess the land of Jerusalem. Wherefore, they shall be restored again to the lands of their inheritance." That's as straightforward a summary as Nephi could possible give us of Isaiah 13–14, isn't it? Babylon will fall, and the Jews in exile will return to their land to rebuild their temple. That's exactly what we saw in the last part of Nephi's quotation of Isaiah. Babylon crumbles, and this is something God makes happen precisely because he means to restore Judah to the land of their inheritance. They're to return and to rule over their former oppressors.

So note well what Nephi's done just in verses 9–11. He's given us, rather quickly, a straightforward summary—appropriately in three parts, along with an aside that serves as a bridge—a straightforward summary of the three sequences of Isaiah he's quoted in the preceding chapters. This is pretty deft work. And note that, so far, he apparently doesn't want to say that Isaiah's meaning is supposed to be found outside of the events stretching from Isaiah's days (the Assyrian threat) to Nephi's days (the Babylonian threat). Even when Nephi likens the text in verse 10, he actually stays pretty well within the scope of what Isaiah's texts clearly mean in their original historical context.

But now Nephi will go a good deal further. We've only looked at the first three verses of Nephi's eleven-verse plain prophecy. And it turns out that once he's outlined what we might call the most *immediate* meaning or application of Isaiah's prophecies, he's fully prepared to go on to far more distant possible meanings and applications of Isaiah's words. The three-part story of God's dealings with Judah and Israel between 750 and 550 B.C. can be seen as built on a three-part pattern that outlines God's dealings with Judah and Israel throughout history. And that's where Nephi goes next.

You see, there's a larger historical story that can be told about Israel's relationship with God. Once again it's going to be a matter of iniquity that leads to devastation and destruction. And once again that sort of thing will only happen after God's sent someone to turn his people away from iniquity. And once again the whole thing comes to a conclusion only when God's people are, after so many difficulties, restored to their former state. But now Nephi turns his attention from his own era to one that for him was still far in the future. Nephi hass of course seen that future history in vision, and so he sees a way of reading it into Isaiah's prophecies. Or perhaps we should say that because he's such an astute reader of Isaiah's prophecies, he can use Isaiah's prophecies to impose some order on that future history he'd seen in vision. Either way, what we're about to get is a weaving of the larger history of Israel—the history stretching from just after Nephi's time to our own—into chapters 2–14 of Isaiah.

Well, actually, I've said that a bit too sloppily. Here's the funny thing. It's not *really* the larger history of *Israel* Nephi's going to give us next. It's *actually* just the larger history of *Judah* he'll look at. Before this point, whenever Nephi's likened Isaiah's writings, he's done so with an eye to the larger history of Israel, with a focus on the New-World remnant of Israel. But since the last time we got to watch Nephi do that, we've encountered his brother Jacob's attempts to grapple with Isaiah. Remember, Jacob focused his own likening of Isaiah not so much on the whole of Israel, or even on the New-World remnant of Israel, but on Judah, "the Jews," specifically. And here, it seems, Nephi's been influenced by Jacob's reading. Where before Nephi's more or less said nothing about the Jews when he's read Isaiah, now he's going to focus his prophetic reading of Isaiah's writings almost exclusively on the Jews. It's as if Nephi's got to wrestle his way through Jacob's provocative interpretation before he can get back in earnest to his own reading. And let me note that he *will* get back to his own reading. It won't be long before Nephi's back to finding traces in Isaiah of what's to happen with the New-World remnant of Israel. But here in 2 Nephi 25, he takes a look at Jewish history.

Let's take a look.

Nephi's History of the Jews

Verse 11 left us with the Jews of the sixth century returning from exile in Babylon. It ended, remember, with this: "They shall be restored again to the lands of their inheritance." So now we pick up the story with a focus exclusively on post-exilic Judah. Here's what Nephi tells us next in his plain prophecy: "But behold, they shall have wars and rumors of wars" (2 Ne. 25:12). That's a pretty decent summary of events during the six or seven centuries following Judah's return from Babylon to their own lands. A whole lot of contention resulted right away from their return, with fights over who could be called true Israelites, intense debates about who should be involved in the rebuilding of Jerusalem's walls and its temple, and political intrigues that even resulted in the murder of a regional governor. It took a century or so before these situations settled into a kind of stable state. And then it wasn't long before Judah was faced with the rapid rise of the Macedonian empire under Alexander the Great. And that was followed pretty quickly by the conquest of their lands by the Romans. Already with Alexander's conquest, Judah was thrown into a kind of cultural crisis, since Alexander brought Greek culture with him, which split Judah into conservative and liberal factions that responded quite differently to this foreign but startlingly attractive worldview. But when the Romans showed up, this cultural crisis and the consequent split in Jewish self-understanding were radicalized. Rome was a relatively benevolent empire—nothing like Assyria or Babylon!—but Judah's internal division made its relationship to the empire highly unstable. By the time of Jesus, things were barely under control. Only a couple of decades after Jesus's death, there was a national uprising against the empire, and it ended *horribly*.

"Wars and rumors of wars," then. That's exactly right. Nephi correctly sees this leading right up to (and beyond) the time of Jesus. And it's to Jesus that he next turns his attention: "And when the day cometh that the Only Begotten of the Father—yea, even the Father of heaven and of earth—shall manifest himself unto them in the flesh, behold, they will reject him because of their iniquities, and the hardness of their hearts, and the stiffness of their necks. Behold, they will crucify him" (2 Ne.

25:12–13). Notice what Nephi does here. He makes the general history of "wars and rumors of wars" the context and basic motivation for Jesus's rejection. I don't think it's going too far to say that he sees Jesus's rejection as basically *political*. That alone should make Latter-day Saints pause before saying, like Jacob *seems* to do, that Jesus was rejected by the Jews *as a whole*. If political motivations lay behind his crucifixion, then it would seem that his rejection was primarily the work of a few people in power who gained the largely blind support of a population that knew relatively little about what was going on. Apparently, at any rate, it seems we ought to read "iniquities" and "hardness of . . . hearts" and "stiffness of . . . necks" as consequences of politics—deeply unfortunate consequences of a protracted period of real and anticipated conflict.

Of course, Nephi doesn't leave Jesus in the tomb for long: "And after that he is laid in a sepulcher for the space of three days, he shall rise from the dead with healing in his wings. And all they that shall believe on his name shall be saved in the kingdom of God" (2 Ne. 25:13). This is good news—good news, indeed. And Nephi recognizes that. "My soul," he says in a quick aside, "delighteth to prophesy concerning him—for I have seen his day, and my heart doth magnify his holy name" (v. 13). But although Nephi makes this happy remark, he gets back to less-happy business pretty quickly. He sees Christ's resurrection as the context *primarily* for the destruction of Jerusalem again: "And behold, it shall come to pass that, after the Messiah hath risen from the dead and hath manifest himself unto his people—unto as many as will believe on his name—behold, Jerusalem shall be destroyed again" (v. 14). Wars and rumors of wars finally result here in a kind of repetition of the situation experienced by Nephi's people some six and a half centuries earlier. (Ancient Jews themselves often drew parallels between the two events, the destruction of Jerusalem by Babylon and its destruction by Rome.) As Nephi tells the story, what finally tips the scales and leads to Jerusalem's devastation anew is the way the early Christian church is treated: "Woe unto them that fight against God and the people of his church" (v. 14).

Finally, this destruction of Jerusalem results in a scattering: "The Jews shall be scattered among all nations" (2 Ne. 25:15). And Nephi wants to make it clear that this isn't Babylon's doing, since it'll have long since been "destroyed" by this point; "wherefore, the Jews shall be scattered by other nations" (v. 15).

So all this is what Nephi reports for us next. What does it have to do with Isaiah? Well, if this is supposed to be a likening or, perhaps better, a reading of Jewish history in light of the patterns discernible in Isaiah, then I think we can say that we've just reviewed Isaiah 2–12 again—or at least Isaiah 2–9. It isn't hard to see the double theme of Isaiah 2–5 here, is it? Iniquity comes in advance of devastation and destruction. Here the iniquities in question are a matter of political and religious leaders who ruin everything for everyone else—just as they are in Isaiah 2–5 originally. So that's clear. What of Isaiah 6–12? Well, here again we've got God sending someone to warn Judah away from iniquity, but it's no ordinary prophet this time; it's the Son of God. Jesus is, of course, a prophet—*the* Prophet—and he's sent to the covenant people, according to the long-established pattern. But here's the odd thing. He's also a messiah, the fulfillment of the hopes of several texts in Isaiah 6–9 in a richer way than any prophet could be.

Here we begin to see, I think, that Nephi may well have read Isaiah 7 and Isaiah 9 in messianic terms—but at the same time that he may well have seen how these texts could be read otherwise. He seems here to see Isaiah's words anticipating the events of Jesus's day, but perhaps not in the most direct fashion. A young woman gave birth back in the eighth century to fulfill a sign given by Isaiah, by the prophet sent to Judah at that time to warn the people about the destruction they were bringing on themselves. But also, a virgin would eventually conceive and bear a son who would be both prophet and messiah, deliverer of the covenant people in the fullest sense. To the people of the eighth century, a child was born and a son given, a king on whose shoulder the weight of the government rested, and he delivered Judah from the Assyrian threat. But also, a child and a son, king of kings, would eventually be given to Judah to deliver them from every trouble. Nephi seems to see each of these prophecies in two ways, with an eighth-century-or-so fulfillment, and with a first-century-or-so fulfillment. Perhaps.

But he hasn't come to Isaiah 11 yet (with the rod that springs suddenly from the roots of the stump that everyone thinks is dead). We discussed the fact that this text has often been read messianically, though uniquely Mormon scripture suggests otherwise. Well, watch what Nephi does with it. He'll actually make a direct reference back to it as we go on here. And it complicates everything.

"And after that [the Jews] have been scattered," says Nephi,

> and the Lord God hath scourged them by other nations for the space of many generations, yea even down from generation to generation until they shall be persuaded to believe in Christ, the Son of God, and the atonement which is infinite for all mankind—and when that day shall come that they

shall believe in Christ, and worship the Father in his name with pure hearts and clean hands, and look not forward anymore for another messiah (and then at that time, the day will come that it must needs be expedient that they should believe these things), the Lord will set his hand again the second time to restore his people from their lost and fallen state. (2 Ne. 25:16–17)

Wow, there's a lot there. And Nephi has here allowed his excitement to carry him away, producing a rather ridiculous run-on sentence. Let's pick it apart a bit. There's a scattering and a scourging of Jerusalem's Jews, it seems, and that continues for a long time—until, it appears, "they shall be persuaded to believe in Christ, the Son of God, and the atonement which is infinite for all mankind." When *that* happens, a couple of other things happen. Nephi envisions Jews worshiping the Father in Christ's name and ceasing to look forward for a messiah. He also and climactically envisions them coming to "believe these things"—a phrase that's used elsewhere in the Book of Mormon to refer to belief in *the Book of Mormon* specifically. Nephi seems to see that as the culmination of this brief little history. There's a moment where Judah comes eventually to read the writings of the branch that was broken off from them and planted in the New World.

Now note this—the way Nephi describes that event is by returning to the language of Isaiah, and it's Isaiah 11 he draws on: "the Lord will set his hand again the second time to restore his people from their lost and fallen state." That's Isaiah 11:11, and it's essential we see that. It seems that Nephi likens Isaiah 2–5 to the "wars and rumors of wars" that lead up to the time of Christ. And then it seems that he likens Isaiah 6–9 to the arrival of the Messiah, along with his death and resurrection. But it seems that he likens Isaiah 10–12 only to events of a much, much later time. In the Lord's setting his hand "the second time" to restore his people, Nephi sees the events of what we call the last days, the final gathering of Israel when history itself comes to an end. This Nephi goes on to call "a marvelous work and a wonder" (2 Ne. 25:17), drawing on the language of Isaiah 29, and he'll go on to describe it as an event of "bring[ing] forth his words unto them" (v. 18)—presumably, again, a reference to the Book of Mormon. That book or these words will be given to the Jews, "unto the convincing of them that they need not look forward anymore for a messiah to come" (v. 18). And then Nephi spends a few words making clear that there's only the one Messiah, the one who would come "in six hundred years from the time [Lehi] left Jerusalem" (v. 19). That's the end of that, as far as Nephi's concerned.

So let's be quite clear about this. It seems Nephi wants us to see something like this in his lengthy quotation of Isaiah: (1) Isaiah 2–5: (a) a general pattern of iniquity leading to destruction, manifested originally in the eighth century before Christ; (b) the same general pattern of iniquity leading to destruction, manifested again in the centuries leading up to the time of Christ and culminating in the destruction of Jerusalem by Rome; (2) Isaiah 6–9: (a) a general pattern of God's sending a prophet to warn the covenant people away from their iniquities, manifested originally in the eighth century with the preaching of Isaiah; (b) the same general pattern of God's sending a prophet, manifested again when Jesus comes as both prophet and messiah; (3) Isaiah 10–12: (a) a general pattern of God's using destruction for the purpose of establishing a remnant true to the covenant, manifested originally in the eighth century when Assyria purged Judah; (b) the same general pattern of God's producing a remnant, manifested again when God recovers Judah for the last time in part through the emergence of the Book of Mormon. Is all that quite fair? I think that's what I see happening in Nephi's prophecy, here in 2 Nephi 25:9–19.

Puzzles about Nephi's Interpretation

I think that's what I see, but I'm left with a couple of puzzles.

Here's the first one. Did you notice that Nephi doesn't seem to come back to Isaiah 13–14 in this larger likening of sorts? He finds a certain application of Isaiah 2–5 in the events of pre-Christian-but-post-exilic Judah. Then he finds a certain application of Isaiah 6–9 in the events surrounding the rise of Christianity. And finally he finds a certain application of Isaiah 10–12 in the events surrounding the coming forth of the Book of Mormon and the final redemption of Israel. It's *almost* as if he's at this point unsure about whether he should've included the whole of Isaiah 2–14 in his long quotation. Wasn't Isaiah 2–12 enough? And perhaps those eleven chapters could've been divided into three, rather than two, sequences, right? He seems here in 2 Nephi 25:11–19, anyway, to see Isaiah 6–9 and Isaiah 10–12 as focused sequentially on two rather distinct eras: the former on the time of Christ and primitive Christianity, the latter on the time of Joseph Smith and the Restoration.

Maybe? But let's note that it wouldn't be difficult to guess where Nephi might go with things if he wanted to extend his plain prophecy to provide an application of Isaiah 13–14. If Isaiah 10–12 can be applied to the coming forth of the Book of Mormon and the restoration of Israel, wouldn't he just see Isaiah 13–14 as applicable to the final judgment? You'll remember that those two chapters tell a prophetic story about Babylon's total demise, and Isaiah there has all sorts of people making fun of Babylon's king as he dies, a king whose nickname in the King James Version is "Lucifer." Wouldn't Nephi have rather easily seen Isaiah 13–14 as continuing the story, then? After Israel's restoration, there's one last bit of the world's history to recount, namely the final eradication of evil and the punishment of the devil. Couldn't Isaiah's taunt song regarding Babylon's fallen king be applied pretty readily to the final binding of Satan? Nephi's certainly seen such an event in vision. He tells us about it in 1 Nephi 22, making it precisely the sequel to Israel's redemption. Here's the text there: "And the time cometh speedily that the righteous must be led up as calves of the stall, . . . and he gathereth his children from the four quarters of the earth. . . . And because of the righteousness of his people, Satan hath no power—wherefore, he cannot be loosed for the space of many years" (1 Ne. 22:24–26). Isn't that what Nephi *implicitly* applies Isaiah 13–14 to here in 2 Nephi 25?

I'm going to assume that's what Nephi has in mind. In 2 Nephi 30, he'll quote at length again from Isaiah 11, revisiting what he portrays as the key events of the latter days, events surrounding the Restoration. He'll allow the remarkable portrayal of world peace in Isaiah 11 to serve as a fitting conclusion to world history, except that he'll add one detail to it: "And Satan shall have power over the hearts of the children of men no more for a long time" (2 Ne. 30:18). That'll be more or less Nephi's final word on Isaiah. There again, and perhaps more clearly, it's pretty obvious that Nephi sees what follows Isaiah 10–12 as being about Satan's final demise. And what follows Isaiah 10–12 is, of course, Isaiah 13–14.

So maybe we've solved that puzzle, for the moment. But I can't shake the feeling there's another puzzle, much harder to solve, that we're left with at the end of all this. Here's how we've interpreted Nephi's plain prophecy in 2 Nephi 25:9–19. We've understood the first two verses to provide *one* application of Isaiah 2–14. This first application isn't really an application, however, since it seems to draw more or less on the straightforward meaning of Isaiah, the same one most historical-critical readers of Isaiah find there today. And we've understood the remaining nine verses of Nephi's prophecy to provide a *second* application of Isaiah 2–14. This second application really *is* an application, since it extracts the basic narrative arc of Isaiah 2–14 from the text and then applies it to a much larger history, stretching from Judah's return from Babylonian exile in the sixth century before Christ to the emergence of the Book of Mormon and the wrapping up of the latter-day work. Here we're dealing, as we've understood things, with a relatively obvious bit of *likening*.

But then I can't shake the feeling that I mostly just *want* Nephi to distinguish between these two applications of the text. Couldn't we read 2 Nephi 25:9–19 as providing us only *one* application of Isaiah 2–14? And wouldn't we then have to read Nephi as here giving us not so much a *likening* as a *straightforward interpretation* of Isaiah? That is, shouldn't we understand Nephi simply to be telling us *what Isaiah's prophecies straightforwardly mean*? Here we'd still have to understand verse 9 as providing us both a brief summary of Isaiah 2–5 and an explanation of Isaiah's prophetic activity in Isaiah 6–9. But then we'd understand verses 10–13 to be describing the events prophesied of by Isaiah in those very chapters: the coming of the Messiah, and so on. Then, presumably, we'd understand verses 14–15 to be focused on the interpretation of Isaiah 10 before verses 16–19 outline the meaning of Isaiah 11–12. (Isaiah 13–14 would still be implicitly interpreted in terms of Satan's ultimate demise.) Perhaps this is a more coherent a reading of the data, with Nephi not so much seeing a repeating pattern at work as he is seeing a simple prophetic outline of history.

To be honest, I haven't fully decided what I think is happening here. I'm myself still working through the larger implications of what Nephi's up to. I suspect I'll be working through those implications for a long time still. For the moment, I don't want to close the door on either possibility. Perhaps Nephi sees the interpretation of Isaiah's prophecies as a straightforward affair, a simple outline of a larger history Latter-day Saints feel they already know well enough. Or perhaps Nephi sees the interpretation of Isaiah's prophecies as a more complicated matter, something that has to be worked out at two levels.

We'll see starting next time that there are good reasons to think he's himself convinced of the latter much more than the former. We'll have to see if we can't clarify that. And it's been far too long since we've stopped to take stock of our progress. So we'll open next time by drawing up a balance sheet of what we've gained so far.

Lecture XXII

Approaching Isaiah 29

Ah yes, we've got to start today by catching ourselves up. What have we accomplished so far? Where are we in this journey that's far too rapidly coming to an end? But heavens, we've covered a lot of ground. We've given our past *eleven* lectures to Second Nephi, building on all we were able to reconstruct in connection with First Nephi before that. A couple of those lectures focused on Jacob's contribution to Second Nephi, the role his work on Isaiah plays in Nephi's "more sacred things." We had to do that too quickly, you'll remember. But perhaps we culled at least a couple of points of interest from our study of Jacob's use of Isaiah 49–52. What's most important, it seems, is that Jacob was attuned in a way Nephi apparently hadn't been to the immediate relevance of Isaiah's words to Judah, to "the Jews." Sometimes that attunement resulted in texts that don't read terribly comfortably today, but there we are. Now, we've seen just in our last lecture that Jacob seems to have rubbed off on Nephi some. Rather suddenly, without any real fanfare, Nephi's begun talking in 2 Nephi 25 about how Isaiah's prophecies are particularly applicable to Judah. It's a bit of a shock, in fact, that he there doesn't say much of anything about broader Israel. It's not entirely clear how we should understand that change in Nephi's interpretive style, but it certainly seems to have something to do with Jacob's work.

After we spent just a couple of lectures on Jacob's Isaiah, we turned our attention to Nephi's long quotation of Isaiah 2–14. We dedicated seven straight lectures to that. You likely felt it was never going to end! For my part, it felt like it was going too quickly, that we were covering things too rapidly, too irresponsibly. But let's review a point or two. We saw that Nephi divides those chapters into three sequences. In a first one, Isaiah 2–5, the prophet looks at the contrast between Israel's destiny and their then-current situation. And that contrast allowed Isaiah to level some pretty serious accusations against his people, in the name of the Lord, and to predict severe consequences—social disorder, oppression from without, and the like—all this as a result of their systematic mistreatment of the poor. Then comes a second sequence, Isaiah 6–12, where the focus is on a very particular historical era, that of the Syro-Ephraimite crisis. Judah was in a politically delicate position, and the king, Ahaz, didn't handle it well. Isaiah, already commissioned to deliver an unreceiveable message to the people, got involved, but neither the king nor the people would hear what he had to say. He found it necessary to seal up his prophetic message for a later generation, leaving Judah to face the immense danger of the Assyrian empire more or less on its own. Yet Isaiah saw in the events surrounding Assyria's devastation (but not destruction) of Judah an occasion for the Lord to winnow the nation down to just a remnant, a group of sanctified survivors who might be prepared to receive the prophet's message. They'd be led by a king of some sort, a messiah of some kind, whether human or divine. And they'd be ready to read Isaiah's words. Finally, a third and last sequence, Isaiah 13–14, focused on Babylon's fall and Israel's eventual redemption. We looked at those chapters rather quickly.

That was a lot to handle, I'm sure. But we've seen in our last two lectures that Nephi doesn't leave us without help. In 2 Nephi 25, he tells us a bit about why he could himself make sense of Isaiah's writings. It was in part a question of his familiarity with Jewish history, geography, culture, and tradition. But it was much more a question of his having experienced apocalyptic visions, his having access—unlike so many of us—to the spirit of prophecy. He'd been given a remarkable gift to know the larger history of the world, or really the larger history of the Abrahamic covenant that underpins the history of the world. He'd seen it unfold in a remarkable vision, recorded in as much detail as Nephi could get away with in 1 Nephi 11–14. And that vision allowed him to see things in Isaiah that the rest of us can't see. Really, it seems, that vision allowed him to see how he might find a sort of correspondence between the immediate focus of Isaiah's writings—events in the eighth, seventh, and sixth centuries before Christ—and the larger covenantal history of the human race. Crucially, once Nephi tells us that he *had* this resource, he then begins (still in 2 Nephi 25) to outline his vision anew, now with a clear focus on how it provides a map of Isaiah 2–14. That, of course, is what we looked at last time.

Nephi and the Remnant

So this is what we've come to. We've seen in Second Nephi, so far, three things: (1) Jacob's more emphatically Judah-focused interpretation of Isaiah; (2) Nephi's long quotation of a three-part stretch of Isaianic text, tracing the development of a remnant of Israel prepared to receive the sealed writings of the prophet; and (3) Nephi's brief clarification of that quotation in a rather Jacob-like manner, focused on the details of Jewish history. What strikes me as we come to the end of 2 Nephi 25, however, is that Jacob's influence on Nephi's interpretive style, at least as that's manifest in that chapter, has led to an underplaying of the significance of the remnant theme. In fact, when we get to a "plain" prophecy in 2 Nephi 25 that's meant to clarify the basic meaning of Isaiah 2–14, there's no talk of a remnant at all. When Nephi starts thinking of Isaiah as primarily focused on the fate of the Jews, he seems to forget about the central theme of the remnant. And that means that he also seems to forget about the sealing up of the prophetic text for a later generation. Yet these are *unmistakably* central themes in the Book of Mormon. Why should Nephi quote at such length from Isaiah 2–14 and then pretend, when he gives a brief explanation of those chapters, that they've got little or nothing to say to this central theme?

Well, here's the trick. It's quite true that Nephi doesn't say anything about the remnant in 2 Nephi 25. But boy, does he ever do so in 2 Nephi 26–27! It seems as if he's holding back the most important theme from Isaiah 2–14 when he provides his summary in 2 Nephi 25, but that's because he wants to develop it much more fully, over the course of two chapters. That's what we're getting next. Now we turn our attention to the remnant.

And how's Nephi going to develop this remnant theology and its connection to Isaiah? By giving us just a little more of Isaiah's writings. And significantly, what he's going to give us is a bit of the Book of Isaiah that's very closely related to the heart of Isaiah 2–14. He's going to work over Isaiah 29, a text that all commentators agree is deeply intertwined with Isaiah 6–12. So here's what we've got to look at today and next time. What does Nephi do with the remnant theme when he turns his attention to Isaiah 29, and how does that develop the undeveloped theme of Isaiah 6–12?

Are you ready? Let's see what we can learn here.

Oddities about Isaiah 29

So, the *very* first thing we need to say about Nephi's handling of Isaiah 29 in 2 Nephi 26–27 is that it's clear that he isn't just quoting from Isaiah at this point. If you read through what Latter-day Saint scholars have generally had to say about Isaiah 29 in 2 Nephi 26–27, you'll see that it's often been assumed that we're here getting access to a much longer original version of the Isaiah text. I can see how some have come to that conclusion. We've already seen how Book of Mormon quotations of Isaiah can differ pretty drastically from the biblical text you'll find in your King James Version. And so it's relatively natural to assume that the differences between 2 Nephi 26–27 and Isaiah 29 are along the same lines, variations in the Isaiah text that derive from Nephi's brass-plates source. But I don't think that's right in the end. The variants you can track in every other quotation of Isaiah in the Book of Mormon are occasional and largely minimal in nature: little details at most. But here we get long insertions— sometimes as long as a dozen verses or more—and that departs pretty substantially from what we've seen elsewhere. Either we're to conclude that Isaiah 29 was manipulated in a most spectacular fashion after it was written into the brass plates, in a way unlike much of anything else in Isaiah as contained in the brass plates, *or* we're to guess that something rather different is going on here in 2 Nephi 26–27. I think it makes a good deal more sense to conclude the latter.

There's also this interesting detail to consider. Everywhere else in Nephi's record, he warns us when he quotes at length from Isaiah. Have you noticed that? In the last verses of 1 Nephi 19, he tells us he's about to quote at length from Isaiah, and only then does he quote from Isaiah 48–49. And then in 2 Nephi 6, Nephi has Jacob warn us that he's going to quote from Isaiah, and only then does he go on to quote from Isaiah 49–52. Again and perhaps most importantly, when Nephi gives us his *really* lengthy quotation of Isaiah 2–14 in 2 Nephi 12–24, he tells he's going to do so in 2 Nephi 11, and then he comments on his own having done so in 2 Nephi 25, as we've seen. So Nephi's established a clear pattern of quoting large chunks of Isaiah only when he's alerted his readers to the fact that he's going to do so. But here in 2 Nephi 26–27 he breaks the pattern. He quotes most of Isaiah 29 in these two chapters, but he never once tells us that he's drawing on Isaiah. We're left to figure that out on our own. That's peculiar, a break in a pretty well-established pattern by this point. And so we ought to be wondering how Nephi's handling of Isaiah is going to be different this time. And, well, we can already guess that one way it differs is that, *this time*, he isn't going to slavishly copy down Isaiah's writings as he finds them in the brass plates. Rather, he's going to adapt and manipulate them, developing them beyond what they actually say.

Let's notice a crucial consequence of that. If Nephi is here giving us a prophecy that uses but goes well beyond the actual words of Isaiah, we should hesitate before we say some things. We often say that Isaiah prophesied of Martin Harris's visit to Charles Anthon, but let's be clear that that's not exactly correct—at least, it's not exactly correct if we're right that Nephi's doing something new and different here. It's not *Isaiah* but *Nephi* who prophesied of that event, though Nephi used Isaiah's words to clothe his prophecy of it. (Actually, we'll see as we work our way through 2 Nephi 27 that it's not exactly sure whether even *Nephi* prophesied of the Anthon incident. We'll get to that.) At any rate, let's be extremely careful about our language here. In 2 Nephi 26–27, we are getting Nephi's inventive *use* of Isaiah, not his slavish *reproduction* of Isaiah. We should be allowed to assume that Isaiah 29 was in the brass plates largely the same way it is in our copies of the King James Version. There was likely some variation, since we've seen that plenty along the way. And we might even be able to guess at some of that variation from some of the ways that Isaiah 29 is used in 2 Nephi 26–27. But it seems most responsible to assume that *most* of Isaiah 29 was available to Nephi in more or less the form it's available to us in our bibles.

So the question we've got to ask is this: What's Nephi doing with Isaiah 29 here? How does he adopt it to his own purposes? Where's he getting the stuff he says here, the stuff he dresses up in Isaiah's words? If he's not just copying over Isaiah's prophecies, where are these prophecies coming from?

That, I think, isn't terribly difficult to answer. He's getting them from his own visionary experiences. He's just told us in 2 Nephi 25 that he's been gifted with the spirit of prophecy, and he's only just given us an outline of at least one major prophecy he's been privileged to receive. I think we can assume that here we're getting more of what Nephi has seen in his visions—or maybe just in that one major vision contained back in 1 Nephi 11–14. Maybe Nephi saw all this at *that* point, way back in the desert camp his family established near the Red Sea. That seems to me rather attractive. Certainly, what *is* clear is that Nephi has an independent source of prophecy, a source independent of Isaiah. And he thinks that independent source of prophecy has some kind of privileged relationship to Isaiah—the sort of privileged relationship that gives him the liberty to weave this prophecy *right into* the words of Isaiah. But now remember back! That's exactly what Nephi's been preparing us for since the very beginning. The whole of First Nephi, remember, was organized to show how Nephi's vision serves as the key for making sense of Isaiah, just as Isaiah serves as the key for making sense of Nephi's vision. Here, after so much work on Isaiah, Nephi's finally getting to a kind of culmination. He wants to show us what it might mean, in the end, to treat his own vision and Isaiah's writings as working on the same level, as equal partners in helping to clarify events in the future. And he does so by making Isaiah's writings and his own prophecies into a single tapestry, a beautiful weave that's rather difficult to pick apart.

Oh, how difficult to pick apart! We can only recognize what's Isaiah and what's Nephi because we have Isaiah 29 sitting there in our bibles. Only that allows us to see what Nephi is doing. But since we *can* see what Nephi is doing, we find ourselves rather privileged. We're quite free to do some comparison work and see just how Nephi adapts Isaiah 29 to his own prophetic purposes.

Let me note here that I was part of a project some years ago, a project launched by the Mormon Theology Seminar, that brought several scholars together to work on the use of Isaiah 29 in 2 Nephi 26–27. We spent a few months looking at these things in detail. Then we wrote papers, presented them at a conference, and finally published them in a volume. The book is readily available. Jenny Webb and I edited it together, and it's called *Reading Nephi Reading Isaiah*. You'll find a lot of good stuff in there, all of it trying to wrestle with what exactly Nephi's doing with Isaiah's writings here. It's preliminary work, of course. But it's good work, I think. I feel like I've learned a lot since then, and I've got a great many thoughts now that go well beyond anything I had to say in the course of our work on that project. What I'll present as we continue our way through 2 Nephi 26–27 here draws on some of the insights that grew out of that seminar, but also on things I think I've figured out in the years since.

A Variety of Approaches to Isaiah 29

Let's start just by identifying where the various bits and pieces of Isaiah 29 show up in 2 Nephi 26–27, since it's not like they're all just there in a jumble. They come in fits and starts, and it'll be useful if we recognize that from the outset. Here's a list of sorts:

Isaiah 29:1–2	these two verses don't show up at all in 2 Nephi 26–27
Isaiah 29:3–5	these three verses appear in several chunks in 2 Nephi 26:15–18
Isaiah 29:6–10	these five verses come all together in 2 Nephi 27:2–5
Isaiah 29:11–12	these two verses appear in fragments in 2 Nephi 27:6–19
Isaiah 29:13–16	these four verses come as a block in 2 Nephi 27:24–27
Isaiah 29:17–24	these final eight verses come as a block in 2 Nephi 27:28–35

Notice right away a certain unevenness in Nephi's uses of Isaiah 29. Some parts of Isaiah 29 are reproduced without much variation at all. Others are worked over so drastically that they're hardly recognizable—more a matter of allusion than of actual quotation. Nephi's use of the text is deliberately uneven. There's material here in Isaiah 29 that interests him more, and there's material here that interests him less.

In fact, let's note what grabs his attention above all. It's Isaiah 29:11–12. These two verses form the centerpiece of Nephi's prophecy. They're reworked in the most substantial way, but they're nonetheless followed quite closely. They make up the skeletal frame of a fourteen-verse stretch in 2 Nephi 27. It thus appears—quite clearly, I think—that it was these two verses that drew Nephi's attention to Isaiah 29 in the first place. In other words, it seems like Nephi wanted to use these two verses to think through things he'd seen in vision, and their usefulness brought him to see how the rest of Isaiah 29 could *also* be useful to him.

Isaiah 29 and Isaiah 8

So let's ask the obvious question: *Why Isaiah 29:11–12?* What do these two verses say, or what's their focus? Shall we quote them as they stand in the King James Version? "And the vision of all is become unto you as the words of a book that is sealed, which men deliver to one that is learned, saying, Read this, I pray thee: and he saith, I cannot; for it is sealed. And the book is delivered to him that is not learned, saying, Read this, I pray thee: and he saith, I am not learned." They're familiar, aren't they? And because we're so primed to read 2 Nephi 27 in terms of the Charles Anthon incident, we have a too-ready answer to the question I asked just a moment ago. Why was Nephi interested in these two verses? We're happy just to answer that they pretty clearly anticipate what happened in New York City with Martin Harris and the scholars. I think, though, that there are better and deeper answers to this question. Let's see if we can't go further than we're accustomed to go.

Think back to Isaiah 8. Do you remember this? The prophet had already received his commission—that's Isaiah 6—in the course of which he was warned that his people wouldn't believe a word he'd say. And he'd already seen that prediction fulfilled, since his intervention with King Ahaz during the Syro-Ephraimite crisis resulted in exactly nothing, except maybe the necessity of telling Judah they'd have a lot of trouble with Assyria due to their unbelief, and to their king's unbelief. That was Isaiah 7. But then came Isaiah 8, still in the historical context of the Syro-Ephraimite crisis. The prophet was again using the births of local babies to explain to the people of Jerusalem just how soon their fears would prove unwarranted, and he was again finding that no one would listen to him. But as Isaiah 8 progresses, Isaiah makes a kind of public announcement that he's basically done with Judah. He talks about the "strong hand" the Lord has used to keep him from "walk[ing] in the way of this people" (2 Ne. 18:11). He's clear that he's not to buy into their plans to set up "a confederacy" with other local nations that hope to stand against Assyria (v. 12). Instead, his command has been to "sanctify the Lord of hosts himself," his sole "fear" and "dread" (v. 13). Having announced his effective independence of Judah—his having been cleaned from the blood and the sins of his particular generation—he announces his plan to "bind up the testimony" and "seal the law among [his] disciples" (v. 16). Having prophesied orally to a people that wouldn't receive it, he turns his attention to the written word, writing up his prophecies for a later generation—for the remnant that's to be produced through the unhappy events surrounding Assyria's campaign.

Now, isn't that all *exactly* what we've got here in Isaiah 29:11–12? Isaiah's whole vision ("the vision of all") has become just a sealed book to Judah, something they can't possibly read. Those who actually know how to read (remember how few and far between those were in the ancient world!), the actually literate take one look at Isaiah's sealed book and say that they can't do anything with it. It's sealed. So then the book is given to the unlearned, to the illiterate. They seem not even to recognize that it's sealed. All they have to say in response is that they can't read: "I am not learned." Isaiah's prophecies have thus been sealed up such that they can no longer speak to the people who have systematically rejected them. They've got to be saved for a later time. They've got to be saved for the remnant.

Do you remember this further detail from Isaiah 8? Isaiah explains that at some point after his writings are sealed up, but still before the full production of the holy remnant that will cling to the Messiah, there will be people who start to realize that the prophet was right. He seems to have in mind something like the following. When the events of destruction he predicted begin to happen—the beginning of the process through which the remnant will eventually be produced—some of the people experiencing those events will remember that Isaiah predicted this stuff. Suddenly interested in the prophet, but apparently still relatively unrepentant, they'll try to figure out a way to get access to Isaiah's words. Of course, the actual writings of Isaiah are by that point sealed and hidden away. And it seems, moreover, that Isaiah's himself already supposed to have died by that point as well. So what do the people do? They set up a séance in the hopes of getting the *dead* Isaiah to talk to them, to help them out of the difficulties he warned them about. Here's the passage from Isaiah 8: "They shall say unto you: 'Seek unto them that have familiar spirits, and unto wizards that peep and mutter! Should not a people seek unto their God for the living to hear from the dead?'" (2 Ne. 18:19). To make sure you understand the reference here, remember that a "familiar spirit" is an animal body (a toad, an ape, or some such thing) through which the spirits of the dead are made to speak in necromantic practices.

So what's all this have to do with Isaiah 29? Well, a lot. We've already seen that Isaiah 8 and Isaiah 29 share an interest in the sealed record, in prophecies written and hidden away until there's a people actually ready to receive them. They share an interest *also* in this séance business. Here's the relevant verse in Isaiah 29, and it follows immediately after the Lord announces his plan to level Jerusalem and leave many of its inhabitants dead: "Thou shalt be brought down, and shalt speak out of the ground, and thy speech shall be low out of the dust, and thy voice shall be, as of one that hath a familiar spirit, out of the ground, and thy speech shall whisper out of the dust" (Isa. 29:4). Sound familiar (no pun intended)? Of course, it's not exactly the same scenario. Here it's Jerusalem's citizens (rather than the prophet alone) who make up the spirits of the dead, who would speak through familiars to whomever survives. But the close relationship established in both Isaiah 8 and Isaiah 29 among three ideas is crucial: (1) there's a major series of catastrophes coming, all predicted by the prophet;

(2) no one will listen to those predictions, with the result that the record of them has to be sealed up and saved for the survivors of the catastrophe, who'll finally be prepared to hear it; and (3) those passing through the predicted events will find themselves wishing they could speak with the dead, and they'll seek to do so through wizardry and witchcraft.

It's clear, then, that Nephi's interest in Isaiah 29 is closely related to his interest in Isaiah 8. We noted earlier that Nephi says nothing in 2 Nephi 25 about the remnant theme that's so central to Isaiah 6–12, as if he'd forgotten for a moment about the deep relevance to his own situation of the fact that Isaiah was forced to turn his prophetic attention to a generation yet to be born, sealing up his prophecies for that later age. But now we see that Nephi was basically saving the best for last. This theme is *so* essential to his purposes that he wants to tie Isaiah 6–12 to Isaiah 29, highlighting the key moment in Isaiah 8 by drawing on its sister text, forcing us to look at this moment in the story in much more detail. He gives his most mature, his most sustained, his most inventive analysis of Isaiah to *this* theme, drawing out of his lengthy quotation of Isaiah 2–14 its most central theme, and highlighting its deep connection to his apocalyptic vision from 1 Nephi 11–14.

So, with 2 Nephi 26–27, we're being brought *back* to Isaiah 2–14, made to look more closely at the very heart of the historical story Nephi has to tell there. And, still more, we're being forced to see what it looks like to see Isaiah's experience as a writing prophet as somehow symbolic of or parallel to the larger experience of the Nephite prophets, writing their words for a remnant of Israel that wouldn't be able to read their prophecies for hundreds and hundreds of years.

Nephi and Isaiah 29

We've got to start wrapping up our discussion in a minute, so let me turn to one final point before we have to quit. We've seen today that Nephi's treatment of Isaiah 29 in 2 Nephi 26–27 serves as a kind of focusing of all the Isaiah material in 2 Nephi 11–30. It extracts the kernel of Nephi's Isaiah and gives it to us in the most developed form possible. We've also seen today that Nephi's treatment of Isaiah 29 in 2 Nephi 26–27 represents his most mature and most inventive treatment of the prophet. He's no longer just quoting Isaiah in long chunks, or making passing allusions to his prophecies, or giving plain paraphrases of what he takes the prophet to mean. He's now weaving Isaiah's words directly into his own prophetic anticipations, making one whole of Isaiah's Old-World prophecies and his own New-World prophecies. But let's note one more striking thing about Nephi's treatment of Isaiah 29 in 2 Nephi 26–27. It ties up a whole lot of loose ends we're likely not even to have noticed as we've read through First and Second Nephi. The fact is, although we haven't yet mentioned it, that Nephi *constantly* draws on the language of Isaiah 29. It's not just here in 2 Nephi 26–27 that it appears.

So let's mark a few of these passages, shall we? So far as I can reconstruct things, the first borrowing from Isaiah 29 appears all the way back in 1 Nephi 14 (verse 7), where Nephi seems to use the language of Isaiah 29:14. He uses that language again in 1 Nephi 22 (verse 8), where you can find a whole bunch of borrowings from Isaiah 29: verse 4 (in verse 23), verse 8 (twice, in verses 14 and 19), and verse 18 (in verse 12). Remember that 1 Nephi 22, moreover, is that chapter where Nephi's trying to explain Isaiah 49 to his brothers. To clarify that chapter, he seems to think that Isaiah 29 is particularly useful. You can find a couple of possible allusions to Isaiah 29 in 1 Nephi 19 as well (to verse 6 in verse 11 and to verse 21 in verse 9). And then there are borrowings in 2 Nephi 6 (Isaiah 29:6 gets paraphrased in verse 15, Isaiah 29:7–8 in verse 13) and 2 Nephi 25 (Isaiah 29:14 gets paraphrased in verse 17, in the middle of Nephi's plain prophecy). Nephi's been peppering us with Isaiah 29 for a long time now.

And he'll continue to do so, by the way. There are at least five borrowings from Isaiah 29 in 2 Nephi 28, at least one in 2 Nephi 29, and at least one in 2 Nephi 33.

You get the point. What we're dealing with in 2 Nephi 26–27, with its careful working over of Isaiah 29, is something like the gravitational center of Nephi's whole project. Here we get a systematic exposition of the text that's been driving Nephi from the very beginning. It's this chapter he's wanted to get us ready to read above all, and now he's going to read it with us.

I suggest we listen up. Next time.

Lecture XXIII

Nephi and Isaiah 29

Outline of Nephi's Uses of Isaiah 29

Well, we spent most of last time just getting ready to look at 2 Nephi 26–27, didn't we? And of course there's far, far too much to say about these two chapters and the way they handle Isaiah 29. To get started, let's return to the outline of sorts we produced last time, our list of the variety of ways the several verses making up Isaiah 29 get used over the course of 2 Nephi 26–27. Here it is again:

Isaiah 29:1–2	these two verses don't show up at all in 2 Nephi 26–27
Isaiah 29:3–5	these three verses appear in several chunks in 2 Nephi 26:15–18
Isaiah 29:6–10	these five verses come all together in 2 Nephi 27:2–5
Isaiah 29:11–12	these two verses appear in fragments in 2 Nephi 27:6–19
Isaiah 29:13–16	these four verses come as a block in 2 Nephi 27:24–27
Isaiah 29:17–24	these final eight verses come as a block in 2 Nephi 27:28–35

You'll notice just from this list that most of Isaiah 29 appears in 2 Nephi 27. Just three verses show up in 2 Nephi 26 (and another two verses don't show up anywhere). In part that's a consequence of the fact that 2 Nephi 26 doesn't turn to the events Nephi wants to associate with Isaiah 29 until verse 14, pretty late in the chapter, and then the last part of 2 Nephi 26, starting with verse 19, is a long tangent that leaves those events behind all over again. So Isaiah 29 only *could* show up in 2 Nephi 26 in verses

14–18. But all of 2 Nephi 27 is focused on the events Nephi wants to connect to Isaiah 29.

What events does Nephi want to link to Isaiah 29? He's very clear about this: "I prophesy unto you concerning the last days, concerning the days when the Lord God shall bring these things"—that is, the Book of Mormon itself—"forth unto the children of men" (2 Ne. 26:14). There's the set of events Nephi sees reflected in important ways in Isaiah 29: the events surrounding the coming forth of the Book of Mormon. And each little block of verses from Isaiah 29 that Nephi reproduces play their own unique role in giving shape to the events surrounding the Book of Mormon's coming forth. He simply ignores Isaiah 29:1–2 because they don't seem to have anything to say about these events. But then he reads Isaiah 29:3–5 as a sketch of the writing and burying of the gold plates. Isaiah 29:6–10 he takes to provide a helpful description of world conditions at the time the gold plates would be unearthed again. Isaiah 29:11–12 we already discussed last time: Nephi finds in them a profound statement about how poorly the Book of Mormon will be received. In Isaiah 29:13–16, Nephi hears a summary of the Lord's instructions to the prophet who would translate and circulate the Book of Mormon. And finally, Isaiah 29:17–24 looks to Nephi like a straightforward prophecy of the eventual success of the book in redeeming Israel.

That's simple enough, isn't it? Isaiah 29 is like a gallery of images, together telling the story of the Book of Mormon: (1) its production and protection (verses 3–5); (2) the setting of its reemergence (verses 6–10); (3) its initially poor reception (verses 11–12); (4) an explanation to its translator regarding the divine reasons for that poor reception (verses 13–16); and (5) its eventual success in stimulating Israel's deliverance (verses 17–24). It's beautiful in its simplicity. But of course, this simplicity is the product of Nephi's own prophetic inventiveness. Isaiah 29 doesn't come prepackaged this way. Nephi has to do some creative work on the text to make it tell this story so straightforwardly. So we've got to keep a close eye on how Nephi does this.

Isaiah 29:3–5

Let's start with something relatively easy, shall we? Let's look at how Isaiah 29:3–5 gets repurposed in 2 Nephi 26:14–18. How does the biblical text read before Nephi gets involved with it? Well, the first two verses of Isaiah 29—the ones Nephi entirely leaves out of 2 Nephi 26–27—make clear that we're dealing here with a prediction of disaster for Jerusalem. In Isaiah 29:3–5, the Lord announces through Isaiah his plan to "camp against" Judah's capital city, "lay[ing] siege" and "rais[ing] forts" (Isa. 29:3). The result, Isaiah says, is that Jerusalem will "be brought down" and "speak out of the ground"—like, of course, "a familiar spirit," summonable only through a séance (v. 4). Despite all this destruction for Jerusalem, however, Isaiah also predicts that her enemies will be reduced to "small dust," to "chaff that passeth away"—and this "at an instant suddenly" (v. 5). Jerusalem is first to be trampled on by her enemies, but then the Lord will do away with those enemies. You can guess that a remnant is on the horizon.

Okay, so there's Isaiah 29:3–5 as it stands in the biblical text. What does Nephi do with it? Well, first, as we already noted, he reapplies all this to "the days when the Lord God shall bring [the Book of Mormon] forth unto the children of men" (2 Ne. 26:14). Okay, but what does he do with the text of Isaiah?

First he uses his own language by way of prophecy: "After that my seed and the seed of my brethren shall have dwindled in unbelief, and shall have been smitten by the Gentiles . . ." (2 Ne. 26:15). But then he offers up a restatement of his own prophecy, using the words of Isaiah 29:3–4: "yea, after that the Lord shall have camped against them round about, and shall have laid siege against them with a mount, and raised forts against them—and after that they shall have been brought down low in the dust, even that they are not" (2 Ne. 26:16). You see what Nephi's done there? He's taken Isaiah's words, clearly directed to and talking about Jerusalem under Assyrian siege, and he's reapplied them to Lehi's children. It's the Nephites and the Lamanites, in Nephi's borrowing, who get "camped against" and "laid siege" to. It's the Lehites who are "brought down low in the dust, even that they are not." Jerusalem, the clear focus of the biblical prophecy, simply disappears.

But then Nephi gets even more creative. Watch this closely. After all the destruction he has just mentioned, first in his own words and then in Isaiah's, he says this: "yet the words of the righteous shall be written, and the prayers of the faithful shall be heard, and all they which have dwindled in unbelief shall not be forgotten" (2 Ne. 26:15). These are Nephi's own prophetic words again. He's predicting what he has seen in vision: the preservation of Christ's teachings to Lehi's children in the gold plates. And now again he restates this prediction by using Isaiah's words from Isaiah 29:4: "For they which shall be destroyed shall speak unto them out of the ground, and their speech shall be low out of the dust, and their voice shall be as one that hath a familiar spirit" (2 Ne. 26:16). Remember what those words meant in Isaiah's prophecy? In Isaiah 29, they indicate the irreversibility of the deaths of Jerusalem's inhabitants. Those who die in the Assyrian onslaught will only be able to speak to the living through séances. But now notice what Nephi's done with those words. Here again Isaiah's words are reapplied to Lehi's children, and specifically to those who would produce the gold plates. But rather than indicate the irreversibility of their deaths, Isaiah's words serve for Nephi to describe the way the writings of those who died will speak from out of the dust. Nephi makes this even clearer as he continues in the next verse, where he quotes "the Lord God" as saying that the Nephites would "write" things which would be "sealed up in a book," and so on (2 Ne. 26:17).

As if that weren't already inventive enough, Nephi does something more, something really surprising. He tells us that the voice of the dead will speak through their writings, but then he explains that it will do so specifically "as one that hath a familiar spirit." It isn't that the latter-day world will get their writings directly, in the form of the gold plates. We'll see that 2 Nephi 27 is largely dedicated to an explanation of that complicated situation. For now let's just be clear that the writings of the Nephites are supposed to come to the latter-day world only in translation, only in the transcription of a prophet's dictation of the gold plates' content. And how's that to be accomplished? Through something rather like "a familiar spirit." Here's the shock. Nephi takes Isaiah's reference to a necromantic practice—to wizardry!—and turns it into something *positive*. The Nephite prophets will have their voices heard only thanks to an effort at translation that's more like a séance (although it *isn't* a séance, obviously)— than like a work of translation. Nephi has apparently seen the process of translating the Book of Mormon in vision, and he sees that it wasn't at all like the scholarly, academic work of translation. Joseph Smith didn't sit down with dictionaries and lexicons, using years of study of the relevant languages to cast the source text in a target language. He was more like a familiar spirit, like a toad or an ape used by a wizard. He's a medium, the channel through which the Nephites' words are delivered to the latter-day world. As Nephi puts this point, "the words of the faithful should speak as if it were from the dead" (2 Ne. 27:13).

So this is pretty weird, I realize. Of course, we've often as Latter-day Saints found a way around this plain meaning of the text. We overlook the meaning of Isaiah's actual words, taking the words "a familiar spirit" to mean that the Book of Mormon strikes people with open minds and hearts as something they've heard before, as something they already knew. It's got a familiar spirit about it. That's a clever reading, to be sure. But I don't think it's what's going on here in the text. Isaiah's meaning is perfectly clear in the Bible. And Nephi takes that meaning over pretty straightforwardly. We've already seen that he's emphatic that "the words of the faithful should speak as if it were from the dead." So, while this might make us a bit uncomfortable, there's probably no good way around it. Nephi uses Isaiah's image of a séance to sketch a picture of the translation process through which the Book of Mormon reached us. That hardly means that the translation process *was* a séance, and Nephi's clear that this is a simile ("*as* one that hath a familiar spirit," he says). But we're apparently supposed to be able to learn from that comparison. We're talking about channeling the voices of the dead, after all.

Nephi goes on to borrow Isaiah 29:5 as well, but let's not take any more time developing this first bit of Nephi's appropriation. He does much the same thing we've been reviewing, except that now he applies the words Isaiah directed to Jerusalem's enemies (as opposed to Jerusalem itself) to the Lehites, just like he applied the words Isaiah directed to Jerusalem to the Lehites. Nephi, that is, obliterates the distinction Isaiah draws between two different groups that face destruction, applying both predictions to one people. But that's all that we'll bother to say about it. You can take a look yourself by comparing Isaiah 29:5 to 2 Nephi 26:18 sometime. I want to make sure we can say some things about 2 Nephi 27, so let's move on.

We've got all kinds of options when we turn to 2 Nephi 27. What do we want to look at in detail? Do we want to look at the relatively straightforward appropriation of Isaiah 29:6–10, where Nephi applies a few words about Jerusalem to the state of society in the latter days? Do we want to look at the virtuosic appropriation of Isaiah 29:11–12? Do we want to look at how Nephi makes Isaiah 29:13–16 into a divine word spoken to Joseph Smith as the translator and publisher of the Book of Mormon? Or do we want to look at Nephi's presentation of Isaiah 29:17–24 as a prediction concerning the Book of Mormon's eventual success? Unfortunately, we can't do all of these, or even more than one, I think. If we want to give any serious attention to any of them, we'll have to settle on one. And that makes deciding relatively easy. Let's look just at the virtuosic appropriation of Isaiah 29:11–12. These are the verses that connect back up with Isaiah 8, as we discussed last time, resuming the discussion of the remnant that's left after Assyria's devastation of Judah. And these are unquestionably the two verses in Isaiah 29 that most interest Nephi. Moreover, they link up pretty nicely with what we've just been talking about in Isaiah 29:3–5, since Nephi revisits the idea that the translation process has to proceed as if "the faithful" were to "speak . . . from the dead."

So let's focus ourselves on 2 Nephi 27:6–23 for the remainder of our discussion today.

A Book and Its Words

This sequence of 2 Nephi 27 opens with an introduction of sorts: "And it shall come to pass that the Lord God shall bring forth unto you the words of a book, and they shall be the words of them that have slumbered" (2 Ne. 27:6). Note that we're coming back at this point to what we've already been discussing: the words of the Nephite prophets, written and sealed up and saved for the last days. The verses leading up to this passage outline the dire situation in the last days, where the Gentiles have ruined more or less everything and Christianity's basically dying. And these "words of a book" are supposed to solve all these problems, restoring Christianity in its fullness and revitalizing religion in an increasingly secular world. And clearly, the words of the book in question are the Book of Mormon. Nephi's about to use Isaiah 29 to describe the initial reception of the Book of Mormon in the last days. It's not going to be pretty, unfortunately. But it's going to be fascinating to see what Nephi does here with Isaiah's words.

Now, the first thing we've got to note is this: Nephi distinguishes carefully between two things, between "the words of the book" and "the book" itself. We just saw in verse 6 that he sees God bringing forth "the words of a book," but now look at verse 7. There he explains this: "And behold, the book shall be sealed." So there's a clear difference between the book and its words, between what we might call the *physical, material artifact* (the book) and its *transmissible intellectual content* (the words of the book). Nephi's surprisingly careful throughout this whole chapter to keep these distinct. And perhaps we can already see why. The book itself is sealed, while the words are being brought forth to everyone. So what's the book? I think that's clear. It's the gold plates, the actual physical artifact that was buried in the Hill Cumorah. And what are the words of the book? That's just what we call the Book of Mormon, the text we print and circulate and read. That's a fair—if not simply obvious—interpretation, isn't it?

Now notice that Nephi's borrowing these basic concepts directly from Isaiah 29. Verse 11 there speaks of "the words of a book that is sealed," and that little phrase already implicitly distinguishes between a sealed book and its words. But while Isaiah only implicitly draws such a distinction, Nephi's going to make it the centerpiece of his prophecy here.

Nephi says a lot about the sealed book, about the gold plates. They're sealed, and in them is "a revelation from God, from the beginning of the world to the ending thereof" (2 Ne. 27:7). That seems to be a reference to the vision of the brother of Jared, which makes up the so-called sealed portion of the gold plates. (You can go read Ether 3–5 if you're looking for more information about that.) And Nephi then tells us that because this "revelation" is in the gold plates, "the book shall be kept from" the world (2 Ne. 27:8; see verses 10–14 too). But not from everyone. Here's verse 9 in 2 Nephi 27: "But the book shall be delivered unto a man"—it's clear we're talking about Joseph Smith—"and he shall deliver the words of the book . . . unto another." Here we've got a simple description of the translation process, don't we? We've got "a man" with the gold plates in his possession, and he's delivering "the words of the book" to someone else. Well, this *might* be a description of the translation process, but a few verses later it starts to look in retrospect like the description of something else. Let's jump to verse 15:

> The Lord God shall say unto him to whom he shall deliver the book [Joseph Smith]: "Take these words which are *not* sealed, and deliver them to another, that he may shew them unto the learned, saying, 'Read this, I pray thee.'"

Here we're pretty sure we're not talking about translation, but about another event in the early history of the Church, right?

You know the event I've got in mind: Charles Anthon. Martin Harris has a lot of questions about the Prophet's ability to translate, so Joseph copies some characters and a rough translation onto a sheet of paper and sends Martin off to New York City to see what the scholars have to say. After some searching around, Martin meets up with Charles Anthon, a celebrated professor at Columbia University (then Columbia College). As Martin tells the story, Anthon corroborates the translation and writes up a certificate of authentication. But as Martin goes to leave, Anthon asks where the gold plates came from, and Martin tells the story of Moroni's visit. Anthon asks for the certificate, tears it up, and tells Martin there's no such thing as angelic visits in the modern world. He tells Martin to bring the gold plates so that he, the great scholar, can translate them, but Martin tells him they're sealed. And Anthon famously says that he can't translate a sealed book.

You remember the story, right? It's right there in the Pearl of Great Price if you need a refresher (see JS–H 1:61–65). By the way, I'd recommend you grab a copy of a recent book by Mike MacKay and Gerrit Dirkmaat, *From Darkness unto Light*. It goes into the details surrounding this event, and it turns out there's a lot we still have to learn about it. But you're certainly aware of the basics. And it's not hard for us to see this story laid out in some detail right here in 2 Nephi 27. As we come to verse 15, we start to realize that when the man with the book delivers the words of the book to another man, we're probably talking about the whole Anthon incident. And we're primed to read the story beginning in verse 15 in exactly that way.

That's not a *bad* reading of the text, but there's a better reading of it, I think. The words of the book are delivered "to another, that he may shew them unto the learned, saying, 'Read this, I pray thee.'" Here's my question: Is "the learned" singular or plural? We assume it's singular, and that it's simply a reference to Charles Anthon. But notice this. When verse 16 refers back to the learned, it uses the word "they." And then in verse 20, we'll hear God say this: "The learned shall not read [the words of the book], for they have rejected them." Are you catching this? Nephi isn't talking about *one* learned person, but about *the learned in general*. It's got to be right that Charles Anthon is in question here, that the prophecy anticipates what would happen at Columbia with Martin Harris and the professor. But it's clear also that Nephi takes that one event as a kind of symbol for a more general phenomenon. We're not simply getting a prophecy of a one-time event, Martin's trip to New York. We're getting a prophecy that uses that event to describe the *general* reaction to the Book of Mormon in the last days.

So let's go back to the text. What does Nephi actually tell us? The man with the book gives the words to another, who takes those words (never the book) to the learned, plural. And what's their response? What does every learned person say when they're confronted with the Book of Mormon? "And the learned shall say: 'Bring hither the book, and I will read them'" (2 Ne. 27:15). That's the learned response to the Book of Mormon. "I want evidence. I'm not going to give this thing a second thought until you can furnish me with the gold plates themselves. If there isn't physical, tangible, material evidence for this whole thing, why should I bother at all? And how would I know that some rube of a farm kid has given me anything of any substance anyway? Let's get the original text, the gold plates, into the hands of some scholars and see what the thing actually says when we've figured out the underlying language. Who could trust the thing at all until good scholarly work has been undertaken, making sure it's done well?" Isn't that the learned response? It's Charles Anthon's response. And it's our response still today, isn't it?

How is it *our* response? Well, for starters, we're too hungry for evidence. We want Mesoamerican temples and Hebraic poetic structures. We want good explanations for apparent anachronisms, and we want complexity that couldn't have been produced by an uneducated frontier kid. We want reassurance about Second Isaiah's presence in the Book of Mormon, and we want to know how to account for the Sermon on the Mount. Far, far too many of us—and always, certainly, the learned among us—want God to unseal a load of material evidence for the book so that we *really* know that the book's true, or so that we *really* know what the book means. And why do we do it? Well, here's Nephi's explanation: "Because of the glory of the world, and to get gain, will they say this—and not for the glory of God" (2 Ne. 27:16). Ouch. But it's too true, isn't it? Why else do we learned folks struggle so mightily for evidence concerning the Book of Mormon? Why else do we learned folks struggle so mightily when the evidence seems to suggest that the whole thing is a fraud? It's primarily "because of the glory of the world," isn't it? I don't know what else it would be.

At any rate, when Nephi goes on to describe the learned saying that they "cannot read" a sealed book (2 Ne. 27:18), perhaps he's describing the whole lot of us, of the learned among us. That's hard medicine to swallow. But I think he's nailed us. And he goes a good deal farther, too. He tells us pretty clearly here that God's placed a seal on material evidence so that we have to wrestle with the words alone. We're *supposed* to be reading a book that speaks like a voice from the dead, like a ghostly voice during a séance. It's disembodied, cut off in a crucial way from all the material artifacts we prefer to deal with. It speaks like a familiar spirit, and we're uncomfortable with that. Why should God set up a situation like that? Here's Nephi's answer. "I am God, and I am a God of miracles," he has God say. "And I will shew unto the world that I am the same yesterday, today, and forever. And I work not among the children of men save it be according to their faith" (v. 23). God's set all this up in such a way that we're *forced* to take the Book of Mormon on faith. Once we've passed through the trial of our faith, perhaps we'll get some kind of witness, maybe even evidence. But that can't be where we begin. The Book of Mormon is *meant* to work against the dominant conception of knowledge on offer in secular modernity.

And then, along the way, Nephi describes what happens with the Book of Mormon's translator, with Joseph. "The Lord God will deliver again the book and the words thereof to him that is not learned, and the man that is not learned shall say, 'I am not learned'" (2 Ne. 27:19). Joseph's here depicted as the unlearned one, yet he's the one who *does* actually have access to both the material artifact (the gold plates) and the intellectual content (the text of the Book of Mormon). As unlearned, however, he has no idea what to do with any of this. "I'm not learned," he says, and what he seems pretty clearly to mean is that he can't even begin to do the sort of thing a scholar would want to do with these remarkable materials. What training does he have for figuring out ancient languages? How's he supposed to discern the significance of anything on the gold plates? And so he complains to God that he's got what every scholar dreams of, but that he doesn't know where to begin. And God responds by informing him that that's just the point: "Then shall the Lord God say unto him, 'The learned shall not read them, for they have rejected them—and I am able to do mine own work. Wherefore, thou shalt read the words which I shall give unto thee" (v. 20). "There, Joseph. That's enough. Just do the work of translation, which comes by the gift and power of God anyway. Don't try to be a scholar, don't aspire to be among the learned. That's not your task."

So here's the upshot of it all. The learned—that's most of us—are confronted with only half of the equation. The learned get only the words of the book, though they refuse to take them seriously because they only know how to work on the relationship between words and things. And then the unlearned—that's Joseph Smith, for starters—are confronted with the whole equation, but they're too easily scandalized by the fact that they don't know what to do with it. Thankfully, God's there to explain to the unlearned that they're also supposed to focus only on the words. And all this is a beautiful parable of sorts for the larger reception of the Book of Mormon. It's perhaps more fitting today than it was in the nineteenth century.

Well, all this is what I see here, anyway. But I've been getting distracted, haven't I? I've left Isaiah behind just to talk about how rich Nephi's prophecy is, theologically. I've written about this elsewhere (in "The Book, the Words of the Book"), so you can go get your fill on this some other time. But let's get back to Isaiah 29, to what Nephi's doing with Isaiah 29 here.

Nephi's Care with the Text

All this theologically rich stuff we've been looking at for the past few minutes here—all this is something Nephi works out as he manipulates Isaiah 29:11–12. But our question concerns exactly *how* Nephi does that work of manipulation. He takes Isaiah's phrase "the words of a book that is sealed," and he uses that to drive a wedge between *words* and *things*, between the material artifact of the gold plates and the transmissible intellectual content of the Book of Mormon. And then he plays on the ambiguity of the Isaiah text in a crucial way. Here's part of Isaiah 29:11: "the words a book that is sealed, which men deliver to one that is learned, saying, Read this, I pray thee." Nephi seems to fix on an ambiguity here. *What* exactly do "men deliver" to the learned? The book? Or the words of the book? The construction (in English, but also in Hebrew) leaves ambiguous which of the two is meant in the Isaianic text. Commentators almost universally understand Isaiah to be saying that the book itself is delivered to the learned, who refuse to read it because it's sealed. But Nephi plays around with the possibility of taking Isaiah to have meant that just the words of the book are delivered to the learned. Then they refuse to read the words because the book itself is sealed. This opens up all kinds of possibilities in light of what Nephi's seen prophetically in vision.

What's fascinating here already is the *care* with which Nephi seems to be reading the Isaiah text. He's reading it inventively, noticing and exploiting ambiguities in the text. He sees what others largely miss, that there's a subtle distinction between the book and the words of the book. And then he sees that the text is ambiguous about which of these is actually given to the learned, drawing their frustration at the fact that the book's sealed. And the suggestion of the Book of Mormon is that Nephi sees all of this because of what he's seen in vision. And this pattern continues into Nephi's handling of Isaiah 29:12. First, Nephi seems to notice quite sharply that there's no ambiguity in that verse about what's given to the unlearned. It's simply "the book." And Nephi gets interested in the fact that verse 11 *can* be read as having the words of the book delivered to the learned, but then verse 12 *must* be read as having the book itself delivered to the unlearned. That opens all over again onto things Nephi's seen in vision. And this leads him to get inventive in certain ways. We've seen that he pluralizes the word "learned" in his adaptation of verse 11, and in that he departs from the Isaianic original in a way. But then notice that he takes "him that is not learned" in Isaiah's verse 12 to be singular, since it points specifically to Joseph Smith, the prophet who has access to the gold plates but hasn't the foggiest idea what to do with them. Nephi's tracking these details with razor-sharp precision. And that's of real significance.

Argh, we've got to finish up. I spent too much time reveling in Nephi's theological brilliance and left too little time to come back to what's going on with Nephi's inventive reading of Isaiah's actual prophecy. Well, we'll have to lay out a few concluding observations at the beginning next time. And you'll have to accept my apologies for being a philosopher in the meanwhile!

Lecture XXIV

Nephi's Virtuosic Conclusion

Nephi as Exegete

We found ourselves running out of time at the end of our last meeting, and the result was that we weren't able to say nearly enough about how Nephi adapts Isaiah 29:11–12. You'll remember that I let my theological interests get the better of me (I'm a philosopher, after all). So let's say at least a few words by way of general summary here before we turn our attention away from 2 Nephi 26–27.

What I hope you began to get a sense for last time is the startling *care* Nephi uses in adapting Isaiah's text to his own prophetic purposes. There are perhaps two extremes we find in attempting to make sense of 2 Nephi 26–27. On the one extreme (we've said something about this before), we might too easily assume that Nephi's not doing *any* work on Isaiah 29, that he's just reproducing a much-longer original version of that chapter. As I hope I've made clear along the way, that extreme doesn't seem to me to be worth much. It makes a lot more sense if Nephi is inventively and prophetically reworking Isaiah's text, weaving it into the things he's himself seen in vision. And then there's the other extreme, where we might too easily assume that Nephi's just mangling Isaiah 29, forcing it to fit his own interests. We might, that is, assume he's doing a bit of prooftexting, ignoring the original meaning and context of Isaiah's words to make it look like the prophet said what Nephi desperately wants him to say. What I *really* hope you began to see at the end of our discussion last time, though, is that this extreme is as misguided as the other. Nephi's a much more careful reader than we often give him credit for. He's got a close eye on rather tiny details in Isaiah 29, and he's using those tiny details to do something quite rich. He's doing *anything but* mangling Isaiah. He's reading him far more carefully than we do.

What's the evidence for that? We reviewed a bit of it at the end of our discussion last time. Nephi seems to fix on the understated distinction in Isaiah 29:11 between the book and the words of the book, and he notes the remarkable subtle ambiguity of verse 11 regarding what exactly is given to the learned (the book or the words of the book?). After that, he's honest about the lack of ambiguity in verse 12. What's given to the unlearned is just the book, and this is what seems to have led Nephi to exploit the ambiguity of verse 11. Nephi seems to have asked himself what might happen if we read these two verses as distinguishing between what's given to the learned and to the unlearned. Everyone has always read the passage as describing two distinct sorts of people responding to exactly the same thing—to the sealed book. The learned reject it because it's sealed, and the unlearned reject it because it's a book. But Nephi sees another possibility here, one that *is* right there in the text. It can be read as saying the learned and the unlearned are given distinct things: the learned receive the words of the book, while the unlearned receive the book. And that allows Nephi to read in a startlingly novel way the complaint of the learned regarding the fact that the book's sealed, and it allows him to read in an equally novel way the complaint of the unlearned regarding their lack of learning. Nephi's careful attention to minute details in Isaiah's text allows him to see what more or less all interpreters have overlooked.

Of course, let's be clear that Nephi does *some* mangling of Isaiah's text. Who doesn't? But we've got to be just as clear that any changes Nephi makes to Isaiah's original text or its meaning he does because he sees certain possibilities latent in the text of Isaiah that otherwise can't be drawn out. His prophetic inventiveness—almost playfulness—as he works on Isaiah 29 shows that he finds *some* rewording or paraphrasing to be necessary if he's going to help us to see what Isaiah's prophecy *could* mean. And that's striking.

In many ways, Nephi's handling of Isaiah 29 should serve as a particularly informative illustration of what he's been up to all along. He sees implications and possibilities lurking within Isaiah's words that Isaiah himself couldn't have seen. He sees things happening there that are profoundly related to what he's himself seen in vision, but these are things Isaiah likely couldn't have made any real sense of. What if we were to take Nephi's use of Isaiah as giving us a picture of what *we* ought to do with scripture? What if we too were to seek the spirit of prophecy, and then were to read the Book of Mormon closely and inventively enough to see the latent possibilities at work in this text? What if we were to read as faithfully *and* as inventively as Nephi? Does that sound paradoxical? I think it is. But I think it's precisely what we ought to be doing in our close study of scripture. *Real* fidelity to the text also turns out to be creative in a certain sense. We have to read scripture so closely that we see the crosscurrents of meaning that organize the fluid mechanics of the text. There's no one definite meaning. At the same time, we can't make the text say whatever we want. Somehow, we have to read so faithfully that we can see the ways the text calls us to read it against its own grain. That requires more work than we're used to giving to scripture study, *and* it requires more grace than we're used to receiving as we study.

Or so it seems to me. And I can't help feeling at this point like we've tackled these most crucial points too hastily, left them too undeveloped for them to be of any real use to you. And yet here we are at the very climax of Nephi's treatment of Isaiah. But maybe we can move on and *nonetheless* spend some of our time clarifying what we've just been talking about. My plan was to spend our time today looking at 2 Nephi 28–30, looking at how Nephi uses Isaiah's writings in scattered fragments through these final chapters of his own prophecy. But I think we can do that while asking how his use of these Isaianic fragments reproduces what we've been trying to talk about in 2 Nephi 26–27. I think. And it's worth giving it a shot.

So let's turn our attention to 2 Nephi 28–30, but let's keep an eye on what Nephi's been doing in 2 Nephi 26–27.

Isaiah in 2 Nephi 28–30

From all I've been able to figure out, around fifteen passages in 2 Nephi 28–30 borrow from Isaiah's words in one way or another. That includes one rather substantial quotation—of a longer stretch of Isaiah 11 in 2 Nephi 30—and a lot of far less substantial allusions, paraphrases, and borrowings. Maybe we could produce a quick list. I've compiled it by doing some of my own searching for Isaianic language, but also by drawing from lists of traces of Isaiah put together by Royal Skousen and Grant Hardy. (Note that I've reproduced their findings, even when I'm not myself terribly sure they're right to find a trace of Isaiah in the text.) Here's what we've got, then:

> 2 Nephi 28:3 draws on Isaiah 44:5
>
> 2 Nephi 28:7 draws on Isaiah 22:13
>
> 2 Nephi 28:9 draws on Isaiah 29:13, 15
>
> 2 Nephi 28:14 draws on Isaiah 29:13 and Isaiah 53:6

2 Nephi 28:16 draws on Isaiah 29:21

2 Nephi 28:26 draws on Isaiah 29:13

2 Nephi 28:30 draws on Isaiah 28:10, 13

2 Nephi 28:32 draws on Isaiah 65:2

2 Nephi 29:1 draws on Isaiah 11:11 and Isaiah 29:14

2 Nephi 29:2 draws on Isaiah 62:10

2 Nephi 29:2–3 draws on Isaiah 5:26 and Isaiah 49:22

2 Nephi 29:7 draws on Isaiah 24:15

2 Nephi 30:9–15 reproduces (with interspersed interruptions)
Isaiah 11:4–9

That's a lot to work with, isn't it? And this list doesn't include at least two possible allusions to Isaiah in 2 Nephi 31–33. But let's see if we can't systematize all this a bit and get down to business.

Just glancing at the list, you might notice that the majority of Isaiah references I've catalogued here show up in 2 Nephi 28 specifically. Only four passages in 2 Nephi 29 seem to draw on Isaiah, and most of them appear just in the first three verses. And then there's only one borrowing from Isaiah in 2 Nephi 30, though it's a big one: the full quotation of a long stretch of Isaiah 11. So perhaps this is the first thing we should say here: that 2 Nephi 28 and the first verses of 2 Nephi 29 are where Isaiah particularly shows up here, at least with the greatest frequency. And then note this second thing, something we've already mentioned in a previous lecture: by far the most consistent attention given to Isaiah in these final chapters of Nephi's prophecy focus on Isaiah 29, the chapter we've been considering in connection with 2 Nephi 26–27. In fact, almost half of the borrowings from Isaiah in these chapters are from Isaiah 29. However, it's worth noting that there are borrowings in these chapters from two other parts of Isaiah that Nephi is generally obsessed with. In those first verses of 2 Nephi 29, Nephi uses once again the language of Isaiah 49—and specifically of Isaiah 49:22, unquestionably one of his favorite texts from Isaiah. And also in those first verses of 2 Nephi 29, he alludes to a passage from Isaiah 11:11, another of his favorites. And don't forget that it's from Isaiah 11 that he'll quote at length in 2 Nephi 30. So to make a third point: Nephi couples his investment in Isaiah 29 here with a *re*investment, however subtle, in Isaiah 11 and Isaiah 49, his two other favorite bits of Isaiah.

Where does all this leave us? Well, I think it leaves us with good reason to look really closely at the first verses of 2 Nephi 29. There we get a bit of Isaiah 11, a bit of Isaiah 29, and a bit of Isaiah 49. And those verses bring to a kind of culmination the whole series of Isaiah borrowings that litter 2 Nephi 28. So I think if we take some time to look closely at how Nephi uses Isaiah in 2 Nephi 29:1–3, we'll get a sense all over again for the remarkable care with which he reads Isaiah's prophecies.

Concatenating Isaiah 11, 29, and 49

Let's get just a bit of context on the table, shall we? 2 Nephi 28 is largely dedicated to condemning the Gentiles who get in the way of the coming forth of the Book of Mormon. Nephi's seen what things will be like in Joseph Smith's day and in our day. And he's apparently more than a bit upset about the dominant Gentile—that is, European—culture that's made it so difficult for people to believe in or care about the book. So the chapter ends with a warning to the Gentiles: "Woe be unto the Gentiles, saith the Lord God of Hosts, for, notwithstanding I shall lengthen out mine arm unto them from day to day, they will deny me!" (2 Ne. 28:32). That nicely summarizes the whole chapter. But before this last verse of the chapter *quite* ends, Nephi gives us a happy word of promise regarding the Gentiles. They're not entirely lost, it turns out. Here's what Nephi says: "Nevertheless, I will be merciful unto them, saith the Lord God, if they will repent and come unto me—for mine arm is lengthened out all the day long, saith the Lord God of Hosts" (v. 32). That's good news, then, because it means that, even though the Gentiles have caused so many problems, there's still some way they might be involved in the work of God and so be able to become a part of the covenant.

But how? Well, Nephi doesn't get to that right away. In fact, he doesn't get to it until chapter 30. Instead, he gives chapter 29 to *another* critique of Gentile problems in the last days. Here we find his famous diatribe against "the Gentiles [who] say, 'A bible! A bible! We have got a bible! And there cannot be any more bible!'" (2 Ne. 29:3). He's announcing the existence of this criticism right from the beginning of the first verse of chapter 29. But, as Nephi tends to do, he gets a bit sidetracked as he makes his announcement. He *starts* to announce this criticism in verse 1, but then he inserts a lengthy aside that doesn't wrap up until early in verse 3, at which point he comes back to his announcement of Gentile unbelief. Now here's the interesting thing. All of the Isaianic language of these opening verses in 2 Nephi 29 is to be found in the lengthy aside that interrupts Nephi's otherwise straightforward announcement of Gentile skepticism. So that's where we'll want to focus.

The Isaianic aside is really just a wordy description of *when* the Gentiles will make a fuss about the Book of Mormon suggesting there's more scripture. That is, we're getting here a long clarification of what "that day" is when "there shall be many . . . of the Gentiles [who] shall say, 'A bible!'" (2 Ne. 29:1–3). So what's that day? And what does that day have to do with Isaiah?

Here's the passage, finally. The day in question is that day

> when I [it's the Lord who's speaking here] shall proceed to do a marvelous work among them [that is, among the Gentiles], that I may remember my covenants which I have made unto the children of men, that I may set my hand again the second time to recover my people which are of the house of Israel—and also that I may remember the promises which I have made unto thee, Nephi, and also unto thy father that I would remember your seed, and that the words of your seed should proceed forth out of my mouth unto your seed—and my words shall hiss forth unto the ends of the earth for a standard unto my people which are of the house of Israel, and because my words shall hiss forth . . . (2 Ne. 29:1–3)

There it is. What have we got here? Well, the day of the Gentiles' general wickedness is apparently the day when God will "do a marvelous work among them." That's language we're quick to connect with the coming forth of the Book of Mormon, and with good reason. It's pretty clear that this is exactly what Nephi has in mind. And that "marvelous work" has a specific purpose here. It's to launch the fulfillment of the covenant. Nephi puts this in terms of remembrance. "That I may remember my covenants which I have made unto the children of men," he has the Lord say, and "that I may remember the promises which I have made unto [the Nephites] that the words of [their] seed should proceed forth out of my mouth unto [them]" (v.2) The covenant's fulfillment gets moving when God *remembers* the covenant and the associated promises. That's how it gets started, but the actual work of fulfilling the covenant concerns something else. Nephi has the Lord say it this way: "that I may set my hand again the second time to recover my people which are of the house of Israel" (v. 1).

Let's pause there for a moment and note what Nephi's doing with Isaiah here (if in fact it isn't simply God's own use of Isaiah here in speaking to Nephi). Both "a marvelous work" and "set my hand again the second time" are borrowings from Isaiah, the former from Isaiah 29 and the latter from Isaiah 11. Here Nephi is found a way to link those two parts of Isaiah's book. But let's look in more detail at what he's doing, shall we?

This "marvelous work" business comes from Isaiah 29:14. Nephi's already borrowed that verse in 2 Nephi 27, in a part of the chapter we didn't get to spend any time on. There, Nephi makes Isaiah 29:14 into something that God speaks directly to Joseph Smith as the translator of the gold plates: "The Lord shall say unto him that shall read the words that shall be delivered him" (2 Ne. 27:24). And what the Lord says to Joseph is first what you find in Isaiah 29:13, all about the people drawing near to God with their mouths and honoring him with their lips, while nonetheless keeping their hearts far from him. That nicely sums up the Gentile situation Nephi condemns in 2 Nephi 28–29 as well. And back in 2 Nephi 27, as in these opening verses of 2 Nephi 29, the Gentile situation spurs the Lord to do a marvelous work. Here's Isaiah 29:14 as quoted in 2 Nephi 27:26: "Therefore I will proceed to do a marvelous work among this people—yea, a marvelous work and a wonder! For the wisdom of their wise and learned shall perish, and the understanding of their prudent shall be hid." If you remember the larger story Nephi develops in 2 Nephi 27 from our discussion last time, you'll hear how significant this passage is for Nephi's purposes. He finds in Isaiah 29:14 a clear statement that one of the purposes of the Book of Mormon's coming forth is to overturn the wisdom of "the learned." Do you remember that Nephi develops Isaiah 29:11–12 into a massive allegory about how "the learned" respond to the Book of Mormon? Here he finds in Isaiah 29:14 an interesting confirmation of it. Or rather, here he makes that passage into an interesting confirmation of it. There's no reference to "the learned" directly in the biblical version of Isaiah 29:14. It says just that "the wisdom of their wise men shall perish," not that "the wisdom of their wise and learned shall perish." But you get the point. Nephi seems to see right there in Isaiah 29:14 an outline of the events he's seen in vision in connection with the coming forth of the Book of Mormon in the latter days. And that's what he sees reflected in Isaiah's talk of "a marvelous work."

Coming back to 2 Nephi 29, then, you can see how much Nephi's packing into the Lord's reference to "a marvelous work" that's supposed to happen in the midst of an unbelieving Gentile nation. Once again we're dealing with the coming forth of the Book of Mormon, and with the way that volume of scripture has to confront the learning of the secular world. At this point, Nephi can simply use three words from Isaiah 29 to draw our minds back to that rather complicated story.

But he does more, as we've already seen. He connects all of those events to a line from Isaiah 11 about the Lord setting his hand again the second time. That's Isaiah 11:11, which Nephi has *also* already quoted along the way. This new connection appears in 2 Nephi 21, in the middle of the really-long quotation of thirteen chapters from Isaiah. It comes toward the end of the block of Isaiah chapters that tell the story of how Assyria's campaign helps to produce a holy remnant of the people of Judah. It's actually a really crucial moment in that story, because the passage as it appears in both Isaiah 11 and 2 Nephi 21 makes reference to a remnant: "And it shall come to pass in that day, that the Lord shall set his hand again the second time to recover the remnant of his people, which shall be left, from Assyria, and from Egypt, and from Pathros, and from Cush, and from Elam, and from Shinar, and from Hamath, and from the islands of the sea" (2 Ne. 21:11). That's quite a bit of recovering that the Lord does, isn't it? But what's the remnant in question? Is this the same remnant that's produced through the conflict with Assyria? Well, there's some difficulty about that. Isaiah 10, a chapter earlier, speaks of "the remnant" that "shall return" after Assyria's devastation of the land (2 Ne. 20:21). That return is so glorious that Isaiah says—hopefully you'll remember this—that "the consumption decreed shall overflow with righteousness" (2 Ne. 20:22). So there's a remnant there. Is this remnant from Isaiah 11 the same one? Or is it significant that this one's gathered only when the Lord sets his hand "a second time" to recover his people?

It seems that Nephi and his brother understood there to be *two* returning remnants, or *two* returns of the remnant. They draw on the language of Isaiah 11:11 with some frequency, in fact. In 2 Nephi 6:14, Jacob says that "the Messiah will set himself again the second time to recover" the Jews in the last days. In 2 Nephi 25:17, Nephi says basically the same thing, that "the Lord will set his hand again the second time" to restore the Jews—this only after "the space of many generations" (2 Ne. 25:16). (Interestingly, Nephi there *also* connects this language with a reference to Isaiah 29:14: "Wherefore he will proceed to do a marvelous work and a wonder among the children of men.") These passages seem to make clear that Nephi and his brother saw in Isaiah's talk of "the second time" a hint that he's thinking of two *distinct* events of gathering the remnant, one ancient and one modern.

Yet here's the really weird thing. In all these quotations of Isaiah 11:11—except the one in 2 Nephi 21—Nephi and Jacob drop the reference to "the remnant" that appears in the original Isaiah text. Back in 2

Nephi 29, for instance, Nephi quotes the Lord as saying just this: "that I may set my hand again the second time to recover my people which are of the house of Israel." You can find that same move being made in all the other borrowings as well. When he applies it to latter-day events, Nephi seems to want to divorce Isaiah 11:11 from its original context, from the role it plays in a series of prophecies about the remnant. He's interested just in drawing from Isaiah's words the idea that there are distinct times when the Lord goes out to recover his people. And it seems he's here drawing together all of his and Jacob's earlier uses of Isaiah 11 to think about that idea, and he's telling us that we ought to be thinking about the event (the event he sees it pointing to) as closely connected with the appearance of the Book of Mormon in the last days—this "marvelous work" that's talked about in his version of Isaiah 29.

Here again we're getting a sense for how much Nephi can, at this point, pack into just a few words drawn from Isaiah. He borrows a few words from Isaiah 11 here in 2 Nephi 29, but those few words bring together all kinds of ideas. We said the same of his few words from Isaiah 29 just a minute ago. So now we're seeing how much *more* he can accomplish when he draws together two little snippets of Isaiah in one place like this. There's *a lot* that's going on, and we're getting a sense all over again for how carefully Nephi's reading Isaiah—for how much time he's apparently put into close interpretation of the relevant texts. And we've got more to go, since Nephi's about to bring Isaiah 49 into all this as well.

Let's come back to 2 Nephi 29:1–3, for a moment. After Nephi links the coming forth of the Book of Mormon ("a marvelous work") and the beginning of the process of fulfilling the promises to Israel ("set my hand again the second time"), he tells us that the Book of Mormon ("my words," Nephi quotes the Lord as saying) "shall hiss forth unto the ends of the earth for a standard unto my people which are of the house of Israel." Where's he getting this image? Well, the image of hissing comes from Isaiah 5: "He will lift up an ensign to the nations from far, and will hiss unto them from the end of the earth" (Isa 5:26, 2 Ne. 15:26). But note that Nephi's changed it in an important way. He talks about God's words hissing to the ends of the earth, whereas the Isaiah text talks about God himself hissing to nations who are from the end of the earth. Nephi seems to be describing a certain communication of the divine word contained in the Book of Mormon to the extremities of the earth, while Isaiah is pretty clearly describing a gathering of violent nations from far away to lay waste to Judah. So here in 2 Nephi 29 we get Nephi borrowing something from that imagery while reworking it substantially.

But that's not what *really* interests us here. Nephi *also* says that the Book of Mormon, hissing to the ends of the earth, will be "a standard unto my people which are of the house of Israel." Where's that coming from? That's just Isaiah 49:22: "Thus saith the Lord God, Behold, I will lift up mine hand to the Gentiles, and set up my standard to the people: and they shall bring thy sons in their arms, and thy daughters shall be carried upon their shoulders." We've looked in some detail at how carefully both Nephi and Jacob use that passage in their writings. But now note what Nephi's doing with it here. In its original, Isaianic setting, the verse describes God's setting up of a standard for the Gentiles, waving a banner of sorts before them. What's the banner or standard in question? It's the redemption of Israel from captivity—originally in Babylon, of course, but, by way of likening, also in any other form of captivity in the larger history of Israel. The Gentiles see that redemption, they're convinced that Israel's God is the true God, and so they seek to assist Israel in their redemption so that they can become a part of the covenant Israel's received. That's pretty straightforwardly the meaning of Isaiah 49:22 on its own. What does Nephi do with it *this* time? Here in 2 Nephi 29, the banner or standard that God's waving isn't Israel's redemption, but the Book of Mormon itself. And it isn't being waved before the eyes of the Gentiles, but before the remnant of Israel. It's now "a standard unto my people which are of the house of Israel," rather than "a standard to the people" who will assist in Israel's redemption. Nephi's inverted the meaning of the passage.

Is he doing this sloppily, though? Hardly. We've already seen how careful a reader he is of Isaiah 49, so there's something more going on here. What's he doing? He seems to be setting up a kind of parallel between the redemption of the Gentiles and the redemption of Israel. The Book of Mormon is a banner God can wave before the remnant of Israel in order to launch the process of redeeming them, but then, in turn, that redemption of the remnant of Israel becomes the banner that's waved before the Gentiles to invite them to assist in the redemption of Israel. Nephi effectively doubles the scope of the Isaiah passage. By reading Nephi carefully up to this point we can feel the way the verse is being expanded. Nephi's clearly understood it the one way, and now he's clearly using it the other way.

Here once again we can witness how much is buried just beneath the surface of Isaiah's words when Nephi's using them, at least at this late point in his record. And we can see all over again just how careful Nephi is with Isaiah's text. He isn't haphazard with Isaiah's words, but he seems to have studied them carefully enough to see how open they are to multiple interpretations and uses. There's a certain virtuosity about Nephi's handling of these texts.

Perhaps what's most beautiful of all is that at this late point in his record, he's bringing together his favorite passages from Isaiah, weaving them into a single, forceful picture. He's giving us Isaiah 11, with its apparent emphasis on a *second* time—a latter-day time—when God will redeem Israel conclusively. And he's giving us Isaiah 29, with its insistence that God uses a sealed book to overturn the wisdom of the learned, at the very moment he attempts to restore the remnant of Israel. Finally, he's giving us Isaiah 49, with its beautiful depiction of Israel's redemption from among the nations, an event that allows the whole Gentile world to get involved with the covenant at last. Here Nephi's brought all this together, showing us what he's ultimately really after with Isaiah. He wants us to see in *all* of Isaiah's writings just *one* theme, really. There's a single message in Isaiah for Nephi: the story of Israel's redemption and the extension of its covenant to the whole world at that point. Of course, there's a lot that happens in connection with that one story, and Nephi's got an eye on all that as well. But it's still one single story he's trying to piece together.

And he's trying his hardest to help us see that one story as well, to help us piece it together ourselves. We've got to end right now, so we will. We'll be meeting once more, so let's plan on tying things together by getting clear about this one larger story that interests Nephi. I can't think of a better way of bringing this lecture series to an end.

Until then.

Lecture XXV

Isaiah's Big Picture

Welcome to our last meeting! What I hope we'll accomplish today is to wrap things up in a relatively even-handed way. Can we draw together into a single overarching picture all that we've been talking about for a long time now? Is there a way to synthesize all this?

Well, we've covered a lot of ground. To a certain degree, we've covered that ground just by starting at one end of it and then working our way toward the other end. We did a little bit of contextualizing and the like at the outset, but then we started at the beginning of First Nephi, and now we've worked our way right to the end of Second Nephi. What can we say about the terrain we've traveled through? Let's make a couple of general points.

Isaiah Is the Point

First, I hope we've made it unforgettably clear what Nephi's up to in each of his two books—that is, in First Nephi and Second Nephi. A host of little details come together to make it evident that Nephi means us to read Second Nephi as the real heart of his project, and that he's especially interested in having us recognize 2 Nephi 6–30 as "the more sacred things" in his record (1 Ne. 19:5). 2 Nephi 1–5 and 31–33 serve as introduction and conclusion to this important focus in Nephi's writings. And what do we find there in "the more sacred things"? Isaiah, three times over. First we get Isaiah as Jacob understands and likens him—that's 2 Nephi 6–10. And then we get a lengthy quotation of Isaiah 2–14 more or less without comment, just given to us straight—that's 2 Nephi 11–24. And finally we get Isaiah as Nephi wants to use him, weaving the Old-World prophet's writings into a New-World vision of history—that's 2 Nephi 25–30. It's crucial to get clear about all this so that we see what Nephi really wants us to see: that the careful, almost systematic exposition of Isaiah's writings in

2 Nephi 6–30 is Nephi's central concern and the thing his people—and we too!—most need. Isaiah, interpreted.

But if that's Second Nephi, what's First Nephi? Getting clear about First Nephi as a project took some detective work, but we gathered the clues and came to some strong conclusions. It turns out that First Nephi is carefully organized and structured in a most intricate fashion. And that structure is supposed to alert us to the fact that First Nephi is a kind of preliminary handbook on reading Isaiah. First Nephi is meant to get us started, introducing us to the necessary sources—the brass plates, the dream of the tree of life—and then showing us how to bring them together in the right way. First Nephi thus serves as a kind of lengthy introduction to Second Nephi. We get the introductory handbook first. We study that carefully, and then we're ready for what comes next: Second Nephi, an advanced course on Isaiah's meaning, at least as Nephi and Jacob likened it. First and Second Nephi are thus a package deal—semester one, semester two, to be taken in succession.

I hope, as I said a minute ago, that all this is unforgettably clear. To be perfectly honest, I think it's step number one for making *any* sense of Isaiah in Nephi's project—or in the whole of the Book of Mormon. This comes first, I think, along with a few general pointers about reading Isaiah that we took some time to lay out.

Isaiah Has Many Meanings

A second point, then. I've tried to make clear as we've worked through the texts that there's no *one* way we're supposed to be reading Isaiah. We spent a lecture looking at how Lehi reads Isaiah, in those few places where Nephi lets us listen in on Lehi's uses of the prophet's writings. And we saw pretty quickly that Lehi's way of reading Isaiah is fundamentally distinct from Nephi's. Moreover, when we took a couple of lectures to look carefully at Jacob's sermon in 2 Nephi 6–10, we saw that he reads Isaiah in a way that's also largely his own. Jacob seems to have been far more interested than Nephi ever was in understanding the scope of Isaiah's unlikened prophecies. Nephi and Jacob share a lot in their approach to Isaiah, but they don't understand him in exactly the same ways. We even looked at a few passages where Jacob's and Nephi's respective interpretations of certain Isaiah texts seem to contradict one another—or at least to be in some kind of tension with each other. This is crucial. We might come to Isaiah with the idea that our job is to figure out the *one true meaning* of Isaiah's prophecies, but Nephi's record seems to warn us away from any such idea. It seems that Isaiah can be understood in a variety of ways.

Similarly, we've spent a fair bit of time clarifying what Nephi and Jacob understand when they speak of "likening" the prophet's writings. And it's clear that likening involves not only applying the text—which is what we usually say—but also recognizing that there's a difference between, on the one hand, the original setting and context for Isaiah's prophecies and, on the other hand, the setting and context to which Nephi and Jacob (or we) liken them. The very fact that Nephi and Jacob recognize their interpretations as acts of likening makes clear that there's no *one true meaning* of Isaiah's prophecies. They can be understood in several different ways, and they can be likened in several different ways. They're to be read and reread, seen with new eyes again and again. And then they're to be re-reread and re-re-reread, with renewed sight every time.

So here's a second lesson we ought to take away from our discussions: Isaiah's no monolithic prophet, even if there are certain underlying themes that we can't ignore without wresting him. His writings are rich and multifaceted—polysemic, as philosophers like to say. We're to wrestle with the *many* ways he can be read, and we're to be ready to think about how we might liken him to all kinds of situations in the history of Israel.

Isaiah Is Systematic

Let's note a third point, shall we? For all the varieties of ways Isaiah might be read, Nephi and Jacob clearly recommend that we read him in a sustained fashion. We certainly *can* read Isaiah in bits and pieces, a verse here and verse there, looking for ways we might hear something familiar in certain passages extracted from their context. But Nephi and Jacob seem especially interested in having us read whole chapters—or whole sequences of chapters—at a time. And by doing this, they seem especially interested in helping us to see that there's a larger thematic coherence to Isaiah's writings. There's something they're *all* about, even if we're largely oblivious to the fact. They're about what we as Latter-day Saints call the Abrahamic covenant. They're about the responsibility given to Israel to introduce peace to the whole world, reworking the world's deep tendency toward violence. That is, they're organized around Isaiah's vision of the ultimate fulfillment of that responsibility—the day when all nations will join Israel in the worship of the true God, beating their swords into plowshares and their spears into pruning-hooks. Isaiah is trying to bring the

Israel of his own day to see that this is their shared task. And Nephi and Jacob want their readers to see how that organizes the history that surrounds their own nation's experiences.

So it seems we ought to be reading Isaiah with an eye, above all, to what he has to say about Israel's complicated status as a chosen people. We ought to be reading Isaiah as providing a prophetic window onto the long, complex history of Israel. And we've seen, as we've worked through the texts, that the status and history of Israel are organized around a few salient points. It's crucial, apparently, that we keep an eye on the theme of the remnant—that is, on the idea that God uses history (and not usually very *happy* history) to winnow the covenant people down to a holy remnant that's fully ready to assume the task he's assigned to Israel. And it's crucial, apparently, that we keep an eye on the idea of prophecy being written and then sealed up for the use of a later generation—the holy remnant precisely. *And* it's crucial, apparently, that we watch for how the eventual redemption of Israel or of the remnant serves to put God's power and faithfulness on display before the whole world, as a way of getting the Gentiles involved in the covenant that was given for their benefit even if it wasn't given directly to them. All this is central to Isaiah's prophecies, as Nephi sees them.

There's our third point, then. Even while Isaiah can and should be read in a variety of ways, Nephi seems to want us to keep an eye on a few themes as nonetheless central to the prophet's work. We've got to keep an eye on the larger history of the covenant that apparently motivated everything Isaiah wrote.

Isaiah's Theme Is Covenantal

A fourth lesson from our discussions is somewhat related to this last one. We've seen that there are reasons to be a bit hesitant about trying to find Jesus in Isaiah's writings. In a lot of ways, much of our collective confusion about Isaiah comes from our single-minded insistence that the prophets prophesied of little or nothing else. When we start digging in Isaiah's writings for clear prophecies of Christ, we find relatively little that makes sense. And even those places where we *do* think we can find traces of Christ's life and mission in Isaiah are often contested by modern biblical scholarship. That should to make us somewhat cautious, though we ought to be careful not to let it make us overly skeptical. There's plenty of evidence that Nephi saw at least a few major passages in Isaiah's writings as messianic (as pointing directly to Christ), but we've seen in our discussions that there are some places where we or other Christians have been ready to see Christ in Isaiah, but where Nephi himself doesn't seem to see Christ. So we've got to exercise some caution.

But again, it's clear from what Nephi does with Isaiah that we can't get too skeptical. Nephi seems to find Christ in Isaiah on occasion, and so we might do well to be open to that possibility as well. What's interesting is that Nephi seems to find Christ in Isaiah's prophecies only at moments where they seem relevant to a larger story regarding the history of the Jews. I think the same can be said of Jacob. Perhaps it'd be possible to fix some kind of principle or criterion for deciding whether Nephi would find a Christological interpretation of an Isaiah passage viable. We haven't done the work necessary to fix such a principle or criterion in the course of our discussions, but I think it might well be possible to do so—and worth the effort. In the meanwhile, perhaps it's enough just to say that Nephi gives us reason to think that we ought to be rather careful about turning Isaiah into "the fifth gospel," as many early Christian interpreters called it (on that, see John Sawyer's book on the subject). At the same time, we'd be overly hasty if we simply dismissed every messianic reading of the prophet.

So there's our fourth lesson. We should be looking first and foremost for the covenant as we read Isaiah, but a major part of the story of the covenant is the mission of the Messiah. And so we ought to be looking in modest and informed ways for prophecies in Isaiah that might indeed point to the coming of Christ several centuries later.

Nephi Models a Careful Reading of Isaiah

Let's note a fifth point, while we're talking about reading. Our last two lectures began to touch on just how careful Nephi ultimately is as a reader. We've seen strong evidence that Nephi doesn't just take general points from Isaiah's writings, but that he's deeply invested in the minutest of details. He seems to catch subtle aspects of Isaiah's wording, drumming up suggestive implications that lie there, hidden under the surface meaning of the text. And he then exploits those subtle aspects, developing their implications in full. Nephi's work on Isaiah shows years of careful reflection, sustained work at the level of single verses, even as it also—as we've seen—shows broad familiarity with general themes. Nephi seems to have grasped the overarching picture with stark clarity, but he's also turned his attention to tiny nuances of the text, usually at the level of just a verse here and a verse there. This is most fascinating, and it's deeply instructive. We apparently ought to be reading Isaiah in something like the same way. We ought to get clear about the broad themes and basic meaning of Isaiah's text, but then we ought to turn our attention to the minutest of details in his writings to see the deep potential ambiguities of the text and how they might inform all kinds of other considerations.

We've got, then, a kind of model for reading on display in Nephi's handling of Isaiah. We're being invited here to learn how to read in a particularly intense way. Can we spend an hour working over just a verse or two? Can we ask enough illuminating questions to see all the ambiguities that lie there in the text? And then can we think inventively enough to see what the ambiguities might suggest about the potential meanings of the prophecy in question? Are we guided enough by the Spirit to see how we might use the nuances of Isaiah's texts to rethink what we believe we already understand? Can we see useful ways of letting Isaiah's writings shape our reflections on our own situation? Likening is difficult work, it seems. It can't be a kind of too-quick application of the prophet's words to our everyday lives. There's more difficult, sustained effort that's needed.

So there's a fifth point. Nephi gives us a kind of picture of what it looks like to read carefully. Apparently, we ought to be looking at details in a much more sustained way than we're used to, and we have to do this with an eye to understanding our own interpretive situation with greater clarity.

Five lessons so far. Is that enough? Maybe that's enough by way of general points. But it's not enough by way of summarizing what we've accomplished in this lecture series. These five lessons give us a kind of basic orientation, but we've discovered a whole lot along the way. That is, these five lessons outline a kind of program for interpreting Isaiah in Nephi's writings or in a Nephi-like way. But we ought to ask what else we've gained along the way that doesn't immediately cash out in practical terms. What else needs saying about what we've accomplished?

The Significance of Variants

There's one thing we've really only touched on along the way, and that's the presence of textual variants in Book of Mormon Isaiah. Do you remember this? Way back when we were still wrapping up our work on First Nephi, we took a look at the differences between Isaiah 48–49 as they appear in the Bible and Isaiah 48–49 as they appear in the Book of Mormon. There are all these little differences between the two versions of these chapters, and they're all really quite interesting. We looked at them in as much detail as we could get away with, always having to hurry on to make sure we get to say a little something about everything. Did you notice as we went on into Second Nephi that we more or less ignored the question of whether there are variants later in Book of Mormon Isaiah? Well, we did, and it's unfortunate. When Jacob quotes Isaiah 50–51 in 2 Nephi 7–8, he gives us a version of those two chapters just riddled with differences from their biblical version. And then when Nephi quotes the whole of Isaiah 2–14 in 2 Nephi 12–24, there's all over again a whole host of variants that call for attention—and we ignored that call. Well, we *mostly* ignored that call. If I remember right, we spent a little bit of time looking at a variant or two in Isaiah 6. But we literally ignored dozens, maybe hundreds, of variants.

This is something that needs a lot more research. When we talked about variants, I think we spent a minute or two on the major studies of Isaiah variants in the Book of Mormon. The fact of the matter is that they're preliminary at best, and they're concerned primarily just with deciding what the variants in the text might suggest about whether the Book of Mormon is in fact an ancient text. That's just scratching the surface, though. There's a whole lot more work to do reflecting on what each little variant suggests at the interpretive level. How does the meaning of this or that passage change in light of the variants that appear in Book of Mormon Isaiah? And then there's work to do on whether there are patterns in the variants. As I've worked on the variants myself, I've been struck by a few things I've not seen anyone else talk about. Some have noticed the tendency in the Book of Mormon to replace certain singular nouns with plural nouns, when the nouns in question are parts or aspects of human beings—words like "face" or "hand" or "soul." But what I haven't seen anyone discuss is the fact that the Book of Mormon only seems to replace such singular nouns with plural nouns in Second Nephi. It doesn't seem to happen anywhere else in the Book of Mormon. Why's that? And what does it suggest? Should we be thinking that Nephi himself eventually decided that such nouns should be plural, and so he changed the text of Isaiah only after that point? Or what's going on there? These questions haven't even been asked (and perhaps you're thinking they're quite confusing, and maybe that's why no one's asked them).

And there's another question that needs addressing in connection with variants. Some of the variants that appear in Book of Mormon Isaiah change the basic layout of the Book of Isaiah in significant ways. Now that

I think about it, we mentioned one of these along the way that appears at the beginning of Isaiah 5. This is a small variant that makes the whole of Isaiah 2–5 into a single oracle (whereas the biblical Isaiah seems to divide Isaiah 2–5 into two distinct oracles: Isaiah 2–4 and Isaiah 5.) What's really interesting about the way the Book of Mormon groups Isaiah 2–5 all together is that it restructures the whole these chapters. We looked at that in one of our previous lectures. Where Isaiah 2–4, taken separately, seems to open and close with anticipations of the end of history, Isaiah 2–5, grouped together as in the Book of Mormon, couples two anticipations of the end of history with two oracles of disaster. That might seem like a pretty abstract detail, but it's significant. The variants in Book of Mormon Isaiah ultimately give us not only occasionally different *passages*; they also give us a Book of Isaiah with a significantly different *shape*.

Returning to another example we've previously discussed, there is a slight variant in the Book of Mormon's rendering of Isaiah 2:5 that uses language you can find in Isaiah 53 (about everyone turning to their own wicked way). Since Isaiah 53 seems to come at the end of Isaiah's writings in the brass plates, and since Isaiah 2 comes right at the beginning of those writings, this variant creates a close connection between the very beginning and the very end of the Isaiah as Nephi had them. If Nephi's giving us a genuine ancient variant in Isaiah 2:5, then there was once a version of Isaiah's writings that opened and closed with rather different ways of talking about Israelites turning, every one, to their own wicked ways—opening with Isaiah directly accusing them of doing so, and ending with them all confessing that they'd done so. That's striking and, frankly, brilliant. If this is the case, I would love to be able to read Nephi's text of Isaiah in full. Just imagine what other treasures like this it might have contained.

You get the point, though: there's a lot more work to be done on the Isaiah variants in the Book of Mormon. We've really only introduced them here, and they've only been lightly touched on by others. It's time these received serious and sustained treatment—not just pointing them out, but exploring what they mean.

Isaiah's Big Picture

Of course, variants aren't the only thing of real importance that we've only just touched on along the way. Just in our last lecture, we began to piece together what we might call Nephi's overarching interpretation of Isaiah. That's something that needs a great deal more attention than it's received—and, frankly, it's received very little. It's clear that Nephi is especially interested in Isaiah 11, Isaiah 29, and Isaiah 49, and that he sees these as joining together to tell something of a coherent story. We've already begun making that story clear in outline, but what's needed is a systematic investigation of Nephi's (and Jacob's) many allusions to these parts of Isaiah. What would we find if we compiled a list of every reference by Nephi to Isaiah 11, Isaiah 29, and Isaiah 49? Are there passages that seem particularly important? We've seen that he's interested especially in Isaiah 11's talk of God setting his hand a second time to restore his people. And we've seen that he's obsessed with Isaiah 29's talk of a marvelous work and a wonder. And we've also seen that he's fascinated by Isaiah 49's talk of Gentiles carrying the children of Israel home on their shoulders. But how do these interests, obsessions, and fascinations on Nephi part combine into a coherent, overarching interpretation of Isaiah?

Maybe we can say at least *something* by way of an answer to this question, though let's be clear that there's much more to do if we're to say anything actually responsible about it. But here's the picture I think we've begun to work up. It comes in three stages.

Of the three Isaiah texts that especially interest Nephi, it's Isaiah 49 that he *first* quotes. Remember that when he gives us our first real taste of Isaiah at the end of First Nephi, it's Isaiah 48–49 that he provides at length. And it's pretty clear already there (thanks to his commentary in 1 Nephi 22) that Isaiah 49:22–23 especially interests him. And then remember that the very *next* treatment of Isaiah that appears in Nephi's record is also focused on that same passage. Nephi asks Jacob to speak on those two verses precisely, and so they're the focus as much of 2 Nephi 6–10 as they are of 1 Nephi 19–22. So I think it's best if we think of Nephi's interest in Isaiah as beginning with Isaiah 49.

And what do we get in Isaiah 49? There we get the basic story that's at the heart of Nephi's apocalyptic vision back in 1 Nephi 11–14. Israel's history is full of trouble. They find themselves in exile, wondering whether God has abandoned his covenant. It seems like they're left on their own, wallowing in foreign—that is, in Gentile—territory. But then they get reassurances. God sends a prophet to tell them that they will be redeemed and that this has all been part of a larger plan. It turns out that God wants them to have spent some time among the Gentiles, because that means that when God redeems them in a glorious fashion, the Gentiles will get a chance to see the wonders that the true God can accomplish. And if the Gentiles' hearts are open, they'll realize that what they're seeing should spur them to assist in the redemption of God's covenant people. They'll join Israel, becoming a part of the covenant themselves. Eventually, they'll join in the worship of the true God, abandoning their pitiful obsessions with power and wealth—which means that they'll finally give up their warlike ways, suing for peace at last. That's the vision of Isaiah 49. Israel's troubles are part of a larger plan, God's clever way of getting the Gentiles involved in the covenant that promises to see the world delivered at last of its long history of violence and wickedness.

Of course, for Nephi, this story provides a basic pattern that he then wants to apply to the future history of his own people. He wants to "liken" Isaiah 49. So he narrows the focus of the word "Gentiles" to mean European Christianity. And he narrows the focus of the word "Israel" to mean just the remnant of his father's children in the New World, after the demise of the Nephite nation. The destruction of Jerusalem becomes the decimation of latter-day Lamanites, and the exile becomes the subjugation of native American peoples to European power and culture. But then comes redemption, with at least some of the Gentiles being called to turn Christianity back to its Jewish and covenantal roots. Their hearts are turned to the remnant of New-World Israel, and they give themselves to the work of systematically redeeming that remnant. And so they're given a chance to get involved, themselves, in the covenant. All this is, of course, what we'd call the Restoration, which is still very much underway.

So *there's* Isaiah 49, as Nephi views it. Once he's given us that general picture, he turns his attention to Isaiah 11, which he only gives us in the rather complicated larger context of the whole of Isaiah 2–14. What does he take from Isaiah 11, especially as it's contextualized by Isaiah 2–14? Well, we've already seen what especially draws his attention—it's this suggestion that God doesn't redeem his people only *once*, but at least *twice*, setting his hand "the second time" to redeem his scattered people. We get the sense that ancient history isn't enough, that we can't assume that Isaiah's prophecies concerned just a set of events that would happen within a generation or two, starting from the time Isaiah originally gave his prophecies. Nephi sees in Isaiah's talk of a second redemption the hint that ancient events are supposed to anticipate what we'd call modern events. God got involved with the covenant people in one way back then. And apparently he's going to do it all over again, now, in the latter days.

Again, though, Nephi—at least after he's listened carefully to Jacob—sees this as something Isaiah didn't himself apply to Nephi's people. He was talking about Judah, about the history of the Jews. But Nephi wants to liken it again. And so he sees in Isaiah's talk of a "second" redemption the possibility of projecting a redemption of Lehi's children into the last days. And we've just been talking about what Nephi thought that would look like. So we've already got the picture clear, I should think. Isaiah 11 helps Nephi to see how the redemption of his brothers' children is secure, even if it lay quite far off in the future. The Lord would set his hand a second time to recover the Lehites.

Finally, Isaiah 29. It's interesting that Nephi only comes to this quite late in his record, after he has already worked through Isaiah 48–52 and Isaiah 2–14. And what does he see there? There he sees the story that he wants to tell about the latter days get *really* specific. What he finds in Isaiah 29 is a story about a sealed book, buried up and then brought forth. He also finds in Isaiah 29 a familiar narrative of how the learned can't make heads or tails of the marvelous work of God. Of course, for Isaiah, this was all a way of describing his own poor reception as a prophet. But Nephi's a likener. And so he finds in Isaiah 29 an outline of the specific events through which the redemption of the remnant of New-World Israel would take place: the appearance of the Book of Mormon. It's that book that binds the exiled remnant to the New-World Gentiles. It's that book that launches a transformation of European Christianity, turning it back to its Abrahamic roots. And it's that book that marks the beginning of God's final attempt at gathering his people together.

There. Isaiah 11, 29, and 49. It's all one story. And Nephi sees Isaiah laying out the details of that story in remarkable clarity. He understands that Isaiah's not thinking about the New World, about Lehi's children, about European Christianity and the Book of Mormon. He understands that Isaiah's thinking about the history of his own people only, about Judah or the Jews, who would face exile in Babylon, restoration to their lands for a time, the scandal of the Messiah's arrival, and then a protracted period of scattering and persecution. But Nephi thinks all this provides a basic outline of the future history of *his* people as well. And so he's smitten by Isaiah. He delights in Isaiah, who gives the rich patterns followed in every iteration of covenantal history. And he delights in plainness, his own revelatory visions that have helped him to see how his brothers' people would live out the patterns Isaiah describes. Isaiah, plus plainness—that's Nephi's whole program in a word.

Inconclusive Conclusion

Well, we're out of time once more. Hopefully we've gotten somewhere in this last discussion, wrapping things up as neatly as possible when we're racing through our materials, never sure we'll be able to cover even the basics. But maybe you've got an elementary sense for what Nephi's up to now. Maybe you see it possible to study Isaiah in the Book of Mormon more straightforwardly than you have in the past. It's not mysterious. At all. It just takes some work, some commitment, and some openness to new ideas.

Of course, if you hope to turn to Book of Mormon Isaiah texts *outside* of Nephi, then it's a whole different story! Well, it's partially different, or it's different in places. Perhaps we'll have to have another lecture series and see what we can say about Isaiah in the rest of the Book of Mormon.

In the meanwhile, I'll just give you my thanks for listening. It's been a rich experience for me, and I can only hope you've enjoyed it as well. In my view, there's little that's more rewarding than talking about the Book of Mormon. Isaiah is, at root, the story of covenant and community, and reading and thinking together has put the text to work in my heart, and, I hope, in yours.

Resources Mentioned Along the Way

Blenkinsopp, Joseph. *Isaiah 1–39: A New Translation with Introduction and Commentary*. New Haven: Yale University Press, 2000.

———. *Isaiah 40–55: A New Translation with Introduction and Commentary*. New Haven: Yale University Press, 2000.

———. *Isaiah 56–66: A New Translation with Introduction and Commentary*. New Haven: Yale University Press, 2000.

Conrad, Edgar W. *Reading Isaiah*. Minneapolis: Fortress Press, 1991.

———. "Reading Isaiah and the Twelve as Prophetic Books." In *Writing and Reading the Scroll of Iasiah: Studies of an Interpretive Tradition*, 2 vols., edited by Craig C. Broyles and Craig A. Evans (New York: Brill, 1997), 1:3–17.

Coogan, Michael D., ed. *The Oxford History of the Biblical World*. New York: Oxford University Press, 1998.

Duhm, Berhard. *Der Prophet Jesaia*. Leipzig: Hirzel, 1890.

Epperson, Steven. *Mormons and Jews: Early Mormon Theologies of Israel*. Salt Lake City: Signature Books, 1992.

Evans, Craig A. *To See and Not Perceive: Isaiah 6.9–10 in Early Jewish and Christian Interpretation*. Sheffield: Sheffield Academic Press, 1989.

Fitzmyer, Joseph A. *The One Who Is To Come*. Grand Rapids, Mich.: Eerdmans, 2007.

Gileadi, Avraham. *The Book of Isaiah: A New Translation with Interpretive Keys from the Book of Mormon*. Salt Lake City: Deseret Book, 1988.

Goldingay, John. *The Theology of the Book of Isaiah*. Downers Grove, Ill.: InterVarsity Press, 2014.

Gorton, H. Clay. *The Legacy of the Brass Plates of Laban: A Comparison of Biblical and Book of Mormon Isaiah Texts*. Bountiful, Utah: Horizon Publishers, 1994.

Hardy, Grant, ed. *The Book of Mormon: A Reader's Edition*. Urbana and Chicago: University of Illinois Press, 2003.

Hasel, Gerhard F. *The Remnant: The History and Theology of the Remnant Idea from Genesis to Isaiah.* Berrien Springs, Mich.: Andrews University Press, 1974.

Holland, Jeffrey R. *Christ and the New Covenant: The Messianic Message of the Book of Mormon.* Salt Lake City: Deseret Book, 1997.

Holzapfel, Richard Neitzel, Dana M. Pike, and David Rolph Seely. *Jehovah and the World of the Old Testament: An Illustrated Reference for Latter-day Saints.* Salt Lake City: Deseret Book, 2009.

Kimball, Spencer W. "The False Gods We Worship." *Ensign*, June 1976, 3–6. [This talk can be readily accessed online: https://www.lds.org/ensign/1976/06/the-false-gods-we-worship.]

Kramer, Bradley J. *Beholding the Tree of Life: A Rabbinic Approach to the Book of Mormon.* Salt Lake City: Greg Kofford Books, 2014.

Laato, Antti. *A Star Is Rising: The Historical Development of the Old Testament Royal Ideology and the Rise of the Jewish Messianic Expectations.* Atlanta: Scholars Press, 1997.

MacKay, Michael Hubbard, and Gerrit J. Dirkmaat. *From Darkness unto Light: Joseph Smith's Translation and Publication of the Book of Mormon.* Salt Lake City and Provo, Utah: Deseret Book and BYU Religious Studies Center, 2015.

Maffly-Kipp, Laurie F., ed. *The Book of Mormon.* New York: Penguin Books, 2008.

St. Justin Martyr. *Dialogue with Trypho*, edited by Michael Slusser, translated by Thomas B. Falls, revised by Thomas P. Halton. Washington, D.C.: Catholic University of America Press, 2003. [Justin Martyr's writings have been translated a variety of times and are available in many places, including for free online. One such online resource is http://www.newadvent.org/fathers/0128.htm.]

McConkie, Joseph Fielding, and Robert L. Millet. *Doctrinal Commentary on the Book of Mormon, Volume 1: First and Second Nephi.* Salt Lake City: Bookcraft, 1987.

Mettinger, Trygvve N. D. *A Farewell to the Servant Songs: A Critical Examination of an Exegetical Axiom.* Lund, Sweden: Gleerup, 1983.

Motyer, J. Alec. *The Prophecy of Isaiah: An Introduction and Commentary.* Downers Grove, Ill.: InterVarsity Press, 1993.

Nibley, Hugh. *Approaching Zion.* Edited by Don E. Norton. Salt Lake City and Provo, Utah: Deseret Book and FARMS, 1989.

———. *Brother Brigham Challenges the Saints*. Edited by Don E. Norton and Shirley S. Ricks. Salt Lake City and Provo, Utah: Deseret Book and FARMS, 1994.

———. *Eloquent Witness: Nibley on Himself, Others, and the Temple*. Edited by Stephen D. Ricks. Salt Lake City and Provo, Utah: Deseret Book and Neal A. Maxwell Institute Press, 2008.

Oswalt, John N. *The Book of Isaiah: Chapters 1–39*. Grand Rapids, Mich.: Eerdmans, 1998.

———. *The Book of Isaiah: Chapters 40–66*. Grand Rapids, Mich.: Eerdmans, 1998.

Prince, Gregory A., and Wm. Robert Wright. *David O. McKay and the Rise of Modern Mormonism*. Salt Lake City: University of Utah Press, 2005.

Robinson, Stephen E. "Early Christianity and 1 Nephi 13–14." In *First Nephi: The Doctrinal Foundation*, edited by Monte S. Nyman and Charles D. Tate Jr. (Provo, Utah: Brigham Young University Religious Studies Center, 1988), 177–91. [Robinson's article can be read for free online at https://rsc.byu.edu/archived/book-mormon-first-nephi-doctrinal-foundation/12-early-christianity-and-1-nephi-13-14.]

Sawyer, John F. A. *The Fifth Gospel: Isaiah in the History of Christianity*. New York: Cambridge University Press, 1996.

Skousen, Royal. *Analysis of Textual Variants of the Book of Mormon*. 6 vols. Provo, Utah: FARMS and Neal A. Maxwell Institute Press, 2004–2009.

———, ed. *The Book of Mormon: The Earliest Text*. New Haven: Yale University Press, 2009.

Smith, Gary V. *Isaiah 1–39*. Nashville, Tenn.: B&H Publishing, 2007.

———. *Isaiah 40–66*. Nashville, Tenn.: B&H Publishing, 2009.

Spencer, Joseph M. *An Other Testament: On Typology*. 2nd ed. Provo, Utah: Neal A. Maxwell Institute Press, 2016.

———. "The Book, the Words of the Book: What the Book of Mormon Says about Its Own Coming Forth." *Religious Educator: Perspectives on the Restored Gospel* 17, no. 1 (2016): 64–81.

———. *For Zion: A Mormon Theology of Hope*. Salt Lake City: Greg Kofford Books, 2014.

———. "René Girard and Mormon Scripture: A Response." *Dialogue: A Journal of Mormon Thought* 43, no. 3 (Fall 2010): 6–20.

Spencer, Joseph M., and Jenny Webb, eds. *Reading Nephi Reading Isaiah: 2 Nephi 26–27*. Provo, Utah: Neal A. Maxwell Institute Press, 2016.

Tertullian. "Against the Jews." In Geoffrey D. Dunn, *Tertullian* (New York: Routledge, 2004), 63–104. [Tertullian's writings have been translated a variety of times and are available in many places, including for free online. One such online resource is http://www.tertullian.org/anf/anf03/anf03-19.htm.]

Tull Willey, Patricia. *Remember the Former Things: The Recollection of Previous Texts in Second Isaiah*. Atlanta: Scholars Press, 1997.

Tvedtnes, John A. "Isaiah in the Bible and the Book of Mormon." *FARMS Review* 16, no. 2 (2004): 161–72.

———. *The Isaiah Variants in the Book of Mormon*. Provo, Utah: FARMS, 1981. [Tvedtnes's analysis of variants can be accessed online for free. See http://publications.mi.byu.edu/periodicals/past/farms-preliminary-reports/.]

Von Rad, Gerhard. *Old Testament Theology*. 2 vols. Translated by D. M. G. Stalker. New York and Evanston: Harper & Row, 1965.

Webster, Noah. *An American Dictionary of the English Language*. 2 vols. New York: S. Converse, 1828. Reprinted, Chesapeake, Va.: Foundation for American Christian Education, 1995. [Webster's 1828 Dictionary can be accessed and searched for free on a number of websites. An example is http://webstersdictionary1828.com/.]

Wildberger, Hans. *Isaiah 1–12: A Continental Commentary*. Translated by Thomas H. Trapp. Minneapolis: Fortress Press, 1991.

Williamson, H. G. M. *The Book Called Isaiah: Deutero-Isaiah's Role in Composition and Redaction*. New York: Oxford University Press, 1994.

Wright, David P. "Isaiah in the Book of Mormon: Or Joseph Smith in Isaiah." In *American Apocrypha: Essays on the Book of Mormon*, edited by Dan Vogel and Brent Lee Metcalfe (Salt Lake City: Signature Books, 2002), 157–234.

Subject Index

Scripture Index

Note that Isaiah 2–14, 29, 48–49, and 50–51 are correspondingly quoted in 2 Nephi 12–24, 26–27, 1 Nephi 20–21, and 2 Nephi 7–8, such that passages cited from the former appear also in the latter and vice versa.

New Testament

Book of Mormon

Also available from
GREG KOFFORD BOOKS

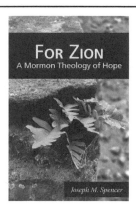

FOR ZION
A Mormon Theology of Hope

Joseph M. Spencer

For Zion:
A Mormon Theology of Hope

Joseph M. Spencer

Paperback, ISBN: 978-1-58958-568-3

What is hope? What is Zion? And what does it mean to hope for Zion? In this insightful book, Joseph Spencer explores these questions through the scriptures of two continents separated by nearly two millennia. In the first half, Spencer engages in a rich study of Paul's letter to the Roman to better understand how the apostle understood hope and what it means to have it. In the second half of the book, Spencer jumps to the early years of the Restoration and the various revelations on consecration to understand how Latter-day Saints are expected to strive for Zion. Between these halves is an interlude examining the hoped-for Zion that both thrived in the Book of Mormon and was hoped to be established again.

Praise for *For Zion*:

"Joseph Spencer is one of the most astute readers of sacred texts working in Mormon Studies. Blending theological savvy, historical grounding, and sensitive readings of scripture, he has produced an original and compelling case for consecration and the life of discipleship." — Terryl Givens, author, *Wrestling the Angel: The Foundations of Mormon Thought*

"*For Zion: A Mormon Theology of Hope* is more than a theological reflection. It also consists of able textual exegesis, historical contextualization, and philosophic exploration. Spencer's careful readings of Paul's focus on hope in Romans and on Joseph Smith's development of consecration in his early revelations, linking them as he does with the Book of Mormon, have provided an intriguing, intertextual avenue for understanding what true stewardship should be for us—now and in the future. As such he has set a new benchmark for solid, innovative Latter-day Saint scholarship that is at once provocative and challenging." — Eric D. Huntsman, author, *The Miracles of Jesus*

Re-reading Job: Understanding the Ancient World's Greatest Poem

Michael Austin

Paperback, ISBN: 978-1-58958-667-3
Hardcover, ISBN: 978-1-58958-668-0

Job is perhaps the most difficult to understand of all books in the Bible. While a cursory reading of the text seems to relay a simple story of a righteous man whose love for God was tested through life's most difficult of challenges and rewarded for his faith through those trials, a closer reading of Job presents something far more complex and challenging. The majority of the text is a work of poetry that authors and artists through the centuries have recognized as being one of--if not the--greatest poem of the ancient world.

In *Re-reading Job: Understanding the Ancient World's Greatest Poem*, author Michael Austin shows how most readers have largely misunderstood this important work of scripture and provides insights that enable us to re-read Job in a drastically new way. In doing so, he shows that the story of Job is far more than that simple story of faith, trials, and blessings that we have all come to know, but is instead a subversive and complex work of scripture meant to inspire readers to rethink all that they thought they knew about God.

Praise for *Re-reading Job*:

"In this remarkable book, Michael Austin employs his considerable skills as a commentator to shed light on the most challenging text in the entire Hebrew Bible. Without question, readers will gain a deeper appreciation for this extraordinary ancient work through Austin's learned analysis. Rereading Job signifies that Latter-day Saints are entering a new age of mature biblical scholarship. It is an exciting time, and a thrilling work." — David Bokovoy, author, *Authoring the Old Testament*

Authoring the Old Testament: Genesis–Deuteronomy

David Bokovoy

Paperback, ISBN: 978-1-58958-588-1
Hardcover, ISBN: 978-1-58958-675-8

For the last two centuries, biblical scholars have made discoveries and insights about the Old Testament that have greatly changed the way in which the authorship of these ancient scriptures has been understood. In the first of three volumes spanning the entire Hebrew Bible, David Bokovoy dives into the Pentateuch, showing how and why textual criticism has led biblical scholars today to understand the first five books of the Bible as an amalgamation of multiple texts into a single, though often complicated narrative; and he discusses what implications those have for Latter-day Saint understandings of the Bible and modern scripture.

Praise for *Authoring the Old Testament:*

"Authoring the Old Testament is a welcome introduction, from a faithful Latter-day Saint perspective, to the academic world of Higher Criticism of the Hebrew Bible. . . . [R]eaders will be positively served and firmly impressed by the many strengths of this book, coupled with Bokovoy's genuine dedication to learning by study and also by faith." — John W. Welch, editor, *BYU Studies Quarterly*

"Bokovoy provides a lucid, insightful lens through which disciple-students can study intelligently LDS scripture. This is first rate scholarship made accessible to a broad audience—nourishing to the heart and mind alike." — Fiona Givens, co-author, *The God Who Weeps: How Mormonism Makes Sense of Life*

"I repeat: this is one of the most important books on Mormon scripture to be published recently. . . . [*Authoring the Old Testament*] has the potential to radically expand understanding and appreciation for not only the Old Testament, but scripture in general. It's really that good. Read it. Share it with your friends. Discuss it." — David Tayman, The Improvement Era: A Mormon Blog

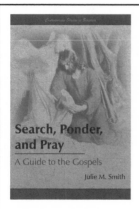

Search, Ponder, and Pray:
A Guide to the Gospels

Julie M. Smith

Paperback, ISBN: 978-1-58958-671-0
Hardcover, ISBN: 978-1-58958-672-7

From the author's preface:

During my graduate studies in theology, I came to realize that there is quite a bit of work done in the field of biblical studies that can be useful to members of the Church as they read the scriptures. Unfortunately, academic jargon usually makes these works impenetrable, and I was unable to find many publications that made this research accessible to the non-specialist. In this book, I have endeavored to present some of the most interesting insights of biblical scholars—in plain language.

It was also important to me that I not present the work of these scholars in a way that would make you feel obligated to accept their conclusions. Since scholars rarely agree with each other, I can see no reason why you should feel compelled to agree with them. My hope is that the format of this book will encourage you to view the insights of scholars as the beginning of a discussion instead of the end of an argument. In some cases, I have presented the positions of scholars (and even some critics of the Church) specifically to encourage you to develop your own responses to these arguments based on your personal scripture study. I certainly don't agree with every idea in this book.

I encourage you to read the Introduction. Although I have endeavored to keep it as short as possible, there are several issues related to the interpretation of the scriptures that should be addressed before you begin interpreting.

It is my experience that thoughtful scripture study leads to personal revelation. I hope that through the process of searching the scriptures, pondering these questions, and praying about the answers, you will be edified.

Life is full of unanswered questions. Here are over 4,500 more of them.

Made in United States
Troutdale, OR
03/17/2024

18532366R00202